THE REVIEW AND ABSTRACT

of the

COUNTY REPORTS

to the

BOARD OF AGRICULTURE

by

WILLIAM MARSHALL

DAVID & CHARLES REPRINTS

7153 4364 5

This edition first
published 1808

Printed in Great Britain by
Clarke, Doble & Brendon Ltd Plymouth
Published by David & Charles (Holdings) Limited
South Devon House Railway Station Newton Abbot

THE

REVIEW AND ABSTRACT

OF THE

COUNTY REPORTS

TO THE

BOARD OF AGRICULTURE;

FROM THE SEVERAL

AGRICULTURAL DEPARTMENTS OF ENGLAND.

By Mr. MARSHALL.

IN FIVE VOLUMES.

VOLUME THE FIRST;

(Which was first Published, in 1808, and is now combined with the other
Volumes of the same Work;)

Comprizing those from the

NORTHERN DEPARTMENT;

Which includes

NORTHUMBERLAND,	WESTMORELAND,
DURHAM,	LANCASHIRE,
CUMBERLAND,	YORKSHIRE;

AND THE

MOUNTAINOUS PARTS OF DERBYSHIRE.

York:

Printed by Thomas Wilson & Sons,

FOR LONGMAN, HURST, REES, ORME, AND BROWN, LONDON; CONSTABLE,
AND CO. EDINBURGH; AND WILSON AND SONS, YORK.

1818.

CONTENTS.

NATURAL ECONOMY.

POLITICAL

POLITICAL ECONOMY.

Public

RURAL ECONOMY.

TENANTED ESTATES.

Improvement

WOODLANDS.

WOODLANDS.

AGRICULTURE.

Working

* On the Winter Management of Store Cattle,—on the Thrashing or Dressing of Corn, on the Expenditure of Hay or Straw, or on the raising of Manure therefrom,—not a word! (excepting the item here referred to, and excepting what may have been incidentally mentioned under other heads). Indeed, those very important concerns of the arable Farmer, appear not to have been thought of, by the framer of the plan of the Board's Reports.

ADVERTISEMENT.

ADVERTISEMENT.

HAVING, in the INTRODUCTION to this volume, explained its plan, what I have to attempt, here, is to point out its utility.

The Reports at large, seeing the magnitude of their bulk, and the comparative smallness of the useful matter they contain, may well be deemed a heavy tax on the time, if not on the purse, of the agricultural public. Their voluminousness certainly debars many practical men from profiting by the useful parts of their contents.

If it shall be found that I have comprized *more* useful information, in one volume than is contained in eight, my endeavors will surely have some claim to utility ; and will, I trust, be entitled to the approbation of the Board whose labors I have thus been rendering superiorly profitable to the public.

The transactions of the Royal Society have been abridged with valuable effect. The volume

I am

I am now offering, however, is not merely an abstract or abridgement of the Reports to the Board of Agriculture, or I should have published it, as such. I have not only concentrated their valuable parts, but have pointed out,—and I believe rectified,—their more dangerous errors; and may have thus rendered my work useful to those who have, as well as to those who have not, the Board's Reports.

Should it be said that I have left many errors, if not absurdities, unnoticed, I would reply—every thing that I have left unnoticed is, I conceive, either erroneous or futile, and, to practical men, of no consideration or avail.

I have a further claim on the agricultural public:—I have not merely separated the better parts, from the confused masses in which I found them dispersed, but have, by appropriate arrangement (as being at once natural and practical) rendered them, I trust, intelligible at sight, and easily to be referred to : and have thus placed them in the most convenient form, not only for *perusal*, but for *study* and *reference*. For, by following each section of the general subject

subject through the several Reports, (by the prefixed Table of Contents) the valuable information, relating to each individual topic, may be read with nearly equal facility, and with the self-same profit, as if the whole were re-cast and arranged systematically. And, allow me to add, the student, by this fresh reading, will inevitably, though perhaps imperceptibly, receive additional advantage from the information collected by the Board.

Lastly, I will venture to prefer a claim on the public at large :—in having (as far as I have yet proceeded) unfolded a view (hitherto unnoticed) of the face of the country, as it relates to TERRITORIAL CONCERNS ; and have thereby furnished an ample field of substantial natural facts, which cannot fail to become of the first utility, whenever the Government of this fair Isle may find it expedient to attend, in some efficient way, to the amelioration of its own territory.

MAY 8, 1808.

INTRODUCTION

INTRODUCTION.

SECTION I.

The ORIGIN and PROGRESS of the BOARD of AGRICULTURE.

BEFORE the Memoirs of the Board can be entered upon with sufficient intelligence, it will be requisite to lay before my reader the rise and progress of my own " PLAN for PROMOTING AGRICULTURE ;" and the subsequent proposal for a " Board of Agriculture :"— the former of which was *publicly* offered six years, and the latter three years, before the Institution, whose transactions form the subject of the present work, took place.

In a public address, prefixed to the RURAL ECONOMY of NORFOLK (first published in 1787) I stated the following particulars ;—which I here reprint for the use of those who may not have that publication at hand.

'The utility of full and faithful Registers of the present practice of Husbandry, in well cultivated Districts, occurred to me about ten years ago ;—when, in a journey of four or five hundred miles through the central parts of the Island, I experienced the inutility of a *transient view ;* but at the same time, clearly saw the advantages which would accrue from a TWELVEMONTH'S RESIDENCE in the immediate District of the practice to be registered. At that time, however, I was too busily employed in registering my own practice* to think of extending my Register, in any way, to the practice of others. But being fortunately released from my connexion

* See MINUTES OF AGRICULTURE in SURREY.

nexion in Surrey, and having prepared for publication my EXPERIMENTS *and* OBSERVATIONS *concerning* AGRICULTURE *and the* WEATHER, I found leisure to reflect more maturely on the means of perfecting the system, which I had, with much deliberation, sketched out, and which I had in part filled up, from my own practice.

'In February 1780, I submitted to the Society of Arts in London, as the first Society, professedly Agricultural, in the kingdom, the following Plan.

PLAN FOR PROMOTING AGRICULTURE.

'THE knowledge of Agriculture either results from experience, simply; or is acquired through the united efforts of experience and theory.

'Theory may facilitate, by analyzing the subject, and giving a comprehensive view of the science in general;—elucidate, by commenting on the experience already acquired;—accelerate, by proposing fit subjects for future investigations;—but cannot convey any certain information without the aid and concurrence of experience.

'The experience of Agriculture is acquired through adequate observation, either on self-practice, or on the practice of others.

'The practice of an individual, however, is generally limited to some particular branch of management, on some certain soil and situation; and a general knowledge of Agriculture must not be expected from the practice of any one man.

'A man, nevertheless, who has spent a long life in the practice of some certain department, must necessarily have acquired a considerable share of knowledge of that particular department: and it is probable, that were the knowledge of the individuals who excel in the several departments of husbandry,—were the knowledge of the

ablest

ablest farmers in the best-cultivated parts of the island collected——English Agriculture would be found, at this day, to be far advanced towards perfection.

' But the individuals who excel in agriculture are unknown to each other ; and, if associated, could not probably communicate their knowledge, with any degree of precision : for their art, being the result of habit, is too familiar to be minutely described. Their farms are the only records in which it is registered, and even there it is as fleeting as the hour in which it is performed. Nothing but actual observation, and immediately registering, in writing, the several operations, as they pass throughout the year, can render the practice of individuals of extensive service to the Public.

' In short, the art of agriculture must ever remain imperfect while it is suffered to languish in the memory, and die with the practitioner : RECORD, only can perpetuate the art; and SYSTEM, alone, render the science comprehensive *.

' Mr. Marshall has already submitted to the Public a register of his own practice during five years; comprehending a plan for acquiring agricultural knowledge, systematically, from self-practice †; which plan is equally applicable to the practice of others; provided the observations be performed without remission, and by one who is accustomed to agricultural observation. He has also endeavored to trace out the foundation of a system, so far as his own practice has extended.

' HIS PRESENT PLAN is, to extend his observations to the practice of others; more especially as it appertains

to

* What Dr. Johnson says of Language is applicable to Agriculture——
" Diction merely vocal is always in its childhood. As no man leaves his
" eloquence behind him, the new generations have all to learn."—*Journey
to the Western Islands of Scotland.*'

' † See Experiments and Observations, as above.'

to the breeding, rearing, and fatting of cattle—to the dairy management—to the management of sheep,—to the draining and watering of meadows,—and to the grass land, or ley-management in general. After he is become proficient in these departments, his intentions are to extend his SURVEY OF PROVINCIAL AGRICULTURE to the arable or plow-management.

' His intended mode of observation is this : Having pitched upon the branch of management to be studied and the district which excels in the practice of that particular branch, he proposes to fix his place of residence, during TWELVE MONTHS, in a farm-house ;—if possible, in the house of the best-informed farmer in the district pitched upon ; and there, with daily attention, minutely observe and register the living practice which surrounds him : not the practice of theoretical, but of professional farmers ; or rather the provincial practice of the district, county, or country observed ; nevertheless attending to improvements and excellencies, by whomsoever practised.

' Nor is his plan confined merely to observation : he means to acquire by self-practice a competent knowledge of the MANUAL OPERATIONS incident to the department of husbandry which is the immediate object of his study; as also to collect such IMPLEMENTS and UTENSILS as may appear peculiarly adapted to the purposes for which they are severally intended; not sketches nor models, but the instruments themselves which he has seen in common use ; and of whose uses he has acquired, by manual practice, an adequate knowledge.

' In order to furnish himself with every advantage which may forward his general design, his further intentions are to employ his leisure in taking a complete RE-VIEW OF WRITTEN AGRICULTURE, from Fitz-Herbert, in 1534, to the present time (excepting the works of such authors as may be living at the time of closing the re-view);

view); and, after his judgement has been matured by a survey of provincial practice, to compress into as narrow a compass as may be, the useful information relative to British Agriculture, which has been already recorded; whether it appears in incidents and experiments sufficiently authenticated, or in hints which may furnish subjects for future experiment.

'Briefly,—his plan is, reciprocally to receive and to offer information;—to communicate provincial practice to the Public at large;—to collect and compress the useful information which is at present widely scattered in almost numberless volumes;—and to reduce these joint accumulations of agricultural knowledge to systematic science: consequently, to offer to the present and succeeding generations a comprehensive SYSTEM OF ENGLISH AGRICULTURE, as it now stands;—and to raise it on a basis so ample and scientific, as that future acquisitions may be added to it from time to time.'

In the RURAL ECONOMY of the MIDLAND COUNTIES,— the first edition of which was published in 1790,—in speaking of Societies of Agriculture, and the inefficiency of those which had then been established, I made a further statement of facts, and ventured to bring forward a proposal which naturally resulted from them; and which, also, I think it right to insert here.

'In the Digest of the Minutes of Agriculture, on the subject Public Agriculture, I proposed an establishment of Agricultural Colleges, to be distributed in different districts as seminaries of rural knowledge.

'It is now more than twelve years since that proposal was written; during which time my attention has been bent, unremittingly, on rural subjects; and the result is that I now see, still more evidently, the want of rural seminaries.

'The seminaries there proposed, are, however, on too
large

large a scale for any thing less than national establishment, and commerce, rather than agriculture, appears
to engage, at present, the more immediate attention of
Government; and this, notwithstanding the present scarcity of corn is such, that we are asking even the Ame-
ricans for a supply; and notwithstanding a very considerable part of the cattle, which now come to market,
are the produce of Ireland.

' I have already said, in the course of this work, that
it is not my intention to obtrude my sentiments un-
seemingly, on national concerns. But possessed of the
mass of information, which, in the nature of my pursuit,
I must necessarily have accumulated,—no man, *perhaps,*
having had a similar opportunity,—I think it a duty I
owe to society, and an inseparable part of my present
undertaking, to register such ideas, whether national or
professional, as result aptly and fairly out of the subject
before me; and, in this place, I think it right to intimate the probable advantages which might arise from a
BOARD of AGRICULTURE,—or, more generally, of RURAL
AFFAIRS :—to take cognizance, not of the state and promotion of agriculture, merely; but also of the cultivation of wastes and the propagation of timber;—bases on
which, not commerce only, but the political existence
of the nation is founded. And when may this country
expect a more favorable opportunity, than the present,
of laying a broad and firm basis of its future prosperity ?'*

In December 1790 (a few months after the publication
of that Proposal) the first President of the Board of
Agriculture did me the honor of making himself known
to me. He was then eagerly employed in collecting
materials for a statistical account of Scotland, and in endeavoring to establish a society, there, for the improvement

* Edition 1790, page 121. Ed. 1796, p. 87.

ment of British wool. He was of course too much engaged, at that time, in Scotland, to make any attempt at the Presidency of a Board of Agriculture, in England; anxiously as he might then eye it, as an honor in reserve.

It was not until the spring of 1793, that the (afterwards) first President apprized me of his intention to bring the proposed Board before Parliament. He showed me his plan, and, during my short stay in London, repeatedly consulted me on the subject.

At the time of my leaving town, there did not appear the smallest probability of the measure being adopted : even its promoter assured me that he had no hope of its being, then, carried into effect. Nevertheless ; I had barely reached my temporary residence in the central Highlands, before the public prints announced the appointment of a Board of Agriculture ; together with the names of the President and Secretary !

How was this mystery to be explained? To me, at five hundred miles distance from the scene of the mysterious transaction, it was impossible even to conjecture the cause of so sudden a change in the sentiments of Ministers, on so *plain* a subject. Upon the spot, however, as I afterwards found, there were only two opinions respecting it ; and these two led to the same point: namely, that it turned on what, in the familiar language of politicians is termed a *job;* and the only doubt that remained appeared to be, whether the measure (weighty as it might be) was adopted to avoid the importunities, and quiet the still more ambitious cravings of the President, or to embrace a *fair* opportunity of rewarding a recent change of political sentiments, in the Secretary.

Thus fled my hope of credit (which I really expected) and all chance of profit (which I had not entertained) from my proposed Board of Agriculture. But as it did not appear, in any direct way, to interfere with my other

plans,

plans, but might in one way or other assist in promoting them, its appointment gave me not much concern :—until I found, by a note from the President, in September following, that he had adopted my plan of provincial surveys : and, with a firmness of nerve which few men are endowed with, inclosed a list of surveyors,—myself among the rest! urging me to take a share in his attempt to supersede a work, in the prosecution of which the most valuable part of my life had been expended!!

My indignation having abated, I returned the following answer :—Mr. Marshall's compliments, &c. &c. "It gave him great satisfaction to hear of the establishment of a Board of Agriculture : an institution which Mr. M. has long been anxious for; as it will give a degree of sanction to rural pursuits, which hitherto they have not had ; and may prove useful to the general work which he has now been so long and laboriously executing. It will of course give him great pleasure to aid the laudable exertions of the Board, in any way that will not clash with his own undertaking. But to render this incomplete, by tearing from it any part of his General Survey of the Rural Affairs of these Kingdoms, would he thinks be altogether improper. If, as he intimated in London, his general knowledge of the practices of the island (Wales excepted) can be rendered beneficial in revising the collections of the raw observers whom the Board must necessarily employ, he shall be happy in lending his assistance. * Taymouth, 11 Sept. 1793."

On more maturely considering this evidently insidious attempt, it occurred to me that the proposed plan of the Board might become subservient to my own design ; by affording

* The above noticed intimation related, not to *agricultural*, but to *statistical*, surveys; which alone were *held out*, in London,

affording me valuable assistance in carrying it into effect. Hence, on further importunity (and a highflying lure thrown out!) I complied with the request to furnish an account of the mountain district, in which I then was residing. Several of the proposed surveyors were respectable; and I now began to consider them, not as *rivals,* nor even as *fellow laborers,* but as a numerous band of *assistants,* which unforeseen circumstances had thus fortunately thrown in my way; to aid me in the more perfect cultivation of my own field! and I am now about to reap the fruits of their labor :—not for myself; but for my country.

Before I quitted the CENTRAL HIGHLANDS, I made excursions into the more recluse and sequestered parts of them (having previously examined the more fruitful and habitable districts, in going over the widely extended estates of the EARL of BRAEDALBANE, in that strongly featured and interesting part of the island); in order to be the better enabled to draw up the promised REPORT; which, in February 1794, I had the honor of *presenting* to the Board; of which I was soon afterward chosen HONORARY MEMBER; and, during a short stay in London, attended its meetings; as well as the more private consultations of the President.

SECTION 2.

The PLAN and EXECUTION of the REPORTS.

THE prosecution of the surveys (or the supposed surveys) was by COUNTIES; each county (Yorkshire excepted) being the subject of one separate REPORT.

This plan of survey, however, is demonstrably wrong for reasons which I trust will plainly appear, in the fol-

lowing extract, from the RURAL ECONOMY of the WEST
of ENGLAND; which was originally published in May
1796; that publication giving me the first convenient
opportunity of stating them, after the surveys of the
Board commenced.

'This popular appellation (the West of England) is
usually given to the four most western counties, namely
Cornwall, Devonshire, Somersetshire, and Dorsetshire.

' But, in examining a country, like England, with a
view to the existing state of its agriculture, and the
other branches of its Rural Economy, the arbitrary lines
of counties are to be wholly disregarded. For if any
plan was observed in determining the outlines of provinces, in this island, it certainly had no reference, or
alliance whatever, to agriculture; unless it were to divide, between opposing claimants, the natural districts,
which required to be studied, separately, and entire.
Natural, not fortuitous, lines are requisite to be traced,
agricultural, not political, distinctions are to be regarded.

' A natural district is marked by a uniformity or similarity, of soil and surface, whether, by such uniformity,
a marsh, a vale, an extent of upland, a range of chalky
heights, or a stretch of barren mountains be produced.
And an agricultural district is discriminated by a uniformity, or similarity, of practice; whether it be characterized by grazing, sheep farming, arable management, or mixed cultivation, or by the production of some
particular article;—as dairy produce, fruit liquor, &c. &c.

' Now it is evident that the boundary lines of counties
pay no regard to these circumstances. On the contrary,
we frequently find the most entire districts, with respect
to nature and agriculture, severed by political lines of
demarcation. The midland district, for instance, a
whole with respect to soil, surface, and established
practice, is reduced to mere fragments by the outlines
of

of the four counties of Leicester, Warwick, Stafford and Derby*. Again, the fruit liquor district, of the Wye and Severn, includes parts of the counties of Hereford, Glocester, and Worcester †. And the dairy district of North Wiltshire receives portions of the counties of Glocester and Berks, within its limits, and extends its practice to the eastern margin of Somersetshire ‡.

‘ Hence, it may be truly said, to prosecute an agricultural survey, by counties, is to set at naught the distinctions of nature, which it is the intention of the Surveyor to examine and describe ; and to separate into parts the distinguished practices, which it is his business to register, entire.

‘ Such a mode of procedure is an impropriety, not only in theory, but in practice. It destroys that simplicity of execution, and perspicuity of arrangement, which alone can render an extensive undertaking pleasurable to him who prosecutes it, or profitable to the public.

‘ Another practical objection, which lies against surveying by counties (beside the repetitions or references it requires) is the unnecessary labor it incurs, and the superfluous volumes to which it necessarily gives rise. For it is not the practice of every township or farm which *can* be registered, nor that of every hundred or county which *requires* it.

‘ It is the superior practices of distinguished natural districts, in different and distant parts of the island (thus separating, and thereby showing in the most intelligible form, its more distinct practices)—and these only, that are *necessary* to be fixed,—as a firm basis

on

---

* See my MIDLAND COUNTIES.

† See my GLOCESTERSHIRE; Section *Fruit Liquor.*

‡ See GLOCESTERSHIRE; Section *Dairy.*

on which to raise future improvements,—and still more enlightened practices.'

THE plan of the original Reports of the Board—if plan they can be said to have—most of them being, literally speaking, " without form and void"—was what may be conceived from some of the heads, of the provincial surveys which I had then published, being turned in a wheel, and arranged in the order in which they happened to be drawn out. They were evidently mine; but so *deranged* and disfigured, as not to be easily recognised.

The originals were printed on quarto paper, in narrow columns or pages, with very wide margins, to receive the additions or corrections of those who might think fit to make them :—a well judged method; by which, in some instances, much additional information was gathered.

Those of the thirty nine counties of England (proper) of which, chiefly, I mean to speak in the present work, were printed in, or nearly in, the following order of time.

Dorsetshire, by Claridge, in . .	1793
Huntingdonshire, by Maxwell,	——
——————, by Stone,	——
Sussex, by Young,	——
Cumberland, by Bailey and Culley, .	Jan. 1794
Essex, by Griggs,	——
Kent, by Boys,	——
Norfolk, by Kent,	——
Oxfordshire, by Davis,	——
Suffolk, by Young,	——
Warwickshire, by Wedge,	——
Wiltshire, by Davis,	——
Glocestershire, by Turner, . .	Feb. 1794
Lancashire, by Holt,	——

Leicestershire, by Monk, . .	Feb. 1794
Lincolnshire, by Stone,	————
Middlesex, by Foot,	————
Northumberland, by Bailey & Culley,	————
Rutlandshire, by Crutchley,	————
Yorkshire, east, by Leatham,	————
————, north, by Tuke,	————
————, west, by Brown, &c.	————
Berkshire, by Pearce, . .	Mar. 1794
Cheshire, by Wedge,	————
Devonshire, by Frazer,	————
Nottinghamshire, by Lowe,	————
Surrey, by James and Malcolm,	————
Buckinghamshire, by the same, .	May 1794
Cornwall, by Frazer,	————
Herefordshire, by Clark,	————
Shropshire, by Bishton,	————
Cambridgeshire, by Vancouver, .	June, 1794
Bedfordshire, by Stone, . .	July, 1794
Derbyshire, by Brown,	————
Durham, by Granger,	————
Hampshire, by Drivers, &c.	————
Northamptonshire, by Donaldson, .	Nov. 1794
Somersetshire, by Billingsley,	————
Staffordshire, by Pitt,	————
Westmoreland, by Pringle,	————
Worcestershire, by Pomeroy, . .	Dec. 1794
Hertfordshire, by Walker, . . .	Jan. 1795
Essex, by Vancouver, . . .	Feb. 1795

Seeing the chaos of Chapters and Sections which was given out by the Board, it was evident that to make use of it, in reviewing the Reports, would have been truly absurd ; and seeing, further, " the confusion worse confounded" by the Reporters ;—who have not unfrequently, and no doubt inadvertantly, spoken of different

subjects

subjects in the same Section; and, sometimes, properly enough, brought forward topics that are not to be found in the plan delivered to them;—I had no alternative, but that of considering the whole as a series of *miscellaneous remarks*, without plan or order; and to mark, in the margins of the several Reports, the proper subject of which each remark belongs; as I have ever done in digesting my own *miscellaneous minutes*. See Minutes in the Southern Counties, Norfolk, Midland Counties, &c.

It is, now, more than twelve years since the first reprinted Report (in the octavo form) was published. Yet, when this volume was put to press, not one half of the English Reports had met the public eye :—for the quarto editions (the original Reports) could not be properly said to be published; the impressions being chiefly distributed, *gratis*.

Some of the octavo editions are little more than literal copies of the original Reports: others are enlarged by additions and notes; and some are the productions of fresh Surveyors: in which instances, there are of course two or more distinct Reports of one and the same county.

Section 3.

QUALIFICATIONS of a REPORTER.

The utility of a work principally arising from its plan and execution, and the plan of the Board's Reports having been already considered, it remains to examine into the qualifications that are requisite to the twofold task of Surveying, and Reporting, the rural practices and improvements of a country.

Before a man can be *fully* qualified to survey, appreciate,

ciate, and report the established practices of a district or county, as they relate to rural affairs, and to point out the means of its improvement, it is essentially requisite that he should possess a practical knowledge of the several branches of the rural profession. It is not enough that he has practised AGRICULTURE, in all its branches, and in different districts, to mature his judgement, dispel local prejudices, and prepare his mind, by due expansion, to form just conceptions of the varying methods and proceedings of other men ;—he should likewise be practically acquainted with the business of PLANTING, and still more with the proper MANAGEMENT of WOODLANDS (a subject of high importance to the lasting welfare of this nation);—as well as with the subject of LANDED PROPERTY,—the right distribution and MANAGEMENT of TENANTED LANDS, and the proper GOVERNMENT of their OCCUPIERS; such as will enable them to exert their respective talents, and cultivate the lands committed to their charge, with full profit to the community: this being a branch of rural economicks, by the improper management of which the public loss, I apprehend, is greater, even than that which is annually caused, by errors in Agriculture.

It is also to be required of him, that he should have a competent knowledge of the different SCIENCES which are intimately connected with rural subjects: particularly Natural History, as it relates to fossils and vegetables; to assist him in registering, intelligibly, facts already known, and in making discoveries that may lead to further improvements; and with mechanics, to enable him to appreciate, with greater ease and certainty, machines and implements in use. Some knowledge of the higher branches of the mathematics, to form his mind to method, and to teach him to think with precision, and decide with clearness, on the subject before him.

him. Moreover it is required that he should possess
an intimate acquaintance with the language in which
he is to draw up his Report; with some practical knowledge of COMPOSITION: in order that he may be enabled
to convey his ideas to others (as well as to form them
in his own mind) with clearness and precision.

But not those, nor any other, acquirements can qualify
a man to make a Report of a county or district, until he
has maturely studied, and become fully acquainted with,
the natural and economical FACTS which belong to it.
If he has been, for some length of time, a resident practitioner, on a sufficiently ample scale, in the best cultivated part of it, and was previously possessed of the
foregoing attainments, he might be deemed preeminently
qualified for the undertaking. If, with those acquirements, he has spent two years, in studying its natural
and acquired properties, as well as its established practices, and the means of its improvement,—by taking a
judicious station, in the best managed part of it, by
deliberately surveying the whole,—by mixing freely
with practical men,—by daily observing their practices,—and cautiously registering facts as they occurred,—
he may be considered as being competent to the task.
By one year's residence, industriously employed, a
man,—who has acquired, by practice, sufficient skill,
in surveying districts, and in *ascertaining* and registering facts—may be allowed to make a public Report, or
to publish his Register.

A mere tourist, it is true, may catch certain facts
which pass under his eye in travelling: and, in this way,
he may gather some general ideas of the nature of a
country, and a few particulars of practice that may
happen to be going on, *at the time of his tour;* and
such facts may be entitled to public notice, *as far as
they go.* But let him not claim, on such slight pretensions,

sions, a right to make a *general Report* of the nature and practice of the country or district thus passed over: even though he may be fully possessed of the qualifications set forth aforegoing. For what a man, even of such acquirements, can collect from *enquiries*, is beneath public attention. An ENQUIRING TOURIST, without a large portion of practical knowledge to assist him in directing his judgement, must be liable to be led into error at every step, and to be imposed upon by every one with whom he may happen to converse.

SECTION 4.

PLAN of REVIEW.

THIS subject, so far as it relates to the plan of the Reports, and the arrangement of the matter therein contained, has been incidentally touched upon, aforegoing. What principally remains to be spoken of, here, are— the manner of reviewing by departments, and the arrangement of the materials, thereby collected.

REVIEWING by DEPARTMENTS.—In the first extract, aforegoing, p. xx, it appears that my original design was to station myself in different Agricultural districts, exemplary for rural knowledge. In another, p. xxvi, I have defined an *Agricultural district,* and shown the impropriety of surveying by fortuitous lines. And I, here, sketch the outlines, and distinguishing characters, of the sixth AGRICULTURAL DEPARTMENTS, into which the kingdom naturally separates :—beginning, geographically, with

The NORTHERN DEPARTMENT ; the outlines of which are shown in the following sketch, and will be spoken of, presently.

Among

Among its natural characteristics are a coolness of climature, and a backwardness of seasons, comparatively with the more southern parts of the island. But its most striking natural feature,—that which distinguishes it from the rest of *this* kingdom,—is given by its MOUN-TAINS:—this being the only part of England, in which the mountain character can be said to prevail *.

Viewed as a field of Rural Economy, it bears strong marks of distinction. On the western side of the department, MANUFACTURES may be said to be in possession of the country. AGRICULTURE, there, is a subservient employment: while, on the eastern, it florishes in all its branches; being, there, carried on with a degree of skill and industry, and with a *rational, well moderated spirit of improvement* that is not equalled in any other department of *this* kingdom.

THE WESTERN DEPARTMENT. This extends from the banks of the Mersey, to the Somersetshire Avon and its banks. On the west, it is bounded by the Welch mountains; on the east, by the minor hills of Staffordshire, and the uplands of Warwickshire, and Oxfordshire; its southern bounds being given by the chalk hills of Wiltshire, and the Sedgemoors of Somersetshire.

It comprizes an almost uninterrupted succession of VALE DISTRICTS; which accompany the Mersey, the Dee, the Severn, and the Avon, to their respective confluxes with the sea. Thus, by natural character it is discriminately marked.

And it is not less so, by Agricultural produce. The entire department,—except the higher lands of Shropshire, and Herefordshire, the Cotswold hills of Glocestershire,

* Those, in the West of England, mostly rise in detached masses, and are of comparatively small extent.

shire, and the higher parts of the Mendip hills of Somersetshire, may be said to be almost wholly applied to
the produce of the DAIRY : cheeses, of different qualities,
being its common production. Fruit liquor, however,
may be mentioned as another product that signalizes
this natural division of the kingdom.

THE MIDLAND DEPARTMENT. This part of the kingdom, too, possesses an aptly distinguishing natural
character. When compared with the great variety of
soil and surface, which most of the other departments
exhibits, this may be considered as one widely extended plain of fertile lands, which are almost uniformly
suitable to the purposes of MIXED CULTIVATION; and
without a single *eminence* within its extensive area;—
excepting the Charnwood hills; which form an insulated mountain height, from whence almost every
square mile of the department may be discerned, from
the mountains of the northern, to the chalk hills of the
southern, department; and from the rising grounds that
separate it from the western, to the banks of the marshes
where the eastern, department commences*.

As a wide field of Agriculture, in which every branch
of the profession is highly cultivated, it has long been
popularly known. Here, not only the spirit of improvement, but of *enterprize*, may well be said to inhabit.
The art, science, and mystery of BREEDING has here
been carried to a height which in any other country,
probably, it has never attained;—the same enterprizing
spirit, which led to this preeminence, still continuing,
with little if any abatement.

THE EASTERN DEPARTMENT is marked by its FENS and
MARSHES; as well as by the light SANDY quality of its
UPLANDS :—

* See Midland Counties, Vol. I. p. 11.

UPLANDS:—joint natural qualities that belong to no other extensive division of the kingdom.

The agricultural pursuits of this department are directed, in a singular manner, to GRAZING,—to the fatting of cattle and sheep:—not only in the marshes and lower grounds; but on the uplands; on which the TURNEP HUSBANDRY has long been, and until of later years exclusively, practised.

THE SOUTHERN DEPARTMENT. The CHALK HILLS, which occupy the principal part of this division, strongly mark its natural character.

Its agricultural distinctions arise, in a great degree, out of its situation with respect to the METROPOLIS:—a vortex, this, which not only draws much of its produce in a summary way, to market; but causes a demand for particular objects of husbandry.

THE SOUTHWESTERN DEPARTMENT. The situation of this extremity of the island is remarkable. It stretches away from the main body, in a narrow headland, or peninsula, nearly two hundred miles in length, into the western sea; which is its common boundary; unless where it joins the extremes of the western and southern departments.

The natural characters of its area are likewise singular. The midland and the western parts of it, are chiefly composed of SLATE-ROCK HILLS: a species of country which is unknown, in the rest of the kingdom; excepting a comparatively small district of its northern department; and excepting the insulated hills of Charnwood, which rise near its center! Indeed, the surface, almost throughout the department (its northeastern angle excepted) is of a singular cast: namely, tall, steepsided hills, severed by narrow vallies; the hills being, in most instances, productive to their summits.

Its

Its agricultural distinguishments are not less remarkable. The DAMNONIAN HUSBANDRY is as foreign to the practice of the kingdom at large, as the lands on which it has been nurtured are to those of its other departments. See the RURAL ECONOMY of the WEST of ENGLAND.

No one can be more aware, than I am, of the want of perfection, in the foregoing division of the kingdom into DEPARTMENTS that are at once *natural* and *agricultural;* each having its *distinguishing character.* But whoever will maturely consider the subject, cannot fail of being struck with *the degree of perfection* by which they are severally marked. To find the kingdom at large separating into six divisions—of nearly equal extent, and uniform distribution, and which, in a very considerable degree, are at once natural and agricultural,—is more than any man, without previous examination, could have reasonably hoped for, much less have expected.

THE ADVANTAGES to arise from reviewing the Reports of the Board, BY DEPARTMENTS, though in a degree obvious, will be here enumerated.

Each department may aptly be considered as a distinct country, having its own association of natural and acquired facts,—and its own objects in view; but with varying means of obtaining them. By bringing the different methods together, they will be easily compared, and the most eligible selected :—not only by the practitioners of that particular department; but by those, of the empire, at large, who have similar objects before them. For, although each department has its prominent natural characters, and leading objects of practice, the latter, at least, are not wholly confined to that particular department; but are many of them more or less

sought

sought after, in almost every district; though, it must be admitted, in a less eligible manner, than where they are PURSUED, on a LARGE SCALE, in the ESTABLISHED and LEADING PRACTICE OF A COUNTRY.

Thus, an occupier of mountain lands, in Devonshire or Cornwall, may see, in the northern or mountain department, what useful matter the Board has collected in the management of alpine districts. In like manner, a dairy farmer of Yorkshire, by examining the western or dairy department, will find the useful ideas that have been drawn together on the management of dairy farms. Any man who is desireous to encrease his information on the subject of breeding Livestock, will of course turn his attention to the midland or breeding department. And, for marshland grazing-and the turnep husbandry, to the eastern or grazing department. A wold farmer of Yorkshire or Lincolnshire, by referring to the southern department, will find what has been usefully adduced by the Board, on the management of chalk hills: and the occupiers of lands in the vicinities of great towns, may there find what relates to established practices, in the neighbourhood of the metropolis. Finally, in the southwestern department, any occupier of lands, that lie out of it, may find practices foreign to his own, and therein will see that the same objects may be obtained, by different means; yet perhaps with nearly equal propriety of management, and, in contemplating these facts,—whether in the southwestern or other department,—will imperceptibly lose his provincial prejudices.

I now proceed to explain my plan, more fully, respecting the ARRANGEMENT of the MATERIALS that may arise in executing it; by pointing out the principal branches into which the main subject before us, naturally separates.

The

The GENERAL ECONOMY of a country,—which is under efficient government, and whose lands are appropriated,—is composed of three obviously differential parts, or separable subjects: namely,

1. The NATURAL ECONOMY of the country itself;— its situation, extent, and conformation;—the materials of which it is formed,—their arrangement and natural characters.

2. Its POLITICAL ECONOMY;—comprizing whatever relates to public concerns, connected with

3. Its RURAL ECONOMY;—including what belongs to private property and its management, relative to rural concerns.

The last, in like manner, naturally separates into three divisions: namely,

Landed estates and their management.

Woodlands and their management.

Farm lands and their management.

In reviewing the Board's Reports, I propose (for reasons assigned in p. xxix) to arrange what may be found entitled to notice, under its proper head, in one of those divisions of the general subject;—in conformity with the plan of my own provincial Registers.

ERRATA.

P. 16. Dele the turned commas, line 17; and the whole of the
        Quotation, l. 18 to 28.

P. 132. L. 13. from bottom, after QUARRIES, insert p. 13.

P. 144. The paragraph, l. 15 to 34 should close the Division,
        Political Economy, p. 143.

P. 278. L. 22. Before Covenants, insert p. 23.

P. 483. L. 12. For *set*, read *sown*.

THE

NORTHERN DEPARTMENT

OF

ENGLAND.

THIS DIVISION OF THE KINGDOM includes
the principal parts of NORTHUMBERLAND and DUR-
HAM; the whole of CUMBERLAND, WESTMORELAND,
LANCASHIRE, and YORKSHIRE (excepting the fens
and marshes, bordering on Lincolnshire);—with
parts of Cheshire, Staffordshire, and Derbyshire.

It contains the following NATURAL DISTRICTS;
which are situated as in the annexed map*

The District of Wooler.
The Seacoast of Northumberland.
The Cheviot Hills.
The " Moors" or Heathlands of this county.
The Cultivated Uplands.
The Valley or District of Hexham.
The Seacoast of Durham.
The Central District of Durham.
The Morelands of the five counties.
The District of Carlisle.
The Seacoast of Cumberland.

The

* SKETCH of the NORTHERN DEPARTMENT. The sketch, which is
here offered, is merely intended to convey a general idea of the relative situation, and the extent, of each district. Nothing but
actual, and deliberate, survey can determine their outlines, with
precision.

The Slate-stone Mountains of Cumberland, &c.
The Valley of Appleby.
The District of Kendal.
The Cultivated Lands of Lancashire.
The Morelands of Lancashire.
Craven.
The Western Morelands of Yorkshire.
The Manufacturing Districts of Yorkshire.
The Limestone Lands of West Yorkshire.
The Vale of York.
The Vale of Stockton.
The Northern Seacoast of Yorkshire.
The Eastern Morelands.
The Limestone Lands of East Yorkshire.
The Vale of Pickering.
The Wolds of Yorkshire.
Holderness.
The Southern Mountains of Lancashire, York
     shire, Cheshire, Staffordshire, and Derby-
     shire.

These districts, collectively, comprize the objects of
the Board's Surveyors, and form the subjects of
the several REPORTS, for the NORTHERN DEPART-
MENT; which are these:

Northumberland; by Bailey and Culley.
Durham; by Granger.
Cumberland; by Bailey and Culley.
Westmoreland; by Pringle.
Lancashire; by Holt.
West Yorkshire; by Brown, &c.
North Yorkshire; by Tuke.
East Yorkshire; by Leatham.
Cheshire, by Wedge; Staffordshire, by Pitt;
     Derbyshire, by Brown.

NORTHUMBERLAND.

B Y the preceding MAP, it will be perceived that
I have abandoned the extreme northern point of the
kingdom : having resigned it, rich and highly cultivated as it is, to the more immediate promoters of the
Rural Economy of Scotland; to which, by situation, as
well as by established practice, it properly belongs.
It is in the plain of Wooler, an Englishman is first
struck with the rural appearances of the south of
Scotland; the style of management being similar, to
some distance, on both sides of the Tweed.

Nevertheless, the DISTRICT OF WOOLER being the
STATION, or district of residence, of both the RE-
PORTERS of the practice of Northumberland, it would
be an impropriety to exclude it out of a review of
their joint report. But " TWEEDSIDE"—as the more
immediate banks of the river are emphatically named
—being, in natural character, and rural management,
the same on either bank, and partaking much more
of Scottish than of English husbandry, I forbear to
separate them.

The northern extremity of England belongs, not to
Northumberland; but to the *town* of *Berwick*, and
the *county* of *Durham**.

Therefore,

* " About 72 square miles of well enclosed, cultivated country."
belong to the latter.

Therefore, what are to be brought forward, here, as the NATURAL DISTRICTS of NORTHUMBERLAND, are the following : namely,

The District of Wooler.
The Seacoast of Northumberland.
The Cheviot Hills.
The Morelands, or Heaths, of this county.
The Cultivated Uplands.
The Valley, or District, of Hexham.

But, before I attempt to define those several districts, or to offer my opinion on the merits of a report which is founded on them, it will be proper to declare my pretensions to so arduous, if not presumptuous, an undertaking.

In May 1792, I viewed the line of country, between Newcastle and Alnwick; and from thence proceeded to the district of Wooler; where I spent a week, agreeably and profitably, in viewing, not only that district, but also the Cheviot Hills, and Tweedside to its extremity at Berwick,—as well as its opposite banks;—and in conversing with the enlightened occupiers of this favored part of the island *: receiving marked civilities, from agriculturists of every class: and among whom I have the pleasure of naming Messrs. Bailey and Culley,—authors of the Northumbrian Report.

In April 1793, I crossed the county, by a somewhat different route; proceeding from Morpeth, by the direct line, to the district of Wooler: thus passing through the middle of the cultivated uplands, and over the eastern skirts of the morelands.

And, in November 1793, I took a deliberate view of the country between Berwick and Alnwick: therein gaining some knowledge of the seacoast district; and making good my general view of the midland, northern, and eastern, parts of the county.

In

---

* The extraordinary sale of farm stock, belonging to Mr. Wilkie of Dorrington (one of the largest occupiers in the island) furnished x e with a singular opportunity of seeing them drawn together.

In August 1798, I took a cursory survey of its south-western quarter: entering it by the great road, between Carlisle and Newcastle, at Glenwhelt; and following the southern branch of the Tyne (down South Tyndale) to Hexham:—where I stayed a few days, to examine its rich and beautiful environs. By an excursion from thence, I penetrated the wider and better parts of North Tyndale; and traced its lofty banks, until I gained an ocean view, not only of the moreland mountains of Northumberland, toward the north, but of those of Cumberland and Durham, to the west and south: commanding, from an eminence, one of the most extensive and barren circle of views (some cultivation to the eastward excepted) which England—if not the Island—contains. From Hexham, I proceeded, by the upper road, to Newcastle; and thereby compleated my general view of the cultivated uplands.

Finally, in March 1799, I examined, with much interest, the lovely bason of Belford; and traced the vale lands of the coast, from Bamburgh castle, toward Alnwick; and, from thence, by Warkworth, and Witherington castle, to Morpeth: thus finishing my general view of the county.

In these several excursions and examinations, I made travelling notes; and also registered, analytically, such evident facts as a stranger may safely collect,— wherever I remained in any way stationary.

These various notices are now before me: and from them I will give a sketch of each of the six districts that are above enumerated: by which the reader will be enabled to form a just conception of the natural features of the county; and I may thereby be better able to appreciate and explain the report which is given of it, than I might without such data to refer to.

The reporters (in this and other instances) have divided the county according to its *political*, not its *natural*, or *agricultural*, lines of separation:—an erroneous

roneous plan of proceeding, which is similar to that
of surveying, by counties. See INTRODUCTION.
Sect. 2.

THE DISTRICT of WOOLER.—This is incident to
the river, Till, which falls into the Tweed, a few miles
below Coldstream. Its principal area is formed by
a remarkable flat of low absorbent land, some miles
across, called " Millfield Plain ;"—whose margins
spread irregularly, in various directions; following
the different branches of the Till; particularly its
main branch, whose valley extends several miles to
the southward. As a district, however, it is but of
small extent.

The soil appears to be pretty uniformly of a sandy
or gravelly nature, what in Scotland is termed " sharp
land ;" and is frequently seen incumbent on a pebbly
substratum ; such as abounds in various districts of
that kingdom : in other parts, however, there are evidences of a more retentive subsoil, and cooler land.

The SEACOAST of NORTHUMBERLAND.—This well-
defined natural District extends from Bamborough,
on the north (being there cut off from the more
northern coast by a ridge of rock) to the southern
bank of the Wansbeck, below Morpeth, on the
south:—an extent of about thirty miles. Its width
is remarkably uniform, considering its length. If
we include the lower skirts of the western banks,
which rise with an easy slope to the upland district,
we may lay the mean width at five miles; and if we
further add the mouths or lower ends of the valleys
which open into it,—as those of the Aln, the Coquet,
and the Wans,—we may fairly, I think, estimate the
contents of the whole district, at more than one
hundred and fifty square miles.

Its elevation and surface are perfectly those of a
low lying vale district. Some of the lower lands are
barely out of the tide's way : and the higher grounds
of the area are seldom more than gentle swells.
Viewed

Viewed lengthway, from various points, it has every appearance of half a rivered vale.

In soil, too, it strictly bears the vale character. It is almost uniformly of a retentive nature, and of a productive quality; but varies in fertility. Toward the northern extremity, there is much deep strong land, of a superior quality. But near the midway of the district the most fertile lands are found. Between the Aln and the Coquet, and on the eastern banks of the former, lie some of the most valuable lands in the island; westward of the Coquet, the surface is flatter, and the soil of a paler color, and a cooler nature.

THE CHEVIOT HILLS.—These remarkable mountain heights are situated "on the borders;" part of them stand within the political bounds of Scotland. But the whole being, by nature and agricultural management the same; and the principal hill, "the Cheviot"—from which they take their name—being situated in Northumberland, I consider the whole as a district of the northern department of England.

The extent of these hills would be difficult to estimate; as they unite with the moreland district to the southward, and are continued, to the westward, by similar green hills in Scotland. Admitting that their bases occupy a circle of about fifteen miles in diameter, their contents may be set down at one hundred and fifty, to two hundred, square miles.

The surface or form of these hills is extraordinary. Many of them are of a conical mould;—some of them, nearly perfect Cones; others of irregular shape; but generally pointed; with smooth steep sides; and with their bases nearly in contact with each other.

The soil, on the lower slopes, has every appearance of considerable fertility; and, with a better climature, might doubtlessly be rendered productive, in a state of mixed cultivation. On the higher steeper acclivities, points of rock, and loose stones appear.

The produce, at present, is grass,—a continued
sheet

sheet of greensward,—from base to summit ; excepting where stones prevail ; and excepting the heads of the higher hills, especially of the Cheviot,—whose upper regions are maculate with blotches of heath. Formerly, many or most of the lower grounds, where any degree of flatness would easily admit the plow, have evidently been cultivated ;—probably at a time when these borders were fuller of people, than they are at present ; when a few very large sheep farmers (each perhaps holding a parish of several thousand acres in extent) and their shepherds, are the only inhabitants : and, even to supply these few, the arable crops, that are at present grown, are insufficient.

THE MORELANDS, or HEATHY WASTES.—I have had little opportunity of *examining* these unprofitable lands ; which occupy, I apprehend, much more than one third of the surface of the county. From the summit of one of the more elevated and western of the Cheviot hills, I had an extensive view of the northwest quarter of these barren tracts. From the commanding point, mentioned aforegoing, page 5, I probably completed my *general view*,—not only of the western, but of the southern, morelands of Northumberland ; the latter being incorporated with those of Durham, &c. Moreover, in travelling the Coldstream road, between Framlington and Whittingham, I had an opportunity of seeing something of the natural character of those wild lands : And my observations, in these superficial views, corresponding with the cursory remarks of the reporters, which will presently appear, it is unnecessary to say more, in this place, respecting them.

THE CULTIVATED UPLANDS.—These, it is probable, extend over one fourth of the county ; occupying the more central parts of its area.

Their elevation and their extent being jointly considered, they may be said to be peculiar to this part of the island. They are not confined to Northumberland,

land, but extend to the adjoining county of Durham;—whose cultivated upper lands are of a similar nature. In low lying vale districts, we frequently meet with lands of a like description; particularly, in the wealds of Sussex and Kent: and with contracted plots of upland, in various parts of the kingdom.

The surface, notwithstanding its elevation, and its extent, approaches nearly to flatness!—unless where it is grooved or furrowed by the rivered vallies which cross it; and which, I believe, are uniformly of a more fertile nature.

The soil of these high lying lands is mostly of a pale color; in some places, approaching to whiteness: in others, it is variegated. But it is uniformly, or nearly so, of a cold weak quality. The substrata are of course retentive; and, beneath them, coals are perhaps invariably deposited.

THE DISTRICT of HEXHAM.—This consists of the principal valley of the Tyne, and its two branches; namely, north and south Tyndales; which divaricate a few miles above Hexham.

The immediate environs, the bason of Hexham (the appearance, in almost every point of view, is that of a deep oval dish) is formed by a dilation of the principal valley; which, here, partakes of the vale character. Its length may be nine or ten miles; its *greatest* width, including the feet of its tall banks, three or four miles. South Tyndale is nearly of an even width—namely about a mile wide—for more than ten miles. North Tyndale is wider, above the conflux of the two branches of the river; but does not continue its width, more than four or five miles; contracting, above, to a moreland dale.

The lands of these vallies are of a friable loamy nature. In south Tyndale, and in some parts of the valley of Hexham, the soil is of a sharp sandy or gravelly quality, incumbent on a pebbly, water-formed base: such as is commonly found in mountain-skirt situations. But the prevailing soil, especially

in

in the principal valley, is a rich deep loam, on limestone: limestone land of the very first quality. No
sooner, however, is the rim of the bason (of Hexham)
surmounted, on either side, than pale, weak, cold-
land heights, and coal pits, meet the eye.

HAVING now endeavored to clear the ground,
and smooth the way, to my present undertaking;
by removing obstacles, and explaining difficulties, that might otherwise have interrupted its progress; I will not longer delay to enter upon the execution.

———

" GENERAL VIEW
OF THE
AGRICULTURE
OF THE
COUNTY
OF
NORTHUMBERLAND;

WITH

OBSERVATIONS ON THE MEANS OF ITS IMPROVEMENT.

DRAWN UP FOR THE CONSIDERATION OF

THE BOARD OF AGRICULTURE

AND INTERNAL IMPROVEMENT.

BY J. BAILEY AND G. CULLEY.

THE THIRD EDITION*."

1805.

THE AUTHORITY of a work of this kind depending
wholely on the ability and application with which it
has been executed, the primary facts to be ascertained relate to the skill and judgment of the author,
and the sort of attention wherewith he has employed
them.

In

* The second reprinted Edition. See the Introduction.

In the present instance, I am happy in being able to speak, from personal knowledge, respecting the QUALIFICATIONS of the REPORTERS. Mr. CULLEY is publicly and well known, as an author on the subject of LIVE STOCK. He is, I believe, of South Durham—from the banks of the Tees—a district which has, for some length of time, taken a distinguished lead in English agriculture. He was, moreover, in early life, a pupil of Mr. Bakewell of Leicestershire :—joint advantages which few men can claim. Add to these, Mr. C. has for many years been an extensive occupier in the county under review; namely, in the district of Wooler, and on the southern bank of the Tweed. His breed of sheep are known, even to the " farthest Thule," by the popular name of the " Culley breed." Mr. Culley is also an arable farmer of high distinction; and has perhaps, as much or more than any man, been instrumental in raising the agriculture of Tweedside to its present eminence.

Mr. BAILEY, too, has long been resident in the district of Wooler; as manager of the extensive landed property of the Earl of Tankerville, in that neighbourhood. His practical knowledge of the management of tenanted estates, and woodlands, must of course be considerable ; and his scientific acquirements are evident in different parts of the REPORT ; of which, from expressions that occur in it, Mr. B. is to be considered as *editor*. Mr. Bailey's practical knowledge as an agriculturist, I cannot so well appreciate. But this was the less required, as the mature experience of his able coadjutor, rendered it in a manner unnecessary.

Jointly, Messrs. BAILEY and CULLEY were peculiarly qualified for the task they undertook. I gladly embrace them ;—and welcome them to a field in which I have long been laboring.

Their MODE of SURVEY, or the QUANTITY of ATTENTION bestowed upon it, does not appear. Indeed, from their long residence within the county, the
northern

northern and eastern parts of it, at least, must have been sufficiently familiar to them, without much further examination. What we learn from their publication, respecting its execution, is contained in the following modest " PRELIMINARY OBSERVATIONS." p. 19.

" In drawing up this Report, according to the plan laid down by the Board of Agriculture, we have endeavoured to be as concise as possible, except in those articles which are in a great measure peculiar to this district; some of which, we have reason to think, may be adopted with advantage in others."

" It is scarcely possible, in an undertaking of this kind, to describe all the minutiæ of practice, or to notice every local improvement; but we hope that the most prominent features of the Agriculture of Northumberland, as existing in 1793, will be found faithfully recorded in the following sheets."

A MAP (by Mr. Bailey) distinguishes the cultivated, from the uncultivated, lands, by appropriate engraving.

This intelligible and permanent method of distinction may, perhaps, have been taken from a sketch which I had previously given of the county of York, and in which I endeavored to separate the lands of the county, by different modes or *colors* of engraving, agreeably to their natural divisions, into MOUNTAIN, UPLAND, and VALE : modes of discrimination which strike the eye at once, and show the surface of a country with nearly the same effect, as that which could be produced by a model or mold. (See the map prefixed to the Rural Economy of Yorkshire.) Mr. B. however, has distinguished the morelands, only; having left the whole of the cultivated surface, indiscriminate.

SUBJECT

THE NATURAL ECONOMY OF

NORTHUMBERLAND.

SITUATION. In defining a NATURAL DISTRICT, it is requisite to describe its boundaries. But not so, in speaking of a COUNTY,—whose outlines appear in every map of the kingdom.

The EXTENT is estimated, by Mr. Bailey, at 1980 square miles, or 1,267,200 acres; 817,200 of which he thinks " are or may be cultivated by the plough;" the remaining 450,000 he considers as incident to " mountainous districts, improper for tillage." p. 2.

Supposing the whole of the six natural districts, described aforegoing, to contain 1850 square miles, they may be divided, in round numbers, to convey a sufficiently intelligible idea of the extent of each, in the following manner.

District of Wooler 100
Sea Coast 150
Cheviot Hills 200
Morelands 800
Uplands 500
District of Hexham 100

1850

All that we find in the Report, relating to the nature of the SOIL, the SURFACE, and the CHARACTER-ISTIC APPEARANCE, of the six natural districts that are sketched, aforegoing, is included in the following extract.

P. 4. " *A strong fertile clayey loam* occupies the level tract of country along the coast, and reaches as far up in general as the great post-road. It is well adapted to the culture of wheat, pulse, clover, and grazing.

" *Sandy,*

" *Sandy, gravelly, and dry loam*—or what is here more generally understood by turnip soil, is found on the banks of the Tyne, from Newburn to Haltwhistle; on the Coquet, about and above Rothbury ; on the Aln, from its mouth to Alnwick ; and down Tweed-side : but the greatest quantity of this kind of soil is found in the vales of Breamish, Till, and Beaumont. The hills surrounding the Cheviot mountains are mostly a dry, sharp-pointed, gravelly loam.

" *Moist loams*—on a wet, cold, clayey bottom, occupy a large portion of this county : being unsafe for sheep, and unfit for turnips, they are principally employed in growing grain, rearing young cattle, and feeding ewes and lambs. This soil prevails most in the middle and south-east parts of the county.

" *Black peat earth*—is the prevailing soil in most of the mountainous districts, and is found in many places through the lower parts of the county.

" The aspect of this county, in respect to surface, is marked with great variety : along the sea-coast, it is nearly level ; towards the middle, the surface is more diversified, and thrown into large swelling ridges, formed by the principal rivers. These parts are well enclosed ; in some places enriched with wood and recent plantations, but the general appearance is des-titute of those ornaments. The western part (except a few intervening vales" (vallies *) " is an extensive
scene

---

* This provincial error is common to the North of England. The following explanations may, there, be useful.

VALE—English ; YSTRAD—Welch ; STRATH—Erse :—an extent of low country, some miles in width ; lying between ranges of higher grounds.

VALLEY—South of England ; DALE—North of England, and South of Scotland ; COOM—Welch ; GLEN—Erse :—the diminutive of Vale ;—the lower grounds narrow,—as from half a mile to a mile or two in width ; generally with a high steep bank rising on either side.

DELL—South of England ; GRAIN or GILL—North of England ; CLEUGH—South of Scotland ; CEUNANT—Welch ; CURRY, or CUR-ROCH—Erse :—the diminutive of Dale, or Valley ; generally, the branch of a Valley :—a short, or otherwise inferior Valley.

DINGLE :—the diminutive of Dell.

scene of open, mountainous district, where the hand of cultivation is rarely to be traced.

" Of the mountainous districts, those around Cheviot are the most valuable, being in general fine green hills, thrown into a numberless variety of forms, enclosing and sheltering many deep, narrow, sequestered glens : they extend from the head of Coquet down to Allenton ; from thence northward to Prendwick, Branton, Ilderton, Wooler, Kirknewton, and Mindrim, and occupy at least an area of 90,000 acres.

" The other mountainous districts lie chiefly on the western part of the county, some of which adjoin the county of Durham ; but the largest portion extends from the Roman Wall to the river Coquet (with a few intervening enclosed vales" (vallies or dales), " and to the moors north of Rothbury. They are not marked by any striking irregularities of surface, being in general extensive, open, solitary wastes, growing little else but heath, and affording a hard subsistence to the flocks that depasture them."

On CLIMATURE, the subjoined remarks are valuable. P. 3. " The *Climate*, in regard to temperature, is subject to great variation : upon the mountains, snow will often continue for several months (and may frequently be seen there of a considerable depth), when there is none in the lower districts. The weather is very inconstant, but mostly runs in extremes. In the spring months, the cold, piercing, easterly winds are most prevalent ; and our longest droughts are always accompanied by them : in some places they have acquired the name of *sea-pines*, from the slow progress vegetation makes whenever they continue for a few weeks. Rain is of little use while they prevail, from the great cold which always attends them.

" The mild western and southern breezes rarely take place before June ; they are certain harbingers of rain and vigorous vegetation, and are the most prevailing winds through the summer and autumn : in the latter season, they often blow with tempestuous fury, dash out the corn, and disappoint the just hopes of the industrious farmer.

" Our

" Our greatest falls of snow, or rain, are from the south, or south-east; and whenever we have a very high *west wind*, it is a certain sign that a great quantity of rain is falling to the westward, in Cumberland and Roxburghshire."

P. 110. "The *Corn Harvest*—in the vale" (valley) "of Till, and upon Tyneside, near Hexham, frequently begins the first week in August; while upon the cold backward soils and situations, oats will be often uncut the latter end of October, or beginning of November; but the most general harvest is in September."

P. 21. WATERS.—" The principal rivers, which act as estuaries" (no) " to the rest, are the Tyne, Blyth, Wansbeck, Coquet, Aln, and Tweed. The innumerable streams which lose their names in the above, spread in every direction through the county."

" A valuable natural produce, of these waters, is the *salmon*, of which we find these particulars: P.21. "The Tyne and Tweed are the most eminent for their navigation, the tide flowing up the former sixteen miles, and up the latter eight or ten. The navigation of the other rivers is confined to a small distance from their mouths: of these, the Blyth and Aln are of the most importance, from the convenience which the first affords to its neighbourhood, for the exportation of considerable quantities of coals; and both of them for corn, &c. and the importation of timber, iron, and other useful articles.

" The Tyne and Tweed have been long celebrated for their salmon fisheries: in the latter, a rent of 800*l.* a year is paid for a fishing of two hundred yards in length, near the mouth of the river; and the same rent is paid for other two fishings above the bridge, not more than two hundred and fifty yards in length each. The fish taken here are, the salmon, bulltrout, whitling, and large common trout, and nearly the whole of them sent to London; in the conveyance of which, a great improvement has taken place of late years, by packing them in pounded ice: by this means they are presented nearly as fresh at the

London

London market, as when taken out of the river. For the purpose of carrying them, and keeping up a constant and regular supply, vessels called smacks, sail three times a week, and being purposely constructed for swift sailing, frequently make their run in 48 hours. These vessels are from 70 to 120 tons burden; on an average twelve men are employed in each vessel, (?) and make about fourteen voyages in a year: and not less than 75 boats, and 300 fishermen, are employed in taking the fish in the river Tweed."

Fossils. P. 17. "*Limestone*—of an excellent quality, abounds through all Bamborough ward, Islandshire, and that part of Glendale ward situated on the east side of the river Till; it stretches from thence, in a south-westerly direction, through the central parts of the county, and is found at Shilbottle, Longframlington, Hartburn, Rial, Corbridge, &c. and at numberless other places to the westward of these; but the south-east quarter, which is so rich in coal, is destitute of lime*; as is also that part of Glendale ward west of the river Till."

P. 17. "*Shell marl* is found in a few places in Glendale ward. The greatest quantity is at Wark, Sunnylaws, and Learmouth, where it has been formed by a deposit of various kinds of shells, both univalve and bivalve, many of which are yet perfect, forming a stratum, several feet in depth, of pure calcareous earth; but the exact depth of this bed of marl has never yet been ascertained, for want of a proper level to carry off the water." And, in a note, p. 18, we are informed that, "Since the first impression of this Report, in 1794, shell marl has been found in several other places, by boring with an auger, as at Mindrim, The Hagg, Learmouth, Newtown, Hopper, &c.; and in every instance, in flat, boggy, mossy grounds, which have formerly been lakes."

As

" * Except a small patch at Whitley, near Tynemouth."

As this note does not appear in the first reprinted
Report, in 1797, the discoveries, here mentioned, are
probably of recent date ;—perhaps, since April 1804.
See TREATISE on LANDED PROPERTY, page 225.

P. 20. " *Iron ore*—may be had in many parts of the
county; of late years, the convenience of shipping it
at Holy Island has induced the Carron Company to
have considerable quantites from thence."

P. 20. " *Freestones*—of various kinds, abound in
almost every part of the county, and are applied to all
the purposes of building.   Many of the quarries afford
tolerable slates for roofing, and flags for floors: at
some of them, excellent grindstones are got, of which
a great many are exported from Camus and Warkworth."   The gritstone quarries which furnish the
far-famed " Newcastle grindstones" are situated on
the south-side of the Tyne, in the county of Durham.

P. 20. " *Whinstones*—of the blue kind, are found
in many parts of the county, particularly along the
sea-coast in Bamboroughshire; and the district on the
western side of the river Till, including all the Cheviot
mountains, produces scarcely any other mineral substance than brown, red, or grey whinstone.   For
making roads, they are superior to any other materials we ever saw, and are led several miles for that
purpose, even where freestones are to be had upon
the spot."

MINERALS.   Among these are mentioned *lead ore*,
and the *ore of zinc* :—

But it is to the COALS of Northumberland the
surveyors have very properly paid their especial attention; and have, by their industry, been enabled to
present to the public much valuable information on
the subject.

Collieries are intimately connected with agriculture.
Fuel is a necessary of life; and if it cannot be drawn
from subterranean sources, agriculture must give up,
in many situations, a considerable portion of the surface soil to supply it.   I therefore most readily
embrace an opportunity, which the Northumbrian
                                                      Report

Report affords me, of laying up some valuable facts on a topic so nearly concerning the lasting welfare of the country.

P. 5. " Coal—is found in abundance through the greatest part of this county, particularly in the lower district; in the south-east quarter it is of the best quality *, and the most numerous and thickest seams, from whence those vast quantities are exported which supply the great consumption of the London market, as well as the coasting and foreign trade.—This coal trade is the foundation of the commerce of the county, and the principal source of its wealth, as well as a never-failing nursery for some of the best seamen in the British Navy.—Of the quantity of coals raised in this county, we have not been able to form a probable conjecture, for want of sufficient data to estimate the quantity used at home; but have obtained what are exported from the river Tyne, in which a considerable portion raised in the county of Durham is included, and which may probably come near a balance for those consumed in this county. Some idea of the magnitude of this trade may be formed, by the following statement of

" THE EXPORTS OF COALS FROM NEWCASTLE.

In 1772 .... 351,890 Newcastle chaldrons.
     1776 380,000
     1791 444,909
     1792 490,682
     1793 486,133
     1794 .... 426,384 †
     1795 505,650

From

" * The coals found in this district are of the variety called "caking coals," which melt in the fire, burn to a strong cinder in the open air, and the best kinds produce very few ashes."

" † This is the only year in which we find the quantities raised in Northumberland and Durham are kept distinct, and which are,

In the county of Northumberland, - - - 257,462 chaldrons.
In the county of Durham, - - - - - - 168,922

In all - - - - 426,384"

"From hence it appears, that this trade is increasing at an amazing rate, there being not less than one-third more coals exported now than were exported twenty years since. From Hartley and Blythe there are exported yearly between 30,000 and 40,000 chaldrons: if these be added to the average export from Newcastle for the last three or four years, the quantity exported from this county may be fairly estimated at 510,000 Newcastle chaldrons, or 956,250 London chaldrons; the Newcastle chaldron being to the London chaldron in the ratio of 8 to 15."

P. 10. "To the coal-owners the winning and working these collieries are very expensive, and frequently attended with considerable risk; for though very large fortunes have been made in this businnss, yet many have been lost: the unexpected alteration of the strata, from dykes and other troubles; the frequent and dreadful explosions from inflammable air; the great depth of the shafts, and increasing quantities of water to be raised, baffle the most experienced artists, and overcome the amazing powers of the fire-engine, which of late years has received many improvements, and been made to perform what was thought absolutely impossible at its first introduction*.

"These powerful machines are now applied to the purposes of drawing coals, which business was formerly universally performed by horses; frequently eight to a shaft, where great quantities were drawn, and dispatch was necessary; but by the invention and application of the drawing machines, a great many horses were dismissed from the collieries, which has considerably reduced the consumption of oats in this neighbourhood.

"Many of the collieries are situated at a considerable distance from the river, to which the coals are conveyed

---

"* We were informed, that there was only one fire-engine in the neighbourhood of Newcastle, about 50 years since; that it raised the water only 40 yards, which, at that time, was thought a wonderful performance: at present, water is raised, and probably in greater abundance, 160 yards and upwards."

veyed from the pits in a peculiar kind of carriage, called a *Newcastle coal-waggon.*"

Having thus been informed of the method of raising coals, and conveying them to the ships, we are led down the lengthened shaft, and shown, not only the different seams of coals, but the intermediate strata, by which they are separated from each other. For the latter part of this interesting information, however, I am obliged to have recourse to a former edition; the seams of coals, only, without the intermediate strata, being given in the last.

P. 12. " It has been asserted, that " *the coals in this county are inexhaustible.*"—Mr. WILLIAMS, in his Natural History of the Mineral Kingdom, is of a different opinion, and thinks it a matter of such importance as to deserve the serious attention of the Legislature. Towards elucidating this point, it may be of some use to estimate what number of acres are wrought yearly in this county to supply the above quantity of coals. In order to accomplish this object, the thickness and number of workable seams of coal must be first ascertained; for which purpose we have been favoured with sections* exhibiting the thickness and depth of the various strata, in some of the deepest pits in the county; which will not only be useful for the present purpose, but we hope will be acceptable to many of our readers, who are curious in researches of subterraneous geography."

As a valuable fact in geological science, I copy one of those sections, from the first reprinted edition, of 1797.

P. 11. " At St. Anthon's Colliery (3 miles east of Newcastle) the strata from the surface to the LOW MAIN coal, are:—

Soil

" * One at St. Anthon's, about three miles below Newcastle, by Mr. JOHNSON ; the other of Montague Main, about three miles above Newcastle, by Mr. THOMAS. "

	Yds.	Ft.	Ins.
Soil and clay - - - - - - -	10	0	0*
Brown post - - - - - -	24	0	0
1. COAL - - - - - - - -	0	0	6
Blue-metal stone - - - - -	5	2	0
White girdles - - - - -	4	1	0
2. COAL - - - - - - - -	0	0	8
White and grey post - - -	12	0	0
Soft blue metal stone - - -	10	0	0
3. COAL - - - - - - - -	0	0	6
White post girdles - - - -	6	0	0
Whin - - - - - - - -	3	1	6
Strong white post - - - -	6	1	0
4. COAL - - - - - - - -	0	1	0
Soft blue thill - - - - - -	3	2	0
Soft girdles mixed with whin -	7	2	0
5. COAL - - - - - - - -	0	0	6
Blue and black stone - - -	7	1	0
6. COAL - - - - - - - -	0	0	8
Strong white post - - - -	3	0	0
Grey metal stone - - - -	3	1	0
7. COAL - - - - - - - -	0	0	8
Grey post mixed with whin -	8	1	0
Grey girdles - - - - - -	6	1	0
Blue and black stone - - -	4	2	0
8. COAL - - - - - - - -	0	1	0
Grey metal stone - - - -	4	0	0
Strong white post - - - -	12	0	0
Black metal stone with hard girdles	6	0	0
9. HIGH MAIN COAL - - - -	2	0	0—152
Grey metal - - - - - -	9	0	0
Post girdles - - - - - -	0	2	0
Blue metal - - - - - -	1	1	0
Girdles - - - - - - - -	0	1	2
Blue metal stone - - - - -	10	0	0
Post - - - - - - - -	0	1	0
Blue metal stone - - - -	6	0	0
Carried over	179	2	4

Whin

* Hence, no doubt, the peculiar coldness of the land. *Rev.*

	Yds.	Ft.	Ins.
Brought over	179	2	4
Whin and blue metal - - -	0	1	6
Strong white post - - - -	7	0	0
Brown post with water - - -	0	0	7
Blue metal stone with grey girdles	4	2	0
10. COAL - - - - - - - -	1	0	0
Blue metal stone - - - -	6	0	3
White post - - - - - -	1	1	0
11. COAL - - - - - - - -	0	0	6
Strong grey metal with post girdles	4	0	6
Strong white post - - - -	2	1	0
Whin - - - - - - - -	0	1	0
Blue metal stone - - - -	2	2	7
Grey metal stone with post girdles	5	1	5
Blue metal stone with whin girdles	3	1	3
12. COAL - - - - - - - -	0	1	6
Blue grey metal - - - - -	1	0	8
White post - - - - - -	4	0	7
White post mixed with whin -	4	0	0
White post - - - - - -	2	2	0
Dark blue metal and coal - -	0	2	2
Grey metal stone and girdles -	4	2	0
White post mixed with whin -	6	0	7
Whin - - - - - - - -	0	1	0
White post mixed with whin -	2	0	6
13. COAL - - - - - - - -	1	0	3
Dark grey metal stone - - -	1	0	6
Grey metal and whin girdles -	3	1	10
Grey metal and girdles - - -	3	0	0
White post - - - - - -	1	0	0
14. COAL - - - - - - - -	1	0	2
Blue and grey metal - - -	1	1	0
15. COAL - - - - - - - -	0	0	9
Blue and grey metal - - -	4	0	0
White post mixed with whin -	1	1	6
Grey metal - - - - - -	2	0	6
Grey metal and girdles - -	2	0	9
16. LOW MAIN COAL - - - -	2	0	6
Total	270	1	8

" In the above pit or shaft, which is nearly* the deepest in the kingdom, there are no less than 16 seams of coals. But many of these, from their thinness, are not workable. The 9th, called the *high main coal*, and the 16th, the *low main coal*, are the two principal seams for affording quantities of coal, being together 12½ feet thick, and are those most generally wrought. But the 10th, 13th, and 14th, are all workable seams, and will afford considerable quantities of coal; the aggregate of the three making nearly 9½ feet thick; so that the total thickness of the workable seams in this colliery amount to 22 feet."

The other Section I take from the last Edition.

P. 14. " In Montague Main colliery (three miles west of Newcastle) the different seams of coal are as follow:

Seams.	Thickness of each seam.		Depth to each seam.		
	Ft.	In.	Yds.	Ft.	In.
1. Coal	0	4	5	2	0
2. Ditto	0	6	44	1	0
3. Ditto	0	9	63	2	9
4. Benwell Main	5	3	69	1	10
5. Coal	1	0	79	2	10
6. Ditto	0	8	133	1	6
7. Ditto	3	4	137	1	10
8. Ditto	1	6	143	1	3
9. Ditto	1	3	147	2	2
10. Ditto	0	8	162	2	6
11. Low Main Coal	2	11	176	0	4
12. Lower Main Coal	2	10	199	2	10
13. Coal	0	6	226	0	10
14. Ditto	0	5	233	1	5
15. Ditto	0	3	241	1	10

" In this shaft there are 15 seams of coal, of which only four are workable, viz. the 4th, 7th, 11th, and 12th, making together four yards, one foot, seven inches of workable coal. If the medium be taken betwixt this and St. Anthon's, it will be nearly six

" * A pit has been lately sunk at Willington, 5 miles north-east from Newcastle, which is 280 yards deep, to the low main coal."

yards thick of workable coal, from which may be formed

A calculation of the quantity of Coal in an acre of ground, supposing the aggregate thickness of the various seams amount to six yards.

An acre of ground contains .... 4840 square yards
which, multiplied by the thickness,   6 yards,

gives .... 29040 cubic yards
in an acre.

From which deduct ⅓ for waste, ⎫
  and the part or pillars necessary ⎬ 9680
  to be left in working .... ⎭

there remains .... 19360 cubic yards
to be wrought.

And as three cubic yards of coal, when wrought, afford a Newcastle chaldron,

therefore .... 19360 ⎱ gives 6453 Newcastle chaldrons
divided by .....   3 ⎰   per acre.

" The coals exported yearly from the rivers Tyne and Wear, with Hartley and Blythe, amount to about 825,000 chaldrons*, which, with the home consumption of the two counties of Northumberland and Durham, will make the quantity of coals raised yearly, about 1,000,000 chaldrons.

And the chaldrons raised yearly, 1,000,000 ⎱ gives 155
           —————— ⎬ acres near-
divided by the chaldrons per acre   6453 ⎰ ly per year,
cleared of coal
6 yards thick.

" And by estimating the breadth occupied by the caking coals to be on an average eight miles broad, and twenty-five miles long, in the two counties, we shall find there will be about 200 square miles, or 128,000 acres of coal proper for exportation.

Then

* From Newcastle, — — 510,000 chaldrons.
  —— Sunderland, — — 315,000 ditto.

In all   — — 825,000

Then the whole area 128,000 ⎞ gives 825 years, the time
divided by the yearly ————— ⎬ before this space will
consumption ....   155 ⎠ be wrought out.

"But there are some reasons to think that a thickness of seam, equal to six yards, will not be obtained over an extent of 200 square miles; probably not more, on an average, than four yards; in which case, the coal will be exhausted in 550 years: and if the aggregate thickness of the seams to be obtained, should prove only three yards, then little more than 400 years will be the term of continuance; but it is probable that, before the half of that time be elapsed, the price to the consumer will be considerably increased, from the increased expense of obtaining them, and the increased length of carriage from the pits to the river. This last, we presume, may be reduced in some situations, by adopting canals instead of waggon-ways, which, we have often wondered, have never yet been attempted."

Those calculations I copy on the faith of the surveyors: and the following geological facts I insert, here, on the same authority.

P. 16. "Of the coal found all through Bamborough ward, Islandshire, and those parts of Glendale ward east of the river Till, the seams are very thin, mostly from one to three feet thick, and of a very inferior quality, yielding a great quantity of ashes, and neither caking in the fire nor burning to a cinder: they are used only for home-consumption, and for burning lime; for the latter purpose they are well adapted, by their property of neither caking nor burning to a cinder; and it luckily happens, that through all this district, the coal and lime are generally found together; a circumstance which greatly facilitates, and lessens the expense of, burning lime.

"If a line be drawn from Alemouth to a little west of Bywell, on the river Tyne, very little of this kind of coal and limestone will be found to the east of it; and from this line to the sea-coast, no limestone whatever appears, except a small patch of a different
limestone

limestone that puts in at **Whitley**, near Tynemouth, and runs from thence in a south-westerly direction, through the county of Durham, &c. In this space, betwixt those two ranges of limestone, lie the caking coals of superior quality above-described; and the same breadth of coal may be traced through the county of Durham, stretching in the same direction, and bounded on the east and west in a similar manner, by stretches of limestone of different kinds."

SUBJECT THE SECOND.

POLITICAL ECONOMY.

POLITICAL DIVISIONS. P. 2. " The county of Northumberland is divided into six Wards, viz. Tindale Ward, Coquetdale Ward, Glendale Ward, Bamborough Ward, Morpeth Ward, and Castle Ward. The three first are situated in the western part of the county, *and include the whole of the mountainous district, with a considerable portion of enclosed cultivated country:* the three latter adjoin the sea-coast, and, being exempt from mountainous district, have been long under cultivation*; the vast resources of coal, which Castle ward in particular possesses, and the increased population the coal trade occasions, give them a decided preference in point of riches and population; though in point of magnitude, considerably the smallest, occupying less than one-fourth of the county."

STATE OF APPROPRIATION. P. 127. "*The Extent of Waste Lands,* or open mountainous districts, incapable of affording profit by cultivating with the plough, is very great, as we have before stated; considerable quantities of which are private property, and, of course, may be depastured by sheep, or other stock, to the greatest advantage; of those that are common, it would certainly be best for every man to know his own share."

P. 126.

---

* But include *Uplands* and *Vale,* within their respective limits.

P. 126. " *The commons*—in this county capable of being converted into profitable tillage land, are now very trifling, the greatest part having been enclosed within the last 30 years; the whole amounting to near 120,000 acres. Of this, the commons belonging to the manors of Hexhamshire and Allendale contain 50,000 acres, a great part (35,000) of which are high, exposed, heathy mountains. These are to be converted into stinted pastures, being thought incapable of any other improvement."

STATE OF SOCIETY. The only particulars, relating to this subject, which appear in the Report before me, are the subjoined notices, respecting provisions, and fuel, in this extreme northern part of the kingdom, in 1794.

Provisions.—P. 167. " The average prices of grain at Berwick, in 1792, were:

	s.	d.	
Wheat	5	0	per bushel.
Rye .	3	4	ditto.
Barley	2	6	ditto.
Oats	2	2	ditto.
Peas	3	6	ditto.

" Fat stock being easily driven from one place to another, keeps the price of butchers' meat more upon an equality in all the markets of the county.

" The average price of butchers' meat is from fourpence to fivepence per pound; but in May and June it generally gets to fivepence halfpenny; and the two last years has been sixpence and sevenpence.

	s.	d.		
Butter	0	6	a pound, of 16 ounces.	
Skim-milk and ewe cheese	0	3½	ditto.	
Fat goose	2	0		
Turkey	3	0		
Duck	0	8		
Chicken	0	6	s.	d.
Eggs, per dozen	0	3 to 0	6	
Potatoes, per bushel	1	0 — 1	6	

P. 30

P. 80. "The principal part of the rye grown in this district, as well as considerable quantities imported from abroad, is consumed in the southern parts of the county, it being the most general bread of the labouring people in that quarter. After being leavened, until it gains a considerable degree of acidity, it is made into loaves, and baked in a large brick oven, or made into thick cakes, one and a half, or two inches thick, called " sour-cakes," and baked on the girdle: the bread is very firm and solid, dark coloured, and retains its moisture or juiciness, longer than any other bread we know."

P. 82. " Barley, or barley mixed with grey peas or beans, is the common bread of labouring people in the northern parts of this county: previous to grinding, they are mixed in the proportion of two parts barley, and one of peas or beans; after being ground, the meal is sifted through a fine sieve, made of wood, to take out the rough husks and coarse bran; it is then kneaded with water, made into thin *unleavened cakes*, and immediately baked on a girdle.

" In this district, barley or mixed meal is seldom, if ever, *leavened* and *baked in loaves*."

P. 85. Oatmeal is " a principal article of food with the great mass of inhabitants, not as bread, but in *crowdies*, or *hasty-pudding* (provincially " *meal-kail*"), for breakfast and supper, eaten with butter, or more commonly skimmed-milk: the latter is an agreeable, nutritive, and healthy food, and is the general breakfast and supper of the labouring people in the northern parts of the county."

Fuel.—P. 168. " Upon the edges of the moors, towards the western parts of the county, a few peats are burnt; but in every other part, we believe, coals are universally used.

" The quantity consumed by a poor family, is from 5 to 7 cart-loads a year."

LOCAL TAXES. Under this head are to be classed the subsequent remarks on tithes and poors rates.

Tithes

Tithes.—P. 31. " Of this burthen of agriculture, we
do not find any thing peculiar to this county, which is
not common to the rest. In some parts, the tithes
are collected with moderation; in others, with severity
of law: some let for a term of years at a fair rent,
whilst others value and let every year."

So far, as to the *gathering* of *tithes*, in Northumberland. In a subsequent chapter, entitled " Obstacles
to Improvement," are the following sensible and dispassionate observations, on their *political operation*,
in the present state of society.

P. 178. " *The payment of Tithes in kind* is universally
agreed to be a material obstacle to the advancement of
agriculture. According to the present mode of collecting tithes, it is not a tenth of the *natural produce* of
the land, but a tenth of the *capital employed in trade.*
If a man employs 100*l.* in trade, he receives his
profits without any deduction: but if he should lay
out this 100*l.* on a speculation of improving a piece
of land (say, draining a bog), he finds, if his scheme
succeeds, that the produce is not all his own; the
tithe-owner comes, and takes away *one-tenth* (which
is probably *all the profit*, after deducting common interest for the money expended), and this from off
land that never afforded any tithe since the creation,
nor *ever would have done*, had not this spirited im-
prover laid out his 100*l.* on improving this bog, rather
than employing it in trade, where he could have
received at least 10*l.* per cent. for his money: the bog
would then have continued unprofitable, and the
tithe-owner would have received *no injury*; for neither
he, nor any of his predecessors, had ever reaped any
advantage from it.—Such a payment, so often the
source of dissentions betwixt the clergy and their
parishioners, should, if possible, be removed, either
by purchase, commutation, or any other means, by
which a *fair equivalent* can be rendered for it; for so
long as it exists, it is impossible to expect that agricultural improvements will be carried to the extent of
which they are capable.—In the above instance we
have

have shewn the great uncertainty of employing money in speculations of improving land, and that the tithes, in such cases, are a large portion of a man's capital in trade, and not a tenth of the natural produce of the earth, which some have thought was all that was intended by the original imposers, who, no doubt, meant them for a good purpose; but if, through a succession of ages, a change of manners, of sentiments, and of cultivation, has taken place, and the ill effects of tithes be universally felt, and acknowledged to lessen the quantity of food obtainable from a considerable portion of this kingdom, a change in the mode of paying them would also be desirable; for the proprietors of such lands are not only losers, but the community at large. It is surprizing that this matter should have so long escaped the regulation of the Legislature, and that it should be always so strenuously opposed by the clergy, there never having been a wish to take any thing from them, but to render a *fair equivalent* for what is their due, and which there would be little difficulty in doing, notwithstanding the many objections that have been invented to perplex this most interesting question."

Poor Rates.—P. 31. " In Newcastle, they vary from 2s. 6d. to 4s. 6d. in the pound, in times of peace; but at present, All-Saint's parish is as high as 6s. per pound, owing to the seafaring people living mostly in this parish; and the sailors being impressed, their wives and children come for support upon the parish.— At Hexham they are 2s. 6d.—Morpeth 3s. 6d.— Alnwick 1s. 10d.—Belford 2s. 6d.—Berwick 2s. 8d.— Wooler 1s. 6d.; and in other parts of the county we find they vary from 6d. to 2s. per pound. In 1804 the above rates are increased at least one-third" *.

PUBLIC

---

* GENERAL REMARK on POORS RATES. These particulars, as isolated facts, are not of much *public* import. But, by continuing to register such facts, as they may occur in other Reports, (when they can be relied upon, as in the present instance) they may, collectively, be found useful, in meliorating, on rational principles, the condition of the indigent,

PUBLIC WORKS. Relating to the public works of Northumberland, I find little collected that requires to be concentrated, here.

River Navigation. P. 21. " The Tyne and Tweed are the most eminent for their navigation, the tide flowing up the former sixteen miles, and up the latter eight or ten. The navigation of the other rivers is confined to a small distance from their mouths : of these, the Blyth and Aln are of the most importance, from the convenience which the first affords to its neighbourhood, for the exportation of considerable quantities of coals; and both of them for corn, &c. and the importation of timber, iron, and other useful articles."

Of *navigable canals* the country is, at present, I believe destitute. One between Newcastle and Carlisle has been proposed; and, to the eye of a traveller, paying some attention to the line, it is evidently and aptly practicable: thereby to join the eastern and western seas. But, through the clashing of interests, the misapprehensions of land-owners, and the rivalship of surveyors, the plan, I understand, still remains unexecuted.

The *Railways* of the Newcastle collieries have been mentioned.—They are constructed with " long pieces of wood, about four inches square, laid lengthway, upon sleepers of wood." The cost about " five shillings, a yard, or 440*l.* a mile."

P. 12. " A gently-inclined plane is the most desirable position for those waggons-ways; but few situations will admit of this. Upon levels, or easy ascents, a single horse draws the waggon : on such parts of the way where the declination is sufficient for the waggon to move by the power of gravity, the horse is taken out, and follows behind ; and where the descents are such that the waggon would move with too great rapidity by its own weight (or " *run a-main,*") the motion is regulated by a crooked piece of wood (called a *convoy,*) coming over the top of one of the hind wheels; upon which the waggon man
presses

presses with such force as he finds requisite, to regulate the motion of the waggon."

In a note, the editor adds—" this mode of conveyance has been used, here, upwards of 120 years." !
And this, it may be remarked, without the principle, on which they are constructed, having been introduced, until lately, into *public works !*

The projected plan of appointing professional surveyors, to manage parochial *roads*, has not only been previously recommended, but has long been practised, in different parts of the kingdom. For *road materials* see fossils, p. 18.

Public Markets.—P. 166. " The price of grain in this county fluctuates very much : betwixt the markets of Newcastle and Hexham, and those of Alnwick, Berwick, and Wooler, there is always a considerable difference*; the prices in the northern parts being, in general, the lowest, or amongst the lowest, in the kingdom, owing to the produce being so much greater than the home consumption. This surplus affords large quantities to be yearly exported from Berwick, Alemouth†, (Alnmouth) and other places along the northern part of the coast."

Morpeth has a *weekly market for fat cattle and sheep*, to supply the collieries; as those of Rotherham and Wakefield supply the manufactories of West Yorkshire : P. 174. " of the former, on an average, not less than 80 weekly; and of sheep and lambs 1600 ‡ ; which

" * Wheat and barley, in Newcastle market, are mostly sixpence a bushel higher; and in Hexham ninepence."

† ALEMOUTH. This may be termed corruption refined. By provincial usage, *Alnmouth* became *Yalnmouth ;* and, by a natural contraction, *Yalmouth.* But *Yal* is *Ale ;* hence, *Yalmouth* is *Alemouth :* and such has long been its *English* name !

" ‡ Mr. THOMAS SPOURS, who has attended this market for upwards of 40 years, says, that 30 years since there was not half this number ; and he remembers, that for several weeks in the winter very few sheep or cattle, if any, were exhibited."

which are brought up for the consumption of New-castle, Shields, Sunderland *, &c."

A list of Northumbrian *fairs* is unnecessarily in-serted :—that of Stagshaw Bank on the 4th of July, and that of Newcastle, on the 29th of October, are, however, of sufficient note to be particularized with propriety in a Report to a public Board.

P. 172. " Stagshaw Bank (near Corbridge, near Hexham)—This is one of the largest sheep fairs in the north of England †; principally of the black-faced heath sheep, which mostly come from the south-west of Scotland. There are also great numbers of cattle, horses, and swine."

P. 173. " Newcastle—for horses, cattle, and swine. This is one of the largest fairs in the north of England. The horse fair begins nine or ten days before the 29th, and continues every day in the town, where great numbers of remarkably fine horses for the field, the road, and the carriage, are sold daily. The abundant choice of every kind, brings great numbers of dealers from London, and various other distant places : its ce-lebrity has increased very much of late years, and we believe it may be justly classed among the first horse fairs in the kingdom. The show of cattle is also very great, not only for the breed of the country, but also for large droves of kyloes, (Scotch cattle,) which are purposely driven from the Highlands to be sold at this fair. The fair on the 29th is held on the Town-moor, and is called the *Cow-hill fair*."

The

" * It may be proper to remark, that 30 or 40 years since, the butchers of those places were obliged to purchase a great deal of fat stock in the neighbourhood of Darlington, and other parts of the county of Durham, the produce of the north not being equal to their demands ; but the scales are now turned, the northern farmers being able not only to supply the increased population of those places, but to send great numbers of both fat cattle and sheep every year to Leeds, Wakefield, Manchester &c."

" † Upwards of one hundred thousand sheep are shown at this fair."

The long talked of reform in *weights* and *measures* does not pass unnoticed. An extraordinary list of Northumbrian anomalies are shown. But I find nothing, that is new, advanced on the subject of their abolition.

Public Seminaries of Rural Knowledge. This subject, too, is touched upon ; and public farms are strongly recommended. This, however, is only a scion,—a slight intimation of what I have long been laboring to enforce ; but, hitherto, without effect.

On *Agricultural Societies* we find the following passage.—P. 180. " There never was an agricultural society in this county : and if any ever had existed, it probably would have been soon dissolved, if we may judge from the experiments that have been made in some neighbouring districts, where we find that, after a few years continuance, they have been given up ; but whether from a radical defect in the institutions, the non-attendance and indifference of members, or the *injudicious distribution of prizes*, we are not pre-pared to say ; but think that public farms are much more likely to promote improvements in the science of agriculture."

SUBJECT THE THIRD.

RURAL ECONOMY.

DIVISION THE FIRST.

TENANTED ESTATES,

Their IMPROVEMENT and MANAGEMENT.

ESTATES.—*Sizes.* P. 23. " Estates vary in their annual value from 20 *l.* to upwards of 20,000 *l.* a year ; one, in particular, is upwards of 40,000 *l.* Small estates,

estates, from 20*l.* to 200*l.* a year, are found in the southern and middle parts of the county, but very rarely in the northern."

P. 24. " Of the annual value of the estates in this county, no authentic information could be obtained ; but a probable guess may be formed, by supposing that there are 800,000 acres of cultivatable land, and that this, on an average, is worth 14*s.* per acre; and that 450,000 acres of mountainous district is worth 2*s.* per acre.

Then 800,000 acres, at 14*s.* £560,000
And 450,000 acres, at 2*s.* 45,000
——————
Gives the total value of the lands, per ann. £605,000"

Tenures. P. 25. " The landed property in this county is mostly freehold. Some small parcels of copyhold are found in the southern parts of the county; and in those districts which belong to the county of Durham, some leaseholds for lives, or years, are held under the church. There are also two or three manors of customary tenure, towards the head of South Tyne."

IMPROVEMENT OF ESTATES. On this important branch of rural economics, I find some, but not many, observations ; and, of these, very few that are new to me. Nevertheless, as some of them may corroborate what I have already published on the subject, and as I may have few opportunities, equal to the present, of adducing the practice and opinions of men of ability and experience, I will notice a few particulars, which, otherwise, I should have passed over, in silence.

Embankment. P. 137. " In the vicinity of Wooler, a large tract of low flat ground (called *haughs,)* adjoining the rivers Till and Glen, being subject to be frequently overflowed, the writer of this Report first made the attempt to embank them at Yevering, in the

the year 1787, which answered the purpose, and soon after it was adopted on the haughs of Turvilaws, Doddington, Ewart, &c.; by which the lands that could not be let for more than 15*s.* per acre (from the great hazard of losing the crop,) are now let for more than double the sum."

The editor has given a section of the bank. It is not, however, necessary to its explanation. The height four feet; the base fifteen; the inner face or slope five feet; the outer, toward the water, thirteen feet: the two slopes forming an angle or sharp ridge at the top of the bank:—a frail mode of finishing, that cannot be well recommended. In this bank, I perceive nothing of excellence, except the flatness of the outer slope. And whether this be properly adapted to given circumstances, we are unable to judge; as neither the sort of resistance required, nor the natural propensity of the flooding water, is mentioned. And, unless these be particularized, any description of an embankment, or the materials with which it was formed, must be vague; because on those given circumstances the proper form and materials entirely depend.

In the instance under notice, the bank was formed with earth, taken from a ditch or excavation along the inner or land side of the bank; the inner slope being faced with sods removed, previously to breaking the ground on that side; and the outer, with turf taken off the intended base or site of the bank. But the editor, in a note, (138) says—" In some situations it is best to cut the ditch on the side next the river, leaving checks at proper intervals, to prevent the run of the water. These cavities fill up in a few years, with mud brought by the floods; and the bank is in less danger of breaking when there is no ditch at the back of it."

In *one* situation, and in one only, I conceive, that method can be *safely* practised: namely, where the *weight* of stagnant or very slowly moving water, *alone*, requires

requires to be resisted. Where much *current* is liable
to take place, and especially at a *bend* in its course,
it would be very imprudent to trust to a bank constructed in that manner. This, by way of caution.

P. 128. " *Draining*—is one of those improvements
that has lately made its way into Northumberland,
and is now mostly practised in the middle and northern
parts of the county; the theory is pretty well understood in those districts, and the practice is becoming
more prevalent every year. Hollow-drains are generally used, *filled* with stones, where they can be got;
where they cannot be obtained (but at a great expense), sod-drains are the only resource, especially in
the northern parts, where there is little wood. Of
late years, great improvements have been made upon
the sheep-farms of the Cheviot hills, by cutting surface-
drains, about one foot wide, and as much deep, in an
oblique direction to the declivity of the ground."

Reclaiming wild Lands. In the Section " Wastes,"
P. 126. " The value of such enclosed commons
depends upon the system of cultivation pursued.
Upon Bulbeck common there are lands which,
in a state of common, were not worth more
than 1*s.* an acre, a part of which has been in
ploughing 25 years, and grown three white crops
successively, between one fallowing and another: this
land is now dear enough at 4*s.* an acre; while Mr.
HOPPER's of Black Hedley, is worth 10*s.* or 12*s.*
His system is, when first broke up from heath, to
pare and burn, and plough in the autumn; next
spring, plough across, lime, and sow oats; then fallow and lime, 75 bushels per acre, and sow turnips;
after which, oats and grass-seeds, four pounds red
clover, five pounds white, and one bushel of ray-grass,
and continue in grass six or seven years; then to
plough for oats—turnips—oats—and sow up with
grass-seeds as before. There are instances, where the
increased value is in the ratio of twelve to one, or
even more; but these are, where the commons were
of

of little or no value to the proprietor, which is too often the case *."

On Sod-burning we have some well judged observations; intimately agreeing with my own sentiments on the subject. P. 128. " Paring and burning is not much practised in the eastern and northern parts of the county: in the midland and southern parts it is most prevalent, but even there it is confined to old swards, and coarse, rough, rushy and heathy lands; for the first breaking up of such ground, it is certainly very convenient, and preferable to any other mode we have ever seen; but though we are fully convinced of its beneficial effects in such situations, yet we have our doubts whether it could be used with advantage upon lands that have lain a few years in grass, and that would produce good crops of grain *immediately on being ploughed out*, which is not the case with coarse, rough heathy lands, or even very old swards on rich fertile soils.

" P. 129. It is the *injudicious cropping*, more than the ill effects derived from paring and burning, that has been the chief cause of bringing such an odium on this practice, which is certainly an excellent one in *some situations*, and *properly conducted*.

" The popular clamour against this practice, " that it *destroys the soil*," we can by no means admit; and are inclined to believe that not a single atom of soil is abstracted, though the bulk of the sod or turf be diminished: this arises from the burning of the roots or vegetable substances." P. 130. " The succeeding crops of corn are so very luxuriant, as to tempt the *injudicious cultivator* to pursue it too far; who, for the sake of temporary gain, may be said to rip it up; as the boy did his goose that laid golden eggs."

Farm

" * The stinted common of Holy Island was divided in 1790; the allotments that were gotten for a right, which never lett for more than 2l. are now lett for 14l. or 15l. per ann. and in a few years will be worth upwards of 20l."

Farm Buildings*. On this subject, the Northumbrian Report affords little information that demands
particular notice, here. A diagram of a modern farmstead is explained; and homestalls on the plan offered,
I doubt not, are preferable to those of former times.
The modern cottage-stead is simplicity itself. It
consists of " one apartment, 15 feet by 16, to dwell
in, with a small one at the entrance, for a cow, coals,
working-tools, &c. 9 feet by 16, and are only one
story high." p. 27.

These huts are built in rows, of lengths proportioned to the number of " servants" employed upon
the different farms; and generally at a short distance
from the homestall: the arrangement and general
appearance of a Tweedside farmstead being very much
the same as those of a West India plantation.

Fences. The Northumbrian and south of Scotland
method of planting live hedges has its peculiarities;
but has nothing of excellence to recommend it to
general practice; although it may claim some particulars in its favor. The quicksets are planted at the
foot of a flatly sloping bank of naked earth;—a sort
of half mound; the back part of which is carried up,
perpendicularly, with sods, to about four feet high.
The loose materials of the mound shelve, from the
top of this sod wall, to the line of hedge plants;
which, in ordinary practice, are judiciously set upon
or behind a sod that has been turned upon the natural soil.

The

* In a didactic treatise on landed property, homestalls belong
to the head of improvements and repairs. But in a register of provincial facts, relating to agriculture, as well as to tenanted estates,
a description of farm buildings and fences more aptly comes under
the section FARMS. Hence, in going through these Reports, whenever I find any thing of instruction arise, that may be useful or
interesting to the *managers* of *estates* (as in the present case, in regard to fences) I will register it under the general head of IM-
PROVING ESTATES,—and refer to it from the section FARMS. But
when merely the practice or custom of the district is reported,
I will place it, at once, in that section.

The Northumbrian Reporters, however, think this too low a situation for the plants; as they " always find the quicks grow much better when planted three sods high, with the thickness of two surface sods laid under their roots:"—(p. 60): and doubtlessly they ever will, *for the first year or two of their growth.* But this is of little consideration, in raising a *fence.* It is their state of growth and *stability,* at *seven, fourteen, and twenty years old,* that ought to be looked forward to, by the hedge planter: and I have never found, in my own practice, or in my observations on that of others, any method that will insure his expectations, equal to that of setting the plants *upon the natural soil* (their feeding fibres being bedded of course among the richest of the mould raised in the operation;) as, by this means, their roots are immediately led into an extended field of pasturage; in which their *crowns form,* and become *firmly established;* while their ramifications spread without a check;—enjoying the same, or nearly the same, freedom as that which the roots of similar plants have, in a state of Nature*.

On the art of *Hanging Gates* the editor has given some directions: and he expresses a degree of surprize (in a note to his last edition, p. 64) to see that a pamphleteer should hold forth the principle of his method, as a *new discovery.* I have, at least, equal cause of surprize, to find the editor of the Northumbrian Report publishing, in 1797, as his own, a principle of Gate Hanging which *I discovered,* in 1785, and *published,* in 1790. See MINUTES in the MIDLAND COUNTIES, No. 36 and 54.

EXECUTIVE

* These remarks are applicable to all lands on which the hawthorn naturally florishes; which are (when it is properly planted) nine-tenths of the cultivated lands of the kingdom: and particularly to the " sharp lands" of the district of Wooler, &c. Over very repellent, cold, chilly substrata, setting the plants somewhat above the level of the natural soil may be eligible. An instance, in point, will be noticed in the county of DURHAM. On such land, I have seen even the Oak planted on moundlets, with success.

EXECUTIVE MANAGEMENT of ESTATES. On the *General Management* of Landed Property, we find the following remarks:

P. 23. "There are probably few parts of the kingdom where estates have made such rapid *improvements* as in this county; there being several instances of the value being more than trebled within the last 40 years. Many causes have certainly been aiding to produce this great effect; but the principal one is attributed to letting large farms, and leases for 21 years; by which means the tenants of capital were encouraged to make those great exertions, from which such advantages have resulted, not only to themselves and proprietors of the land, but to the community at large, from the very increased produce, and superiority of its quality.

" The usual mode of letting farms is, to fix a rent, under certain conditions and covenants, six or twelve months before the expiration of the lease; but upon one of the largest estates in the county *, the tenants have an offer of their farms *two years and a half or three years* before the expiration of the lease, which is a mutual benefit to both landlord and tenant; and is attended with so many advantages, that it is in a fair way of being generally adopted."

Here, again, the editor I conceive is silently incroaching upon me. For this principle too, I discovered in 1785,—have ever since been recommending it,—and had formed a lease upon it, before 1797; when the editor, I find, first mentioned it. See TREATISE on LANDED PROPERTY, Section *Tenancy*. It is *possible*, however, that, in this as in the former instance, we may have been separately led to the same point.

The editor continues, p. 24. " On some estates, the practice of letting farms by *secret proposals*, is still in use. This is a dark and mysterious mode, which

" * The Earl of TANKERVILLE'S."

which frequently defeats the end it is intended to accomplish, and instead of obtaining an *excessive high rent*, the prize has been often gained at a *very inferior value;* and, in the language of the turf (where only one has entered the lists), " by walking the course;" and we have known some of the first farmers in the county forego their farms, rather than submit to contend in the dark."

Tenancy. P. 82. " *Leases*—for twenty-one years, are lett on most of the principal estates, especially in the northern parts of the county. Some proprietors of land in the other districts, lett only for nine, twelve, or fifteen years; and a few lett no leases. The general time of entry is the 12th of May*.

" The *covenants* vary with circumstances; but we think the following the best calculated for improvement, and the benefit of both landlord and tenant:

" After the usual reservations of mines, woods, &c. and provisoes of re-entry on non-payment of rent or alienation, &c. the tenant covenants to pay the rent—all taxes—keep and leave all in repair—not to sell hay, straw, or other fodder, but convert the same into manure, for the benefit of the premises—to lay the dung on the premises (except that bred the last year, which is left for the in-coming tenant)—not to sow any hemp, flax, mustard, or rape, except the last for green food—not to depasture more stints the last six months, than were depastured in the winters of preceding years—to destroy the moles yearly, and scale the grass-grounds—to thrash the way-going crop in an uniform manner, and deliver a daily supply of straw to the next tenant—to keep uneaten the lands sown with grass-seeds in the last year of the term, from the first of October to the end of the term—to permit the lessor to sow grass-seeds on the way-going crop—and to plough the lands intended for fallow, five months before the expiration of the term—to have

" * Upon the Duke of NORTHUMBERLAND's estate, the time of entry is Lady-Day, and the off-going tenant has no way-going crop."

have no more in ploughing than * —— acres at one
time—to fallow yearly ior wheat, turnips, or other
green crops, one-third of the ploughing lands, and
lay upon every acre   cart-loads of dung; or, in
lieu thereof,   cart-loads of lime†—not to keep
any land in ploughing more than three years at one
time—to lay to grass yearly, one-third of the ploughing lands fallowed in the preceding year, and sow
upon every acre   pounds of clover, &c. (or other
seeds suited to the soil;) to keep such lands in grass
at least two or three years‡, before they are ploughed
out again—to keep in grass during the whole of the
term, and at the end thereof leave in grass, all those
fields called§
          and all such lands as shall be converted
into watered meadows—to be at one half the expense
of making new quick fences, and of cleaning and
rearing them for seven years after first planted—*and
others, that situation or circumstances may require.*

" The lessor covenants, that the tenants shall have
peaceable possession, and a way-going crop from off
two-thirds of the ploughing lands, with the use of the
stack-yards, barns, and granaries, for twelve months
after the expiration of the term; also to be at one-
half the expense of making new quick fences, and
of cleaning and rearing them for seven years after
first planted; with other covenants that may be agreed
on respecting building, &c."

In

" * Generally, from one-third to near one-half, on the larger
farms; but on some small farms it is more."

" † This covenant is only inserted where the soil is known to
want lime, which is generally the case on all the dry lands of this
district."

" ‡ Weak soils, improper for corn, should continue in grass five,
six, or seven years, or until it is thought they want refreshing by
ploughing, which is only used in such situations as being subservient to stock."

" § These are, generally, old rich grazing pastures or meadows."

In p. 27, we are informed, that " *Repairs* are mostly done by tenants."

Rent. P. 30. " The rent per acre must vary with the quality of the land, and other circumstances: at a distance from towns, and for the purposes of farming only, lands may be had from one shilling per acre up to thirty and forty shillings: in the year 1795 a farm of upwards of 2000 acres, was lett for 20*s*. an acre, unenclosed, but tithe-free of grain: one of 600 acres, at 24*s*. per acre, pays all tithes: another of 300 acres, at 35*s*. per acre, tithe-free, well enclosed, and in high condition, and several other large farms, that pay tithes of every kind, have been lett as high as from 27 to 37*s*. per acre; and some old rich grazing pastures along the sea-coast, lett for 40*s*. per acre.

And, in a note, p. 31. " These were the rents per acre in 1795; but in 1804 the advance has been such, that the dry fertile loams, let for 50 to 55*s*. per acre; and rich old grazing pastures for 60 to 70*s*. per acre, tithe-free."

These prices, seeing the remoteness of the situation, are almost incredible: for the acre by which they are regulated appears, in a short Glossary prefixed to the Report, to be the statute acre. But the border lands may have frequently lain uncultivated; and, when occupied, had probably little power of exertion, either from tillage or manure. Whereas, of late years, the improvements in management, and, doubtlessly more than all the rest, the application of *lime* as a *fresh* manure, has roused them into action:— while the neighbouring ports and the collieries afford ready markets for their produce. The grazing grounds below Morpeth are of an extraordinary quality; and such lands, every where, have borne high prices.

Receiving Rents. P. 30. " The *rent* of lands in this county used formerly to be clogged with payments in kind, and personal services; but these have been long disused, and the whole is now paid in money. The rents are mostly due on the 12th of May and the 22d of November; but payment is seldom required till four or five months after being due."

DIVISION THE SECOND.

WOODLANDS,

Their PROPAGATION and MANAGEMENT.

W OODS. P. 124. " Woods growing in a natural state are found mostly on the banks of rivers; those of the North and South Tyne, the Wansbeck, Coquet, and their tributary streams, have by far the greatest quantity. Of old oak timber, from eighty to one hundred and forty years growth, the probable value may be about 60,000*l.* of which two-thirds can only be said to be proper for building ships of great burthen.

" The demand by the collieries and lead mines for small wood, has induced the proprietors of woods on the Derwent, Tyne, &c. to cut them at an early age. From twenty-five to thirty years growth is the general term for oak, elm, and ash; but birch, willow, and aller, are cut sooner; and hazle for corf-rods* once in three or four years."

P. 125. " In the management of these woods, the general practice is to cut all away together. The system of ANTHONY SURTEES, Esq. of Newbiggen, we think preferable. He takes his away in *patches;* and as the older trees interfere with the younger springs, and where a thriving healthy oak is in a convenient situation, he lets it stand for timber; by this means the young spring is sheltered, and an annual produce of upwards of 100*l.* is obtained from sixty acres of woodland."—I insert this passage, though I confess I do not clearly understand any part of it, except the conclusion.

PLANTATIONS.

" * Corves are a kind of large wicker-work baskets, used for bringing coals out of pits, made of rods from one-half to one inch diameter."

PLANTATIONS. P. 125. " Plantations on an extensive scale, are rising in every part of the county; and are almost in every instance doing well, and promise not only to repay the spirited exertions of the proprietors, but will add greatly to the ornament and improvement of the country.

" Amongst the great variety of trees we have observed in those plantations, the larch rises proudly pre-eminent above the rest, and in almost every situation far out-strips the various species of firs and pines, wherever we have noticed them planted promiscuously together. In many plantations in the northern parts of the county, the *spruce firs*, between 20 and 30 years old, have *died off*, and this in so many very different soils and situations, that they are now in a great measure discarded from the plantations that have been made of late years : the cause of this failure has not been yet satisfactorily accounted for."

This fact is elsewhere observable ; and it may have its use to suggest, that the Norway spruce is not well adapted to the soil, or the climature, of England.

DIVISION THE THIRD.

AGRICULTURE:

OR,

FARM LANDS and their MANAGEMENT.

FARMS. P. 29. " The *sizes* of farms vary considerably in this county: in Glendale and Bamborough wards, the farms are large, from 500*l.* to 1500*l.* a year ; very few under 100*l.* In the other parts of the county, they are from 50*l.* to 300*l.* a year : some tenants in the northern parts of the county, farm from 2000*l.* to 4000*l.* a year, and upwards."

For *homestalls, fences* &c. see p. 40.

OCCUPIERS.

OCCUPIERS. P. 29. " The capitals necessary for
such farms, entitles them" (their occupiers) " to a
good education, and give them a spirit of independence and enterprise, that is rarely found amongst
the occupiers of small farms and short leases. Their
minds being open to conviction, they are ready to try
new experiments, and adopt every beneficial improvement, that can be learnt in other districts : for this
purpose, many of them have traversed the most distant
parts of the kingdom to obtain agricultural knowledge,
and have transplanted every practice they thought
superior to those they were acquainted with, or that
could be advantageously pursued in their own situation ; and scarcely a year passes, without some of
them making extensive agricultural tours, for the sole
purpose of examining the modes of culture, of purchasing or hiring the most improved breeds of stock,
and seeing the operations of new-invented and most
useful implements.

" The character of a farmer is here so respectable,
that gentlemen who possess landed property from
500l. to 1500l. a year, think it no debasement to
follow the profession ; and so high a name have many
of the farmers obtained, for their superior knowledge
in rural affairs, that they are seldom without pupils
from various and distant parts of the kingdom, with
whom they have very handsome premiums*. Amongst
the present pupils may be reckoned the son of an
Earl, and the son of a Baronet ; who, from their
abilities, attention, and anxious readiness to learn and
work at every operation, we hope will do credit to the
profession, and render the most essential services to
their respective districts."

MANAGEMENT of FARMS. On the general management of farm lands,—or the ECONOMY of AGRI-
CULTURE,—we find nothing in this Report, excepting
what is contained in its " conclusion" (of which hereafter ;) and, there, we only have that recommended,
as

" * Generally 100l. per annum."

as of late invention, which has long been the established practice of the MIDLAND COUNTIES, and the
WEST of ENGLAND; and which, for some length of
time, I have been endeavouring to inculcate, in the
kingdom at large: namely, the plan of subjecting
lands that are proper for mixed cultivation, to the alternate production of arable crops and herbage; in
equal proportion; or according to the nature of soils,
and the dictates of other circumstances: a system of
management, which, in contradistinction to the common field or feudal system, is well termed MODERN
HUSBANDRY.

On the " *Rotation* of *Crops*," in Northumberland
we have the subjoined particulars. P. 69. " The
most prevailing rotation was:
1. Fallow,
2. Wheat,
3. Oats,
4. Fallow, &c.

repeated for two, three, or four fallowings. Upon the
strong lands along the sea-coast, instead of oats after
wheat, they generally substitute pease or beans, or
beans and pease mixed; when laid down to grass, it
is sown with grass-seeds, and continued in grass seven
or more years.

" *On dry soils*, after ploughing out from grass, the
rotation was:
1. Oats,
2. Oats,
3. Turnips, sown broad-cast, lined and dunged,
   and twice hand-hoed.
4. Barley or wheat, sown up with clover and ray-
   grass, and continued in grass from four to
   seven or more years, depastured principally
   with *sheep*.

" The *best cultivators* use the following rotations,
according to soil, situation, and circumstances.

" *Clayey soils:*
1. Fallow,

2. Wheat,

2. Wheat,
3. Clover for 1 or 2 years, depastured with sheep,
4. Beans or pease.

" *Dry strong loams:*
1. Turnips, drilled at 30 inches invervals, or cabbages at 36;
2. Barley,
3. ⎫ Clover and grass-seeds; for 2 or 3 years de-
   ⎬ pastured with sheep, and a small propor-
4. ⎭ tion of cattle;
5. Oats,
6. Beans, or pease, drilled at 30 inches intervals, horse and hand-hoed;
7. Wheat, drilled from 9 to 12 inches intervals, horse and hand-hoed.

" *Sandy and dry light loams*—after being ploughed out from grass:
1. Oats,
2. Turnips, drilled at 30 inches intervals.
3. Barley or wheat, drilled from 9 to 12 inches intervals, hoed and sown up with clover and grass-seeds, depastured with sheep (and a small proportion of cattle) for *three* or *more years.*

" This last rotation has been practised of late years, and is becoming more general, not only upon the turnip soils, but upon the strong clayey lands, substituting naked fallows, or beans drilled at 30 inches intervals, instead of turnips; and those who have tried it on such strong lands find, that after two or three years clover and grass-seeds, depastured with sheep, the land will grow good crops of oats, which they could never get it to do under their old system.

" Those who have practised the Norfolk system on thin light soils, find their crops grow worse, especially the turnips and clover, and many have been obliged to adopt this system, by which they find their lands renovated; and, instead of having to complain that their soil was " *tired of turnips and clover,*" they now find

find that it produces abundant crops, and that every rotation brings it nearer its former fertility."

I have copied Mr. Bailey's remarks, at length, as they appear to have been made with a degree of consideration. But, I suspect, Mr. B. is not well acquainted with the Norfolk husbandry, which he indirectly condemns; for the Norfolk system and Mr. B's. system are the very same; except that the Norfolk farmer takes three crops of corn and two crops of herbage, in six years; Mr. B. two crops of corn and three of herbage; and, in this respect, his plan may be allowed (in *spirit* at least) to have a preference; provided his land will lie three years in profitable herbage. But, in regard to " turnips and clover" the two systems are precisely the same. Each of them comes round every six years, and in the very same succession of turnips—barley—clover.

WORK PEOPLE. The following particulars relating to the *Northumbrian Pesantry*, will afford matter of amusement, if not of astonishment, to *English* farmers. The practice of Northumberland is, doubtlessly, a relick of the vassal system, which still prevails in the more northern parts of Europe, where farm laborers belong to the land;—make part of the live stock of the farm.

The practice of paying laborers, *in kind*, originated in the same necessity as that of paying landlords and the clergy, in kind: practices that once prevailed, no doubt, throughout the island, and all Europe. How far it may still be right, in *very recluse situations*, where farm work people are a sort of *fixtures* to the soil, though they do not *belong* to it, I will not attempt to decide; but merely transcribe the Reporters account of the Northumbrian practice, at the close of the eighteenth century.

P. 164. " Through the greatest part of this county, and especially upon the large farms, there are very few servants kept in the house; seldom more than two men and two maids; but the ploughman, carters, barnmen,

barnmen, shepherds, &c. have each a house and garden, or yard, to themselves, and are generally married.   The conditions of servitude for one year are:

	£.	s.	d.
2 Cows kept, or money in lieu, at 3*l.* each	6	0	0
3 Bushels of wheat, at 5*s.* per bushel	0	15	0
33 Ditto of oats, ... at 1*s.* 8*d.* ditto	2	15	0
12 Ditto of barley, .. at 2*s.* 6*d.* ditto	1	10	0
12 Ditto of rye, ... at 3*s.* 4*d.* ditto	2	0	0
10 Ditto of pease, ... at 3*s.* 6*d.* ditto	1	15	0
24 lb. of cast wool, . at 6*d.* per lb.	0	12	0
1 Bushel of potatoes planted, a pig tether-⎱ ed, keeping hens, &c. ....⎰	2	4	0
Carriage of coals, six cart-loads	1	0	0

In all 18 11 0

" They are bound to find a woman laborer to work for the following wages: for harvesting 6*d.* per day; for hoeing turnips, hay-making, scaling, weeding corn, &c. used to be 4*d.* per day, but was last year raised to 6*d.* per day.

" In addition to the above conditions, the shepherd generally has as many sheep kept as are worth four or five pounds a year; but, if he has any under-shepherd to keep to assist him, the number is increased accordingly.   In the hilly districts, their sheep sometimes amount to hundreds, besides six or eight neat cattle.

" An overseer, or head servant, has, in addition to the above, as much money as to make his place worth from 20*l.* to 30*l.* a year.

" Thrashing is mostly done by the piece; a twenty-fifth part of the corn thrashed being the general custom, if the straw be taken away unfolded; but if the thrasher folds the straw, he has a twenty-first part, and finds a woman to dress the corn, and to work at all other work, for the same wages as the others: he

has

has straw for his cow in winter, but pays for her summer's grass."

The *money payments* are as follow.—P. 165. " The yearly wages of house-servants are, for men, from 8*l*. to 12*l*.; for women, 3*l*. to 5*l* *.

" The wages of day-laborers, without victuals, or any allowance of beer, are:

	s.	*d.*	*s.*	*d.*
For men in summer	1	2 to 1	4†	
winter	1	0 — 1	2	
harvest	1	6 — 1	9	
Women, ditto	1	0 — 1	3	
———- for other work	0	6 — 0	8	
Masons	1	8 — 2	0	
Carpenters	1	6 — 2	0	

" Upon some of the large farms, a carpenter and smith are hired by the year.

" The *hours of working* are from six in the morning to six in the evening, when the length of day will permit, with the following intervals of rest:

	H.	M.
At breakfast	0	30
Ten o'clock	0	30
Dinner	1	30
Four o'clock	0	30

In all	3	0 hours of rest.
And	9	0 hours of labor."

WORKING ANIMALS. In the original Report, printed in 1794, we had the following accounts of the animals of draft, in Northumberland.

Quarto

" * These were the wages in 1793; but in 1804, the wages for men were from 15 to 18*l*. a year; and for women from 6 to 7 *l*."

" † In 1796, the wages got up to 2*s*. and in harvest to 2*s*. 6*d*. for men ; and for women to 1*s*. 9*d*.; and in 1804 are at least one-third more than those above stated."

Quarto edition, p. 15.—" The best draught horses used in this county are brought from Clydsdale in Scotland: they are in general from 15¼ to 16 hands high ; strong, hardy, remarkably good and true pullers: a restive horse being rarely found among them."

And in p. 29.—"A few years since, the ploughing and various other purposes, for which draughts are wanted upon a farm, were performed by horses; oxen being only used by a few individuals. But since the great advance in the price of horses, oxen are become more general, especially for the purposes of ploughing, and carting *about home*. They are harnessed both" (either) " with yokes and" (or) " collars. When four are used, a boy is allowed to drive; when two, the man that holds the plough drives with cords. They only plough half a day at a time: each ploughman having four oxen, a pair of which he uses in the forenoon, and the other in the afternoon. Their food in winter is straw and a few turneps, in the summer grass.

" Horses are always yoked double, and driven with cords by the ploughman, and in general plough an acre a day: but in the season of sowing turneps, one and a half or even two acres, are frequently ploughed on fine light soils.

" A pair of tolerable draught horses cannot now be bought under 40*l.* At the high price oats have been for the last two years, the expense of keeping is very great: most farmers allow four bushels of oats per week to two horses, in the busy months in the spring; and turnep seed time, they get more. But then in the summer season, their quantity is reduced, so that upon the whole, two horses consume about 200 bushels of oats in a year, which, at 2*s.* per bushel, is 20*l.* a year, for corn only, for a two horse draught."

In 1797, however, the editor of the reprinted Report had greatly altered his sentiments on this subject; telling

telling us, in a note, p. 67, that "after a few years trial, they were given up, and horses again substituted in their stead; and at present (1804), there are probably not half a dozen farmers in the county who use them:"—and, in a "comparative statement between horses and oxen for the purpose of the draught" (p. 155.) the editor brings forward some extraordinary calculations. But if those calculations are meant to include *oxen, generally,* (we are not told that they are intended for *Northumbrian oxen exclusively)* they are formed on a false foundation. They are made on the extravagant supposition that one horse is equal to four, or at least three, oxen!!! For the Northumbrian oxen are only able, or are only allowed, to do half a day's work.

Now, in Devonshire, an ox is able and allowed, to do a day's work, every day; four of them, small-sized as they are, and with a clumsy imperfect implement, *constantly plow* (during the plowing seasons) *an acre, a day.* I have known two of them, with a lighter better implement, do nearly as much work, and in the most perfect manner.

Oxen, as horses, should be bred for the purpose intended. Who ever thought of sending an unwieldy dray horse to start at Newmarket. And who, but a Northumbrian, could have thought of putting an elephantine Northumberland ox to the plow, and then publicly exposing his inability for such valuable employment.

Had the editor of the Northumberland Report bestowed the same attention to the breeding of draught oxen, which, I understand (I may have been misinformed), he has paid to the breeding of draught horses, he would have produced animals nearly, if not quite, equal to Northumberland cart horses. A man of much less ability would, I verily believe,— from the experience I have had in working oxen of different breeds, as well as horses of different countries,—have bred oxen, three of which would have been

been more than equal, for the purposes of plowing, at least, to two cart horses, of any breed in the king-don.. Hence, I will not hesitate to say, the editor's calculations fall, as a baseless fabric, to the ground.

A few of the fragments, however, may be made useful. The editor calculates the yearly expence of a working ox, at 8 l. 5s. (p. 157.), of a working horse, at 16l. (p. 158.); consequently, of two horses, at 32l.: whereas, the annual expence of three oxen, according to his calculation, is only 24l. 15s. Beside, in those calculations, nothing is allowed for the growth of oxen, from three to six years old*! And *every* horse is supposed, not only to *live*, but to *last* (of course in full work, and with the same maintenance as younger horses) until he be twenty years old ! ! ! —N. p. 158.—" This is calculated on the supposition, that a horse bought at 4 years old will work 16 years."

Nor must we, yet, quit the subject: for, to use the writer's own words, p. 159,—" it may be necessary to examine this subject in another point of view, before any proper conclusions can be drawn, whether *ox teams* or *horses* are the most eligible; and in this case we must consider whether the quantity of land employed in supporting those animals, be used in the most profitable mode to the community, as well as the occupier."

In order to prove how impolitic it is, in a FARMER, to work oxen instead of horses, he is shown, pp. 159 and 160, that (on the false ground of calculation set forth aforegoing) eight oxen cost more by twenty pounds †, a year, in keeping, than their work is worth.

Whereas,

---

* Giving, as a reason, the following assertion. N. p. 157.—"No-thing is allowed for the yearly increased value of an ox; as it is now well ascertained, that an ox fatted at 3½ years old, is worth more to the butcher than one at 6½, that has been wrought from 3 to 6 years old."

† On the writer's principles of calculation, it ought to stand thirty pounds ($£8:5:0 \times 8 = 66 - 36 = 30$). But no matter. It is all the same.

Whereas, " the same oxen, put to graze," would pay
" the farmer much better than their earnings by
working." (p. 160.)

To show how much the COMMUNITY would be
gainers by—" the system of breeding oxen for fatting
only, instead of working (and using horses for the
purpose of cultivation)"—(p. 160.)—a statement is
made of the quantities of land that would be respectively required, to support oxen and horses, as working animals in tillage : for this writer does not appear to have considered them in any other character.

P. 161.---" In this respect the community wonld
be considereble gainers, as will appear by the following statement :

An ox, for summering and wintering, requires 4 acres;
Therefore a six ox team will require .... —24 do.
And 2 horses, for grass and hay per ann. require 7 do.
For corn and straw .... 4 do.
Land necessary for keeping 2 horses per ann. —11 do.
                                                 —

The difference in the quantity of land requir-⎰
ed for a team of oxen more than horses ..⎱ 13 do.

" Hence it appears, that a team of *six oxen* requires 13 acres more land to maintain them, than a
team of *two horses*, which will do the same work; and
of course, the produce which might be derived from
these 13 acres is lost to the community: suppose it
to be one-half in grass, and the other half in ploughing, and to avoid fractional parts, we will call it 12
acres ; then we shall have :

    6 acres of clover, or grass,
    2 ditto of oats,
    2 ditto of turnips, or fallow
    2 ditto of wheat.

" It would then send to market yearly, at the lowest
computation :

    8 cwt. of beef,
    10 quarters of oats, and
    5 ditto of wheat.

" From

" From this view of the subject it appears, that if oxen were universally used for the draught, in the room of horses, there would be a considerable defalcation in the supply of the markets, both in corn and animal food."

And, in a final note, are the subsequent calculations on the loss that would be sustained, in the county of Northumberland, alone. N. p. 161.—" In this county it is estimated that there are capable of cultivation 800,000 acres ; and allowing one-third of this to be in tillage, that is, 266,666 acres, and that every 50 acres in tillage will require a team to manage it properly, of course there will be at least 5333 teams; but, for the sake of round numbers, call it 5000 teams :

Then 5000 × 8 cwts. of beef = 40,000 cwts.

   of beef, at 30s. -   -   -   -   - £60,000

Then 5000 × 10 qrs. oats = 50,000 qrs. of

   oats, at 16s. -   -   -   -   - 40,000

Then 5000 × 5 qrs. wheat = 25,000 qrs. of

   wheat, at 40s. -   -   -   -   - 50,000

The value in provisions that would be lost to this county yearly, if horse teams were abolished, and oxen used in their stead } 150,000

Now all this has doubtlessly been seen, as it were in a vision. And I willingly believe that whoever unfortunately saw it was really entranced,—was insensible of the error into which his mistaken calculations were leading him.

If two oxen can be kept with the same expenditure as one horse, which, according to the writer's calculations, they may within a fraction (as appears aforegoing) then, even at the extravagant rate of two oxen to one horse, the community (let us *here* allow) would neither be gainers nor losers, by the change : for working oxen would cost the community no more keeping,—would consume no more, in value, of marketable produce,—than working horses are now consuming,

consuming, where no oxen are at present worked. Consequently, there would be the same land, manure, and labor, jointly, for unworked cattle, as there now are, in such situations.

But, on the less unreasonable calculation of three oxen to two horses,—equally well bred for the purposes of draft in husbandry,—of equal ages, and equally in their prime of work,—as from five to ten years old,—there would be a very considerable extent of land, for the grazing of unworked cattle, over and above what there is, at present : and, moreover, the carcases of the entire increase of working oxen, occasioned by the change, would be thrown into the markets, as store cattle: and, of course, the lands which are at present occupied in rearing cattle, equal to their whole amount as such, would be an immense increase of territory to the community.

To convey, to the readers of this volume, some idea of the vast acquisition of human food which would accrue to the community, by carrying on the works of husbandry, with cattle, instead of horses, I will insert, here, what I published on the subject, in the year 1790, in the first edition of the Rural Economy of the MIDLAND COUNTIES, vol. i. p. 468 *.

" On all soils, and in every situation, mountains and fens excepted, cattle are requisite in their three capacities of

Dairy Stock,
Beasts of Draft, and
Grazing Stock.

" It may, however be proper, before I proceed farther,

---

* These remarks occur in " General Observations on the Improvement of Livestock;" which belonging rather to a general work, than a provincial register, I did not reprint them in the succeeding edition ; reserving them for their proper place. Nevertheless, I think, that part of them which relates to "cattle as beasts of draft in husbandry," may be usefully brought forward here; more especially as it views the subject, under discussion, in a different light to that in which I have here been kindly led to place it.

farther, to produce some evidence that they are, in the present state of agriculture and population, and under the present customs of the country, requisite, as beasts of draft, in husbandry.

" That they are not under present circumstances, *necessary*, in this capacity,—at least not in any great degree,—is evident in the smallness of the number worked at present, compared with the number of horses now in use for that purpose. It is probable that, in England, not more than one sixth of the works of husbandry is at present done by cattle*.

" But great and interesting as the subject of beasts of draft in husbandry undoubtedly is, it would be improper to enter largely into it, in this place. I have already touched upon it, repeatedly ; and may hereafter have occasion to enter fully into its discussion. Therefore all I shall offer, at present, will be a statement of the COMPARATIVE EFFECTS of horses and cattle, as beasts of draft in husbandry.

" This kingdom contains (near enough at least for our present purpose) thirty thousand square miles of *cultivated* surface.

" Supposing the works of husbandry to be carried on solely by HORSES, and supposing twenty horses employed on each square mile (or about three to every hundred acres) the number of horses employed in husbandry, would be six hundred thousand : from which deduct one sixth, for the proportion of cattle worked at present, and there are, on this statement, five hundred thousand horses now employed in agriculture.

" Admitting that each horse *works* ten years, the number of farm horses that die, annually, in this kingdom alone, is fifty thousand :—each of which requires four years keep, before he be fit for full work:

---

* This estimate must be received as in a great measure conjectural. It would be difficult to adduce data sufficient for all accurate estimate.

work * :—for which consumption of vegetable produce, he returns not to the community, a single article of food, clothing or commerce †.

" Hence, it is evident, that, by the practice of working horses in husbandry, the community is losing, annually, the amount of two hundred thousand years' keep of a growing horse ; which, at the low estimate of five pounds a year, arises to a million of money, annually.

" On the contrary, supposing the business of husbandry to be done solely by CATTLE, and admitting that oxen may be *fatted* with the same expenditure of vegetable produce, as that which *old horses* require to fit them for *full work*,—and that instead of fifty thousand horses dying, fifty thousand oxen, of no more than *fifty-two* stones each, were slaughtered, annually,—it is evident that a quantity of beef, nearly equal to that which the metropolis now consumes, would be annually thrown into the market; or, in other words, a hundred thousand additional inhabitants might be supplied with one pound of annual food, a day each : and this without consuming one additional blade of grass."

Further, it remains to be noticed, that CATTLE, in their natural habitudes, require *herbage*, only, to fit them for their task:—whereas, HORSES consume — must consume—a very considerable portion of the insufficient supply of *human food* which the country produces, to enable them to perform their labor, with due effect. And this brings to light a still further advantage of cattle. Herbage, especially if depastured, does not exhaust the soil that produces it; but,

on

* It is true that horses are *broke* in, at three, some at two, years old; but they are or ought to be indulged, in keeping and work, until they be six : so that the cost of rearing, and fitting for full work, may be safely laid at four years ordinary keep.

† Even his skin, for economical purposes, is barely worth the trouble of taking off. 1807. Was not, then.

on the contrary, invigorates it, most effectually, for
the production of *corn:* while grain crops (oats most
particularly) foul and exhaust the lands they grow on;
so as to require an expenditure of manure and tillage,
to reinvigorate them;—which manure and tillage
would, otherwise, be applied to the more immediate
subsistence of the species *.

It was with the greatest reluctance I sat down to
rectify the errors which I had perceived in the Reporters' calculations on this subject; being concerned
that I had to contend, in any way, with either of the
authors of the Northumberland Report. But, in pursuing my present undertaking, it would be highly
criminal to suffer dangerous errors to pass unnoticed;
more especially those of men whose suggestions may
have weight with the public. In the present instance
I have been gratefully repaid for the time and attention bestowed; for I am thereby more and more convinced of the propriety of cultivating the soil with
edible animals that require only herbage to support
them,—and of lessening, without delay, the number
of those which are deemed inedible, yet cannot exert
their powers with sufficient effect, without eating the
bread of the inhabitants of this circumscribed territory,—which (judging from the immense quantities
of corn imported) has long been unable to provide
them with a sufficient supply,—under the improvident
practice which we have found recommended to general observance,—through the medium of the Board of
Agriculture.

IMPLEMENTS. A full chapter on this subject gives
us ample proof of Mr. Bailey's abilities, as a mechan-
ist,

---

* In the foregoing quotation, p. 54, a plow horse, according to
the estimate of the editor, consumes one hundred bushels of oats,
yearly:—a quantity which is equal to the produce of three or four
acres of middling oat land; and which is adequate to the maintain-
ance of a Glendale Ward cottager, his wife, and half a dozen children:—and this " for corn only."

ist, and as a draftsman: Mr. B. having invented, or improved, a variety of useful implements and machines of husbandry; and has represented them in clear, intelligible engravings, from his own drawings.

Part of those drawing are copied from " An ESSAY on the CONSTRUCTION of the PLOUGH, deduced from mathematical principles;"—which Mr. B. published some years ago; and to which I have great pleasure in referring my readers,—as an ingenious and useful performance.

The other engravings and verbal descriptions of implements of Agriculture, in the volume before me, relate to—*a single horse plough* for cleaning the intervals of turnips in rows, having a mold board that moves on hinges. *A horse hoe*, for the intervals of beans in rows: in which, however, I perceive nothing of superior excellence.—*A hand hoe*, for the rows of beans. This " consists of two ends, about six inches long each from the eye; one of which is two inches broad, and the other one inch. With this hoe the weeds amongst the stems of beans may be easily eradicated" p. 43: a valuable little tool which I have seen used, in Yorkshire, for hoing broadcast wheat, and for cutting off thistles, and other strong weeds, within the ground, in grass lands, for which it is greatly preferable to the spaddle or spud that is in ordinary use for that purpose. Quere, has it travelled, southward, from Northumberland?. A *drill* for *turneps* on *ridges:* on the ordinary principle of the indented roller. It sows only one row on each ridge.—A *drill* for *all sorts* of *grain*. This is on the same principle: and it appears to be at least equal to any of the numerous patented, and unpatented, machines for that purpose.—*A thrashing mill*. The same may be literally said of this. Mr. Bailey gives a description, and a perspective engraving of one (worked by water) which was erected (doubtlessly under his own directions) at Chillingham, the place of his residence, in 1789:—probably the best of the kind which had then been erected.

But

But by far the most *interesting* part, of the chapter on implements, is the HISTORY of the THRASHING MILL;—the most valuable machine of Agriculture that has been discovered, for ages past; and every particular relating to its origin, will be eagerly sought after, in ages to come.   It is to be observed, however, that another account, given by the Reporters of the West Riding of Yorkshire, regarding the rise and progress of this valuable invention, varies, in some particulars, from that which is here inserted.

P. 49. " *Thrashing Machines*—are now become general in the northern parts of the county; they are all upon the principle of the flax-mill; which principle was first introduced into this county for thrashing corn, by Mr. EDWARD GREGSON, near 32 years since*: the machine he used was worked by a man, who could thrash with it twelve bushels of wheat in a day; but being hard work, and Mr. GREGSON dying soon after, it was neglected.   Mr. WILLIAM MENZIE, who was servant with Mr. GREGSON at the time, says, " that his master took the idea from a small flax-mill which a Scotchman travelled the country with, for the purpose of swingling the flax which the farmers grew for their own use.   This portable flax-mill was carried in a cart from one farm house to another, being a cylinder of five, or five feet and a half diameter, and eighteen inches wide; the switchers were driven by his foot, with a crank like a cutler's wheel; and that the thrashing-machine Mr. GREGSON had, was made at that time, and exactly the same as the said flax-mill†."   Mr. THOMAS GREGSON thinks that

---

* In the original Report, in 1794, we read " near 20 years since;" by which it would seem that the *principle* of the present machine was first known, in England, about the year 1774: whereas, the above statement, in 1797, throws its introduction back to 1765.

" † This machine wanted only a pair of fluted rollers for taking in the corn, to make it complete: had these been added, it would have been the same as the machines used at present."

that his brother EDWARD had seen something of a similar nature in Scotland, probably the same which Mr. D. MELDRUM gives an account of, about the same time, in a letter to Mr. WILLIAM CHARGE, of Cleasby, in the county of York, which he describes as being the same as the flax-mill; that it thrashed 150 bushels of oats a day, which dropped through a skreen into a winnowing-machine, that dressed it at the same time.

" Some time after this, Mr. OXLEY erected a thrashing-machine at Flodden, moved by horses, in which the corn was fed-in between two *fluted rollers*, and struck by switchers *hung on hinges;* those in use now are *fixed*, as were those of Mr. GREGSON. The complaint of Mr. OXLEY's machine was, that it did not thrash common oats clean, probably for want of velocity: for it is found in the machines now used, that if the switchers move with a velocity of 1500 feet per minute, they will not thrash clean; and experience has proved, that to thrash common oats clean, requires a velocity of 2500 feet per minute.

" Mr. ILDERTON erected two thrashing-machines, one at Ilderton and another at Hawkhill, worked by horses; the principle of which was to rub the grain out by projecting pieces of wood (on the circumference of a large cylinder), rubbing against several rollers, either fluted or set with small iron staples. He used it many years; but it was frequently necessary to put the straw twice through, before it was perfectly clean.

" We were informed by the late Sir FRANCIS KINLOCH, bart. of Gilmerton, in Scotland, that while he was attempting to perfect Mr. ILDERTON's machine, he saw a portable flax-mill, made for the use of poor families, worked by a man. It struck him that it would thrash corn, and he got one made, with the addition of two smooth rollers for taking in the corn : the work being too hard for a man, he sent it to Mr. MEIKLE's mill, to have it tried it by water.

water. Soon after, Mr. MEIKLE's son built a thrashing-mill at Kilbagie; and after ten or twelve had been
erected in the neighbourhood by other workmen, he
applied to Mr. KINLOCH.to take out a patent, who
told him that he did not look upon it as an original
invention, and that a patent would be of no use.
Some time after this, Mr. MEIKLE took out a patent
(for England only) in his own name."

P. 51. " From a review of the whole, it appears
that the principle of the flax-mill had been thought
on and applied by different persons, at different times,
for the purpose of thrashing corn; but that Mr.
MEIKLE was most probably the first person who
made a machine on those principles, of perfect utility;
at least, it is pretty certain, that the first *effective
machine* was the one built by his son, for Mr. STEIN,
of Kilbagie.

" At their first introduction into this county, the
corn and straw were thrown out together upon the
floor, and caused great confusion : to remedy this, a
skreen was added, through which the grain dropped
into a winnowing-machine, and from off the skreen
the straw was taken by a man: but a *circular rake*,
invented* about ten years since, performs the operation much better, and at the same time saves a considerable expense. This rake is now added to all
those that have been lately erected; which only
causes an addition to the machinery of one light
wheel."

The *history* of the *winnowing mill*, likewise, is
spoken

---

* In the original, as well as in the first reprinted edition, the following note is added to the word *invented*,—" by Mr. BAILEY, who
first applied it in his machine at Chillingham ;" which appears, by
the title of the plate of its description, was erected in 1789 ; only
one year after that of Mr. STEIN. But, in the last edition, that
note is omitted.

This wheel rake is a very material—might be deemed an
essential—improvement of the thrashing-mill, be the inventor of
it who he may.

spoken to in the Northumbrian Report. But what is said of it merely corroborates what I made out, in 1787; namely, that Europe is indebted for it to China; and that it reached this island by the way of Holland. See YORKSHIRE, section *Implements*.

MANURES.—*Yard Manure.* P. 130. " In some parts of this county, where the turnip culture is carried to such extent, every exertion. of ingenuity is practised to raise a large portion of *farm-yard dung:* for without this valuable article, it is well known that good turnip crops are not to be expected; and the farmers of strong soils are sufficiently sensible of the advantage of dung to their crops, not to use every endeavour to increase its quantity.

" The farmers of turnip soils, in order to have their dung sufficiently rotted, lead it out of the fold-yard in the winter, make it up in large dunghills, in order to increase the putrefactive process."

Lime.—On the *effects* of lime, I am happy in being able to collect, from the Northumbrian Report, some valuable incidents and observations.

P. 131. " In Bamborough ward, where it has been long used, many intelligent farmers begin to doubt of its efficacy, and the propriety of continuing to lay it upon their *old tillage lands.* Upon the dry soils in Glendale ward, where it has not been used much above 40 years*, its effects are more conspicuous, especially upon such lands as have been seldom or never limed. In its natural state, the soil of this district is dry, duffy, light, full of fibrous roots; and when in fallow, on passing over it, you sink to the ancles: after being sufficiently limed, the fibrous

roots

" * Mr. JAMES HALL, of Thornington, was the first person that ever carried a cart-load of lime across the river Till, at Ford, for laying upon land: the first year he prevailed upon his father to allow him to lead ten cart-loads, which had so wonderful an effect, that the quantity was increased next year, and in a few years after the use of it became general."

roots disappear, the soil becomes denser, firm to the tread, retentive of moisture, and produces better and more abundant crops of grain than before; when laid to grass, the effects of the lime appear to an inch, by the superior verdure which takes place as far as it has gone*. Many of these dry soils, after being limed, grow white clover naturally; where not limed, it seldom appears; but they cover principally with *agrostis capillaris* (fine bent), which is seldom eaten by any kind of stock, if they can get other food: when land has been sufficiently limed, this plant disappears; and wherever it is found, it may be safely concluded, that the soil on which it grows has not had its due quantity of lime.

" About seven years since, Mr. GEORGE REED, of South Middleton, near Wooler, cleared from broom 30 or 40 acres of light, dry, poor, gravelly soil, that had *never been limed*, which was sown with rye; the rye stubble was ploughed in the autumn, and the worst part of it limed, at the rate of 100 bushels per acre;

" * About twelve years since, when looking over the farm of Thornington, with Mr. JAMES HALL (the late tenant), I was surprized with the sudden alteration in the verdure of the land, which took place immediately at the junction of two ridges: one side was a fine dark green, *eaten very bare*, and covered with a thick mat of *white clover and ray-grass;* the other was a dingy brown, principally composed of *fine bent* and *sheep's fescue*, and in a great measure *neglected by the sheep.* An explanation was desired for so great a contrast; and Mr. HALL informed me, that when this parcel of land was last in fallow, the part which was *eaten so bare,* and looked so green, was *well limed;* the other, which the sheep neglected, had *never been limed.*

" It has been said, and repeatedly copied by writers on Agriculture and Botany, that " *sheep prefer the 'festuca ovina' to all other plants:*" in the above instance it was quite the contrary; from which, and from other observations I have made, I am inclined to believe, that the idea has probably originated more in conjecture than experiment. It has also been remarked by botanical writers, that sheep refuse to eat ragwort *(senecio jacobæa).* The fact is, they are so very fond of it, they will not allow a plant to flower wherever they depasture."—A fact that has been long known to observant husbandmen.

acre; next summer the whole was drilled with
turnips (dunged, &c. as described page 67), which
came up all alike, and continued to do equally well
for three or four weeks; but little or no rain falling in
that period, and the weather continuing droughty,
those turnips upon the land which had *no lime,* died
away; whilst those upon that part which *was limed,*
were discernible *to an inch,* flourished with unabated
vigour, and produced an excellent crop (for such
land), worth at least 4*l.* 10*s.* an acre. Many similar
instances might be produced, but this is the most
striking we recollect to have noted."—Again, p. 134,
" The opinions respecting the good or ill effects of
lime are exceedingly various; some asserting that
it can never be used in too large a quantity; whilst
others contend it is of no use whatever. Our own
practice authorises us to say, that upon some soils,
the application of lime (or calcareous earth in some
other form) in considerable quantities, is absolutely
necessary, in order to bring them to their most fertile
state, and to prepare them for the action of other
manures,; whilst upon other soils, lime produces no
sensible effect; and if used in large quantities, will
prove very detrimental. Thus may one of the most
valuable applications for the improvement of many
soils, be condemned by those who draw *positive conclusions* from *partial observations of facts.* The practice
of paring and burning, we believe, owes the oppro-
brium which some have thrown upon it, to *a similar
mode of reasoning.*"—Finally, n. p. 79. " The soils
which formerly were occupied in growing rye, are
now so much consolidated and improved by the use
of lime, that they produce abundant crops of excellent wheat; several thousand acres of which are now
grown every year after turnips, where, thirty years
since, scarcely a single bushel was ever produced."

Lime is *burnt* in drawing kilns,—in the form of
inverted cones. The *price,* at the kiln, 3s. to 4s. 6d.
for 25 upheaped bushels. The *quantity used,* 75 to
150

150 bushels, an acre. It is sometimes *horded* up, before winter, in large heaps turfed or thatched over (as in the midland counties) ; to be used for the turnip ground, the ensuing spring.

Shell Marl. P. 134. " Shell marl is used with great advantage, at the rate of 20 or 30 cart-loads an acre, on the farms of Wark, Sunnylaws, and Learmouth." See, afore, p. 17.

Sea Weed. P. 134. " Sea Wrack, Sea Ware, or Marine Plants—driven ashore by the tide, are used with great effect wherever they can be had. Of these, the *fucus vesiculosus*, and its relatives, *f. serratus* and *inflatus* (skeir ware,) are not held in much estimation, and when used, require to be laid up in large heaps to putrefy. If laid upon the land, as the others are, when taken immediately from the shore, they dry, and turn to a black coriaceous substance. The *fucus digitalus* (wassels) is the great favourite; and another species, called *May-weed*, which we cannot point out by its Linnæan name, not having had an opportunity of seeing it ; but, from the descriptions we have heard, suspect it to be the young plants of the *fucus digitalus.*"

On the OPERATIONS of AGRICULTURE, viewed, abstractedly, from particular crops, we are favored with the following articles of information, in the volume under Review.

On TILLAGE, we find some dispassionate, judicious Remarks, in the section *Fallowing*.

P. 67. " The practice of making naked fallows on all kinds of soils, once in three or four years, was general through this county till the introduction of turnips ; in a few years the fallows of the dry lands were covered with this valuable plant. On such other soils as were found improper for this root, the naked fallows still prevail, with an almost universal opinion, that it is absolutely necessary to the fertility of the land ; yet there are some few who dare to doubt this long-established doctrine, and presume to think, that
                                               naked

naked fallows might be dispensed with in *many si-tuations*, by cultivating leguminous crops, *drilled at wide intervals*, to admit being *ploughed*, or *horse-hoed* between; to which, if *proper hand-hoeings* be added, the land will be nearly as well prepared for wheat, as if it had been a complete naked fallow.

" This is not advanced on speculation or theory; instances can be produced, where no naked fallows have been made on fields of strong loam for twelve years, yet they are as clear of quickens, couch-grass, or other pernicious weeds, as any fields in the district, that have been under naked fallow two or three times in the same period *."

Again. P. 68. " Though we are diffident in giving a decided opinion upon so important a subject, yet from observations made on the above facts, we cannot help being inclined to think, that the quantity of naked fallow might be very much reduced, and in another century will probably be totally abolished, if no fortuitous circumstances arise to check the ex-ertions and spirit for improvement which have been so prevalent of late years, and so generally diffused through this district."

Much, however, it may be proper to add, will ever depend on substrata and seasons, in regard to *occasional* fallowing.

SEMINATION. The editor of the Northumberland Report is not only a *drillist*, but, as has been shown, a drill inventor, and has moreover struck out a par-ticular mode of drilling. Nevertheless, Mr. Bailey, as a driller, is a moderate man : we find nothing *offensive* in his remarks or recommendations. Indeed he does not *urge* the practice, any farther than as it relates to *pulse* and *roots*; and these ought, undoubt-edly (unless under particular circumstances) to be cultivated

" * It may be necessary to observe, that, previous to the adoption of this system, the land was cleared of quicken, or couch-grass, by a complete summer fallowing."

cultivated in rows. Beside, Mr. B. has good sense and experience enough to know that land requires to be well cleaned, previously to drilling, even *pulse*, with *wide intervals* (see the foregoing note) : and he is doubtlessly well aware, that, before *corn* can be properly drilled, with *narrow intervals*, the soil should undergo a complete purification. Now this is all I ask, or ever have asked, of drillists. Let them clean their lands, thoroughly, before seed time, and I will give them free liberty to put in their seed, in any way which to them may seem most meet.

Having already stated my opinion, fully, on the DRILL HUSBANDRY, in the Rural Economy of the Southern Counties, I shall probably have no farther occasion to explain myself on the subject, in going through the Board's Reports. It is my intention, however, to give its advocates the most attentive and cordial hearing; and I shall be very happy, if, by so doing, I shall be able, in any sort, to add to the TRUE INTEREST of AGRICULTURE.

In pursuit of that principle of conduct, I was desirous to convey to my readers Mr. Bailey's mode of drilling; for although it occurs in the section, *wheat*, it is, no doubt, applicable to other species of *corn*. But as Mr. B. has had recourse to diagrams for its explanation, I must forego my intention. I have the less to regret, however, as, on mature examination, it appears to contain nothing that is *materially* different from other methods in use, for performing that *mysterious* operation ; which has given birth to various *persuasions*.

GROWING CROPS. P. 135. " *Weeding* corn is universally practised : *the broad-cast crops* are hand-weeded; in which operation, the thistles (being rather unpleasant to handle) are in some parts drawn by a pair of large pliers."—" The drilled crops are both horse and hand-hoed, and with so much attention, that no kinds of weeds are suffered to remain; the whole

whole being kept in the cleanest and completest garden-like culture."

The only species of *vermin* mentioned as being injurious to corn crops, in the field, are " Crows" (Rooks) which (p. 182) " of late years, have become a very great nuisance, not only for rooting up wheat and other grain in a sprouting state, but clover and potatoes, corn stacks, and young plantations, are greatly injured by them. Last spring, a collection of sixpence a plough was made by a few farmers in Glendale ward, for pulling down their nests. Many thousands were destroyed by this means; and we hope the practice will be continued until they are found less pernicious."

HARVESTING. The harvest management of Northumberland is nearly the same as that of YORKSHIRE ; which I have minutely described. In the operation of reaping, however, there is a shade of difference, in favor of the Northumbrian practice. P. 110. " Most of the corn is cut with sickles, by women; seven of whom, with a man to bind after them, generally reap two acres per day. Oats and barley are sometimes mown:" but are more generally reaped; according to the practice of Scotland.

WHEAT. The *varieties* of wheat, that are, or rather were, cultivated in Northumberland, are enumerated, in the Report. But, as the cultivated varieties of wheat, as of oats, potatoes, and cider fruits, in the kingdom at large, are almost endless, and only temporary, many of them being local, it is not my intention to notice them, in the present work ; unless when they are peculiarly valuable in themselves, or give rise to useful reflections; as in the present instance.

The editor divides the Northumbrian varieties of wheat into two orders,—the *smooth chaffed*, and the *downy chaffed ;* on which he makes some sensible remarks.

P. 73. " The downy-chaffed wheats have shorter straw,

straw, and are less liable to have the grain shaken out
by winds (the chaff embracing the grain more closely)
than the smooth-chaffed tribes, which is a considerable
advantage; but then we are apprehensive that this
downiness makes them retain the dews and moisture
upon the ear much longer than the smooth-chaffed
kinds, and probably renders them much more liable
to be affected by those diseases which give a dusky
dark shade to the chaff, and a rusty cankering upon
the straw; as we recollect few instances of smooth-
chaffed or red wheat being troubled with this disease,
of course the downy-chaffed kinds are most proper
for windy open situations, and the smooth-chaffed to
well-sheltered inclosed districts."

A variety of wheat, capable of withstanding the
attacks of *mildew*, would be, indeed, a valuable acquisition. At present, I much fear, no one enjoys
that power.

P. 71. " The *preparation* of the soil, for the greatest quantity of wheat raised in this county, is naked
summer-fallow: of late years, considerable quantities
have been grown after turnips; it is also grown after
rape, clover, beans, pease, tares, and potatoes."

Trench ploughing is recommended, p. 66, for clover
leys that are intended to be drilled. And, for the
loose free lands of the district of Wooler, which are
well suited to the operation of drilling, trench ploughing may, no doubt, be often practicable, in the proper
season of sowing.

Semination. P. 73. " The *seed* is selected with
great attention, from the most perfect samples; and
the practice of *changing seed* is thought to be advantageous; for this purpose more or less new seed is
every year imported from distant parts, as Kent,
Essex, Huntingdonshire, Cambridgeshire, &c. New
seed is preferred to old, and that immediately after
being thrashed, rather than what has lain long in a
granary." I copy these *opinions*, merely as such.

Preparing the *Seed.* P. 73. " *Steeping* in chamber-
lye, and powdering with quick-lime immediately after,
                                                      to

to make it sufficiently dry for sowing, is generally practised; the smut is seldom seen where this is properly performed, and some go so far as to say, that it will cure smutty seed."—This being as it may, Mr. B. gives some striking instances, which fell under his own observation, of the efficacy of this heretofore prevalent practice of the north of England.

The process is this: P. 73. " It is done by throwing the wheat into a vessel full of chamber-lye, stirring it about with a strong stick, and skimming off the light grains as they appear on the surface: when this is done, the liquor is let off (by a plug or cock at the bottom of the vessel), and the wheat taken out and mixed with quick-lime: after this, the sooner it is sown the better, because it is apt to heat and spoil if suffered to continue in the sacks, or in large heaps; but if dried and spread thin on a granary floor, it will keep several days.

" If the grain remains too long in very putrid chamber-lye, its vegetative powers will be injured: five or ten minutes are as long as it should be suffered to continue."

The *quantity* of seed sown, p. 74, " is from two to three bushels per acre, *broad-cast*, according to the times of sowing, nature and condition of the land, &c. Those who drill at ten or twelve inch intervals, find one bushel and a half per acre amply sufficient."

P. 74. " The *time* of *sowing*, on the lands that receive a naked summer-fallow, is September and October: after *drilled beans*, October and November; and after *turnips*, all through the winter (as the land is cleared, and weather suitable), until the middle of March. In the year 1795, many hundred acres were sown in Glendale ward so late as *the beginning of April*, which were all well harvested, and produced, on an average, about 24 bushels per acre, of excellent grain, in many cases superior to that sown in the autumn; which was rather singular, as it is generally thought that wheat, sown so late, does not produce

duce the grain so well perfected as that which is sown earlier. This lateness of sowing was occasioned by the snow lying so late in the spring; and we are disposed to think, from many experiments, that on those light soils, the month of February is the best and safest seed time for wheat, maslin, and rye, of all others in the year."

If this opinion be formed, principally, on the incident of 1795, which was attended by a peculiar circumstance, it might be dangerous to rely on it; even in Glendale ward. Nevertheless, the incidental fact is valuable.

P. 76. " The *culture whilst growing*, of the broadcast crops, consists only in hand-weeding: such as are drilled, are hoed once or twice, as well as handweeded where wanted. These hoeings not only destroy the weeds, but make a fine preparation for the clover and grass-seeds, which seldom fail where this operation is properly performed."

P. 76. " *The produce* varies considerably, according to soils, seasons, culture, &c.; from 24 to 30 bushels per acre, may be taken as a fair average crop; under favourable circumstances, as high as 50, and even 60 bushels per acre, sometimes occur."

RYE. P. 79. " Rye was formerly the principal grain grown upon all the dry, sandy, and light soils; but since the use of lime, and the introduction of turnips and artificial grasses, it is rarely cultivated, except upon *very sandy* soils."

MESLIN. A remark, which is new to me, has been made in Northumberland, respecting this crop. —P. 80. " It has been remarked, that when wheat and rye are grown mixed in this manner, the grains of each are larger and more perfect than when grown singly, without any admixture." Do they separately prefer somewhat different sorts of nourishment?

BARLEY. In addition to the ordinary *species* of Barley, a *variety* of the long-eared, or common sort,

is

is cultivated, in Northumberland. P. 81. "The awns of which drop, or are easily shaken off when ripe; from the grain being shorter, plumper, and rounder-bodied than the common sort, it is preferred by the millers for making into pearl-barley. This variety ripens later than the common kind, or red-stroked barley, by near a fortnight, and is distinguished from it by the grains being closer set, and the skin having a light yellowish tinge, and not being marked by *dark red* lines; it is also shorter in the straw, and may be called the *yellow*, or *pale-skinned* long-ear'd barley.

"*Battle-door*, or *Sprat Barley*, is sometimes grown, and is preferred for sowing upon land in high condition, where there is danger of the other kinds lodging."—A well judged precaution.

Succession. P. 81. "It is generally sown after turnips."

Semination. P. 81. "In Glendale ward, a few farmers cultivate it in drills, with 9 or 12 inch intervals."

P. 82. "The *quantity sown* is from two to three bushels per acre broad-cast: when drilled at nine to twelve inch intervals, it is found that from one and a half to two bushels per acre, are sufficient.

"*The time of sowing*, from the beginning of April to the latter end of May.

"*The produce*, from 30 to 60 bushels per acre.

Markets. P. 82. "Great quantities are made into *pot* or *shelled barley*, not only for home consumption, but for exportation: in the northern parts of the county, very few corn-mills are now to be found without the appendage of a barley-mill."

P. 81. "*Beer, Bigg*, or *four-rowed Barley*, used to be the only species of barley cultivated in the county: it is now rarely sown, except upon raw, crude soils, on which it is found to answer better than any other, more especially if late sown, owing to the
turnips

turnips having been kept longer than usual in a cold
backward spring, for the use of the feeding, and store
stock."

OATS. Several *varieties* are enumerated, and among
them "Church's oat;" which prevailed, on the borders,
several years; but which is now, I believe, nearly out
of fashion; the " potatoe oat,"—a truly *accidental*
variety,—being of later discovery*. And even this,
I understand, (though it is, or was, of a very superior
quality) is already growing into disrepute†. So transient appear to be the varieties of oats.

Tartarian oats (pretty evidently a distinct species),
after having been given up, are now " cultivated in
the midland parts of the county, on rather an extensive scale, being found, there, more productive than
any other kind they have tried."—(p. 84.) In travelling between Berwick and Darlington, in 1799,
I observed scarcely any other sort of oats in cultivation. On cold weak lands, in general, they may
perhaps be found eligible. They are at least a fit
subject of experiment, on such lands.

Quantity of *seed* of oats:—seven bushels down to
four or five, according to the sorts. As no mention
is made of the quantity used in drilling, are we to
infer that oats are not drilled in Glendale ward?

P. 85. " The *time* of *sowing* is March or April:
and the early kinds are sown sometimes as late as
the middle of May." This is a late season for sowing
oats. But vegetation is rapid in northern climates.

Produce,—twenty to eighty bushels an acre.

BEANS. P. 86. " Beans have, time immemorial,
been a prevailing crop upon all the strong lands in
the county, especially along the *sea-coast* to the southward ;

---

* See CUMBERLAND, Sect. *Oats*.

† Owing principally, or wholely, I believe, to its being found (in
Yorkshire at least) peculiarly, and destructively, liable to the disease of *smut*.

ward; they generally succeed wheat, clover, or old grass. *The kinds cultivated*, are the large and the small horse bean, and sometimes the mazagan; they are sown in February, four bushels and a half per acre *broad-cast*, and never hoed: the produce very uncertain; 20 bushels per acre a fair average *broad-cast* crop.

" In this district, the soil of which is so well adapted to the growth of beans, it is surprizing that drilling them should be so much neglected, and that this beneficial mode of culture for both beans and pease, should be confined to a few farmers in Glendale ward and Tweed-side: with those few they are drilled from 27 to 34 inches distance, horse-hoed or ploughed between, and hand-hoed; the crops good, and the wheat that succeeds, equal to that upon the summer-fallows adjoining. We find that two or three ploughings or horse-hoeings between the rows, and twice hand-hoeing in the rows, are generally sufficient."

To the above passage is added the Glendale method of *drilling beans,* It would be unreasonable, however, to expect any thing of general excellence, in the practice of a district in which it is not only a new process, but where it is confined to a few individuals. Nevertheless, we not unfrequently find a superior degree of ingenuity and exertion manifested, in the introduction of a new practice; and, sometimes, useful ideas struck out, which had not before been thought of. The practice under notice fortunately discloses a valuable minutia, which I have not elsewhere met with. It relates to the *covering* of the *seed.*

P. 87. " The seed is covered in by going once over with a light harrow, or, what is better, by a double mould-board plough running up between the rows, and making a hollow interval between them, which keeps the seed dry in wet weather. Another advantage of having the earth raised in this manner is, that the beans may be much sooner hoed, the earth falling into

into the hollow interval rather than upon the young plants.''

At the close of the section, we have the following general, and sensible, observations on the varieties or sorts of beans.   P. 89. " We find the large horse-bean ripens earlier by near a fortnight than the smaller kind, for which reason it is more eligible for northern climates and late situations. A variety of bean, that would ripen earlier than the large horse-bean and be *equally productive**, would |be a great acquisition to the bean culture. We ought not to despair but that such a variety may be found, when it is considered that fifty years since, the farmers of this district thought it very improbable that varieties of oats could be had, which would ripen a *month earlier*, and be *more productive*, than the kind they then cultivated.''

PEAS,—we are informed, in p. 90,—" are mostly grown upon such lands as have been worn out by too long continuance in ploughing."—And, in a note,— " on such old tillage lands, it is found, that wheat, peas, and vetches, or tares, are the only species of grain that can be raised to advantage."

POTATOES.   P. 90. " Of this invaluable root, the *varieties* cultivated here are very numerous, and frequently changing; many of the kinds that were formerly in repute, being now in a manner lost; as the the *True Kidney*, the *Rough White*, the *Blood Red*, the *Tawny*, &c.; and their places supplied by others."

P. 91. " They are generally *cultivated*, in drills, from 32 to 40 inches distance."

P. 91. " They are seldom grown for the use of stock; except for horses; to which they are given raw."

TURNIPS.   P. 92. " Turnips have not been used in this county, as food for supporting cattle and sheep,

" * The mazagan ripens earlier, but is not so productive."

sheep, much above seventy years*: for this purpose they were first grown in the northern parts of the county; it is but of late years they have been cultivated on part of Tyne-side."

The *Culture* of *Turnips*. P. 92. " At their first introduction they were sown broad-cast, and hoed by gardeners and other men, at extravagant wages. The late Mr. ILDERTON, about thirty years since, had the merit of first reducing the price of hoeing, by teaching boys, girls, and women, to perform the work equally as well, if not better, than men. The mode he took was simple and ingenious: by a light plough, without a mould-board, he divided the field into small squares of equal magnitude, and directed the boys and girls to leave a certain number of plants in each square. In a short time they became accurate, regular, and expert hoers ; and, in a few years, all the turnips in the country were hoed by women and boys, at half the expence, and better than by men.

" The present mode of drilling turnips was first introduced into this county about the year 1780 : the advantages with which it is attended, have so far recommended the practice, that very few are now sown broad-cast †; and, as we think it an operation that

" * Mr. EDWARD NISBET, in the year 1797, then near 90 years of age, said that it was *upwards of 70 years* since Mr. PROCTOR, the proprietor of Rock, brought ANDREW WILLEY, a gardener, to cultivate turnips at Rock, for the purpose of feeding cattle; that WILLEY afterwards settled at Lesbury, as a gardener, and was employed for many years to sow turnips for all the neighbourhood ; and his business this way was so great, he was obliged to ride and sow, that he might dispatch the greater quantity. The practice of hoeing was also introduced at this time."

" † The broad-cast culture of turnips, in the northern parts of the county, for many years previous to this, was not inferior to any we ever saw; and in respect to *accurate, regular, clean hoeing,* superior to what we ever observed in Norfolk, Suffolk, or other turnip districts which we have frequently examined." And, in a note to "hoeing turnips," in the section *Labour*, p. 165, this excellency of practice is given to the WOMEN of the borders.—" In this

that may be serviceable in other districts, we shall be more particular in describing the manner of performing it."

The *Northumbrian practice* is then explained. But it falls short of what might have been expected to have risen, in the experience of twenty-five years constant practice, among men of intellect and exertion *. The method of first ridging up the soil, and then setting on the dung by hand, has probably been copied from the potatoe culture. It is rather extraordinary, however, that, during twenty-five years experience, no one should have noticed, that potatoes are produced *within* or *beneath* the soil,—turnips *upon* it: for although they strike down tap-roots, to give stability to the plants, in the state of fructification, they throw out their feeding fibres, superficially,—frequently exposing them upon the surface. And how much more convenient, as well as rational, it is, to spread the dung, (provided it be in a proper state of ripeness,) evenly over the surface, as for a broadcast crop: and, then, to form the ridges for the seed; —to be deposited among the dung and fine mould collected together, in the middles of the ridges, by the operation.

But comparatively simple and eligible, as this method doubtlessly is, a gentleman of Cornwall,— Mr. GWATKIN,—has fallen upon one which is still more so. Mr. G. has, for the last twelve years, and with uniform success, been in the practice of spreading,

this branch of labour, the women in the northern parts of the county excel: the writer of this note has at different times visited *Norfolk*, *Suffolk*, and all the principal turnip districts in the island; but never saw turnips *so well hoed* and *completely cleaned*, or kept in such *garden-like culture*, as on these borders."

* PRESERVING TURNIP SEED. The Northumbrian practice, in this particular, is most eligible.—P. 97. " It is generally reaped, tied up in sheaves, and when dry, put into a *long stack*, where it is kept through the winter, and thrashed out in April or May."

ing, not only his manure, but his seed, evenly over the whole surface, before he form his ridges: thus burying the seeds at different depths; yet at every depth dispersing them among manure and fine mould, —to push on the growth of the plants, and enable them to escape their enemies: and thus securing a crop, be the season what it may. For, if the season prove moist, the crop is immediately given by the more superficially covered seeds,—if dry, those that have been buried deeper continue to rise, in succession, according to the depth at which they happened to be deposited. This plan is so rational, that theory alone, might almost venture to decide in its favour, without the corroborating evidence of twelve years successful practice.

In 1804, I constructed a machine, for *watering turnips on ridges;* and described it in a new edition of the Rural Economy of the WEST of ENGLAND, *Minute* 64. It lodges the water *within,* not upon the *tops* of the ridges:—either before, or after, the drilling of the seed: through which mean, where water is to be had, a crop of turnips may be secured, let the droughtiness of the season be what it may. This method of moistening the soil is equally applicable to the practice above described. By filling the ridges with moisture, immediately after they be formed, in a dry season, they would be able not only to throw out, but support the crop, in the first instance.

It may be useful to those who are unacquainted with the practice of raising turnips on ridges, to mention that it is, in most cases, proper, and, unless in a very wet season, requisite, to draw a lightish roller (of a weight proportioned to the soil and the season) lengthway along the ridges; to flatten and smooth their tops, and give their upper parts the required firmness.

The ridges may be formed either with a common plough, laying two plits, or furrows, back to back;

cr

or with a double mouldboard plough, which is more expeditious. In either way it is useful, especially if the watering machine is to be used, to have a *marking wheel* running along the land-side of the plough, to direct the ploughman in setting out the ridges, at exactly equal distances. A proper medium is thirty-three inches: In some cases three feet may be preferable. The intervals are cleared with a horse hoe, or a small plough; and the rows hand-hoed, as often as may be required; the plants being set out, at six to nine inches distance. If they stand in two rows, or if promiscuously, as in the practice above described, they require to be set out, alternately, on each side of the ridge; in order that the roots, as well as the tops, may have better room to spread in, and a greater freedom of air and pasturage. A full crop of turnips, thus disposed, fill up the entire area of the field,—appear to occupy the whole ground,— as if they stood at regular and short distances.

I have, here, purposely entered, at large, on the subject of CULTIVATING TURNIPS on RIDGES; as NORTHUMBERLAND is not only the first English county into which this method was introduced, to the notice of professional men, but the only one, in which it has, for any length of time, been an ESTABLISHED PRACTICE. For it has ever been a leading object of my own surveys to study and register, with increased attention, the practices which are peculiar to—or which are superiorly pursued in—the district or department under examination; and, in going through the Board's Reports, I intend to adhere to the same principle.

Another principle of conduct which I have observed in my former Works on provincial practice, is that of endeavoring to collect materials concerning the ORIGIN and PROGRESS of SUPERIOR PRACTICES. And this, also, I mean to abide by, in my present undertaking.

In the Northumberland Report, I find some valuable

able particulars relating to the HISTORY of the
TURNIP CULTURE, as it is there practised;—of which
the following is an abstract. For, although the cultivation of turnips on ridges is not a discovery of
magnitude,—or to be named with that of the thrashing mill,—great praise is due to its promoters.

The Northumbrian Reporters, after giving the
merit of the invention to Mr. TULL (who, having
tried drilling in *every* shape, without success, may, in
like manner, be considered as the inventor of *all*
the methods that ever have been, or ever will be,
practised) inform us, not as from their own knowledge, but from information ; that the first successful
practitioner of the method under notice, was Mr.
CRAIG of Dumfrieshire, in the SOUTH of SCOTLAND
(the great agricultural luminary, for a length of years,
in that quarter of the island); who so early as
" about 1745," pursued the following method :—
P. 100. " In the autumn, as soon as the corn crop
was off, he ploughed his land into two-bout ridges, in
which state it continued all winter: next spring these
ridges were ploughed and harrowed until sufficiently
pulverized, and at last split, to make a hollow furrow
for depositing the dung, which was covered in by the
plough going twice about, making a ridge near four
feet wide; then this two-bout ridge was harrowed :
a single-wheel drill, turning round a hollow cylinder
of tin with holes in it, deposited the seed directly
over the dung : the drill had a small roller behind to
cover in the seed, and was drawn by one horse. When
the plants were ready for hoeing, they were set out
at ten or twelve inches distance from one another,
in the rows, and the intervals ploughed between
through the summer, as often as necessary."

From ARDBIGLAND, Mr. CRAIG'S place on the
northern coast of Solway Firth, the Reporters conjecture, the practice travelled into CUMBERLAND;
where, " in the year 1755, PHILIP HOWARD, esq. of
Corby, first cultivated turnips in that county, in drills
with

with four feet intervals: finding the distance too wide, he reduced it to two feet, and continued it for ten years before it was followed by the farmers, who now pursue the same mode with little variation, except that they make the distance of the intervals about twenty-seven inches. The one-bout ridges, in which the dung is deposited, are here called *stitches*, and are flattened at the top by drawing a piece of wood over them, instead of a roller or a harrow.

"About the year 1756, or 1757, Mr. PRINGLE, formerly a surgeon in the army, who had an estate near Coldstream, in Berwickshire, was the first person in that neighbourhood who cultivated turnips in this manner: his drills were at three feet and a half distance." p. 101.

But it was left for the superior ability of Mr. DAWSON of FROGDEN, near Kelso, in Scotland (one of the most accurate managers, whose practices I have had opportunities of observing) to ESTABLISH the PRACTICE.

P. 101. "Mr. WILLIAM DAWSON, who was well acquainted with the turnip culture in England, having been purposely sent to reside in those districts, for six or seven years, where the best cultivation was pursued, with an intention not only of seeing, but of making himself master of the manual operations, and of every minutiæ in the practice, was convinced of the superiority of Mr. PRINGLE's mode over every other he had seen, either in Norfolk or elsewhere; and in 1762, when he entered to Frogden farm, near Kelso, in Roxburghshire, he immediately adopted the practice upon a large scale, to the amount of 100 acres yearly. He began by drilling at three feet distance; but a few years after, trying various widths of intervals, he reduced it to two feet and a half, which he still continues. As far as we have been able to obtain information, he was the first that used *a roller for flattening* the tops of the one-bout ridges."

The

The Reporters add, p. 102,—and I cordially thank them for it,—"it may not be improper to remark, that Mr. PRINGLE pursued this mode for several years, yet none of his neighbours followed the example; but no sooner did Mr. DAWSON (an actual farmer) adopt the same system, than it was immediately followed, not only by several farmers in his vicinity, but by those very farmers adjoining Mr. PRINGLE, whose crops they had seen for ten or twelve years so much superior to their own. It is also deserving of notice, that when Mr. DAWSON settled at Frogden, the whole of that district was under the most wretched system of cultivation, and the farmers unacquainted with the value of turnips, artificial grasses, and lime. At first, his practice met with many opponents, and was ridiculed by the old, the ignorant, and the prejudiced; but his superior crops and profits soon made converts: the practice in a few years became general; and this district is now amongst the best cultivated in the kingdom, the land trebled in value, and the aspect of the country greatly improved. It is a pleasing reflection, that the example and exertions of one man, have been capable of producing so great, so lasting, and inestimable benefits; and it is more than probable, that this mode of cultivating turnips would have died away with Mr. PRINGLE, and the practice been lost to this district, had it not been for the discernment and intelligence of this individual."

This powerfully corroborates what I have long been desirous to inculcate; well knowing the ground of my motive. It belongs to the higher order of PROFESSIONAL MEN, to a DAWSON, to ESTABLISH IMPROVEMENTS. How wise, then, in men of fortune, to introduce and encourage on their estates, men who are so useful to their prosperity. Be it the amusement and ambition of landed gentlemen to be instrumental in *discovering* and *promoting* improve-

ments

ments that may be profitable to their estates and the community.

CULTIVATED HERBAGE. In this section of the Report under review, though of some length, we find nothing that is peculiarly entitled to notice. Nevertheless, a few of the remarks it contains may serve to corroborate, if not enrich, what I have already collected, on the subject.

P. 112. "The *Artificial Grasses** most commonly cultivated in this county are, Red Clover *(trifolium pratense)*, White Clover *(trifoliuu repens)*, and Ray Grass *(lolium perenne)*. With these some people mix Rib-Grass *(plantago lanceolata)*, and upon sandy soils, Hop Medic *(medicago lupulina)* is sown with success. Few of these grasses are ever grown alone, except red clover, when intended to continue only one year; and even then, a small portion of ray-grass (from one to three gallons per acre) is generally sown with it, we think with much propriety, as it not only comes early in the spring, but thickens the crop, and facilitates making the clover into hay."

P. 115. " *Ray-Grass*, is universally sown through every part of this county, and its merits justly appreciated. The seed from the London market used to be held in high estimation; but, of late years, great quantities of an annual variety have been introduced from that quarter, and considerable losses occasioned,

---

* ARTIFICIAL GRASSES. I do not mean to censure the Northumberland Reporters for this *unnatural phrase;* because it was put into their mouths. It was probably first used in antithesis to *natural* grasses: and I find that I have, but not of late, unthinkingly written it. We have, to be sure, *artificial flowers;* and *artificial grasses*, too, might doubtlessly be picked up in Bond-street.

When speaking of the food of animals, the most proper epithet to be used, in contradistinction to *natural,* is *cultivated:*—and, when nothing but *grasses* were raised, the phrase *cultivated grasses* would be most applicable. But the *trifolia* are legumes, not grasses. Both of them, however, produce *herbage*. When a term, or a technical phrase, is to be used, one which is appropriate ought certainly to be preferred to one that is absurd.

casioned, by the ground being left totally bare, or without a single plant of ray-grass, the second year: this having so frequently happened, has induced many principal farmers to grow their own ray-grass seed, which they know to be of the true perennial kind."

P. 116. " In order to ascertain which of the above plants were most grateful to sheep, the following experiment was made, in a field (of good dry loam) sown with a mixture, of red clover 10lb. white 3lb. yellow 3lb. rib-grass 2lb. and ray-grass 1 peck per acre; five parcels of ground, adjoining each other, were selected, for sowing each of the seeds separately : the result was, that the red and the white clovers, and the rib-grass, were eaten perfectly bare, while the yellow was in a manner untouched, and got to such a length as to be obliged to be mown ;—at the same time, it was eaten equally with the other plants in those parts of the field where they were sown promiscuously as above."

A precaution that is used, by the Reporters, on turning cattle upon a full bite of clover, is valuable.— P. 114. " When cattle are turned into a fresh clover " fog," especially in wet weather, they are sometimes hove, by the sudden fermentation of the clover : to prevent this inconvenience, cattle are put upon it in the middle of the day, when it is free from dew, or any moisture, they being first filled with natural grass, which hinders them from eating so greedily as if put on hungry : if the clover once pass, they seldom take any harm afterwards. By using this precaution, we have not had any cattle hoven for several years."

NATURAL HERBAGE, or GRASS LAND.—P. 111. " What is generally understood by natural meadows, are such lands as are overflowed by rivers*, and produce

* No: MEADOW is applied, in most parts of the kingdom, to low lying *mowing grounds;* whether they are, or not, liable to be overflowed; in distinction to *marshes, grazing grounds,* and other PASTURE LANDS.

duce a crop of hay every year, without any returns
of manure. Of this description of meadows we have
very few in this county : what are called meadows
here, are such old grass lands as are employed for
growing hay almost every year, the greatest part of
which are uplands. To enable them to stand this
severe cropping, they are, or ought to be, manured
on the surface every third or fourth year : if this
operation be neglected, they impoverish very fast.
Where they cannot conveniently be dunged as above,
they are depastured one year, and mown the other ;
or, what is better, depastured two years, and mown
the third : the produce, from one to a ton and a half
per acre, a fair crop."

Meadow Haymaking. Of the Northumbrian method, the Reporters speak slightingly. " The mowers
cut from half an acre to three quarters a day, and
that very ill : the haymakers are equally indolent and
inactive." (p. 117.) The best practice of Northumberland, as described in the Report, is, however,
no way inferior to the par practice of the kingdom.
It, in most respects, resembles that of YORKSHIRE ;
which I have described, The only particular that
has struck me as requiring notice here, is the method
of conveying the load cocks, pikes, or stacklets, to
the aggregate stack in the field.—P. 118. " When
the large stack is made in the field, the " pikes" are
drawn to it, by putting a strong rope round their
bottom, the two ends of which are fastened to the
hind part of a cart, in which are yoked three or four
horses. This saves the trouble of forking and loading
them in carts, and is done in much less time."

Grazing Grounds.—P. 112. " Natural pastures, or
old grass land, are most prevalent along the sea coast :
these are depastured with both sheep and oxen ; the
general mode of stocking being two acres to an ox,
and the same quantity of ground to eight or ten
sheep, through the summer, and from one to two
sheep per acre through the winter; the latter are
                                                        either

either the store flock, or ewes for fat lambs. Sometimes Cheviot wethers, three years and a half old, in
good condition, are put in those pastures after the
fatting cattle are taken out, and pay well, if they
get sufficiently fat to be sold to the butchers about
Christmas."

P. 120. " Some few graziers follow the old custom
of keeping only one kind of stock upon the same
ground; whilst others, we think with more propriety,
intermix, with oxen and cows, a few sheep, and two
or three colts in each pasture; which both turn to
good account, and do little injury to the grazing
cattle: in some cases sheep are a real benefit, by
eating down and destroying the ragwort *(senecio
jacobæa,)* which disgraces some of the best pastures
in the county where *oxen only* are grazed."

HORSES. P 155. " Those bred in the county are
of various sorts, descended from stallions of different
kinds, from the full-blood racer to the strong, heavy,
rough-legged black. From the full-blood stallions
and country mares, are bred excellent hunters, road
and carriage horses; and from the other kinds of
stallions are bred the draught horses, which in general
are middle-sized, active animals, well adapted to the
husbandry of the country."

CATTLE *.—*Breeds.*—P. 139. " The different kinds
of cattle bred in this county, are the short-horned,
the Devonshire, the long-horned, and the wild
cattle.

" The *short-horned kind* have been long established
over the whole county; the other kinds are found
only in the hands of a few individuals, who have introduced them with a laudable view of comparing their
merits with the established breed of the country."

Again.

* On this important subject of the rural concerns of a country,
we find less than might have been expected, from Messrs. Bailey
and Culley. But Mr. CULLEY had, previously published, in one
volume octavo, a valuable TREATISE on LIVE STOCK, in general.

Again. " Their color is much varied, but they are mostly an agreeable mixture of red and white. From their being in many places called the Dutch breed, it is probable they were originally brought from the Continent.

" They have been much improved of late years, by the exertions and attention of enterprising breeders ; who have already improved them so far, as to be sold fat to the butchers at three years and a half old. The weight of the carcase is in general from 60 to 80 stone (14lb. to the stone,) but there are instances of individuals attaining much greater weight."

P. 140. " The *long horns* have been introduced from the improved stocks of the Midland counties, at different times, and by different breeders, but have in most instances given way again to the improved breed of short horns *."

Again.—" The *Wild Cattle* are only found in Chillingham Park, belonging to the Earl of TANKERVILLE; and as it is probable they are the only remains of the *true and genuine* breed of that species of cattle†, we shall be more particular in our description.

" Their colour is invariably white, muzzle black ; the whole of the inside of the ear, and about one-third of the outside from the tip, downwards, red : horns white, with black tips, very fine, and bent upwards ; some of the bulls have a thin upright mane, about an inch and a half, or two inches long : the weight of the oxen is from 35 to 45 stone ; and the cows from

25

" * At this time (1804) they are totally abandoned by every breeder in the county ; the improved breed of short horns (from the stock of Messrs. COLLINGS,) having proved themselves much superior."

" † We are no strangers that there may be found in two or three different parks of the kingdom, breeds of cattle which pass under the denomination of Wild Cattle ; but are inclined to believe that they have been contaminated by crossing, and that those in Chillingham Park are the only remains, which answer the description given by BOETHIUS, of this species of cattle."

25 to 35 stone, the four quarters; 14lb. to the stone. The beef is finely marbled, and of excellent flavour.

" From the nature of their pasture, and the frequent agitation they are put into, by the curiosity of strangers, it cannot be expected they should get very fat; yet the six-years old oxen are generally very good beef; from whence it may be fairly supposed that, in proper situations, they would feed well.

" At the first appearance of any person they set off at full speed, and gallop to a considerable distance; when they make a wheel round, and come boldly up again, tossing their heads in a menacing manner: on a sudden they make a full stop, at the distance of forty or fifty yards, looking wildly at the object of their surprise; but upon the least motion being made, they again turn round, and gallop off with equal speed; but forming a shorter circle, and returning with a bolder and more threatening aspect, they approach much nearer, when they make another stand; and again gallop off. This they do several times, shortening their distance, and advancing nearer, till they come within a few yards, when most people think it prudent to leave them.

" The mode of killing them was, perhaps, the only modern remains of the grandeur of ancient hunting. On notice being given that a wild bull would be killed upon a certain day, the inhabitants of the neighbourhood came in great numbers, both horse and foot: the horsemen rode off the bull from the rest of the herd until he stood at bay; when a marksman dismounted and shot. At some of these huntings, twenty or thirty shots have been fired before he was subdued: on such occasions, the bleeding victim grew desperately furious, from the smarting of his wounds, and the shouts of savage joy that were echoing from every side. From the number of accidents that happened, this dangerous mode has been seldom practised of late years; the park-keeper alone generally shooting them with a rifled gun, at one shot.

" When

" When the cows calve, they hide their calves, for a week or ten days, in some sequestered situation, and go and suckle them two or three times a day. If any person come near the calves, they clap their heads close to the ground, and lie like a hare in form, to hide themselves. This is a proof of their native wildness, and is corroborated by the following circumstance, that happened to the writer of this narrative, who found a hidden calf, two days old, very lean, and very weak: on stroking its head, it got up, pawed two or three times like an old bull, bellowed very loud, retired a few steps, and bolted at his legs with all its force; it then began to paw again, bellowed, stepped back, and bolted as before; but knowing its intention, and stepping aside, it missed him, fell, and was so very weak that it could not rise, though it made several efforts; but it had done enough, the whole herd were alarmed; and, coming to its rescue, obliged him to retire; for the dams will allow no person to touch their calves without attacking them with impetuous ferocity.

" When any one happens to be wounded, or grown weak and feeble through age or sickness, the rest of the herd set upon it, and gore it to death."

Mr. Bailey does not even conjecture how these cattle became immured within the demesne of Gillingham. I understood, when I had the great satisfaction of seeing them, that tradition (having perhaps no other equally plausible way of accounting for the fact) spoke of their being inclosed by the park wall, when it was first built. If the wall was raised while this breed of cattle were in a state of nature, in that part of the country, and surrounded a wood, or other fastness, which was their favorite haunt, tradition may be right.

What seems to prove them to be a *natural breed,* or a variety of ancient formation, is their identity, in regard

regard to color and other distinguishments; perfectly resembling, in these things, other wild animals *.

Breeding. P. 143.—" *Hiring Bulls*—for the season, is practised in this county : as high as 50 guineas have been paid for a bull of the short-horned breed for one season, and from three to five guineas given for serving a cow; but the more common premium is a guinea."

Rearing. P. 143.—" *Breeding Young Cattle*—is practised in almost every part of the county. Upon the large farms, cows are kept more for this purpose than the profit of dairying. There are instances of fifty or sixty calves being brought up in one season, by one farmer, who did not milk more than fifteen cows. Calves are certainly best reared with milk; but where such numbers are bred, many different things have been mixed with, or substituted for, this nutritive and natural diet: oats and bean-meal, oil-cake, lintseed, boiled turnips, &c. are used, and have their various advocates; but lintseed is most approved: eggs are excellent for mixing in the calf's food; when cheap in the spring, perhaps they cannot be better employed †. In the summer the calves are turned to grass, and in the first winter get turnips and straw. After being a year old, they are kept in summer on coarse pasture; and in winter on straw only."

Dairy

---

* Quere, had each horde, tribe, or patriarchy, while in the pastoral state, cattle of known color, or distinguishing natural mark ; as red,—black,—white,—white with red ears,—white with black ears, &c. &c. (the two last being, I believe, the distinguishing characteristics of the two varieties of " wild cattle" now extant in England) ; to the end that they might be the more easily separated, when accidentally intermixed; as well as more readily to obtain information of—and claim with greater certainty—those which might happen to stray ?

† This, I confess, is to me a new idea, in the *rearing* of cattle. Nevertheless, on the borders, where eggs are not uncommonly sold for threepence a dozen, they may be profitably employed as the food of calves. Eggs and milk appear to be of a kindred nature,—

and,

Dairy Management of Northumberland. P. 143.
" This county cannot boast of its dairies; those who
live in the vicinity of Newcastle, and other populous
places, make a handsome return by the sale of milk,
fresh butter, &c. but upon most of the large farms in
this county, dairies are not held in much estimation."
Yet we are told, p. 139. of " there being instances
of cows giving 36 quarts of milk per day, and of 48
firkins of butter being made from a dairy of twelve
cows; but the more general quantity is three firkins
per cow in a season, and 24 quarts of milk per day."
But rearing calves,—rather than butter or cheese,—is
the leading object of the Northumbrian dairy. We
are not informed, however, from whence the supply,
of supernumerary calves, is drawn.

Grazing Cattle. P. 119. " Oxen are mostly grazed
in the eastern part of the county, and a few in the
vicinity of Whittingham; they are bought in May or
June, and sold as they become ready to supply the
large fleets of colliers and other trading vessels belonging to Newcastle, Shields, Sunderland, Hartley, and
Blythe.

" Some few graziers buy only such oxen as are in
forward condition, by having got turnips in the spring;
those generally go off in June, and are followed by
cows, heifers, or kyloes*; of which those that do not
get fat on the pasture, to be sold through the summer, are put upon " fogs" (aftermaths), and sold in
November and December. The cows are also bought
in the spring months, and are chiefly used for home
consumption. The kyloes are bought at Falkirk
trysts *(" meetings")*, or at Newcastle fair, in the
autumn, and wintered upon coarse rough ground, or
straw (sometimes a few turnips are given in the
spring),

and, perhaps, may interchangeably afford nourishment, not only to
infant animals, but to those of every age,—whether oviparous, or
mammalian.

" * An excellent breed of small cattle from the Highlands of
Scotland."

spring,) and are sold all through the summer, as they become fit for the butcher, to supply Newcastle, and other markets. Those that are ready to go off in June, always leave the most profit, beef being frequently sold at that season for a shilling a stone more than the ordinary prices.

" The profit of grazing, like all other speculations, varies with circumstances ; but we believe we may venture to average it at 3*l.* or 3*l.* 10*s.* for keeping on grass from May-day to Michaelmas. Cows, in general, leave more than oxen, in proportion to their weight; but they are subject to disorders of the udder, that frequently reduce the profit, and deter many people from grazing them."

SHEEP. On this important species of live stock, we have a full and valuable Section. I will select such parts of it, as I conceive to be sufficiently entitled to admission, here.

The *Breeds* of Sheep, in Northumberland. P. 144. " In this county there are three distinct breeds—the Cheviot sheep, the heath sheep, and the long-woolled sheep.

" *The Cheviot Sheep*—are hornless ; the faces and legs, in general, white*. The *best breeds* have a fine open countenance, with lively prominent eyes ; body long, fore-quarters wanting depth in the breast, and breadth, both there and on the chine ; fine clean small-boned legs ; thin pelts ; weight of carcass, when fat, from 12 to 18 lb. per quarter ; fleeces from $2\frac{1}{2}$ to

" * Many of the Cheviot sheep have dark faces, and were more so formerly. We were informed by Mr. CHISHOLM, Mr. REDHEAD, Mr. MARSHALL, &c. that these dark-faced ones grew equally as fine wool, were as hardy, and equally as good thrivers as the white-faced ones ; but that the people to whom they sold their sheep, and especially tups, preferred white faces ; for which reason they have endeavoured to get quit of black faces."

This is good evidence of their being merely a selected variety, from the native alpine stock of the kingdom ; as will be more evidently shown.

$2\frac{1}{2}$ to $3\frac{1}{2}$ lb. each, and sold in 1792 for 11d. per lb. The wool is not at all fine, there being in a fleece of 3 lb. weight, only 2 lb. of fine wool, worth 1s. per lb. (when the whole fleece sells at 10d. per lb.) and 1 lb. of coarse, worth only 6d. per lb.

" They are bred only upon the hilly districts in the north-west part of the county, and do not extend much farther south than Reedwater.

" The *best kind* of these sheep are certainly a very hardy and valuable mountain sheep, where the *pasture is mostly green sward*, or contains a large portion of that kind of herbage, which is the case with all the hills around Cheviot where these sheep are bred; for as to the mountain of Cheviot itself, no kind of sheep whatever are bred upon it; and we find it an universal practice amongst the most experienced sheep farmers, to depasture the *heathy districts* with old sheep; but they never attempt to keep a breeding flock upon them *."

P. 148. " The *Heath Sheep* have large spiral horns, black faces and legs, a fierce wild-looking eye, and short firm carcases (weighing from 12 to 16 lb. per quarter,) covered with long, open, coarse, shagged wool. The fleeces weigh from three to four pounds each, and sold, in 1792, for 6d. per lb. They are an exceedingly active and hardy race, and seem the best adapted, of all others, to high exposed *heathy* districts; such as we find them in possession of here, from the western parts of the county of Durham to North Tyne."

P. 149. " The breeders of this kind of sheep on the south-west corner of the county, are very confident that they are a *much hardier sheep* than the Cheviot

---

" * Mr. Robson, of Chatto, informed us, that ewes and lambs would not do upon his farms of *Common Burn*, near Wooler, and *Felhope* and *Carshope*, at the head of Coquet. On such situations the gimmers are found to be hardier or do better than the wether sheep of the same age, called Dinmonts."

Cheviot breed; and, upon their high exposed heathy mountains, where there is *very little green herbage*, much more profitable : while the Cheviot farmers assert that theirs are equally hardy, and that the greater value of the fleece gives them a decided superiority."

Having suggested a fair trial to be made, by the promoters of those two very different breeds, the Reporters, with much good sense and moderation, proceed to give their own opinion on the subject.—P. 149.

" Until some experiment of this kind determine the matter, we hope we shall not give offence to either party by stating, that we have seen the heath sheep bred with advantage, upon higher and coarser pastures than *Common Burn*, or those others around Cheviot which are deemed improper for a breeding flock of the Cheviot kind; and that it may probably turn out, that each breed is peculiarly adapted to particular situations; the one to *coarse, exposed mountains*, where the luxury of green herbage is thinly scattered, or rarely to be found ; the other, to *hilly pastures*, where considerable portions of verdant surface predominate, such as characterize the pastoral districts around Cheviot.".

P. 150. " *The long woolled sheep*—which formerly occupied the lower district of this county, were called *Mugs*, probably from their faces being covered with a muff of wool, close to their eyes*. These being a slow-feeding tribe, have given way to the Dishley breed, which were first introduced into this county in the year 1766†, and by their superior merit, have so far made their way against every prejudice and opposition, that it is probable in a few years there will be a difficulty in finding a flock that is not more or less related to the Dishley blood.

" *The*

---

* In Yorkshire, " Mud Sheep :" doubtlessly *Mudland Sheep*. *Rev.*

" † By Messrs Culley."

" *The improved breed of long-woolled sheep*—are* distinguished from other long-woolled kinds by their fine lively eyes, clean heads, straight broad flat backs, round barrel-like bodies, very fine small bones, thin pelts ; and that singular property of making fat at an early age, perhaps more than any thing else, gives them a superiority over the other breeds in this island †.

" The weight of the carcass in general is, ewes three or four years old, from 18 to 26lb. per quarter ; the wool, upon an average, 7½lb. a fleece ; the length from 6 to 14 inches ; sold, in 1792, at 10d per lb."

Engravings are given of those three distinct breeds or varieties of Northumbrian sheep, from the accurate pencil of Mr. Bailey. To amateurs, engravings of farm stock may be amusing.

The *Management* of Sheep. That which is observed on the *Cheviot Hills* is the most interesting. Many of the flocks are immensely large ; and " Sheep Farming" is the sole employment of their owners :— the same, or a similar mode of management extending to a great distance, over a range of similar green hills which form the Scottish border.

P. 147. " *The mode of management*—amongst the sheep farmers of those hills is, to divide their flocks into different parcels, viz. lambs, hogs, gimmers, ewes, and wethers, and each parcel kept on such pasturage as is thought most proper for them. Every parcel is attended by a shepherd, who is bound to return the number of sheep delivered to him, either alive, or in his account of dead sheep, which are in general sold at different prices, according to their goodness. (?)

" The ewes are two years and a half old before they are put to the tup, and are kept till five or six years

* Which, I believe, were, in 1794, chiefly confined to the northern parts of the county.
† This assertion may be objected to. A Southdown Rambreeder may deem it too broad.

years old : the loss of lambs is sometimes very considerable, not only on being dropped, but also from other disorders, as the " *milk-ill,*" which attacks them from three to seven days old ; the " *quarter-ill,*" &c. which Mr. CHISHOLM, of Clennell, estimates at not less than 15 per cent. taking one year with another. And Mr. SMITH, of Woodhall, says, that " although the Cheviot breed be as healthy as perhaps any, yet there can hardly be an instance adducible, of any of the different flocks coming all to the shears, much less the hogs ; out of which it is common to allow two out of each score."

In the management of the *long-woolled breed,* in Northumberland, I perceive little that is different from what I have already described in the MIDLAND COUNTIES ;—the acknowledged source of the breed, and their management. Nevertheless, in the Northern Department, the " Culley breed" is entitled to consideration ; and the subjoined notices may have their use.

P. 152. " *Letting Tups*—to serve ewes for the season, has been a practice in this county for near 30 years, and is becoming more prevalent daily : the prices vary from five to one hundred guineas, for the use of one sheep ; and ewes are frequently taken in to be served by a favourite ram, at as high rates as from three to five guineas each. The number of ewes to be served by a shearling tup, is generally stipulated not to exceed 80, and for an aged sheep 120."

Ewe Flocks.—P. 150. " The most approved mode of management of this breed of sheep is as follows : the ewes generally lamb in March, when we give them a few turnips to increase their milk. The latter end of June, or beginning of July, the lambs are weaned, and sent to middling pasture ; but a good pasture would certainly be a more eligible practice. The ewes are milked two or three times, to ease their udders, and such as are not intended to be continued

for

for breeding are culled or draughted out, and put to clover; when this fails, they get turnips, and are sold about Christmas to the butchers, very fat."

P. 151. " We generally reckon one-third of the ewes to have twin lambs. They are put to the tup, so as to have lambs at two years old, and kept for breeding until three or four years old, except such as are of particular good forms, or have other valuable properties : these we keep as long as ever they will breed. Such as are defective in shape, suspected of being slow feeders, or other unprofitable qualities, we never put to the tup, or attempt to breed from."

Store and *fatting* sheep.—P. 151. " The lambs, after being weaned, take the name of hogs. They are generally put to turnips the beginning of November, and continue at them till the middle of April or beginning of May; when the wether hogs are put upon good pasture, or second year's clover. The second winter they have turnips until the clovers are sufficiently grown to receive them, which is generally about the middle of April : they are clipped or shorn about the middle of May, when we begin to sell them, and are mostly all sold by the middle or end of June. Morpeth is our best market."——" Of late years it has been customary to sell the shearling wethers in June or July, to the butchers, fatter than most other breeds will be at two or three years old; the weight of these shearling wethers is from 18 to 21 lb. per quarter."—P. 120. " *Sheep*—that have been wintered upon turnips, are put to the earliest grass that can be obtained; the clovers and ray-grass are generally ready in April; the old grass-lands not before May. In both situations they are continued till shorn, and sold off, from the latter end of May through all June and part of July. The draught ewes, or shearling wethers, intended for turnips next winter, succeed them, and thus a regular rotation is kept up. Of late years, some farmers have sold their shearling

shearling wethers in July (when only fifteen months old) to the butchers.

" A large portion of the lands of this county being liable to the rot, and unsafe for a breeding flock, the occupiers of such situations venture ewes for fat lambs for one year; these are bought in the autumn, put to tup early (some in August,) the lambs sold in May, June, and July; after which the ewes are fatted, and sold in October and November."

On *milking ewes*, we find these judicious remarks. P. 154. " It used to be a general practice through all this county to milk ewes after the lambs were weaned, for six, eight, or ten weeks; from this milk great quantities of cheese were made, and sold for about 3*d*. per pound. When kept to three or four years old, it is exceedingly pungent, and on that account some people prefer it to cheese of a much better quality.

" To milk ewes two or three times after the lambs are weaned, is a useful practice; but when continued to eight or ten weeks, it becomes very detrimental, keeps the ewes lean, and ill prepared for meeting the severities of winter.

" This custom has been long disused by the intelligent farmers in the lower districts; and we are glad to find it much laid aside by the most considerable hill farmers. The profit of milking ewes for six or eight weeks, is estimated at 8*d*. per ewe; and it is generally agreed they are decreased in value, at least, 1*s*. 6*d*. per head; of course there is a loss of about 1*s*. per head by milking. In one instance of milking long-woolled ewes, last summer, there was a loss of, at least, 3*s*. per head."

The practice of *salving* sheep (see YORKSHIRE) is going out of fashion.—P. 154. " In the lower districts it is now almost totally disused; and some of the hill farmers have laid it aside, and find their flocks do equally well as before."

Among the *vermin* of *sheep* are here classed the

fox

fox and the *dog*. Respecting the latter, we have the following novel remarks. P. 183. " Dogs, in every place are swarming : two-thirds of them at least are kept by people who have no manner of use for them, and are constantly complaining of their inability to obtain food for their families. It would be doing these people an act of justice, to exempt them from performing statute duty on the highways, on condition they did not keep a dog ; and to supply the deficiency by laying a tax upon dogs, which tax should be applied towards repairing the roads." And, in a note to the above, " Since the first edition of this Report, the legislature have thought proper to lay a tax upon a certain description of dogs, but have exempted the only ones which are a nuisance to the community."

Finally, on the *improvement* of the two native breeds of Northumberland, namely, the *Cheviot* and the *heath* sheep,—I find, in the Reporter's " Conclusion," the subsequent observations, which I insert, without comment, in this place.

P. 190. " We have before noticed, that the Cheviot sheep might probably be improved by a cross with the South Down, and are now happy to add, that there has been formed a Society for the Improvement of Cheviot Sheep, who, amongst other laudable exertions, have hired, from Mr. ELMAN, of Glynd, in Sussex, two South Down rams, from which, it is hoped, a material improvement in the Cheviot fleece may be expected; and that a few years experience will determine the proportion of South Down blood that will suit the different situations of climate, pasture, &c. Whatever may be the result, there is certainly great praise due to the promoters of such undertakings.

" There are *some situations*, amongst the Cheviot pastures, on which we are inclined to believe a valuable sheep might be raised, from a cross with a small, lively, fine-woolled ram of the Dishley kind, and Cheviot ewes : and from a mixture of the three kinds, viz.
Cheviot,

Cheviot, South Down, and Dishley, it is probable that
the Cheviot breed would give hardiness of constitution, the South Down fine wool, and the Dishley a
good carcass, and inclination to fatten.

" We would also beg leave to recommend a similar
association to the gentlemen on the southern parts of
the county, for the improvement of the Heath sheep,
the most material objection to which is, the uncommon
coarseness of their wool: to make the fleece finer,
and at the same time preserve the hardiness of constitution of the present race, would be a considerable
improvement; probably some advantages might be
obtained by a cross with the Herdwick sheep, a breed
peculiar to the mountainous district on the south-
west part of Cumberland."—A breed that will be
particularly mentioned in reviewing the Report of
that county.

GOATS.—P. 162. " Goats are kept in small numbers on many parts of the Cheviot hills, not so much
as an object of profit; but the shepherds assert, that
the sheep flocks are healthier where a few goats
depasture This probably may be the case, as it is
well known that goats eat some plants with impu-
nity, that are deadly poison to other kinds of domestic
animals.

" The chief profit made of these goats, is from their
milk being sold to invalids, who come to Wooler in
the summer season."

RABBITS do not appear to be *propagated* in Northumberland. They are found, in considerable numbers, among the sand hills along the coast.

SWINE,—in Northumberland, appear to be, at
present, in the state of revolution.—P. 162. " The
Berkshire pigs, and the large *white breed*, were formerly the most prevalent in this county; but the
small *black Chinese breed* has in a great measure sup-
planted them, especially upon the large farms; and
these are likely to give way to a small white breed
lately introduced, remarkably quiet, inoffensive animals;

mals; on which account they are principally preferred to the Chinese breed."

POULTRY.—What is said of this unprofitable species
of farm stock, makes one smile. Who, *in England,*
ever imagined that "labouring people" are in the
habit of rearing poultry,—*for their own eating!* There
is much truth, however, in what the Northumberland
Reporters say on this subject. P. 163. " Poultry, in
a district like this, where they are sold so low, are
the most unprofitable stock kept upon a farm, the
value of the corn consumed by them being generally
double what they are sold for; and the labouring
people are so well convinced of their inutility, that
they constantly and universally sell them, knowing
from experience, that if the value received for them
be laid out in either beef or mutton, it will be much
more serviceable; and this piece of economy is so
well understood, that we believe there is scarcely an
instance of a labouring person ever making use of
poultry for his own family; they are always considered as articles *purposely bred to pamper luxury.*"

CHAPTER EXTRAORDINARY.

PROFITS OF FARMING.—In a section of the general
plan of the reprinted Reports, entitled, " Expense
and Profit,"—(as if every surveyor was expected to be
able to look into the pockets, as into the fields, of
the farmers he might happen to be sent among),—the
Northumberland Reporters (in excuse for not com-
plying with the sillily conceived instructions given
them) properly enough make the subjoined observations: P. 34. " The expense upon a farm may be
estimated pretty near the truth, for a certain number
of acres ; but the profits depend upon so many precarious circumstances, such as seasons, mode of culture, produce, markets, &c. that we think any estimate of profits upon a particular farm, would be a
                                          very

very vague criterion for judging of the rest, and most probably would not suit any other farm of the same rent or magnitude in the county."

But thinking it their duty, perhaps, to say something more on the subject, they have offered a pretty long statement of the expense of cultivating an acre of land; and of the *profit*, or rather *rent*, that may arise therefrom, on lands of different degrees of *productiveness;* but without specifying their natural characteristics; on which the expenses of cultivation very materially depend :—closing their calculations with the following inferences: P. 37. "From the above statement it appears, that nearly the same capital will be required to carry on a farm *in ploughing* at 7s. per acre, that it does one at 26s. per acre : therefore, a farm of *good land,* of 100*l.* per year, will require less capital than a farm of *bad land* of 100*l.* per year; and also, that when the value of the crops in six years amounts to no more than 12*l.* such lands are improper for arable, and will pay no rent; of course, the most profitable mode of employing such soils, is to let them remain in pasturage."

Those calculations, however, want many qualifications and provisoes, with respect to situation, surface, soil, manures, &c. &c. to render them useful, *for any purpose:* unless inasmuch as they may give rise to more matured statements: and I cannot let them pass without further notice. I must, therefore, copy them at length.

In continuation of the passage, first above quoted, the Reporters (or the Editor) proceed :—" We shall therefore state the expense of cultivating an acre, supposing a farm in the rotation of three years arable and three years grass, viz.

1 year oats,
2 ...... turnips,
3 ...... barley,
4 ...... clover and other grasses,
5 ...... ditto,
6 ...... ditto,   and

and that the first year's clover carries six sheep per acre, the second year four, and the third year two sheep per acre. Then the expense will be as follows;

First year—for oats:

	£.	s.	d.
Ploughing and harrowing	0	6	0
Seed, and sowing	0	14	0
Weeding	0	1	0
Harvesting	0	6	0
Thrashing and winnowing	0	5	0
Market expenses and carriage	0	6	0
		1 18	0

Second year—for turnips, *drilled at 30 inch intervals.*

Ploughing and harrowing 5 times..	1	5	0
Lime, leading and laying on	1	5	0
Leading dung	0	8	0
Spreading ditto	0	2	0
Seed and drilling	0	1	6
Hand-hoeing twice	0	6	0
Horse-hoeing twice	0	1	6
		3 9	0

Third year—for barley, *sown broad-cast.*

Ploughing and harrowing twice ..	0	10	0
Seed, 3 bushels *, and sowing	0	8	0
Weeding	0	1	0
Harvesting, thrashing, marketing } and carriage ....}	0	17	0
		1 16	0
		7 3	0

"* This is the quantity commonly sown, but we think two bushels, or two bushels and a half, very sufficient; and where drilled at nine or twelve inches intervals, one bushel and a half we find a proper quantity; which saving of seed will pay for horse and hand-hoeing, when the crop is drilled."

	£.	s.	d.
Brought forward	7	3	0

4th, 5th, and 6th years—clover and other grasses.

Grass-seeds sown on the barley crop	0	14	0
Harrowing and rolling in	0	1	0
Stoning, scaling, and catching moles for 3 years	0	5	0
Attendance, and other expenses of sheep for 3 years	0	12	0
	1	12	0
Taxes and cesses for 6 years	0	18	0
Capital employed for cultivation, &c.	9	13	0
Ditto for 12 sheep, at 26s. each	15	12	0
Total capital employed on 6 acres	25	5	0
The interest of which, allowing 10 per cent. is	2	10	6
To which must be added the expense of cultivation	9	13	0
Gives the expense per year for 6 acres * ...	12	3	6
Or per acre	2	0	6

" The expenses incurred for cultivation will be nearly the same, whatever the soil; but the produce will vary according to the quality of the land.

On good lands the produce may be:

1st year, Oats, 45 bush. per acre, at 2s. per bushel	4	10	0
2d year, Turnips, per acre, ...	5	0	0
3d ditto, Barley, 36 bushels per acre, at 2s. 6d. ditto, ...	4	10	0

4th,

" * These were the expenses in 1793; but in 1804 the advances of workmen's wages, taxes, &c. have increased the expense to at least one-third more."

	£.	s.	d.
4th do. Clover and grasses	3	0	0
5th do. Ditto	2	0	0
6th do. Ditto	1	0	0
Value of produce in 6 years	20	0	0
Deduct expense of cultivation, &c. ...	12	3	6
Leaves the rent for 6 years	7	16	6
Or per acre, per year	1	6	1

If the value of the crops be,

	£.	s.	d.
1st year, Oats, 30 bush. per acre, at 2s. per bushel. .... }	3	0	0
2d do. Turnips.	3	10	0
3d do. Barley, 24 bush. per acre, at 2s.6d. ditto. .... }	3	0	0
4th do. Clover and grasses.	2	10	0
5th do. Ditto.	1	10	0
6th do. Ditto.	0	15	0
Value of produce in 6 years	14	5	0
Deduct expense of cultivation, &c. ...	12	3	6
Gives the rent for 6 years	2	1	6
Or per acre, per year	0	7	0

Now what is the use of these calculations? It needed neither mathematics, nor logic, to prove that two hundred acres of land costs more working—requires a larger capital—than one hundred of a similar texture, &c. &c. &c. And as to the final inference, above quoted, it is altogether vague; or, at most, only serves to show that the calculators system cannot be *generalized* *.

But

* See note (‡) p. 33 of Rep. P. 44 of Rev.

But these calculations being before us, let us look into their merits, and see whether they will not afford inferences of a different nature. By them it evidently appears that an acre of land, which is kept three years in arable crops, and three years in herbage, and whose marketable stock is long wooled sheep, requires a capital of four guineas;—the occupier being entitled to five per cent. on the amount of the said capital, as his profit ; over and above another five per cent. for legal interest thereon;—together making up the ten per cent. above charged. For, if this extra five per cent. is not intended as an equivalent for the farmer's skill and industry, the whole statement is void; there being no other allowance made for these two valuable considerations. Hence a farmer who holds a hundred acres of land, worth 40s. an acre, and pays two hundred pounds a year, will, on the calculations under notice, be entitled to a profit of no more than twenty-one pounds:—an income which is not equal to that of a common day laborer; and, for this pittance, he is to stand to the loss of stock, seasons, and other risques, perhaps to three times the amount: no allowance for those things appearing in the statement. Hence, secondly, the calculators favorite system, of six shifts and long wooled sheep, leaves, on the first statement, twenty-six shillings an acre, for the landlord, but nothing, or worse than nothing, for the tenant; and, on the second part, only seven shillings an acre, rent, for tolerable turnip, barley, and clover land. Hence, thirdly, let us venture to conclude, that there must be more than one radical error in those calculations;—or that the *improved* system of management which has been rather exultingly recommended, is not proper to be adopted *.

The reader may be assured that the remarks, here brought

* It is possible that I may, in my turn, have been inadvertently led into error, in my investigation of this or other subject. If I have, I will gratefully thank any one who will set me right.

brought forward, were not suggested by a desire of
lowering the Northumberland Reporters, jointly or
separately, in the opinion of the public; but to show
how dangerous, to be depended upon, are complex
calculations, on general subjects, in Agriculture. If
such men as the authors of the Northumberland Report are liable to error in Agricultural statements,
what egregious blunders must not the common order
of Agricultural writers commit! And what opportunities have designing men to enforce their interests,
or their prejudices, by such calculations;—even as
an adroit barrister, who is arguing a complex case,
in which a multitude of facts are interwoven, is
enabled, by bringing forward, and magnifying, those
which best suit his purpose, and keeping others in
the back ground,—to make the better cause the
worse, or the worse the better, as may be most convenient to his views. Yet a very large portion of
written Agriculture is formed of such *imposing* materials *.

It is scarcely necessary to add, that the observations, which I have here deemed proper to offer, are
meant to put well intentioned writers on their guard,
in making calculations of that kind, and inexperienced
readers, in appreciating them. But I conceive it to
be essentially necessary in me to say, that I am far
from wishing to decry agricultural calculations, altogether. Simplex statements, of ascertained facts,
may be, on many occasions, of the greatest use.
When founded on real data, the results, if carefully
drawn, become certain; and are the surest guides in
practice. What I am desirous to show is the fallacy
which may arise from speculative calculations, on
complex subjects, with no better foundation, perhaps,
than

* When such materials become *embodied,* by men without the
slightest pretensions to practical knowledge, or, perhaps, one accurate idea relating to the subject, what chaotic masses of ignorance
and error must necessarily be produced.

than assumed premises; or partial facts so much bent as to give a false bias to the whole. When statements of this nature are applied to that most complex subject, the " expense and profit" of Agriculture,— there being so many things requisite to be taken into the account,—they required a compass of mind, a patience in study, and a maturity of experience and judgment, which few men possess.

IN the " CONCLUSION" of this Report, the writer takes a general view of the Northumberland practice. P. 184. " The most striking parts in a view of the Agriculture" (of Northumberland) " are, the great extent of farms, leases for 21 years, and the opulence, intelligence, and enterprizing spirit of the farmers: but the most prominent feature is, keeping a due balance betwixt the arable and grass lands, so as always to have a large breeding live stock, especially of sheep. Various systems of husbandry have been tried, and the boasted one of turnips, barley, clover, and wheat, has been pursued till the crops have evidently declined, particularly the turnips and clover; and the only means of restoring such lands, has been by adopting the system of three years arable, and three years grass, *depastured with sheep,* and a small proportion of cattle: by this mode, Nature has time to prepare a sufficient lea-clod, which being turned up for the turnip fallow, will ensure a vigorous crop of turnips, as it is well known they always flourish upon fresh land, or where they find the remains of a lea-clod to vegetate in. It is from this circumstance, and the peculiar and excellent mode of cultivating them, that such great crops are produced, with not more than *ten or twelve cart-loads* of dung per acre: crops that are seldom worth less than 4, 5, or 6*l.* per acre for the purposes of feeding cattle and sheep, and have in many instances been sold for 7 and 8*l.* per acre. This mode of cultivating turnips in drills, is also of great importance, being much superior to the
broad-

broad-cast culture, not only for the turnip crop, but for every other crop that succeeds them.

" The proportion betwixt the quantities in arable and grass, varies according to the quality of the soil, and other circumstances; but in most situations it is usual to keep a certain portion of the best and richest old grazing lands constantly in grass, as a *corps de reserve*, in case the artificial grasses fail; and on strong clayey soils, for depasturing a portion of the store flock upon in winter; for this purpose, it is necessary, upon such soils, to have a much larger portion of old grass land, than upon dry loams; and which is generally eaten lightly in the latter part of summer, that there may be a good aftermath, against the time the artificial grasses fail.

" It is this union of stock and tillage, and pursuing the systems mentioned in page 70, that enables the farmers to pay such high rents; and which keeps the land always in a *due state of fertility*, to produce the most profitable crops*; and at the same time is managed and kept clear of weeds at the least expense. The portion that is kept in grass for three years, breeds and fattens such a number of sheep, as leave a considerable profit, probably equal, if not more than the arable crops."

There is much good sense in these general observations. But the writer does not appear to be sufficiently

---

" * There is a certain state of fertility necessary for producing maximum crops of grain: land may be too rich as well as too poor, for growing corn: we have frequently seen crops of wheat rendered of little or no value, by the injudicious application of a few cart-loads of manure per acre more than was necessary: upon lands made too rich, corn is very apt to lodge; which not only injures the crop of grain, but entirely destroys the clover and artificial grasses sown along with it."

This is a valuable passage; though it contains nothing which is not known to observant husbandmen. The matter and the manner are equally good. It is in the best style of Agricultural writing. *Rev.*

ciently aware of the peculiarity of the situation in which he writes,—when he speaks, in general terms, or with so little reserve, of stocking arable lands with *sheep*. Were it not for populous collieries and a crowded port, in its neighbourhood, where would even the circumscribed district of Wooler find a market for its fat mutton?—for its inhabitants, we learn, live chiefly on vegetable foods. And what would be the result, were every district of the kingdom, to follow the example of the district of Wooler?

The foregoing Remarks, however, are followed up by some ingenious calculations on *long-wooled sheep;*— and these, by a somewhat contemptuous sneer at *" folding breeds."* Who can the writer have met with, that recommends the folding of sheep, in rich lowland inclosures, adapted to heavy long-wooled sheep?

But long-wooled sheep are the theme; and severer taunts are thrown at those who are childish enough to argue in favor of the *established breed of a country.* Yet this is the writer's own argument, when he recommends the *black-faced Moreland breed*, for the heathy mountain lands, on which they have long been the established breed (p. 148 and 149—Rev. 98) and the *Cheviot breed*, for high, bleak, but grass-grown pastures; namely the Cheviot hills; on which they have been, perhaps, still longer established (p. 150— Rev. 99) moreover recommending the improvement of these two established breeds. And, in these things I perfectly agree with him : but not, in the means of improvement:—which, I conceive, ought not to be affected by *strange crosses*,—(see Rep. p. 190—Rev. p. 104); but by JUDICIOUS SELECTIONS, from the established breeds;—after the manner, by which the immortalized BAKEWELL improved the established breed of his country.

RETROSPECTIVE VIEW

OF THE

NORTHUMBERLAND REPORT.

It were needless to remark, to those who have read the foregoing extracts, that the public are indebted to Messrs. BAILEY and CULLEY for much valuable information. Their errors are comparatively few. But my having bestowed more than ordinary attention upon them,—for reasons already given,—they may appear the more prominent. Errors of greater magnitude may, in other instances, be suffered to sink, in silence;—leaving them to pass away, quietly, into oblivion.

Viewing the Report of NORTHUMBERLAND, in the aggregate, it is much to be apprehended, that, in going the round of the Boards' Reports, *we shall not see its like again.*

DURHAM.

THE NATURAL DISTRICTS, of this division of the kingdom, are fewer, and less distinct, than those of Northumberland. Nevertheless, the Bishoprick of Durham, though its culturable lands are remarkably uniform, in soil and substrata, has its distinguishable features.

The Sea Coast is marked by a flatness or tameness of surface, comparatively with the more central parts of the province.

The Banks of the Tees are distinguished by lowness of situation, and productiveness of soils.

The Morelands, that occupy the western parts of the county, are, on the contrary, characterized by elevation and barrenness.

While the interior of the county is marked by the irregularity of its surface; and the diversity of its soils, comparatively with the rest of the county. In *this* dictrict the capital is situated.

And beside those four principal divisions, Weardale, or the Valley of Wolsingham, claims attention. It rises out of the midland district, and extends, westward, to near the extreme of the county; dividing the Morelands to near their greatest height.

MY own observations, in this county, have been made in repeatedly travelling through its more central parts, in the line between Darlington and Newcastle; in varying that line, from Durham, by Sedgefield, to Stockton; and in deliberately viewing the country along the coast,—from Newcastle to Sunderland,
and

and, thence, through the midway of that district, to Stockton: Thus gaining some general knowledge of the county at large; the morelands, and the valleys which penetrate them, excepted.

In this place, however, what I shall attempt to describe, is the sea coast, and the central district; and to speak of that congeries of morelands, of which those of the county of Durham form the principal part.

The vale of Stockton I refrain to particularize, here; as only a part of it lies within the limits of Durham ; and it will be more consonant with my general arrangement, to speak of it, in another place.

The SEA COAST of DURHAM. This line of country is little known ; and, in the *Report* under view, it is unnoticed *. Yet it is well entitled to consideration. I will therefore transcribe such of my travelling notices, as may serve to convey a general idea of its natural economy; together with such particulars of management as met the eye, at the time of viewing it;—namely the 28th and 29th of August, 1798.

NEWCASTLE to SUNDERLAND.

Twelve miles.

Climb up the village of Gateshead.
Coal Pits and double Railways close to it.
Reach the first stage of upland: cool, but productive.

Steam

---

* In the *Appendix,* there is a letter from DOCTOR COLLINGWOOD of Sunderland, to the President of the Board ; concerning the more northern part of this district,—particularly the neighbourhoods of Shields and Sunderland. But it appears to have been written upon the spur of the occasion,—perhaps to stem a torrent of importunity,—and I do not perceive any thing in it that demands particular mention.

Steam Engines, and clouds of smoke.

Oaks and Beeches in hedgerows.

The substratum of a pale clayey nature.

See the Banks of the Tyne : steep and wooded.

Still pale, deep, earthy subsoil.

Various clouds of smoke rising towards Shields.

Many clean fallows observable—(3 miles.

A new line of road well kept :

The milestones in two steps.

Meet large parties of female reapers and gleaners.

Limed fallows ;—and clean clovers.

Stone and pantile buildings, with ridge stones and coped gables, universal.

A wide flat of country opens to the right ; between Gateshead Fell and the Sea.

Cows on gross clover, in head.

Pale strong land ; with more and more clean fallows.

South Shields road branches off : wind to the right.

See rising grounds, on the left, and in front, with broken uplands, on the right.

Strong bay horses, in carts.

Neat, clean short horned cows.

A distant ragged hill, seen to the right.

Clean good crops : wheat shucks uncovered !— (6 miles.

Pass an immense quarry, in the face of a knoll ; with limekilns in front ;—

And West Baldon, on a swell of limestone.

Catch a reach of the Tyne ; with columns of smoke,—its accompaniment !

Beyond a rich flat of country, the sea breaks in front.

Rising grounds, with wind-mills, on the left.

Not a tree in the whole flat !

Much wheat yet uncut.

Still a new line of road.

Old grass lands, in high ridges.

Remarkably

Remarkably clean good husbandry; with very few exceptions.

The entire flat is deep, cool, clayey land.

A paved drinking place on the side of the road.

Approach a low flat coast: (9 miles.

Join a new road, between Shields and Sunderland.

Sklrt a rising ground : deep strong soil, on gravel and limestone rock ! desirable land: the hop ground of Maidstone.

A quarry of close rock, and a large kiln.

Sunderland opens to the view; with high grounds, westward of the Wear.

Cross the Wear, by the iron bridge, at Bishop Wearmouth, near Sunderland.

Recollections.

In elevation, the country passed through may be termed a vale passage; though not defined by regular lines of hills.

The surface remarkably flat ; even as a vale district.

The climature is backward: somewhat behind the heights of Harlow (in Northumberland) : owing probably to the coolness of the substrata.

Waters:—scarcely a brook, or rivulet, observable.

The soil—most uniform : a pale clayey loam.

The subsoil—the same.

Roads:—at present good : the materials soft; the tolls exorbitant.

The whole inclosed in well sized fields ; apparently of recent date.

Products :—arable crops : very little old grass land: no wood; and few hedge trees ; in most parts none. No unreclaimed lands, observed : one small plot of furze-ground excepted.

Farms,—apparently of the middle size.

Arable crops—wheat, barley, oats, clover.

Tillage.—Clean fallows are most abundant: the clovers and stubbles are of course clean.

Manure.

Manure.—Much lime evidently burnt; but not much, at present, apparent on the lands.

Harvesting.—Not one instance, yet, of corn being mown. The whole reaped.

Horses;—as above noticed.

Cattle.—Few seen.

Sheep.—Still fewer!

How is the fertility of the country kept up?

Lime may fertilize fresh land for a time; but if not duly assisted by other manures, will fail in its effects.

SUNDERLAND LIME.

The channel of the Wear, above the bridge, is a narrow chasm, 80 to 100 feet deep (across the lower end of which the bridge is thrown); apparently formed by a rent or parting of an extraordinary mass of limestone; which rises perpendicularly on either side of the river; and is quarried for lime on both sides of it.

On the south side of the Wear, the face of the rock, now in work, is not less than fifty feet high; and is covered with ten feet, or more, of coping—a pale coloured clay: this being, probably, a fair specimen of the substructure of the neighbourhood.

The rock is not a uniform mass; nor has it regular seams. It is rather composed of huge blocks of stone; the irregular interstices being filled with " marl;"—a pale earth, probably calcareous. Where the masses of rock are large and " strong," they are blasted; and the fragments " prised " out, with great labour, and some risk *.

The kilns, that are situated upon the immediate banks

* The LIMESTONE of SUNDERLAND, in contexture and general appearance, resembles that of the Mendip Hills, and the Plymouth quarter of Devonshire; but is less variegated than the latter, being of a lightish grey or "stone color." It is doubtlessly capable of a good polish as marble.

By analysis, one hundred grains yield ninety-seven grains of calcareous earth: in this respect ranking with the purest of the English limestones.

banks of the river, are three large ones, on each side; united in clusters. Each having three eyes or draft-holes; with sheds, or penthouses, projecting over them.

The stones are drawn to the kilns in single horse carts; which are backed over the fire, and the stones shot into the kilns!—of any size, as large as a man can lift! But coals are cheap: being brought down the river to the kilns.

The price eleven shillings a chaldron, of thirty-six Winchester bushels.

It is measured in wheel-barrows, holding three bushels each; having previously lain to cool, under the penthouses; from whence it is wheeled, by hand, down to the vessels, which lie along a quay, in front of the kilns, but considerably below them, and tilted into the holds.

Great quantities are sent off, in this manner, to the lower parts of the vale of Stockton, and other parts of the Yorkshire coast; and still greater, I believe, to the north of Scotland; as far as Inverness and even to Caithness.

Summer is the season of burning: letting the kilns go out in October: lime being dangerous lading in winter.

SUNDERLAND to CASTLE EDEN INN.

Thirteen Miles.

A flat country near Bishop Wearmouth. mostly good grass land.

A beautiful short-horned cow.

The sea opens to the left: an oval hill, on the right.

Hedges, and even the ash, cut by the east winds.

A heavy crop of wheat.

White limestone and red pantile buildings still prevail: but without ridge stones or coping.

Several windmills seen.

A flock of lambs: the first flock of sheep observed.

The surface wavey: the soil various in colour.

Pass Rhyhope:—(3 miles.

Several clean stiffland fallows.

A field of bad beans: the second observed.

Cross a dingle: deep pale earthy subsoil; and cool weak land.

Lime in load heaps, and some spread on fallows.

A foul fallow; and a foul ley ground adjoining: inseparable companions.

The surface breaks into swells and vallies; with the road *crossing* them.

Some very strong upland.

A billowy country on the right:—(5 miles.

The land and its management fall off.

Thin wheat, thinly eared, and foul with wild oats.

The climature late. Oats greenish; and some awned wheat still green!

Wild, among cultivated, oats: the former shed: the chaffy panicles standing erect.

Much fallow appears: some foul with coltsfoot: yet several pieces of tolerable clover.

An extent of billowy surface forward.

Cross another valley: at Daleton.

Still pale, deep, apparently calcareous substratum.

The sea spread with ships: the sails white as snow; the water blue as indigo. The day fine.

Reach high uplands.

Poled sheep on old pasture ground.

A wide view on the right, toward Durham.

A lime-kiln and quarry, in a hollow;—beneath the deep earthy superstratum.

The land improves.

A piece of turnips: the first observed.

A flock of black faced lambs, travelling northward. Q. From the eastern morelands?

Another deep dell: (8 miles). The line of road under improvement.

Cross

Cross a gently billowy, chalkhill-like surface.

The country continues to improve: (9 miles.

Tolerable grass land on the swell of Easington.

A circle of views, south of Easington: the eastern morelands of Yorkshire, in front; those of Durham on the right; and quere, the Fells of Northumberland to the north? with the ocean on the east.

Hartlepool seen, as it were, *in* the sea.

A dairy or two of cows: the first observed! and a few very large sheep.

Haymaking on the high grounds.

Some weak gravelly lands.

A wide view forward, of tree-less inclosures.

A striking *mountain dingle*, in a cultivated country! Cross the extraordinary chasm. Its steep sides drained and planted. The substratum of a loose earthy nature, worn away by a small stream; by which, perhaps, the whole has been formed!

Still weak ungrateful land: brick earth, sand, and gravel, intermixed.

Instance of brick buildings: the first.

Recollections.

Elevation—very considerable: mostly high upland; grooved, in the manner mentioned.

The surface—billowy; and rendered very uneven, by the deep vallies that cross it. In glancing the eye over it, it appears to be a tame, flattish extent of upland, similar to that of Northumberland.

Climature—backward: behind the uplands of Northumberland, thirty miles further northward.

The only *land* waters are the short rivulets above noticed; running separately to the sea.

The soil, throughout, is of a cool retentive nature: though somewhat varying in quality.

Substrata—deep pale earth and limestone.

The road—most unlevel; the surface hard but rough: some parts of it apparently of whinstone.

The

The whole inclosed: mostly in large, but not regular fields? The fences chiefly thorn: some walls.

Products—wheat, oats, some peas, a few beans, much clover, and very much perennial grass land: mowing grounds, even on the heights. No woodland; and very few hedge trees; these ashes, and mostly stunted.

The farms, apparently, of the middle size.

The prevailing road team—two strong bay horses.

Cattle—wholely short horned, and uniformly good.

Sheep—none observed; but those noticed.

Castle Eden Inn to Stockton.

Thirteen miles.

Dip into a shallow bason of clean land: grass grounds, in high crooked ridges? milking galloway cows, in the field: a fresh style of country.

Rotund swells appear in front: clean-skinned, inclosed *down*-like lands.

Pale colored fallows, very clean, and landed up in a husbandlike manner.

The climature still backward: wheat not yet ripe on the rotund heights.

A more genial better country succeeds: (16 miles.

The estuary of the Tees, and the Yorkshire morelands, appear, at hand. Cleveland is here seen, from end to end, and the entire width, between the river and the feet of the hills:—how inconsiderable a space it seems, in this point of view, to occupy.

The country improves; yet the climature continues backward.

Large grass fields without stock?

The summit of Rossbury *rises* to the view.

Still deep earthy subsoil.

Descend towards a lower, flatter stage of country.

Well colored fallows, and good grass land:—(18 miles.

Two large bay horses, of the coach mold, drawing corn, in a long, shallow, spreading, open-bodied cart;—common in this country.

Drop still lower towards the vale.

Wheat, here, mostly carried.

More well colored fallows.

How little live stock appears.

A flock of poled sheep: (19 miles.

Grassy swells, in high ridges; stocked with cows.

A few unhoed turnips; and a ridge of potatoes, in rows.

Now, mostly grass land; yet little stock appears!

A wide flat country extends, far, on the right: the vale of Stockton, and the head of the vale of York.

Another plot of unhoed turnips; and another land of potatoes! the only specimens yet seen.

Old grass land, over deep earthy subsoil.

A good vale district:—(22 miles.

Ash trees, *here*, thrive in hedges.

A few small flocks of good sheep.

Still deep earthy substratum; but the color is altered to somewhat red; the depth 10 or 12 feet.

Now, many good hoed turnips.

A remarkably flat vale district:—(23 miles.

Pass through Billingham.

Cross a flat of meadows; with cattle now in them.

Cross a brook; and reascend the upper grounds.

The day closes in.

Recollections.

The elevation and surface, as in the notes.

The VALE of STOCKTON is defined by the rotund, prominent hills which rise about nine miles northward of the Tees; its flat vale lands spreading seven or eight miles from the river.

The soils, throughout this stage, of a retentive nature.

Subsoil, of the vale, deep clay; apparently of an unctuous rich quality, and of great depth:—a quantity sufficient to furnish an extent of country with fertility.

Buildings.—The walling materials changed about Castle Eden, from limestone to red bricks. But the covering is the same throughout: not a slated nor a thatched farm building observed.

Fences.—Observed several thriving thorn hedges, planted pretty high in the bank; and, where the soil is strong and the base of a cool, moist quality, it may be proper to plant quicks somewhat above the natural level of the soil.

Farms apparently of the middle sizes: if the sizes of fields and farmsteads be any guide.

Road team—still two horse carts.

Tillage.—Fallows still abound: but not so uniformly free from greenness, as in the more northern parts of the county.

Harvesting.—Every thing yet "shorn"—reaped. Wheat mostly set up in uncovered shucks of twelve sheaves: Oats invariably "gaited."

Horses—throughout, of the tall, bay breed.

Cattle—short horned; with some galloway cows.

Sheep—of the long wooled breed.

Swine, Poultry, Bees—very few seen.

The CENTRAL DISTRICT of DURHAM. This large portion of the county commences at the foot of Gateshead Fell; and spreads southward to the vale of Stockton. Its eastern boundary is the sea coast district; and its western, the Morelands, with the valley of Wolsingham.

Its surface is characterised by the hills and minor hillocks, with which it is studded. This style of surface, however, is most observable in the northern parts of the district; its southern area being less strongly featured.

The soil and substratum of the lower lands, or

what might be termed the *base*, floor, or ground of the district, are similar to those of the sea coast of Durham,—of the uplands of Northumberland,—and of Cleveland in Yorkshire: namely, a pale clayey loam, on a deep retentive substratum:—a description of land which reaches, with little interruption, I believe, from the feet of the Cheviot hills, to those of the eastern morelands. It is to be remarked, however, that the lands of the south of Durham, and of Cleveland, are in general of a better quality, than those (of a somewhat similar formation) in Northumberland : owing, in part, at least, to their elevation being less; thereby enjoying a better climature *. In the neighbourhood of the city, there are some vale lands of superior value. Of the soils of the *hills*, of this district, I am less able to speak. The swell, on which Sedgefield is seated, is covered with a well textured loam, incumbent on a gravelly substratum; forming land of a valuable quality.

The MORELANDS of the FIVE COUNTIES—of Durham, Northumberland, Cumberland, Westmoreland, and the northern extreme of Yorkshire. This range, or rather congeries, of mountain heights, form one united mass; which is separated, on the north, from the main body of the Northumbrian morelands, by the valley of the Irthing; and, on the south, by that of the Greta, from the western morelands of Yorkshire.

This department of English mountains I have had opportunities of viewing, from elevated points, on almost every side. In general appearance, and surface produce, it classes with the Northumberland and Yorkshire morelands. But, by internal structure, it is entitled to superiority. It not only abounds in *coals*, but is much more productive of *lead* than any

other

---

* It may, I believe, be further remarked, that the vale of Stockton is not incumbent on coal.

other division, I believe, of the heathlands of the northern provinces.

Respecting these hills, and the valleys that intersect them, viewed as a widely extended field of rural economy, the five Reports, in which they have some claim to notice, will not, I fear, afford much satisfactory information.

" GENERAL VIEW

OF THE

AGRICULTURE

OF THE

COUNTY OF DURHAM,

Particularly that part of it extending from the TYNE to the TEES * :

WITH

OBSERVATIONS ON THE MEANS OF ITS IMPROVEMENT.

By JOSEPH GRANGER, LAND-SURVEYOR,

HEUGH, NEAR DURHAM.

TOGETHER WITH

THE PRELIMINARY OBSERVATIONS OF SIR WILLIAM APPLEBY,

(OF DURHAM.)

DRAWN UP FOR THE CONSIDERATION OF

THE BOARD OF AGRICULURE AND INTERNAL

IMPROVEMENT.

1794."

OF the REPORTER of the county of Durham, his QUALIFICATIONS, or MODE of SURVEY, I have not the slightest knowledge. Mr. GRANGER writes like a man of business ; and is probably a man of some eminence in his profession.

The

---

* The entire county may be said to be included between the Tyne and the Tees. It is the CENTRAL DISTRICT that appears to be more particularly spoken of by the Reporter.

The copy, before me, being a first sketch,—there being, as yet, I understand, no reprinted Report of this county,—it will require to be examined with indulgence. No complaint can lay against the *length* of it. The body of the Report is made up of thirty-four pages.

Respecting the PRELIMINARY OBSERVATIONS of Sir WILLIAM APPLEBY (set forth in the title page), little is required to be said. Sir William, it pretty plainly appears, was *urged* to say *something:* and he has, doubtlessly, done his best. Of Durham (city) and its environs, he has favored us with a florid account,—almost flaming! On the subterranean productions of the county, however, and especially respecting coal tar, Sir William Appleby has brought forward some interesting facts, that are well entitled to notice.

The CONTRIBUTORS to the APPENDIX, too, appear as conscripts—" dragged into the service;" as if it had been found an arduous task to make up any thing, in the shape of a Report, for this county ;— well as it merits to be recorded, in the annals of rural economy.

A SKETCH of the COUNTY is prefixed to the body of the Report; to show its surface and soils. But instead of their being discriminated by the permanent marks of the graver, as in the map of Northumberland, they are (or have been) distinguished by water colors; which are already so far fled, that, were it not for a *straight line* dotted across the county (to show the natural division of its soils!) it would be difficult, or impossible, to distinguish, even the morelands from the cultivated country.

SUBJECT THE FIRST.

NATURAL ECONOMY.

ELEVATION and SURFACE. P. 31. "The general aspect of this county is hilly, and naked, but not a little enlivened by the comfortable view of farm houses standing in the midst of the farms. Cross-Fell, although situated beyond the western limit of this county, may, it is presumed, with propriety enough be called the *natural* head of it, for, from the eastern side of that mountain issue the sources of the river Tees, and take an eastern course, accompanied on the north by a lofty ridge, from the north side of which issue the sources of South Tyne, and take a northern course; the ridge then bends to the north, and forms the western limit of this county to Kilhope-Cross. From the eastern side of this lofty ridge, and from those of the mountainous ridges which branch eastward from it, issues the Weare, and other brooks, or rivers, that take their courses, with some rapidity for the most part, eastward to the sea; and from those mountains other ranges of hills branching off, and still decreasing in height as they approach the sea-coast, spread themselves in various directions over the whole county."

SOILS.---P. 31. "Near the river Tees, the soil is loamy, or rich clay; as it is likewise in some spots near the other rivers and brooks in this county: at a further distance from these rivers and brooks, the soil is of a poorer nature, commonly called *water-shaken*, with here and there spots of gravel interspersed; but these are of small extent, the middle of none of them being half a mile from clay: the hills between the sea, and an imaginary line drawn from Bernard-castle on the Tees, to Alan's-ford on the Derwent, are for the most part covered with a dry loam, the fertility of which varies in proportion to its depth; and, but
where

where thinnest, it affords wholesome pasturage for
sheep, and from the above-mentioned line westward,
the summits as well as the sides, are moorish wastes."

CLIMATURE.---P. 32. " The climate is uncertain
in all the seasons of the year, insomuch that the
cultivator seldom reaps all his crops to such advantage, as from the nature of the soil might
be expected, the weather in the spring being either
too harsh, or in the beginning of summer too cold
and dry, and in the autumn too wet and windy;
and the whole face of this county declining from west
to east, is exposed to, and annoyed by, the north-east
wind, which often prevails long in the spring."—
P. 42. " Hay-harvest, upon new laid lands, commences soon after midsummer, and old meadows
generally are cut in July. Corn harvest adjoining
the Tees, the sea, and some of the rivers, often begins
towards the end of August ; in other parts of this
county it is a fortnight or three weeks later, and
commonly lasts throughout September; beans throughout October, and sometimes not finished till the middle
of November."

FOSSILS and MINERALS. For some valuable information respecting these subjects, the public are indebted to Sir William Appleby; who appears to have
paid especial attention to them.

QUARRIES. " The neighbourhood of Walsingham
produces a beautiful black spotted marble for chimney
pieces, hearths, mortars, and many other uses, and is
the only place in the county for the large grey mill-
stone for grinding of corn.

" The whole county is well stored with excellent
quarries of fine stone slates, flags, &c. for building ;
also with numerous sorts of lime, brick and tile kilns
of various kinds. Gateshead Fell in this county is
peculiarly noted, through the whole habitable globe,
for producing and exporting what are vulgarly,
though erroneously, called Newcastle grind-stones, on
account of their being shipped from thence. There
are

are also several equally noted quarries of excellent fire-stone, which is in high estimation and use for furnaces, ovens, &c. and is exported in immense quantities to different countries."

On *coal mines*, or the method of working them, we find nothing that requires transcription,—after the ample detail which the Northumbrian Report has furnished. But,

On the subject of *coal tar*, Sir William Appleby's Remarks are, at least, interesting. The properties of this powerful extract, and the purposes to which it may be profitably applied, have long been involved in a depth of mystery, which the public have not been able to fathom. Is it deficient in virtue? or has it been unfairly dealt with? or have its advocates imprudently ascribed to it more merit than it, in reality, possesses?—and thereby disgusted those who might otherwise have given it due encouragement;—while something *newer*, and of course more *fashionable*, stepped in, and supplied its place.

If, in the process of converting coals into coke, or cinders, for the various uses of manufactures, the bituminous or oleaginous matters they contain, can be preserved, and applied to valuable purposes, instead of their being suffered to foul the atmosphere, and become injurious, perhaps, to the animals and vegetables they may assail, it appears, demonstrably, that there may be circumstances under which they ought to be preserved. And, further, it may be remarked, that, when the copper mines of this country shall be less productive than they are at present; and its commerce less able to command a foreign supply of pitch and tar *;—it may be expedient to pay some public attention to the process now under notice. I therefore transcribe Sir W. A's account, at length : as I may not, in prosecuting my present Work, have another

* The above Remarks were written long before the ports of the north of Europe were shut against the commerce of this country.

another opportunity, equally favorable, for bringing forward the subject.

P. 15.—" COAL TAR and PITCH. These two important and invaluable articles for the paying of ships bottoms, are an infallible preservative against those destructive animalculæ, the sea worms, and this county appears to be peculiarly adapted for its manufacture to any extent required. Both coal tar and pitch, I understand, were made fifty years ago by the ancestors of Mr. George Dixon, a coal owner in this county, and also by himself, during the American war, in large quantities, and sent to Newcastle, Sunderland, &c. but for some reason or other he has discontinued the business, owing, perhaps, to the heavy expense of land carriage. I am informed, that at the time they were first invented, a vessel was actually payed therewith, and sent under the directions of Government to the West-Indies, by way of experiment, which returned perfectly sound and clean as when it was sent out, and which every vessel payed with such *genuine coal tar* will ever infallibly do ; but certain it is, proper attention and encouragement had not then been, and, I am afraid, is not yet given to their production and application, otherwise they must have ere now been generally used, to great private and public advantage, independent of their being great internal commercial articles.

" There are many processes for making the above-mentioned articles, prior to that for which Lord Dundonald obtained a patent, and parliamentary extension. Some of them are so productive, (owing perhaps to the coal containing much bitumen) as to require only 4½ ton of coal to a barrel of tar. Several manufactories for making them have been erected in this county lately ; but such establishments ought only to be made contiguous to coal pits communicating with a navigable river, in order to avoid the heavy expense of land-carriage, and none but the most bituminous coal applied to these purposes ;
even

even the smallest of such coal, which is scarcely vendible by the coal-owner, is the properest, and two ton of some will produce a barrel of tar. I have tried various pieces of coal, both of my own and other owners, and find some amazingly productive, particularly one of Mr. Lambton's (the greatest proprietor and owner upon the river Weare) in so great a degree, that one-fourth part of a single stratum in one of his coal pits, if made into tar, would be much more lucrative than the whole produce of such pit, great as the profit of such mines is known to be; on which account, I am certain it would be much the interest of such owners to establish large apparatuses for its manufacture, and highly incumbent upon Government and ship-owners to encourage the general use of such *genuine coal tar* ONLY.

" The cautionary word ONLY must be carefully and peculiarly attended to by every person who buys and supplies these invaluable articles, particularly to the above-mentioned purpose, or indeed to any other exposed to air or water, as it is usual for the manufacturer (though highly impolitic and unjust, and arising either from ignorance or avarice) to extract the essential oil thereout, which is absolutely essential or necessary to their efficient application, renders the residuum a mere *caput mortuum*, by totally depriving them of their adhesive and preserving qualities, and I am afraid, nay I am certain, has much discouraged their consumption, as Mr. Fiott, and many other gentlemen of my acquaintance, in London and elsewhere, have made various complaints to me of their inefficacy, desiring me to inform them (thinking I could and would so do) why in so many instances they failed of success?—I gave them, as I now give the Public, the same serious and concise caution, and there being no apparent difference between the original tar, and that which has undergone the second process, I know of no other security the purchaser can have, but the word and honour of such manufacturer,

facturer, though I should be inclined to purchase none but of those who made the *original tar only.*

" I am also certain, that the liquid arising and produced before the tar comes over, is equally invaluable for the purposes of curing the scab, and many other disorders in all animals, by simply rubbing them therewith, as the ingredient is totally hostile to every species of animalculæ, which, it is well known, are the sole cause of such diseases. The Gentleman, as well as the Farmer, will therefore find his account in its application; but if not to be had in sufficient quantities, (or if too strong it should be reduced with water) I naturally suppose the original tar boiled in water, and such water applied, would answer the same beneficial purposes, at least it might be strong enough to rub sheep with. It certainly would be well worth the while of every farmer to make the experiment, more especially as one or the other will infallibly answer his most sanguine hope, and cost him nothing but his labour, and such persons would do the community a great service, by communicating their effects to the Board of Agriculture and the Public.

" Every application of the original tar, or its oil, for sheep, without their being well qualified with grease, should be carefully avoided; perhaps the same caution may not be necessary for larger animals.

" Why Government, the Board of Admiralty, and the East India Company, will not encourage its general use, notwithstanding the numerous proofs given, and the reiterated representations made to them all by Lord Dundonald, myself, and many respectable persons, the reader must form his own conjecture, for it is undoubtedly a hundred times more valuable for the above-mentioned purpose, and many others, than any foreign vegetable tar whatever. And though this is a subject more connected with commerce than agiculture, yet it is well entitled to the consideration
of

of the Board, in consequence of its probable utility in curing the disorders of sheep, and in the benefit that would result, from applying it as a paint, for implements of husbandry."

Moreover in a note, p. 18, Sir William states the following strong facts. " In order to elucidate their beneficial effects more fully, relative to shipping, I will take the liberty to report two or three curious anecdotes that occurred, before Lord Dundonald's process was known.

" Being once in company with Captain Take, of a Jamaica packet, I mentioned my having made some experiments upon Coal Tar, and stating to him the infinite advantage and security the navy would derive therefrom, if used by it, he replied, " Sir, I can give you and the public stronger proofs of its infallible good effects than any man in this kingdom." He informed me that Mr. Campion, a capital Tar-maker in Bristol, had desired him to take out two planks done with coal and foreign tar, and caused them to be sunk in Port Royal harbour for two months, which when drawn out, it was found that the first mentioned was as clean and sound as when immersed, and the latter a complete riddle.

" One morning I called upon my friends, Messrs. Twiss and Jennour, agents to the East-India Company, when the conversation turned upon the singular virtues and efficacy of Coal Tar, and the great benefit the Company would derive from its use, and save the immense expense they were at in coppering their large ships. They were so fully convinced by the irrefragable proofs given them, that they earnestly entreated I would wait upon Mr. Oliver, Secretary to the Company, and make the like important representation to him, who would undoubtedly make a report of it to the Court of Directors. Accordingly I waited upon him the next morning, and in the course of our conversation, he ordered a piece of the wreck of an East-Indiaman to be brought for my inspection

spection (which is well worth every curious person's seeing, more especially those concerned in shipping) when I said, " This specimen of the destructive and dangerous effects of the sea worm speaks more than a thousand tongues can express."—He then proceeded to inform me that it was part of the bottom of an East-India ship just arrived, most luckily, at a crisis when it had many feet water in its hold, and 400,000l. cargo on board, and when examined to know the cause, was actually found to be totally eaten through in a hundred places, and many of them, I am certain, above an inch in diameter. " Now Sir," I replied, " if this vessel had been well payed with genuine Coal Tar, no such accident could have happened, for such application is infallible in its effects, in all climates and seas.

" At that time I found Mr. Oliver had never been informed of its consequence, and deeming such information of much importance to the Company's interest, he desired I would wait upon the then Chairman, and communicate it to him. Next morning I had an interview with the Chairman, told him who I was sent by, reciting every particular before mentioned, and the specimen I had seen, as a most corroborating argument in favour of what I advanced ; when with great composure he told me it was of no importance to the Company, *for—they—only—hired— their—ships.*—" Would it do (said he) for—Ropes ?" I replied, " Sir, I came to tell you, as a favour, what it will do for, not what perhaps it may not do for."

" A worthy respectable friend of mine, Mr. Thomas Richardson of Sunderland, informed me, a few weeks since, that he had gone on purpose very lately to examine a large ship that had been well payed with Coal Tar, and sent to the West-Indies, and after her return into the Baltic for some months, when he found her bottom, and every other part, perfectly sound and clean, and not so much as a single barnacle upon it."

Lead

Lead Mines. P. 20. " The principal lead mines in the county of Durham, are in the parish of Middleton in Teasdale, and the parish of Stanhope in Wearedale."

Salt Springs. P. 21. " There is a very singular salt spring at Birtley in this county, and one of the great arcana of nature, which, like many more, will never be explored by man, and displays the wonderful works of the Omnipotent in an eminent degree. —It arises at the depth of seventy fathoms, in an engine pit erected for drawing water out of coal mines, at the extremity of a stone drift, drove 200 yards north-east therein, for the purpose of draining the water from the coal works, and what is more extraordinary, springs only in such drift in every direction, though such pit, and every other contiguous thereto, have been excavated both above and below it many fathoms, where, and when it might naturally be supposed the same spring would have been found. Its mixing itself with the fresh water in the same pit, would have occasioned its remaining totally unnoticed to this day, but for an accident which happened to the boiler of the engine soon after its erection. One morning the bottom of the boiler suddenly dropt out; the engine man amazed thereat, as well he might, informed the undertakers, who upon examination found it incrusted with a vast quantity of strong salt, and the iron totally corroded. Upon tasting the water, though incorporated with immense quantities of fresh, it was found exceedingly brackish and salt, whereupon they explored the workings, and found the above-mentioned very valuable salt spring arise in such drift only, and which has for these nine years produced, and may for eternity produce, 20,000 gallons per day, four times stronger than any sea water whatever, therefore it can have no communication with the sea.

" In consequence of which valuable discovery, a large and extensive manufactory of salt has been established

blished by a company of gentlemen, who, after encountering many difficulties, as are usual at first in great speculative undertakings, have brought it to very great perfection, of a most excellent quality, and send it to most parts of the kingdom.   There is a very considerable quantity of a strong saline residuum, called bittern, to the amount of 2000 gallons per day; which at present is of no use to the manufactory.   It will therefore be a very necessary inquiry, whether it could not be used as manure in agricultural improvements."

And P. 23. "There is another very curious salt spring at Butterby near this city, that rises out of a rock in the river Weare, and is only visible and visitable at very low water.   A small excavated bason has been made therein, perhaps many centuries ago, but its production is so trifling, though equally as strong as that of Birtley, that the proprietors have never thought it an object worth attending to, nor perhaps never will, for the reasons given."

Wherever there is a salt spring, we may, I believe, conclude that a salt rock is situated in its vicinity. The descending waters of rain coming in contact with the saline mass, are impregnated by it.   If they remain a sufficient time in contact with it, they of course become saturated.   Hence the salt wells of Cheshire; out of which a principal part of its produce of salt is raised.   A hint, this, to the miners of Durham.

SUBJECT THE SECOND.

POLITICAL ECONOMY.

STATE OF APPROPRIATION.   On this important subject, Mr. Granger, as a professional man, has probably had some experience.   He speaks of it with judgment and intelligence.   I wish, however, that he had been fuller and more explicit, respecting the
                                                        " perverse

" perverse custom of Intercommon," on " ancient Inclosures."

P. 43. " In this county the lands, or common fields of townships, were for the most part inclosed soon after the Restoration."

Again, " The common fields are few in number, and of small extent : in the western part they are more numerous, but no division of any of them is in agitation, the expense necessary to procure Acts of Parliament being thought too great. Some general law, or process of light expense, for the division of uninclosed lands, is a frequent and a fervent wish, among the proprietors and the most intelligent farmers of this county.

" The waste lands are situated mostly in the western parts of the county, and may, by probable conjecture, amount to 130,000 acres, and being of different qualities, are capable of various improvements; much may be converted into arable, much into pasture, much into woodland; and even of the mosses, it would be found that many might be drained, and the rest not left unuseful for the production of peat. Lime, of an excellent quality, is at hand, and although the frequency of heavy showers in the western parts, may endanger corn by lodging it, &c. yet the culture of rape, turnips, and potatoes, for all which in many parts it is well adapted, would produce immediate profit, and prepare the land for being laid down to permanent grass. Within the last thirty years, large quantities of waste lands in the lower parts of the county have been inclosed, and it is certain, that the resulting advantages, in regard to improvement in quantity and quality of produce, stock, rent, and increase of population, have been, and continue to be very considerable. It is impossible to treat this subject of wastes, without lamenting that in some of the rich parts of the county, particularly in the neighbourhood of the capital of it, large quantities of land should still lie totally deprived of the benefit

fit of cultivation, in commons; and that ancient inclosures, by being subject to the perverse custom of intercommon, be prevented from that degree of fertilization, to which the easy opportunity of procuring manure, in most cases, would certainly soon carry the improvement of them : in their present state, little or no benefit is derived to any person whatsoever, intitled either to common, or intercommon, from the use of them. By an Act of Parliament passed about twenty years ago, for dividing Elvet-Moor, and for extinguishing all right of common, in certain inclosed intercommon lands, it was enacted, that the lands subject to intercommon shall be discharged therefrom, on the proprietors thereof paying an equivalent, to be ascertained by the Commissioners under the said Act. Their adjudications were executed without any difficulty, and with general approbation."

STATE OF SOCIETY.—*Provisions.* The following were their moderate prices, in Durham, in the year 1793. —P. 49. "Provisions are higher than they were twenty years ago, without any appearance of a tendency to fall. Wheat, upon an average, from five shillings to five shillings and sixpence per Winchester bushel; beef, from three shillings and sixpence to four shillings and sixpence per stone, fourteen pounds to the stone; mutton, four-pence per pound."

Commerce. P.59. "The commerce of this county depends upon the export of the produce of the mines and manufactures. The mines are of lead, exported from Newcastle and Stockton; and coals, exported from Newcastle and Sunderland; and there is a considerable land-sale of coal from this county into the North Riding of Yorkshire. There is a quarry which produces mill-stones in the Forest of Weardale. There are upon Gateshead-Fell, in this county, quarries of grind-stones of great fame and extensive sale, under the denomination of Newcastle grind-stones. There is also a vend of lime to a very considerable amount from this county into the North Riding of Yorkshire."

The

The *Manufactures*, here enumerated, are many. But none of them appear to be of a nature or extent to interfere with the legitimate industry and morality of the county; excepting a few cotton mills.

SUBJECT THE THIRD.

RURAL ECONOMY.

DIVISION THE FIRST.

TENANTED ESTATES; their IMPROVE-MENT and MANAGEMENT.

Estates.—P. 33. " A third part of this county is supposed to be of ecclesiastical tenure; of the remainder, part is possessed by great, part by middling, and part by small proprietors."

Improvement of Estates.—*Laying out Farm Lands.* The following are Mr. Granger's sentiments respecting the proper *size* of a *Farm*, in the county of Durham. They are well expressed; and are admissible, to a certain extent, in any county.

P. 40. " According to the average quality of the land in this county, three hundred acres, seem to be the proper quantity, to constitute a farm most advantageously; because, being of that size, it may be managed with less force, particularly of horses, than if divided into more farms, and the whole be within the eye of the master."

Reclaiming rough Grounds. P. 46. " Paring and burning is of ancient use, and continues in practice for lands that have been long in grass, and are grown mossy. The sods are pared thin, and dried; laid together in small heaps, set on fire, and burnt to ashes, which are spread upon the ground, together with two cart loads of lime upon each acre, and ploughed in. This practice has been found to have the best effect, when the old benty grass, or moss of the sod, are con-

sumed

sumed by the fire, and the earth left unburnt; but too generally the earth is burnt along with the grass, or moss, to red ashes."

This distinction does credit to the discernment of the husbandmen of Durham. On thin, light, porous lands, the soil, I am of opinion, should be *baked*, rather than *burnt*. The roots and seeds of weeds, with the animalcules, and their eggs, which the soil is infested with, ought to be deprived of life, by the action of the fire. But whether the same principle be equally applicable to the cool, closely textured lands of the Bishopric of Durham, may remain perhaps to be proved, by attention and repeated experiments. See YORKSHIRE, Sect. *Sodburning*.

PUBLIC WORKS.—*Roads*. On this subject, the Reporter speaks as a practical man; though nothing of excellence occurs in his Remarks. The following observations, however, on parochial Surveyors, though not new, are judicious.—P. 49. " The public roads are in good condition, but the private township roads are in a very indifferent state; for the Surveyors appointed in the present mode, in each township, wishing to avoid quarrels with their neighbours, are apt to be too remiss in the execution of their authority. But it is probable these roads would soon be improved, if the Justices would please to appoint Surveyors, with a salary, for a few adjoining townships throughout the county, with authority to demand the performance of the statutable labour, and to direct what places shall be repaired, and the mode of performing the work." This regulation has been established, in different parts of the kingdom; and every where with good effect, I believe, where proper men are employed.

EXECUTIVE MANAGEMENT OF ESTATES.—*Leases*. P. 53. " The leases are generally for short terms, seldom exceeding six years, with the usual covenants to secure to the landlord a due payment of rent, and to the tenant a quiet possession of the farm, and of his

away-

away-going crop. That the landlord shall at the commencement of the term put all into tenantable repair, and the farmer shall leave all in equal good condition at the end of it. That during the term the landlord shall uphold the main walls, timbers, and roof, and the tenant all other parts at his own expense, and lead all necessary materials. That the tenant shall scour and dress a quantity of hedge annually, &c. There are other covenants generally inserted, which are of a more doubtful nature, as, that the tenant shall be confined to pursue a scheme of husbandry annexed to the lease, by which he is restrained to fallow one third part of the tillage land annually, and consequently to take no more than two crops to a fallow; whereas a skilful husbandman having, by frequent ploughings, and other proper management, got his fallow early into condition, might, much to his own benefit, and not less to the improvement of the soil, have a crop of turnips, or where the land is not fit for turnips, of rape, coleseed, &c. The produce to be eaten down where grown, or the crops might be varied in other respects. The covenant therefore should be, as it seems, not to take two crops of white corn without a green crop interposed."

These restrictions are objected to by Mr. Granger: —the first, because a good farmer may sometimes throw in a fallow crop with advantage:—the latter, for reasons which will appear, under the article *Lime*. And Mr. Silas Angus, " land-agent to the Earl of Shaftsbury,"—in a letter addressed to Sir William Appleby, and inserted in the Appendix to this Report,—says, p. 68, " Agents are too apt to make out the same scheme of husbandry for all varieties of ground, and when that is the case, some are great sufferers when they are tied down to fulfil their engagements by which they may be obliged to keep a piece of ground for two years in an unproductive state, when others who are under the same conditions may

may lose nothing by it, having land adapted for the purpose."

These several Remarks tend to show, that, during the currency of a lease, until the last three years of its termination, a tenant should have few restrictions. Nevertheless, that during the last three years, of the term, he should strictly conform with such regulations, as may tend to place and leave the farm in a state which will induce a proper tenant to enter upon it, at a full rent, for a fresh term.

DIVISION THE SECOND.

WOODLANDS and PLANTATIONS.

It must naturally excite some surprise, in a person who has been accustomed to make observations on woods, and the lands on which they are wont to florish, to find a cool, clayey country in a manner destitute of *oak trees!* In the hedgerows of most parts of the county, the ash is common. But, unless in the neighbourhood of Durham, an oak is rarely seen. Yet the soil and the substrata appear to be very similar to those of the Wealds of Kent and Sussex: the latter of which, more particularly, has long been celebrated for its oak timber.

In Northumberland, however, on lands of a kindred nature to those of Durham, the oak does not continue to thrive as timber; but loses its top, and becomes stagheaded. The climate is certainly against the growth of trees that are exposed to easterly winds, immediately from the sea; and there may be something in the substrata of Durham and Northumberland, which is ungenial to their growth, in its more advanced stages: so that the present nakedness of the country may have arisen from the conviction of its owners, that the *oak*, in ordinary situations, is unprofitable, as *timber;* while *coppice wood*, is of little value,

value, as fuel, in a country that abounds with coals. The *ash*, however, being a necessary article in husbandry, and useful, as timber, at an earlier age than the oak, and moreover braving the sea winds better, has, on the contrary, been found profitable to be reared; and has, no doubt, heretofore, engaged the attention of land owners.

The Board's Reporter, however, ascribes the country's nakedness to another cause:—namely, to the " eclesiastical tenure;"—" for who will plant a tree, which, the moment it takes root, will be no longer his property"—p. 47. But to this cannot well be owing the *general* nakedness that exists. For we are told, above, that only one third of the county belongs to the church. Yet the other two thirds,— saving a " little wood about some seats of noblemen and gentlemen,"—are equally nude.

There are, doubtlessly, sheltered situations in the more broken and unevenly surfaced parts of the county, where wood might be raised on lands that are unfit for corn or herbage. And Mr. Granger mentions an instance, p. 48, in which a clause was inserted in a bill of appropriation and inclosure, by virtue of which the life lessee " shall and may, at all times hereafter, fully, and freely, and peaceably, and quietly, have, hold, and enjoy, to, and for their respective uses and behoofs, and sell and dispose of the whole of such woods, underwoods, and trees, and other plantings as are now growing, or standing, or as they shall respectively hereafter plant, or set, or shall grow, in or upon their same copyhold or customary allotments; and the said leasehold premises respectively, any custom or right heretofore used or enjoyed by the said Lord Bishop of Durham, or any of his predecessors, or which might be used or enjoyed by him or any of his successors, to the contrary thereof in anywise notwithstanding."

" In consequence of this clause, some thousand of acres of new copyhold and leasehold inclosures have been

been covered with trees, which are thriving wonderfully on ground utterly incapable of any other improvement."

DIVISION THE THIRD.

AGRICULTURE.

FARMS.—P. 39. " The farms are generally of a middle size ; few exceeding 200*l.* annual rent."

HOMESTEAD.—P. 52. " The houses in general are well situated in the midst of the farms, and tolerably commodious ; the offices too frequently scanty ; the fold-yards too few and too small, which is a great hinderance to getting the ground freed in the spring."

Of the OCCUPIERS, or rather let us say AGRICULTURISTS, of the county of Durham, the Reporter (or other hand) in the " Conclusion," writes in these high terms. P. 62. " Upon the whole, he thinks there is ground to indulge the pleasing hope, that we are still advancing towards perfection in agriculture; for it may with truth be said, that proposals for improvements are received with attention, and judged of with candour. Experiments are prosecuted with a liberality highly meritorious, and never to be enough commended; nor is any character in more esteem, than that of a skilful communicative cultivator."

PLAN OF MANAGEMENT.—P. 54. " The fertility of lands of old inclosure in this county, is thought, in general, to have suffered a considerable decrease of late: probably that decrease may have been occasioned by the proportion of tillage to the grass land in each farm having been too great, considering the general thinness of the soil ; to rectify which, it seems recommendable, that the quantity of tillage should be reduced to one third, instead of one half of the whole farm, which is now too general."

P. 38. " The present usual rotation of crops is, after summer fallow, wheat, oats, or beans, or peas,
and

and sometimes a crop of broad clover is taken in lieu of oats, beans, or peas: in some spots of gravelly soil, which are rare, there are turnips and barley in perpetual succession, with now and then a crop of clover interposed."

Mr. G. should have said where this extraordinary " rotation " is practised. It is not likely to be carried on upon the " water shaken lands," of which the cultivated parts of the county chiefly consists. See p. 131, aforegoing, article Soil.

WORKPEOPLE.—*Wages.*—Taking for granted, that Mr. Granger speaks from his own knowledge and experience, respecting the prices of labor (as well as of provisions), in 1794, I insert them with a degree of confidence.—P. 44. " Annual wages of a man servant in husbandry, having meat, drink, washing and lodging, are from 10*l.* to 14*l.* : of a woman servant in husbandry, from 4*l.* to 6*l.* Price of labour by the day, from 1s. to 1s. 6d. and in harvest sometimes, as exigencies may require, it is advanced to 2s. 6d. or upwards. To a woman for common work in the fields, 6d. per day, for weeding corn, and in hay harvest, 8d. ; and in corn harvest, as exigencies may require, the price rises to 2s. or 2s. 6d."

The annual wages may appear to be exorbitant, to a south of England occupier. But they were equally high in Yorkshire, at that time.

WORKING ANIMALS.—P. 42. " Horses only for the most part are employed in the team ; in some situations oxen would perform the work better, especially upon our steep declivities, and are fed at a lower rate in winter, upon straw alone ; except that occasionally, upon hard work, a sheaf of oats is given them once in the day, and in case an accident should render them unfit for labour, or the state of the farmer's stock should make it proper to sell them, they will sell to profit ; whereas the horse, after having required a greater expense in keeping, in
case

case of accidents, to which he is more liable, or of age, will produce a mere nothing."

IMPLEMENTS. P. 41. " The Rotherham plough, harrows, and rollers. Carts with two wheels, containing about twenty-four bushels, or one ton weight, drawn by three horses, and used for the purposes of leadiug coal, lime, dung, &c. Long carts of a good form, with two wheels also, and drawn by three horses, used for leading hay, and corn in the sheaf. Few waggons with four wheels used."

MANURES.—P. 41. " The produce of the fold-yard and lime, with the farmers in general, are the only manures used. In situations near the coast, abundance of sea weed may be collected, which, with a mixture of sand, would be valuable manure for their clayey land, but which is not sufficiently attended to, perhaps principally owing to the exact quantum for improvement not being accurately ascertained."— Further—" It is remarked that the manure produced in towns, where sea sand is used to lay on the floors of houses, is infinitely more valuable than any other common manures." I insert the last passage, though it seems to want explaining.

Lime. Mr. Granger, speaking of covenants of leases, p. 53, says, " another covenant very frequent in leases, is, that the tenant shall spread two cart loads of lime on every acre of fallow; whereas the best judges are now agreed in opinion, that lime is prejudicial to old arable, and only beneficial to new lands."

But has not Mr. G. already sufficiently accounted for the deterioration of the lands of Durham, without their ungrateful occupiers bringing an unreasonable charge against lime? (see p. 148).—Lime is able to give fertility to *fresh land,* without the co-operation of live stock:—but not to *continue* to enable it to throw out corn crops, without a due return of animal or vegetable manure. Cleveland (which is naturally
a part

a part of the same country), has, for some time, been experiencing a similar effect. The surest remedy, or mean of renovation, at present known, I believe, is, in effect, what Mr. G. recommends; namely, to PASTURE MORE, and PLOW LESS.

PRODUCE OF GRAIN CROPS.—P. 38. "Of wheat upon good land, the produce may be estimated from twenty to thirty bushels per acre; upon the inferior land from ten to twenty bushels per acre; the average price, from five shillings to five shillings and sixpence per Winchester bushel. Of barley, never attempted but upon dry ground, inclined to gravel or sand, from thirty to forty bushels; average price, from three shillings to three shillings and sixpence. Of oats, from twenty to forty bushels per acre; average price, two shillings and sixpence per bushel. Of beans, from fourteen to twenty bushels per acre; average price, four shillings and sixpence per bushel. Of peas, from eight to twelve bushels per acre; average price, three shillings and sixpence per bushel."

CULTIVATED HERBAGE.—P. 33. "The grasses chiefly cultivated are rye and duffil grass; red, white, and hop clover; and rib and oat grass; but the two latter are justly falling into disrepute."—Again, "Rye-grass is much esteemed, because it is of earliest growth, continues late in the autumn, and thrives in all soils and climates."

GRASS LANDS. The natural sterility of the lands of Durham is seen in the scanty produce of *mowing grounds*. P. 38. "There are acres of meadow ground which sometimes produce two tons of hay per acre, but in general the produce is below half a ton."

On stocking *pasture grounds* we have this passage:—P. 61. "The rage for overstocking, which hath been too general, is restrained. By some, fields are saved from the scythe or depasturage, between May and December, and then come into good use for their stock."

This appears to be flying from one extreme to another.

another. But we are not told on what land, nor in what situation, the practice is used. Where much *snow* lies, *long* grass is liable to be injured or spoiled. I insert the notice as containing something new;— though it may have arisen out of an erratum. Quere, for May, read September?

I have heard an expedient of that sort spoken well of in Yorkshire: not, however, as affording winter pasturage; but as meliorating—manuring—the land, for future crops.

The following ingenious method of freeing the surface of repellant grass lands, from rain water, with the plough, is well entitled to a place here. P. 45. " Sometimes superficial drains are made with draining ploughs, of various inventions; sometimes, by opening the furrows with a common plough, the wing of the share being generally raised nearly to a perpendicular, which cuts the one side of the furrow in a slope, while the coulter, being bent at a right angle, immediately under the plough beam, to the land side, an inch and a half, and then again to the furrow a little acutely, and descending obliquely to its point, where it meets the perpendicular, cuts the other side of the furrow likewise in a slope, and under proper management turns out a sod six inches deep, four inches and a half broad at the bottom, and six inches broad at the top."

ORCHARDS.—P. 52. " Orchards are uncommon, unless in the southern parts of this county, where they are general and profitable."

These, I believe, may be considered as the most northerly orchards, of any considerable extent, in England.

LIVESTOCK. The Reporter having had the permission of " Mr. CULLEY, (p. 33) to insert in this work his accurate description of the horse, bull, and ram of the county of Durham, as stated in his Observations on Live Stock,"—there was the less occasion for his own observations on the subject;—" A few additional

additional reflections, however, (continues Mr. G.) have occurred, and will follow after the descriptions, for consideration. Stock being the peculiar boast of this part of the north of England, it seems a duty to give it that attention which it deserves:" And, afterward (willing that his countrymen should lose no part of the credit they have gained), he further adds, p. 38, " Although, perhaps, there may be in this part of the kingdom some favourable peculiarity of soil or climate, we have also traditional assurance, that our ancestors were careful in the selection of the animals from which they bred, in the several kinds of stock, to which attention, the pre-eminence of character it still bears in the market, is perhaps principally to be attributed." Mr. G.'s descriptions are as follow :

HORSES.—P. 36. " The horses are fit for the field, the saddle, and the harness, and sold at good prices to the London dealers."

CATTLE.—P. 36. " The cattle are short-horned of a good kind, still improving, by the attention of some breeders to a judicious selection of bulls and cows; and perhaps upon every consideration of form, weight, produce of milk and butter, and above all, quickness of grazing, not inferior to any in England."

SHEEP.—P. 36. " The sheep are large, with long wool. They have of late been crossed by some, with the Leicestershire kind, and several think with advantage; others are of opinion that the cross hath been disadvantageous, because, although it must be allowed that the form has been improved, the weight certainly hath been found to be diminished; and that in those of the age of a year and a half, the usual time of sale, diminishes the value, perhaps not less than a crown per head; nor hath the pasture admitted of greater number, nor have they fattened sooner to compensate that loss; nor hath it been found, that by keeping them longer, a greater increase of profit hath accrued from them than from the other. They wish therefore to preserve the old,
which

which hath acquired the name of the Tees-water breed, and hath been long most deservedly in high esteem; and they recommend, in order still to improve it, a careful attention in the choice of ewes and rams in the propagation. In Weardale, where the sheep is of a small kind, weighing, when fat, from fourteen to eighteen pounds a quarter, part horned, with mottled faces, the wool fine, care is taken to preserve the breed pure; the ewes are constantly, in breeding time, brought off the moors, and put to approved rams, in their inclosed pastures. Those that run at large upon other wastes, are a promiscuous kind, and in a perpetual state of degeneracy. It is usual for our farmers of water-shaken ground, in the lower parts of the county, to purchase from the north-western moors, ewes in the latter end of harvest, and putting them to rams of the Tees-water breed, to sell them with their produce the summer following, it not being safe, on account of the rot, to keep them longer."

SWINE.—P. 37. "There is reason for caution, in the introduction of new breeds, where the breeds are already good. A breed of swine brought from Germany of a round form, and pleasing appearance, spotted black, red, and white, tempted many to propagate them; and yet by experience they have been found unprofitable, because they require a greater proportion of food, than our old breed, to fatten them, and when fat, are deficient in the weight that might have been expected from their bulk; the cause of which may, perhaps, be ascribed to a great quantity of woolly hair growing amongst their bristles, and draining, perhaps for its support, the nourishment which should have been distributed in the flesh: and the old breed thinly covered with bristles only, which had been nearly lost, is coming again into general request."

I cordially agree with Mr. Granger in his first position. The rest I do not so clearly comprehend.

BEFORE

BEFORE I put aside the Durham Report, I think it right to observe, that its deficiency, in regard to the number of subjects treated of, serves to show the writer's good sense, in not obtruding his sentiments, unless where he conceived himself sufficiently informed. Had Mr. Granger been as conversant in agriculture, as he appears to be in estate agency, he would, no doubt, have favored us with a fuller Report.

CUMBERLAND.

THE NATURAL DISTRICTS that are included, wholely or in part, within the outlines of this county, are,

The district of Carlisle ;

The sea-coast of Cumberland, &c. ;

Great part of the slate-stone mountains of Cumberland, Westmoreland, &c. ;

With a smaller portion of the morelands of the five counties, above mentioned.

THE KNOWLEDGE, which I have incidentally gained of these districts, has arisen in the manner, following.

In 1798, I passed through the more central parts of the county;—by Penrith, Carlisle, and Longtown ; a line that I have, since, repeatedly travelled.

In the autumn of the same year, I gained a general idea of the north-eastern quarter ; in crossing it from Longtown, to Brampton; and, thence, passing by the great road between Carlisle and Newcastle (with a deviation toward the Gillsland Hills) to the eastern extremity of the county. See P. 5. aforegoing.

In 1799, I had a general view of the western mountains; in traveling from Kendal to Keswick ; in an excursion from thence, by the lower road, along the side of Basenthwaite Lake, to Cockermouth ; extending my ride toward Worthington ; returning to Keswick by the Upper or Mountain Road ; after-ward,

ward, crossing the foot of Skiddaw, to Ireby and
Wigtown: and, from thence, after taking a cursory
view of the surrounding country, I proceeded to
" Bowness;" where I crossed the Firth of Solway,—
on my way to the north of Scotland.

In 1800, I crossed the Firth, near its head, from
Old Gretna, to Rockclif: and by that means saw
the fertile country which lies to the north of Carlisle.

And, in 1801, I examined the country, to the
westward of Carlisle,—toward Wigtown.

To the sea-coast district, I still remain a stranger;
excepting what I saw of it, in my excursion from
Keswick.   But I have the less to regret, on that
account; as it appears to have engaged more than
ordinary attention of the Surveyors, whose Report will
presently come under consideration.

The DISTRICT of CARLISLE.   This is a well defined
natural district.   It may, with little latitude, be
deemed an extensive plain, surrounded by mountains
and the sea (the estuary of Solway)—above which
its lower, and more prevalent lands, are but little
elevated; these lower parts bearing the true vale
character.   The elevation of its southern margin,
however, is somewhat greater.

Its boundaries, on the north, are the estuary, and
the moss, of Solway ;—on the north-east, the broken
mountain heights of Gillsland ; on the east, the morelands of Cumberland ; on the south, the valley of
Appleby, and the point of the hill which rises between that and the environs of Penrith ;—and, on
the west, the slate-rock mountains, and the northern
extreme of the sea-coast district ;—from which it is
partially cut off, by the inlet or estuary of Abbey
Holm, and the feet of the mountains.   The extent
cannot be less than four or five hundred square
miles.

For several miles round Carlisle, the north-eastern
side excepted, the country is rich; forming a vale
                                        district

district of the first quality : the surface is well varied, and the soil, mostly, a red loam of superior fertility.

On the north-east of Carlisle, toward Longtown, and from thence to near Brampton, the surface is singularly flat, and the soil of a loose sandy texture; the substrata being, in many parts, evidently of a cool, moist quality :—and much, surely, might be done toward its improvement ; by a well regulated commission of drainage. It appears to be mostly of recent inclosure; from a state of moist heathy common.

Round Brampton, the soil is still sandy : but it obviously rests on a warmer more genial base, than the last mentioned; and covers a widely different surface;—which rises in hillocks of the most grotesque shapes; as if the sands, by which they appear to have been formed, had been tossed up by tempest, or whirlwinds. And a similar description of land accompanies the Irthing, to the confines of Northumberland :—thus dividing the Carrick Castle Morelands, from the Gillsland Hills and the main body of the heathlands of Northumberland.

The southern margin of the district, though somewhat more elevated, is smoothly surfaced; shelving, gently, from the environs of Penrith, to Upper Hesketh, where what might be strictly termed the *Vale* of *Carlisle* commences.

The soil, throughout, this extended tract, ten miles in length and some miles in width, is red loam, on a sound absorbent base : forming land (its climature apart) of a superior quality for mixed cultivation. Yet the principal part of this fair passage of country —some twenty or thirty square miles in extent—is still suffered to lie (a few years ago lay) in the unprofitable state of commonage !

Much of the western extreme of this district, likewise, remains in the same unproductive state. Many of the commons, on the shore of the estuary, about Boldness, are, it is true, of a mean quality ; the soil weak,

weak,—the produce heath or peat earth. But, in the neighbourhood of Wigtown, there are commons, which are superior in soil to those of Hesketh, and much superior in climature. Some extraordinary causes, surely, must operate in preventing the appropriation of so much valuable land.*

The MOUNTAINS of CUMBERLAND, &c. This extraordinary passage of the mountain department being " one and indivisible," and by much the largest portion of it lying within the county of Cumberland, I will offer, in this place, a sketch of the entire natural district; which forms a singular variety of British mountain.

From every outward appearance, whether at the bases or the upper stages of these mountains, the ordinary materials of which they are formed is shistous, or slatey, rock; very similar to that of which the minor hills of Devonshire and Cornwall are constructed; as well as the minor mountains of South Wales. But, there, especially in the former situation, scarcely any thing of rock appears: the hills, though steep, have generally a covering of soil: while the mountains of Cumberland vie with the granite rocks of the Grampian Hills, in ruggedness of surface; and with the calcareous mountains of North Wales, in picturesque effect.

In the disposition of these mountains, we find nothing of regularity: no lengthened ridge, nor continuous chain of hills. The whole appears as a congeries of broken, and mostly pointed, masses—of immense bulk—whose bases are united, or nearly approach each other; unless where they are *superficially* divided by the lakes that are dispersed among them. Very little valley land is seen; except on the margins

* It is remarkable, that the worst-soiled commons, as those between Longtown and Brampton, have been first appropriated. Perhaps their being unsafe for sheep induced the customary tenants to give them up the more readily.

margins of the lakes; and excepting on the banks of the principal river,—the Derwent.

The lower skirts, and the flatter parts, of the hills are mostly covered with soil; resembling that of the Devonshire Hills: the principal ingredient appearing to be decomposed slate stone.

The Cumbrian, as the Cheviot, hills are green; excepting towards the summit of the higher mountains. Skiddaw, like "the Cheviot," is partially clothed in heath.

The extent of this tract of mountain (in Cumberland, Westmoreland, and Lancashire) cannot be less, I conceive, than five or six hundred square miles; exclusively of the limestone heights, situated on the western bank of the valley of Appleby.

"GENERAL VIEW

OF THE

AGRICULTURE

OF THE

COUNTY OF CUMBERLAND,

WITH

OBSERVATIONS FOR THE MEANS OF ITS IMPROVEMENT.

DRAWN UP FOR THE CONSIDERATION OF

THE BOARD OF AGRICULTURE AND INTERNAL

IMPROVEMENT.

BY J. BAILEY AND G. CULLEY."

THE ACQUIREMENTS and QUALIFICATIONS of these gentlemen, as Reporters, have been already spoken of, in p. 11.

Their MODE of SURVEYING the COUNTY of CUMBERLAND, does not appear. Of the rout they took, or the time they spent in the examination of its

several

several districts, we are not informed. In Northumberland, they were *at home ;* and a detail of the manner in which they acquired the knowledge of the facts, whereon their Report is founded, was the less required, than in Cumberland, where we must of course consider them as *strangers*, previously to their survey ; there being no evidence in their Report to warrant us to conclude, otherwise. We must therefore proceed with greater caution, in appreciating the miscellaneous materials with which they have furnished us.

Prefixed to this Report (which is bound up in the same volume with those of Northumberland and Westmoreland) is a MINIATURE MAP, by Mr. Bailey; in which the more mountainous parts are intended to be distinguished, from the lower, more cultivated, lands ; by the method adopted for the map of Northumberland. And, further, in the present instance, a very ingenious method is used, with the intention of showing the different natures of the soils and substrata of the county, by dotted lines ; with letters of reference placed within each division. How infinitely more scientific, and permanent, is this neat and convenient form, to that of the flaring blotch map of Durham.

SUBJECT THE FIRST.

NATURAL ECONOMY.

EXTENT. P. 197. " The county of Cumberland is situated between the latitudes of 54 deg. 6 min. and 55 deg. 7½ min. North ; and the longitudes of 2 deg. 13 min. and 3 deg. 30 min. west from London. Its length, from St. Bee's Head, in a north-east direction, to Butter Burn, is 58 miles ; and its mean breadth, in a N. W. direction, is 30 miles."—" And contains 1516 square miles, or 970,240 acres."

ELEVATION.

ELEVATION. In a note, p. 198, we find a short list of the highest of the British mountains, with their several degrees of elevation. Those of Cumberland are as follow :—

	Feet.
" Cross Fell,	3,400
Helvellin,	3,324
Skiddaw,	3,270
Saddleback,	3,048."

We are not, however, informed in what manner those heights were ascertained ; or after whom they were copied. I therefore insert them, here, on the authority of the Reporters.

SURFACE. P. 200. " The surface is beautifully diversified with level plains, and rising eminences ; deep sequestered vales (vallies), and stupendous mountains."—P. 201 " The mountainous districts are separated into two divisions, one of which bounds the east side of the county, and is the *highest part* of that ridge of mountains, that divide the eastern and western coasts of the island, from Derbyshire, in England, to Linlithgow, in Scotland. Cross-fell, Hartside-fell, Geltsdale-forest, and Spadeadam-waste, are the names of that portion of the ridge which passes through this county. These mountains are composed of strata of different kinds of stone, and are rich in coal, lime, and lead-ore ; but are no way remarkable for any striking irregularities of surface.

" The other division of mountainous district occupies the south-west part of the county, known by the names of Skiddaw, Saddle-back, Helvellin, Wreynose, Hardknot, Sca-fell, &c. &c. remarkable for their steep, broken, rocky sides, and romantic shapes ; and are, in general, one mass of that kind of stone which produces the beautiful blue slate, so much and so deservedly esteemed for covering the roofs of houses. They are destitute of coal, lime, or metallic ores."

CLIMATURE. P. 198. " In a county like Cumberland, enjoying such an extent of sea-coast, and where

where so large a portion is occupied by mountains, and those reckoned amongst the highest in the kingdom, the climate must be various. Along the coast, and for a considerable way up the rivers, the snow seldom lies above 24 hours; but upon the mountains the snow will continue for six or eight months: of course, the lower parts of the county are mild and temperate, while on the higher grounds, and upon the mountains and their vicinity, the air is cold and piercing; but the whole is healthy, though subject to great and frequent falls of rain, particularly in the autumn, which makes their harvests very precarious and expensive."

WATERS. P. 203. " Though this county enjoys an extent of 67 miles of sea-coast, yet it cannot boast of its navigable rivers; the tide flowing not more than two or three miles up the greatest part of them: even the Eden, by much the largest, is perplexed with shoals, and its navigation cannot be said to reach beyond Sansfield, though the tide flows a few miles further.

" There are few places where water is so abundant and good, as this district is blessed with; for, besides the large rivers Eden, Derwent, Esk, &c. every village, and almost every farm, enjoys the benefit of a pure spring, or is visited by a rivulet. The larger rivers abound with salmon, trout, and various other kinds of fish, and the smaller brooks with trouts and eels. It is also ornamented with many beautiful and extensive lakes; which, with their pleasing accompaniments, have of late years made the tour of the lakes a fashionable amusement, and from whence considerable emoluments have resulted to the neighbouring inhabitants."

SOILS and SUBSOILS. P. 199. " The *Soil* is various, but may be classed under four different heads.

" 1st, *Fertile Clays*, or rather *rich strong Loams*, occupy but a small portion of this county: formerly, this kind of soil was generally employed in grazing,

or

or the dairy; but since the introduction of growing wheat, it has been converted into tillage, and produces excellent crops of grain.

" 2d, *Dry Loams,* including the various degrees, from the rich brown loam to the light sandy soils. This is the most prevalent, occupying a greaer, portion of the county than any other; not only the lower districts, but the steep sides of the mountaints are in general of this soil; and in many places, even their summits are covered with a dry sound earth, producing green sward, with little heath. We suppose at least one half of the lower, or cultivatable district, is of this valuable soil, excellently adapted to the culture of turnips, artificial grasses, the various species of grain, and of breeding and feeding the most improved kinds of stock, particularly sheep, it being perfectly sound, or safe from the rot.

" 3d, *Wet Loam,* generally on a clay bottom. The fertility of this soil is various, depending on the thickness of the staple, and the nature of the clay below: it is dangerous for sheep, but may be applied with advantage to keeping cows for the dairy, breeding young cattle and horses, and to the culture of wheat, oats, clover, and ray-grass.

" 4th, *Black Peat Earth* *, is most prevalent on the mountainous districts, particularly those adjoining Northumberland and Durham: it is also found on moors or commons in the lower parts of the county; in some places only a few inches thick, upon a white sand, well known, by those whose lot it has been to cultivate it, to be an ungrateful and unprofitable soil."

FOSSILS and MINERALS. P. 202. " This county abounds with coal, lime, and lead-ore; it also produces black-lead, copper, gypsum, lapis caliminaris, and excellent slate.

" *Coal*

---

* *Peat Earth* is the produce of bogs and " mosses." What covers the surfaces of heath lands is better defined moory soil, or the black soil of heaths.

" *Coal*—as observed in the last section, (see *Surface*, p. 162.) is found in many parts of the eastern mountains; and, with not many exceptions, all along that tract (extending in different degrees of breadth,) from Sebergham to Whitehaven, and along the coast to Maryport, forming a district of about 100 square miles. Cannel coal is got in large quantities in the parishes of Caldbeck and Bolton.

" *Limestone*—abounds in most parts of the eastern mountains, and in the parishes of Graystock, Dacre, Penrith, Broadfield Common, &c. and in the neighbourhood of Egremont and Whitehaven.

" *Gypsum*—is got in the parishes of Wetheral, and St. Cuthbert's, Carlisle; but has never been applied there as manure.

" *Lead Ore*—is got in great abundance in Alstonmoor; and, in a lesser degree, in the parishes of Caldbeck and Melmerby. In the lead-mines is also found the lapis caliminaris.

" *Copper Ore*—is found also at Caldbeck, Melmerby, and at Hesket, but at present not worked with that success which formerly attended them.

" *Black Lead*—is found only in Borrowdale, a few miles west of Keswick.

" *Blue Slates*—of an excellent quality, are gotten in Borrowdale; and inferior sorts in some of the neighbouring mountains.

" *Freestones*—abound in most parts of the county; some of which split into good slate; but are more heavy, less durable, and require stronger timber to support them, than the blue slate, and are also more subject to imbibe moisture."

SUBJECT

SUBJECT THE SECOND.

POLITICAL ECONOMY.

STATE of APPROPRIATION. In the section " Soil and Surface," we have the subjoined account of the existing state of the lands of the county.

P. 202. " From a map of Cumberland, published by Messrs. HODGKINSON and DONALD, laid down from a scale of two miles to an inch, we calculate that

	Acres.
The mountainous districts contain	342,000
Improvable common	150,000
Old enclosures	470,000
Lakes and waters	8,000
Total quantity of acres in the whole county	970,000"

By this statement, it appears probable, that not more than half of the lands of the county are appropriated : and, certainly, more than half of them still remain in a wild uncultivated state ; and this, while many of them are lands of a valuable quality, for the purposes of cultivation.

These facts, so discreditable to the county, and the kingdom at large, have arrested, with peculiar interest, the attention of the Board's Surveyors ;—who, in different parts of their Report, have dwelt on the subject. I will, here, adduce their remarks ; and endeavour to place them so as to give increased force to their effect.

The present value of those unappropriated Lands.—P. 235. " The present value per acre of these *mountainous districts*, may be nearly estimated from the following data :

" Mr.

" Mr. GREENHOW, of Threlkeld; takes pasturage for his sheep on Skiddaw forest for a year, at 5s. per score, which is 3d. per sheep ; and supposing an acre keeps a sheep, then will 3d. an acre be the yearly value of these mountains. They can scarce be in a less productive state; an acre of wood, if it only grew broom-sticks, would pay much better.

" *Of the Commons*,—in the less elevated parts of the county there are many, with large tracts of excellent soil, capable of being improved by judicious culture, proper draining, and improved breeds of sheep, to many times their present value ; which is certainly very small, probably not more than from 1s. to 2s. per acre."

Their improvable value, in a state of appropriation. P. 214. " *The advantages* that arise from enclosing, *in respect to increase of produce or value*, must entirely depend upon the modes of management pursued after the enclosing takes place."—(A subject that will be brought forward under its legitimate head.)

P. 215. " *The advantages* arising from enclosing of commons, in respect to the *improvement of stock*, is obvious : while in a state of common, every one turns upon it what he pleases, and there is generally double the quantity of stock that there ought to be. The consequence is, they make no improvement; *they barely exist ;* the yearly profits how small ! Should an enlightened breeder wish to improve his sheep, how is he to effect it, while his ewes mix promiscuously with his neighbour's flocks ? If he had the best tup in the kingdom, can he be sure that one of his ewes would be tupped by him, while there are probably not less than a score of his neighbour's to contest the female with him ? On the other hand, if the common were enclosed, every one would stint with that species of stock for which his allotment was best adapted, and in such numbers as would ensure profit : when he can confine his ewes within his own enclosure, he can make whatever experiment he pleases, by putting
a few,

a few, or many ewes, to any particular tup, without any fear or apprehension of having a spurious breed, by the interference of his neighbour's: he is also enabled to keep his flock from many disorders : few commons but have some tracts of land liable to the rot: how are they to be prevented from depasturing upon it ?—or if the scab, or other infectious disorders, have taken place amongst any flock on the common, how is he to avoid it ?"

P. 236.—" In a county like this, that does not raise corn sufficient for the consumption of its in-habitants, and where it is always one-fourth or one-fifth dearer than in an adjoining county, it is lament-able to see such extensive tracts of *good corn land* lying waste, of no value to its owners, and of no benefit to the community. Instead of the present scarcity of grain, large quantities might be yearly ex-ported ; and instead of the ill-formed, poor, starved, meagre animals that depasture the commons at present, an abundant supply of good fat mutton would be had to *grace* the markets of the county, and also to send off large supplies to Newcastle, Liver-pool, Manchester, and other populous manufacturing places.

" It is difficult to say, what would be the increased value of such land under proper management; we think we cannot be wrong in stating, that it would be at least from six to eight times the value to the pro-prietors.—But of what advantage would it be to the public ?"

This question is answered by a calculation; in which the estimated " total value of increased pro-duce" comes out 227,000 *l.* ; for the 150,000 acres of lower common lands, only.

The *Means* of Appropriation.—P. 270. " *Enclosing of Commons,*—we have already pointed out, would be a great source of improvement in this county, could it be done at a moderate expense, and on equitable terms ; the charges of obtaining an Act of Parliament, and

and the various additions made thereto by the practitioners of the law, are in some cases three or four
times more than all the other expenses put together.
Surely this might be avoided by a general act. The
House of Commons has already laid a foundation, by
the standing orders respecting such bills.—If two-
thirds of the proprietors request a division, we see no
reason why they should be put to the expense of obtaining an Act of Parliament, because two or three,
or possibly only one, ignorant or ill-natured person or
persons, are absurd enough to oppose it."

STATE of SOCIETY. *Provisions.*—P. 254. " Grain
of all kinds is generally very high ; the average price,
in 1793, was,

	s.	d.
For wheat, ...	6	6 per bushel.
Barley, ...	3	8 ditto.
Oats, ...	2	8 ditto.
Butchers' meat, from ..	0	3 to 4*d*. per lb.
Butter, from	0	6 to 8*d*. per lb.
Skimmed milk cheese,	0	3 per lb.
Potatoes, ...	1	0 to 1*s*. 4*d*. per bush.

Poultry.—A stubble goose, 2*s*. ; duck, 8*d*. ; a fowl,
6*d*. ; eggs, from 3*d*. to 6*d*. per dozen.

Fish.—Salmon, 6*d*. per lb. ; trout, 3*d*."

Again. " The *Bread* generally used in this county,
is made of barley, or a mixture of barley and rye :
oatmeal is made into hasty-puddings, and eat with
butter, treacle, milk, or beer, for breakfast, and often
for supper."

" *Potatoes*, for several years, have been in general
use, as a principal article of food ; few families dine
without them ; and we believe many a dinner and
supper are made of potatoes, with a little butter, or
cream, for sauce, and in many cases only milk, or,
where this cannot be had, a little salt."

Fuel.—P. 255. " Coals are cheap and plentiful in
most parts of the county ; in several places, from
15*s*.

15*s.* to 30*s.* will procure a year's fuel for a small family."

" Peat and turf also abound, and are used instead of coals in some districts."

Employments. P. 261. " The *Manufactures* are not extensive ; printing cottons at Carlisle, and a check manufacture (on a small scale) in most of the market-towns, with four or five cotton-mills erected of late years near Carlisle, Dalston, and Corby, with a small factory of corduroys at the latter place, is all this county has to boast of." Four or five cotton-mills to *boast* of ! Their effects on the morals of Carlisle, at least, have been, for some time, *notoriously* ascertained.

LOCAL TAXES.—*Poor Rate.* In 1797 ? the poor rate, " at Carlisle, 2*s.* ; Wigton, 2*s.* 6*d.* ; Aldston, 3*s.* ; Harrington, 1*s.* 6*d.* ; Kirkoswald, 1*s.* 8*d.* ; and in many of the country parishes, they vary from 6*d.* to 10*d.* per pound." p. 210.

P. 262. " In most of the country parishes the poor-rates are low, from 6*d.* to 9*d.* per pound, which, we believe, is partly owing to a sort of pride existing amongst the lower classes, of not applying for parochial relief till they cannot possibly subsist without it ; and also to the number of *friendly societies* which have been established, and we hope are still increasing. Such useful institutions are deserving of encouragement by every person whose property is chargeable with poor-rate."

Tithes. P. 210. " Tithes are mostly taken in kind ; a few parishes pay a modus in lieu of tithes, and others are tithe-free, in consequence of a portion of common being given to the impropriator."

PUBLIC WORKS. On this prominent subject, in a Report to a public Board, we find little to notice, in that of Cumberland.

Embankments (public I take for granted) are recommended, P. 272, " on the marshes of Burgh, Rockcliffe, Abbey-Holm, and the mouth of the Duddon."

Duddon." And, in a note, "the Lancaster, Cartmel, and Duddon Sands," are mentioned. But of these in their proper place.

Roads. What the Cumberland Surveyors say on this subject (p. 256.) serves to show that cursory observations on the existing state of roads, at any particular time, must be in some degree vague. The condition of a road is continually varying. The states of the Cumbrian roads, as mentioned by the Reporters, in 1794, might be said to be the reverse, in 1798; when I found the great road, between Carlisle and Newcastle, in high condition: while many of the less public roads were unsufferably bad :—notwithstanding the great plenty of good materials that abound in most parts of Cumberland (not in all); and notwithstanding the carriages of burden which travel upon them are, invariably, single horse carts. My journals, in 1798, 1800, and 1801, are full of complaints, on this subject: amounting to a proof, that the road surveyors of Cumberland are negligent of their duty; or that single horse carts are not so favorable to roads, as theory aptly suggests.

MARKET PRODUCTS of Cumberland. A valuable produce of its *waters* are salmon; of which great quantities are sent to the metropolis.

The products of its *soils* are those of Woodlands and Agriculture, which will be mentioned. The surplus that is shipped off, from this county, consists of "butter, bacon, and hams of an excellent quality, form a part of the commerce of this county. The article of butter is said to amount to 30,000*l.* per ann. the greatest part for the London market." p. 261.

The best produce of its *substrata* appears to be *Coals;* concerning which the following particulars are noticeable

P. 259. "The *commerce* of this county consists principally in the exportation of coals from Whitehaven, Workington, and Maryport, to Ireland, &c. The number of vessels employed in this trade amounts
to

to upwards of 300, from 60 to 120 tons burthen. This lucrative trade has arisen to its present importance within the last hundred years; it originated at Whitehaven, from the exertions of Lord LONSDALE'S ancestors, to whom the coal in that neighbourhood principally belongs."

P. 261. "The quantity of coals exported from these ports, taken on an average of 11 years (from 1781 to 1792), is as follows:

	Chaldrons
From Whitehaven, ...	81,940
Workington, Harrington, and Maryport, ... }	70,870
	152,810"

SUBJECT THE THIRD.

RURAL ECONOMY.

DIVISION THE FIRST.

TENANTED ESTATES; their IMPROVEMENT and MANAGEMENT.

ESTATES.—*Sizes of Estates.* P. 205. " There are probably few counties, where *property in land* is divided into such small parcels as in Cumberland, and those small properties so universally occupied by the owners. The annual value of these tenements varies from 5*l.* to 50*l.* a year; but the generality are from 15*l.* to 30*l.*; some few extend to 100*l.* or a little more.

" The rental of the largest estate in the county, is said to amount to about 13,000*l.* per annum."

Tenure. P. 205. " By far the greatest part of this county is held under lords of manors, by that species

of

of vassalage called *customary tenure ;* subject to the payment of fines and heriots, on alienation, death of the lord, or death of tenant, and the payment of certain annual rents, and performance of various services, called *boon-days ;* such as getting and leading the lord's peats, ploughing and harrowing his land, reaping his corn, hay-making, carrying letters, &c. &c. whenever summoned by the lord.

" We cannot pretend to be accurate, but believe, that two-thirds of the county are held by this kind of tenure, principally in those small tenements described in the last chapter. The remaining part is mostly freehold, which has increased with the enclosure of commons ; and sometimes whole parishes, or manors, have been enfranchised on those occasions. Copyhold and leasehold are rarely met with."

In the chapter, " Obstacles to Improvement," the Reporters make the following well judged and benevolent remarks, on the *customary tenure* of Cumberland.

P. 263. " One great obstacle to improvement, seems to arise from a laudable anxiety in the customary tenants to have their little patrimony descend to their children. These small properties (loaded with fines, heriots, and boon days, joined to the necessary expense of bringing up and educating a numerous family), can only be handed down, from father to son, by the utmost thrift, hard labour, and penurious living ; and every little saving being hoarded up for the payment of the *eventful fine,* leaves nothing for the expenses of travelling, to see improved modes of culture, and to gain a knowledge of the management and profits of different breeds of stock, and be convinced, by ocular proofs, that their own situations are capable of producing similar advantages." And further, " the *customary tenure* is allowed, on all hands, to be a great grievance, and check to improvement. Would not this be best done away on the division of commons, as was the case at Brampton,

&c.

&c. where Lord CARLISLE had one-twelfth for his
consent, as lord of the soil, and for enfranchising the
allotments ? There are other lords who ask one-fourth
for their consent and enfranchising*. The yearly
value of the various customs, fines, &c. might be
easily settled by commissioners, and twenty-five years
purchase on *this value*, be the price of enfranchise-
ment, which might be allowed out of the allotment,
upon the division of a common ; or paid in money,
at the option of the tenant." (p. 264.)

I cordially agree with the Reporters, in the propriety of abolishing those vexatious and impolitic
remnants of feudal vassalage†. But I cannot think
that the precise means, which they propose, are well
calculated to bring about so desireable a change. It
is not merely the estimated annual value of the fines,
heriots, annual rents, and services, that is to be
brought into the account ; but, likewise, the incalcu-
lable benefits to arise on being relieved from the train
of evils, above enumerated ; which must necessarily
gall and fetter every man who holds under so base a
tenure. Twenty-five years purchase is but a moderate offer, for the former considerations. From thirty
to thirty-three years' purchase appears, to me, to be
a more reasonable and fair price, for the whole.

IMPROVEMENT of ESTATES.—*Reclaiming wild
Lands*. On this subject we find the following judicious remarks, concerning the breaking up of *well soiled
commons*.

P. 214. " From the abundant crops produced by
land which has never grown grain before, the occupier
vainly thinks that it will always continue to do
so;

_____

" * The portion given to the lords of manors, for their consent as
lord of the soil, in most parts of the kingdom, is one-sixteenth. The
part to be allowed for enfranchising will depend on the nature of
the tenure."

† See TREATISE on LANDED PROPERTY, Art. *Chief Rents*.

so ; and the deception is still increased by the stimu-
lating effects of lime ; but alas ! after having got nine
or ten crops, the golden prospect vanishes : the farther they proceed, the more they are convinced of
their error ; and growing corn having become a losing
trade, the land is left to grass. But what can it produce ? Already exhausted by repeated corn crops,
and over doses of lime, it remains a spectacle of the
bad effects of such culture, and a warning to others
to avoid the same course. Even under this treatment,
the increased value is in the ratio of three or four to
one. Had these lands been continued in tillage only
three years at one time ; the first year oats ; second,
fallow, turnips, or rape ; the third, wheat or oats, or
(if the soil suited) barley, sown up with clover and
ray-grass, and depastured with sheep for three, four,
or five years, according to circumstances and situations ; we will venture to say, the land would have
gone on improving from rotation to rotation ; would
have been more profitable, and put on a very different aspect to what it does at present, and have been
worth double the rent it now lets for."

The subsequent mode of reclaim belongs to *heathlands.*—P. 241. " At Bleatarn, Mr. RICHARDSON has
made great improvement, on a poor black moory soil,
growing very short heath, in its original state not
worth sixpence per acre. He ploughs in autumn,
and lets it lie till the autumn following ; then ploughs
across ; and the next summer makes a complete
fallow, which he limes, after the rate of one hundred
and fifty bushels per acre ; and in April or May following sows it with grass seeds (without corn) in the
following proportion per acre : white clover, 8 lb. ;
red, 4 lb. ; rib-grass, 4 lb. ; ray-grass, 1 bushel and a
half ; and common hay-seed, 6 bushels."

And the subjoined to *Morasses.*—P. 242. " Near
Naward Castle, Mr. RAMSHAY has made great exertions in reclaiming peat-moss, *by throwing it up with a
spade,* into round ridges seven yards wide ; the top
being

being from twelve to eighteen inches higher than the furrow, which is cut deep enough to act as an open drain. In this state it lies all winter: in the spring following, he covers it nearly an inch thick with a compost, formed of five loads of earth to one of lime; and upon this dressing, sows,

Common hay-seeds, ... 12 bushels per acre. (!)
Ray-grass, ... 2 ditto.
Rib-grass, ... 2 or 3lb. ditto."

Irrigation is recommended, as an improvement of the lands of Cumberland; and with much propriety. Not only the limestone, but the slate-rock, waters would, it is probable, prove highly beneficial, if judiciously applied. It is not, however, on the low flat, dead-lying lands, on the margins of the lakes and the larger rivers, that much, I believe, can be effected. Lakes and sluggish rivers are difficult to lift above their banks. The most probable improvement to be made, on a large scale, by irrigation, in this county, is, I apprehend, that of leading the smaller streams— the brooks and rivulets—of slate-rock water, over the feet and lower skirts of the hills,—in the DEVONSHIRE manner :—by this mean obtaining, at a small expense, a valuable supply of winter fodder for mountain stock.

Markets. A remarkable instance of improvement is mentioned, in this Report, as being effected, by an individual, through the mean of establishing a NEW MARKET and PORT, upon his Estate.

P. 260. " Maryport, in the year 1752, consisted of only one farm-house; in that year another house was built. It is now a neat, well-built, middle-sized market-town, with a small and good harbour, enclosed by two piers; and in 1793 contained 3445 inhabitants, which increase about 100 yearly. The ground upon which the town is built belonged to HUMPHREY SENHOUSE, Esq. To encourage settlers, he sold off house and yard-steads, reserving a ground-rent. The land around it letts for 2 or 3*l.* an acre, which would not
have

have been worth more than 1*l.* had things remained as they were in 1752."

We are not informed, however, of the expense incurred, in bringing about this extraordinary increase of rental value.

On the *introduction* of *improvements,* in Agriculture, this Report brings forward two instances; further corroborating what has been suggested, in the Northumberland Report. See p. 87.

P. 222. " *Turnips*—were first cultivated in this county, to any effect, for the use of cattle, by PHILIP HOWARD, Esq. of Corby, in the year 1755 : his first essay was drilled at four feet distance; the crop amazingly good; the weight, on an average, 10lb. each turnip ; some weighed 25lb. ; he afterwards continued to grow them at two feet, and two feet and a half distance, with constant success, for eight or ten years, before any farmer followed the example ; at last, Mr. COLLINS, of Wetherall, made a trial, and succeeded : others soon followed him."

P. 228. " We were informed, that in 1752, no person in the county had thought of sowing a field down with clover, or even hay-seeds; and that PHILIP HOWARD, Esq. of Corby, was the first who sowed a field with clover, and taught his countrymen the use of artificial grasses ; yet it is but a few that have benefited by his laudable exertions."

On the EXECUTIVE MANAGEMENT of Estates, we find few remarks, in this Report, except what relate to

Leases.—P. 211. " The *Noblemen* and Gentlemen who enjoy the most considerable landed property in this county, *lett no leases;* some have verbal contracts for seven years, which are next to none ; and of those who lett leases, the term is only for five, seven, or nine years ; besides the usual reservations of mines, wood, &c. the tenant covenants to pay the rent, cesses, taxes, and to keep all in repair ; some are confined to a certain quantity of tillage, and to fallow one-
fourth

fourth yearly; others are under no restraint of this
kind; a few others are confined to lay on a certain
quantity of lime, and to sow with white clover and
hay-seeds, the lands that are laid to grass: these are
the principal covenants that affect Agriculture. To
enumerate such as are of a local nature, respecting
the performance of customs, services, grinding corn,
payment of chickens, &c. would add little to the improvement of Agriculture, or enlargement of rural
science."

P. 208. " Repairs are generally made at the joint
expense of landlord or" (and) " tenant ; the former
supporting walls, doors, and timber; and the latter
thatch, slate, glass, &c."

In speaking of " Obstacles to Improvement," the
Reporters introduce the ingenious arguments, subjoined, in favor of *long leases*.

P. 264. " *Letting no Leases*, or leases for five or
seven years, is another great obstacle to improvement.
To such proprietors of land we would beg leave to
hint, that no tenant will ever make improvements
under the uncertainties of a *short lease*, much less
where there is *none*. A tenant may be well convinced, that by proper culture, draining, improved
breeds of stock, &c. he could make his farm, in a few
years, worth *one-third* more than it is at present; but
this cannot be done without laying out money : suppose 100*l*. and suppose, by this means, the increased
yearly value of his crop is 20*l*. Now it is clear, it will
be six years before he can be repaid the principal and
interest of the sum expended. Should his lease expire
in the fifth year, he would be a loser; and should he
have no lease, he might be turned off his farm at the
end of the second year. Under such circumstances,
the chance of loss is much greater than the prospect
of gain. By reasoning in this manner, he concludes,
that it is safer to have his 100*l*. at interest at 5 per
cent. than risk it in improving his farm under such

uncertainties; and that it will be the surest game, to take *every advantage* of the farm in his power.

"On the other hand, if his lease had been for twenty-one years, he would have foreseen, that, by laying out his 100*l.* he would gain 200*l.*; and, as "the hope of reward sweetens labour," he would have doubled his exertions, and gone on from improvement to improvement; and at the expiration of his term, his landlord would have the satisfaction of seeing his tenant had acquired a competency, his farm increased in value, and the community benefited by the increased produce. We have heard, it is true, some arguments urged in favour of letting *no leases*; such as would have been used by a feudal lord, and which, we are persuaded, cannot long be held by liberal and benevolent minds, enlightened by science, or anxious to promote the true interests of their country."

I am well aware, however, that not these nor any other arguments will prevail, at present, with many men of large property, to grant long leases. I therefore embrace this as a favorable opportunity of recommending to proprietors of estates in general, to adopt the TRIENNIAL LEASE, with REMUNERATIONS for UNREAPED IMPROVEMENTS. See TREATISE on LANDED PROPERTY, 4to. ed. pp. 365 and 372, or 8vo. ed. pp. 379 and 385.

Rent.—P. 210. "In the vicinity of towns, land letts (in 1797?) from 2*l.* to 4*l.* an acre; farms at a distance from towns, from 5 to 30*s.* per acre; in general, the average may be stated at about 15*s.* per acre; rent is almost universally paid in money."

DIVISION THE SECOND.

WOODLANDS and PLANTATIONS. ·

THE Reporters' remarks, on these subjects, are concise; but, nevertheless, (except in one particular) satisfactory.

WOODLANDS.

WOODLANDS.—P. 234. "This county is far from
being well wooded. The Irthing, Eden, and Caldew,
are the only rivers whose banks produce any quantity
of *natural wood*; and of these, the banks of the Caldew
seem to have the largest proportion of old oak-timber.
Of the value of the oak-timber proper for the purposes
of ship-building, we could obtain no satisfactory information, but suspect, from what we saw, it is of
small extent; we fear the oak is not suffered to attain
a sufficient age for this purpose; as we saw a wood
near West Ward (now felling) of upwards of two
hundred acres, that was little more than thirty years
old, the whole cut away, without leaving any to stand
for ship timber." But was not this wood, and are
not other tall coppice woods, in Cumberland, cut for
the use of the collieries?

PLANTATIONS.—P. 234. "Of late years, many
plantations have been made near gentlemen's seats,
which shew, by their vigorous growth, how well
adapted the greatest part of this county is for the production of wood. From the nakedness of the country
along the coast, one would naturally conclude, that
the situation was inimical to that production; but
Lord MUNCASTER's extensive and thriving plantations
near Ravenglass, shew that the nakedness of the land
is owing to other causes*."

P. 235. "Many parts of these districts might be
applied to planting with considerable advantage, and
would, probably, in this way, make a better return
than if the soil had been in such a situation as to admit
of being converted into tillage. We were glad to see
a large plantation of larches thriving exceedingly well,
on the steep edge of the west side of Skiddaw, lately
planted by Mr. STORY. We hope the example will
be

"* If a customary tenant plants wood, he cannot cut it without
leave of the lord; in some cases, the lord claims it as his own; which
sufficiently explains why the occupiers do not plant wood."

be speedily and extensively followed by every proprietor of similar situations."

AGRICULTURE.

FARMS.—*Sizes.* P. 209. "On the large estates,
there are some farms from 100*l.* to 150*l.* a year, few
reach 200*l.* and we only heard of four or five, that got
as high as 3 or 400*l.* a year, and one of 600*l.*; but
the most general size of farms in this county, is from
15*l.* to 50*l.* a year."

Homestalls.—The authors of the Cumbrian Report
very justly observe, in the section " Houses of Proprietors," p. 207, that " Descriptions of gentlemen's
seats, we presume, come more under the notice of a
topographical survey, than an agricultural one."

P. 207. " Through the greatest part of this county,
the *farm-houses* are remarkably well built of stone;
the blue slate roofs, and white dashed walls, give
them a look of neatness that is peculiarly pleasing,
and prepossesses a stranger with a favourable idea of
the cleanliness of the inhabitants; an idea which he
finds well founded on further investigation."

This style of building, however, is chiefly confined
to the vallies and margins of the western mountains:
and it is remarkable that the same description of
country habitations prevails, with striking similarity,
in Cumberland, in South Wales, and in Devonshire.
Building materials are nearly the same in all: and
they were once, perhaps, inhabited by the same race
of people.

For the *cottages* of Cumberland, see the section
LABORERS.

OCCUPIERS. P. 209. " Cumberland farmers may
be

be divided into three classes: the occupiers of large farms; the small proprietors (provincially " *lairds*," or " *statesmen*"), and the small farmers.

" It is to the first class, and the gentlemen farmers, that this district owes the introduction of any of the modern improvements in agriculture; and we were glad to find a spirit of enterprize arising amongst them, for the adoption of new modes of culture, and improved breeds of stock.

" *To the small Proprietors*, Agriculture, we presume, is little indebted for its advancement: these " statesmen" seem to inherit with the estates of their ancestors, their notions of cultivating them, and are almost as much attached to the one as the other: they are rarely aspiring, and seem content with their situation, nor is luxury in any shape an object of their desires; their little estates, which they cultivate with their own hands, produce almost every necessary article of food; and clothing, they in part manufacture themselves; and have a high character for sincerity and honesty, and probably few people enjoy more ease and humble happiness.

" *The small Farmer* is obliged to raise such crops as will pay him best for the present, and avoid every expense of which he does not receive the immediate advantage, by which means his farm and himself are always kept in a state of poverty: many of these small farmers are also mechanics, and agricultural laborers, that farm from 5*l.* to 10 or 12*l.* a year."

MANAGEMENT of FARMS. In Cumberland, as in Northumberland, we find the Reporters recommending mixed cultivation; or an alternacy of arable crops and herbage. They, here, enter somewhat into detail; and in a didactic manner. But I do not perceive any thing, in their remarks, which requires particular notice.

SUCCESSION of CROPS. P. 219.—" The most prevalent system, through a great part of this county, is, to have a crop of white corn every year while in
ploughing;

ploughing; such cultivators make no fallows, except ploughing twice, and manuring for barley, can be deemed such.

" Where a a field in ploughed out from grass, they have oats,—oats,—barley,—oats; or, oats,—barley,—oats,—oats, &c. &c. for nine or twelve years, and then left to grass for seven or nine years. Some few sow hay-seeds and a little white clover; but the greatest part leave it to Nature*." These facts are worth preserving, as the remains of a " system," at the close of the eighteenth century, which, at its commencement, was pretty common, I apprehend, to the kingdom at large;—where the feudal system did not interfere.

LABORERS. In the section " Cottages," we are furnished with a general idea of the laborers of Cumberland.—P. 208. " Of this description of buildings there are not many purposely erected for laborers in agriculture, very few of that class being wanted in this county: as the farms are so small, the occupiers and their families are generally sufficient for the work, without any foreign aid."

And, in the chapter " Rural Economy," the Reporters have entered into particulars, respecting this subject.—P. 253. " From the number of small farms, there is an uncertainty of a day-laborer meeting with constant employment, as the occupiers want assistance only on particular occasions.

" On this principle we account for the high wages given in this county; through the whole of which there is an universal custom of giving the laborers *victuals*, both men and women;—the wages are,

" For men, per day, 10*d*. and victuals; in harvest, 1*s*. and victuals. For women, hay-making, 8*d*. and victuals;

" * On asking a farmer at Uldale why they sowed no clover, or grass-seeds, he replied, ' *we have no occasion, for the land is naturally girs-proud.*' "

victuals; harvest, 10*d.* and victuals.   The hours from 6 to 6.

"The victuals are estimated at 8*d.* per day for men, and 6*d.* for women.   Servants kept in the house, are only hired for half a year, to prevent gaining settlements: their wages for that time are, a man, from 5*l.* to 7*l.*; women, 2*l.* to 3*l.*   Masons, without victuals, are from 1*s.* 8*d.* to 2*s.* per day; carpenters, 1*s.* 6*d.*

"When work is done by the piece, the prices are as follows:

		s.	*d.*
Thrashing wheat, per bushel, ...		0	2
———— barley, ditto, ...		0	2
———— oats, ditto, ...		0	1¾
Ploughing, per acre, ...		5	0
Reaping, per acre, ...		5	0
Mowing, per acre, ...		2	6
Walling, per square yard, ...		0	8"

These, I suppose, are to be considered (nothing to that effect is expressed) as the *par* prices, in 1793 or 4.

Working Animals.   P. 218.   "Tillage Land is here commonly ploughed by horses; a team of oxen, we believe, is not to be found in the county: the horses are yoked double, and driven with cords by the ploughman."

P. 250. "The *Horses* are middle-sized, from fourteen to fifteen and a half hands high, of various colours; but bays and chesnuts seem the most prevalent: for a small farm, where horses must answer for both draught and riding, they are probably most suitable; but certainly might be improved by stallions from the North Riding of Yorkshire—the best breed of horses we know for the double purpose above-mentioned.

"About 70 or 80 years since, teams of oxen, or oxen yoked with horses, were very common; from that period draught oxen gradually decreased; and
for

for some years past, we were informed, there has not been an ox-team in the county."

This circumstance may be readily accounted for, by the breed of cattle which the Cumberland farmers had to work. Aukward, thickwinded longhorned oxen* are as improper for working, as heavy slow-paced shorthorns. Beside, as the Reporters justly observe, " horses must answer for both draught and riding," on the small farms of Cumberland. No wonder, then, that oxen are not worked, *there.* And as Messrs. Bailey and Culley cannot be considered as advocates for small two-horse farms, they surely will not be suspected,—from any thing that appears in the Cumberland Report,—of wishing to convey, *generally,* that oxen, of a proper breed and on farms of a proper size, are unfit for the purposes of draft, in husbandry. What they have thought fit to bring forward, on the subject, may rather serve to show, that very small farms are unprofitable to the community; forasmuch as they do not admit of the most profitable mode of culture.

IMPLEMENTS. Under this head, I find nothing to notice; excepting what relates to *single-horse carts:*— on which, at present popular topic, the Reporters' remarks are mostly accurate and just. They are of some length. But the subject being of considerable importance,—not only in regard to Agriculture, but to Roads,—I think it right to transcribe them.

P. 212. " *The Carts,* through the whole of this county, are drawn by a single horse," (single horses) " and probably originated through necessity, from the small farmer keeping no more than one horse. In those times, simplicity and cheapness were only considered: we recollect seeing some of those " *tumble carrs,*" without one piece of iron about them; the wheels were made of three pieces of wood, joined by
pins

---

* See YORKSHIRE. Sect. *Breed* of *Cattle.*

pins of the same material. It is probable they had the name of *tumble carrs*, from the axle being made fast in the wheels, and the whole turning, or tumbling round together: but this construction has given way to the wheel with a nave and spokes, turning round a fixed axle; which is much more manageable, in quick or short turns*.

" The advantages of single-horse carts are so well understood in this county, that we did not see any other used.

" Three single horse-carts are driven, without any difficulty, by a man, or a boy, or even women and girls: along the coast, more than half the carts are driven by females, and many of these under twenty years of age, with as fine forms and complexions as ever Nature bestowed on the softer sex."

P. 272. " *To the Notice of other Districts*, we would beg leave to recommend the use of *single-horse carts:* having been long convinced of their utility,

* THE SINGLE-HORSE CART is merely an improvement of the MOUNTAIN SLEDGE; which is formed with a pair of long shafts, without wheels; the lower and larger ends of the shafts dragging on the ground: a species of single-horse carriage which is still in use, in different mountain districts.

The first and lowest stage of improvement of the shaft sledge, which I have seen, is that of shoeing the ends of the shafts with iron, to prevent their wearing;—the next, to insert a very small wheel (a friction wheel) in the end of each, to ease the draft; the third, to fix two circular pieces of plank, 12 to 15 inches diameter, by square mortices, upon the ends of a round axle, which turns with the wheels, in the manner above mentioned;—the fourth to enlarge the " log wheels," by joining, ingeniously and with some taste, three pieces of plank, and thus increasing the diameter to 20 or 30 inches: but still the ends of the axle are square, and its middle, or bearing parts, round. This is the " Cumberland Cart," and is still in use in that county and its neighbourhood. The last and highest stage of improvement, of the shaft sledge, is the fixed axle-tree, with spoked wheels turning upon it, in the ordinary manner of wheel carriages; but of a small light construction, fit for one horse to draw. This is, at present, the more prevailing carriage of the lower lands of Cumberland. *Rev.*

utility, we are glad to have an opportunity of stating to the public a few facts, which will fully evince their superior advantages.

" The horses of Cumberland are not of a large size: one fifteen hands high, of a light form, that will answer either for riding or drawing, seldom draws less in a single-horse cart than .... 12 *cwt.*

" The common load for a *draught horse* of the above size is, ... 15

" The carriers from Brampton to Newcastle, over a hilly country, carry frequently, ... 18

" We met a carrier's boy driving five carts from Longtown to Newcastle; in which were four ton; or on each cart, ... 16

" A single-horse cart carried ten pigs of lead, of twelve stone each, which is 15

" From the above it may be fairly concluded, that the common load for a single-horse cart, will be about 15 cwt.

" In most countries, a two horse-cart seldom carries more than .... 20 *cwt.*

" Nor a three-horse cart more than 30

" Here a boy or a girl drives two single-horse carts, which carry 30

" Of course, *two horses*, yoked in *single-horse carts*, will draw as much as *three horses* yoked in *one cart*.

" A common carrier at Carlisle, who many years employed a waggon, has laid it aside, and now uses *single-horse carts only;* as he finds he can, by that means, carry much greater weights.

" There are few articles which may not be carried on a carriage of two wheels, equally as well as upon one of four, except long timber; and as waggons are so destructive to roads*, why should their use be longer

" * The superior goodness of the roads in Cumberland may, in a great measure, be attributed to the universal use of single-horse carts.—

longer persisted in, as it is clear that the same number of horses yoked in single-horse carts, will draw
more than when yoked six or eight together;—they
are easier loaded and unloaded, are much more handy,
for almost every purpose; and six or eight may be
driven by a man and a boy, which is a trifling additional expense. If a middle-sized Cumberland horse
draws 15 cwt. a large strong waggon horse will as
easily draw 20 cwt. and which is done in some parts
of the kingdom."

Thus, we are furnished with almost every thing
that can be said *in favor* of single-horse carts. But,
in recommending, to the kingdom at large, a change
of such magnitude, it were but right—only fair—
to enumerate the *disadvantages*, as well as the benefits,
to arise from it. In a revolution, there is generally
some risk ;—and more or less evil, as well as good, to
be expected.

A common objection to changing waggons and
long teams, for single-horse carts, is the increase of
carriages. Beside, where carters and waggoners are
accustomed to the long whip, and where each has only
one carriage to take care of, it would be some length
of time before they could be brought to take the
charge of three or four, each ;—and to help them up
the hills, in the manner I have seen practised,—by
placing the shoulder to the tail of the cart :—not so
much to assist in forcing it forward, as to throw
weight on the horses' back, and thereby enable him
to exert his strength with better effect. This, in a
hilly

carts.—Wherever waggons are used, they are the destruction of
roads, especially in hilly countries, where they are obliged to lock
the wheels; the banks are in a manner ploughed up with them,
and the nine inch wheels are, in reality, no more than three inch
wheels, by the artful mode of laying on the middle course of tyre,
which is *raised an inch above the rest:* instead of being nearly exempted from tolls, every *horse* drawing in a *waggon*, ought to pay
treble to what should be exacted from a *horse* drawing in a *single-
horse cart."*

hilly country is a serious objection to one-horse carts (of the construction now in common use); as, in a long team, the fore horses perform what the man attempts. In a waggon, no such assistance is required. In harvest, carts are unsteady and aukward to load; and a low load is inconvenient at the stack, or a high mow. On public roads, an inconveniency arises, to travellers in carriages, from crowds of carts, haltered together in strings, winding across the road*.

Nevertheless, with those, and other, inconveniences that might doubtlessly be mentioned, one-horse carts may, in some situations, be preferable to long teams: even for a farmer.

Their superiority, in regard to roads, appears to be evident; and I am of opinion that they ought to be favored in tolls:—a measure which, sooner perhaps than any other, would bring them, gradually, into common use. They ought, however, to be restricted, as to weight. For it is observable that horses (most horses) drawing singly, exert themselves, more, than when they are associated; and a horse, in harness, will ever tear up and injure a road, in proportion to his exertions. Beside, it is to be considered, that a *cart* carrying 15 cwt. does the road nearly as much harm, as twice that weight carried upon a *waggon*. There is, however, one considerable advantage of single-horse carts over long teams:—they are not so liable to wear roads into ruts and horse tracks: a circumstance that is well worth the attention of the commissioners of turnpikes.

I have thought it right to discuss this subject, here, with a degree of analytical attention, Cumberland (and its neighbourhood) being the only part of *England*, in which one-horse carts (of different constructions)

---

* An attempt, I understand, was recently made to introduce strings of one-horse carts into the streets of London!

structions) are universally in common use, as carriages of burden.

MANURES. P. 239. " *Lime* is found in great abundance in many parts of this county, and of excellent quality. The quantity laid upon an acre varies from sixty to an hundred and fifty bushels ; we found it a general opinion, that lime did little good to land that had been long accustomed to it ; and that those who had used the large quantity of 150 bushels per acre, found their lands greatly exhausted, and were now fully convinced of their error in continuing it so long, especially in such large quantities." Again,—" Lime is mostly laid on, while the land is in a state of fallow ; but in some places, we found it laid upon the grass land, *one* or *two* years before they intended to plough it out."

" *Tangle*, or *Sea Weed*," p. 239, " is used along the coast, wherever it can be got ; the quantity per acre is fifty or sixty cart-loads. This is known to be a valuable manure, either for corn, turnips, or grass, wherever it can be had.

" *Slake* or *Mud*, left by the tide, is used in the neighbourhood of Ravenglass, with good effect, on the grass lands, fifty or sixty cart-loads per acre.

Muscles, are also used in the neighbourhood of Ravenglass, for manure, after the rate of five or six cart-loads per acre ; they are got on the sands adjoining the coast.

" *Sea Sand*.—An accidental experiment of Lord MUNCASTER'S shewed its utility in destroying moss, but it is not used as a manure.

" *Compost*.—It seems a general practice through every part of the county, to make a compost of lime and earth, in the proportion of one cart-load of lime to four or five of earth : they use it as a top-dressing to their grass lands, and find it very beneficial."

TILLAGE. P. 218.—" Fallowing for wheat and turnips is practised in many parts of this county ; four or five ploughings and harrowings is the general practice: we saw some very clean, and well managed, gathered up into neat narrow ridges, on which the wheat was looking very healthy."

SEMINATION. P. 240. " All kinds of grain are sown broad-cast."

GROWING CROPS. P. 240. " The only weeding it gets is by hand : hoeing a crop of corn, we believe, was never practised in the county. Turnips and potatoes are the only crops in which weeds are destroyed by hoeing."

WHEAT. P. 220. " Wheat is a modern production here; a general opinion used to prevail, that wheat could not be grown in many parts of this county. We were informed, that it is not much more than 40 years since summer-fallows for wheat were first used; and it is not twenty years since Lord MUNCASTER introduced summer-fallows, and the culture of wheat, in the neighbourhood of Ravenglass, where it is now grown in great abundance, as well as all along the coast of Scotland, and in the neighbourhood of Carlisle. The wheat that is sown after turnips or clover, is trifling, the main supply is from summer-fallows; they generally sow two bushels and a half per acre, in September or October, as the season suits, and they reap from sixteen to thirty bushels per acre."

" BARLEY and OATS, (p. 221.) being the grains from which the bread of the inhabitants is made, were probably the first, and only corn grown in this county for many centuries; *bigg*, or *bear*, with four rows of grains on the ear, was the kind of barley formerly cultivated; but lately, the common early sort, with two rows, has been introduced. They sow two and a half bushels per acre, in April or May, and reap twenty-one bushels on an average.

" *The common Oat*—was the only variety grown in this county, and is now by far the most prevalent; but of late years, a few enterprizing individuals have introduced the early varieties of this grain with great advantage." In

In a note, " the potatoe oat is now (1804) very generally grown in the best districts of the county."

This variety of the oat, I believe, is of Cumbrian
origin : and, among many other instances, shows how
readily superior varieties of cultivated crops may be
raised. This may well be termed an *accidental* variety. Its existence literally hung on a thread. A
female laborer (as I was informed on the borders)
observing the fine appearance of a plant of oats which
grew in a potatoe ground, where she was at work,
carried it home, and suspended it, as an ornament,
to the roof of her cottage; where it hung, some
twelve months or more, before it was noticed, by an
enterprising farmer of the neighbourhood ; who planted its produce ; and, by this easy mean, raised a
superior variety ; which has rapidly spread over the
island ;—even to the most distant extreme from the
place of its origin. And, it may be added, valuable
as this variety is allowed to be, it is possible that a
still superior one may be discovered by attending
carefully to the individuals of its produce. But see
note p. 78. aforegoing.

PEAS,—we are informed, are stacked in trees !
(p. 221) to secure them from the wind, and to finish
their drying. In the Highlands of Scotland, I have
seen three tall poles, set up trianglewise, for those
purposes. The peas are piled round a sufficient
number of triangles so set up : thus leaving hollow
cones, or pyramidal spaces, in the middles of the
stacklets. These being small, the wind blows through
the thin light coverings ; which are secured, with
ropes, from being torn off by the wind. In exposed,
tempestuous situations, and in a moist climature, some
expedient of this sort may be eligible.

TURNIPS. See p. 178. aforegoing. In some few
other parts of the county, as well as in the neighbourhood of Weatherall, they are partially cultivated,
p. 222.

CULTIVATED HERBAGE. After what we have
learned,

learned, concerning this subject, we cannot reasonably expect any useful information on the culture of herbage. The Cumberland farmers, however, will I hope listen to the advice of the Reporters, when they recommend "ray-grass," (p. 229) "instead of common hay-seeds, so universally sown in this county, with clover both red and white."

GRASS LAND, or perennial herbage. P. 227.— "Natural meadows are generally found in narrow strips by the sides of rivers. The largest tract of natural meadow in this county, is in the parish of Scaleby, which letts for 28 s. per acre ; also between the lakes of Keswick and Bassenthwaite, there is a considerable extent of natural meadow.

" Natural pastures are not very numerous in the cultivated districts of the county ; unless such may be called natural pasture, which is left to Nature to cover with herbage, after having been exhausted with growing corn. If by natural pastures be understood such as have never been disturbed by the plough, there will be found great abundance in this county, as not only all the commons in the cultivated districts, but the mountains, may come under that denomination."

Grazing Grounds. P. 230. " The best grazing lands we saw were at Pap Castle, near Cockermouth, lett at 3 l. per acre ; and the holm lands on both sides the Eden, near Carlisle, lett at 2 l. 10 s. per acre, for the purposes of *grazing only.*"

Moles in *Grass Lands.* The Reporters of Cumbrian practices extol that by which the moles of Cumberland are nearly extirpated.

P. 274. " A most excellent practice is prevalent here, for every parish to lett the taking of their moles, for a *term of years*, at a certain yearly sum ; which is raised in the same manner as the parochial taxes, and does not now exceed a halfpenny an acre ; which, they justly observe, was much cheaper than they could have the ground *scaled for*, were the moles not destroyed in this manner. It is a pity but there was

a law

a law to oblige every parish in the kingdom to destroy
their moles in the same manner; which is done so
effectually here, that we scarcely ever saw a mole-hill
upon the enclosed grounds of most parts of Cumberland."

These are the unqualified sentiments of men who
practise on light absorbent lands; in which moles
may well be considered as a species of vermin;—particularly while such lands are under a course of arable
crops.   But, in strong closely textured soils, incumbent on uniformly retentive bases, moles are, demonstrably, of great use.   They are the natural, and only
effectual, drainers of such soils; which frequently
baffle human art, in attempting to render them sufficiently dry and open, to enable them to produce the
more valuable species of herbage.   A contrivance to
take moles, alive, in light dry lands, and transfer them
to lands of the above description, would rank high as
an improvement in Agriculture.

The silly, yet common objection, to moles in grass
lands, because they incur some labor in spreading
their hillocks, is truly ridiculous.   Many a spirited
farmer will carry " Maiden Earth,"—" Virgin Mold"
—some distance, of course at some considerable expense, to spread over his grass lands—" to encourage
the finer grasses;"—yet think much of the trouble of
spreading such valuable " top-dressing," when placed,
there, ready to his hands !

But the act of raising fresh mold to the surface, in
a finely pulverized state, is only a minor benefit of
moles, to closely textured retentive lands : freeing
them from superfluous moisture, and furnishing the
roots of herbage, with the requisite supply of air, are
still more valuable advantages.   And these may be
had, with certainty ; by encouraging, or otherwise
stocking them with moles : precaution being previously had to intersect such lands with trenches, deep
enough to receive their discharging drains : namely,
ten or twelve inches deep.

I am

I am not here writing from the suggestions of theory: but from what I have observed in practice. If the mole plough be eligible in retentive soils, though worked at considerable expense, and requiring frequent repetitions, how much more eligible are moles, who make infinitely better work, cost free.

A prevailing, but dangerous, fault of Agricultural writers is that of *generalizing* practices that are liable to *exceptions;* and thereby leading their readers into error, instead of instructing them. And if such men, as Messrs. Bailey and Culley are not free from this oversight, how few men there are who can be safely trusted with pens, to write on rural subjects.

HORSES. The *breed* of horses, in Cumberland, has been mentioned, (Sect. *Working Animals.)* The following short notice, respecting their *breeding* and *disposal*, is all we have further on the subject.

P. 250. " Almost every small farmer breeds his own horses, and generally more than are necessary for the cultivation of his farm; these are often purchased by dealers, for the purpose of supplying the light-horse regiments."

CATTLE. On the *breed* of Cumberland, the Reporters speak as follow :

P. 244. " The *cattle* are a small breed of long-horns, with a few exceptions of the Galloway breed intermixed, particularly along the coast from Whitehaven to Carlisle.

" *This breed of Long-Horns* is not distinguished by any peculiar good qualities, which is not to be wondered at, when it is considered that, probably at this time, there is not one person in the county that pays any attention to its improvement. Twenty years ago, Mr. HAZLE, of Dalemain, had made some progress in this business, and gained a very useful breed of long-horned cattle; but his successors neglected them, and the labours of the good old man are totally lost.

" The long-horned, and the Galloway polled cattle,

are

are probably the best adapted to this county of any other; but the kind of long-horns that occupy it at present, may certainly be much improved by paying proper attention to breed always from the best males and females that can be selected. This end would be the readiest attained by getting good bulls and heifers from the midland counties, where the long-horned breed are brought to great perfection."

These remarks are liable to objections. The Cumbrian breed of cattle are certainly "a small breed of longhorns,"—comparatively, I mean, with that of the midland counties. But I cannot admit that "this breed of longhorns is not distinguished by any peculiarly good qualities." For I find in my journals (formed with the subjects before my eyes) in examining the mountain districts of Cumberland and Westmoreland, abundant evidence to the contrary. The cleanness and symmetry of their form, though frequently striking, is a less admirable distinguishment than that of their thriving on bleak mountain pastures. I observed them, in high condition, on the sides, and even on the heathy summits, of some of the higher hills! their size being rather too large, than too small, for their pastures.

I entirely agree with the Reporters, however, in that they may be improved, by selection:—"by paying proper attention to breed always from the best males and females that can be selected." But I cannot believe that the naturalized breed of these mountains can receive much improvement, by "bulls and heifers from the midland counties." In the *district* of *Carlisle*, such a change might be eligible: but certainly not, on Skiddaw, Saddleback, Wrynose, and Hardknot,—where the descendants of the Canley, the Dishley, or the Rollright breed would, I conceive, find themselves far above their element. No *mountain* farmer, I hope, has followed, in this particular, the advice of the Board's Reporters.

Rearing Cattle. P. 245. "On those farms that have

have a right of common, the grass lands are employed through the summer in growing hay, depasturing their cows, and sometimes young cattle; but the latter are more generally summered on the commons, and in autumn brought into the old enclosures, till the approach of winter, when all the cattle are housed."

Dairies. P. 244. " *The Dairies* are small, and mostly employed in making butter, of an *excellent quality.* Those that are situated in the vicinity of towns, sell it weekly, by the pound, to supply the consumption of the inhabitants. In other situations, it is put into firkins of 56lb. each, and sent to distant markets.

" The average quantity of butter from one cow, is generally estimated from one to two firkins: (?) some cows will give twelve quarts of milk at a meal, and make seven pounds of butter per week ; but the most general average is seven or eight quarts of milk at a meal, and from three to five pounds of butter per week, through the summer.

" Skimmed-milk *cheese* is the principal kind made here, and chiefly consumed at home."

Grazing Cattle. P. 230. " The kinds of cattle usually fatted are, the native country breed, and Scotch cattle, both kyloes and the Galloway kind. Of these, they find the kyloes the quickest feeders, the Galloway next, and their own country breed of longhorns the slowest.

" The profits of grazing cattle depend much on the skill of the buyer, in *selecting* the *quickest feeders* : and, when fat, in selling them for their *full value ;* also, not unfrequently, on the state of markets."

Those observations are not new; but they convey truisms that are well entitled to repetition ; and I am glad to find them in the Cumberland Report.

SHEEP. The following account is valuable ; as in it we find a satisfactory description of a variety of sheep of which extraordinary tales have been told.

P. 245.

P. 245. " The *Sheep* bred in this county are only of *two kinds*, and these two are probably something related : one of them is peculiar to that high, exposed, rocky, mountainous district, at the head of the Duddon and Esk rivers, more particularly known by the names of Hardknot, Scalefell, Wrynose, &c.

" Of this breed of sheep (commonly called *Herd-wicks*), the ewes and wethers are all polled or horn-less, and also many of the tups ; their faces and legs speckled ; but a great portion of white, with a few black spots on those parts, are accounted marks of the purest breed, as are also the hornless tups ; they have fine, small, clean legs. We are told that the lambs, when dropt, are well covered ; the wool is short, and forms a thick matted fleece, much finer than that of the black-faced heath sheep ; with which variety they seem to have been crossed, as we suspect, from some of the rams having spiral horns, and from some *kemps* or *hairs* being intermixed amongst some fleeces of the wool : they are lively little animals, well adapted to seek their food amongst these rocky mountains, which in many places are stony and bare ; and, where covered, the soil is thin, but the herbage mostly green, though heath is found on their summits. They have no hay in winter, and support themselves in the deepest snows by scratching down to the heath, or other herbage ; indeed, it seldom happens but that some parts of the mountains are blown bare, which the sheep find out. They do not face the coming storm, as reported, but, like other sheep, turn their backs on it ; and, in such weather, they generally gather toge-ther, and keep stirring about ; by which means they tread down the snow, keep above it, and are rarely overblown.

The loss per cent. per ann. is, of *hogs**, from 5 to 10.

Ditto ditto, of old sheep, ... from 2 to 5.

                                  " The

" * Provincial term for sheep, from six months old till being first shorn."

" The ewes are kept as long as they will breed lambs, and are often from ten to fifteen years of age before they are sold : the wethers go off at four years and a half old. Both ewes and wethers are sold from these mountains, and killed without being put on any better pasture: we saw a carcass of one of the wethers at Ravenglass, very good mutton, which weighed 11 lb. a quarter, and had 10 or 12 lb. of tallow. The ewes weigh from 6 to 8 lb. a quarter; the fleece weighs 2 lb. and sold last year at 6 d. per pound, which we think much below its value.

" The mountains on which these sheep are bred happen not to be common, but belong to Lord MUNCASTER; as do also the stock that depasture them, which have, time immemorial, been farmed out to *herds*, at a yearly sum. From this circumstance, these farms (three or four in number) have obtained the name of *Herdwicks*; that is, the district of the *herds*; and the sheep, the appellation of *Herdwick sheep.* They have obtained such a character for *hardiness of constitution*, that Mr. TYSON *, who farms the principal flock, sells a number of tups every year into various parts of the county, to *improve the hardiness of other flocks*; the price is often as high as two guineas and a half."

What follows, I cannot admit.—P. 247. " The sheep, through the whole of this county (except the *Herdwicks*), have been descended from the *black-faced, coarse-woolled, heath sheep*; but by crossing with some other kind (probably the *Herdwicks*), many of them have acquired a large portion of *white* on their *faces* and *legs*; some have those parts speckled, and others totally black."

This theory I conceive to be wrong. Its reverse I believe to be right. I have already had occasion to reflect

" * We were told by Lord MUNCASTER's agent. that the family of TYSONS have lived in this sequestered spot above four hundred years."

reflect and write on this subject; in the WEST of ENGLAND, section *Sheep;* and the more I examine it, the fuller is my conviction of the truth of what I have there written. In the SOUTHERN COUNTIES, I had further occasion to speak on the same subject;— in the districts—*Southern Chalk Hills,* and the *Heathlands* of *Surrey.*

It is an interesting fact, that the *unshepherded* sheep, found on common pastures, in Devonshire, in Surrey, in Derbyshire, and in Cumberland, bear a strong resemblance of each other: having, in all those distant parts of the kingdom (as well as in others) the appearance of mixed, mongrel breeds:— some of the individuals being horned, others hornless; some having black, others grey, others white, legs and faces; with wools of different qualities. This motley appearance, this apparent intermixture of breeds, is not observable within the mountainous districts of Cumberland, only; but is seen on the lower lying well soiled commons,—whether between Penrith and Carlisle, Brampton and Gillsland, or Wigtown and " Bowness:" greyfaced, and hornless being the most prevalent characteristic of the unshepherded common sheep of Cumberland.

Sheep that are kept within fences, as well as shepherded flocks in open countries, have generally a similarity, if not a uniformity, of character, in the individuals of each flock. They may well be termed CULTIVATED VARIETIES, raised by selection from the aboriginal, native, or long-established stock of the unappropriated lands of the country. One leading man selected a horned, another a hornless, one a maculate, another an immaculate, variety; as best suited his judgement, or fancy, for the lands he possessed.

These several varieties, or *breeds,* being found more profitable, or becoming more fashionable, in the respective neighbourhoods in which they were selected, than the native stock,—in time became general to the natural districts in which they were, by these evident

evident and easy means, established. Thus, originated—thus were *bred*—The poled, greyfaced breed of Devonshire. The horned, whitefaced breed of Dorsetshire, &c. The poled, black or greyfaced, finewooled breed of Sussex. The horned, blackfaced breed of Norfolk. The large, poled, greyfaced breed of Berkshire. The finewooled, whitefaced, poled breed of Herefordshire. The poled, whitefaced, longwooled breeds of the midland counties and Lincolnshire. The greyfaced, poled, finewooled breed of Shropshire. The horned, blackfaced, coarsewooled breed of the eastern morelands of Yorkshire. The poled, whitefaced breed of the Cheviot Hills :—and many others that might be enumerated. Even on a small district of the Cumberland mountains (p. 199.) where sheep have been *herded*, for a length of time, a distinct variety is found : while on the adjacent *unshepherded commons*, the *uncultivated* stock remain in possession *. The old sheep farmer's reply, p. 249, to the surveyors, when asked from whence they had their breed, was not ill put :—" Lord, Sir, they are sik as God set upon the land : we never change any." They are, no doubt, what circumstances and time have stocked the country with; having, in all probability, descended, without *foreign* admixture, from the time when this country was in the pastoral state.

A man of much less ingenuity and experience, than either of the Board's Surveyors of Cumberland, would,

---

* It may be said that the breed of the Yorkshire morelands, above-mentioned, are not strictly *shepherded*. Each flock, however, has its separate " heaf," or distinct walk, several miles perhaps in circuit. The flocks do not *intermix*. Nevertheless, in rutting time, the rams will sometimes stray ; and this will serve to account for the less pure state of this breed, on the Yorkshire morelands, than in Scotland, where they are more strictly shepherded. On the eastern skirts of the morelands—the *commons* of the northern seacoast of Yorkshire—the *intermixed stock* resemble that of the commons of Devonshire and of Cumberland !

would, in the course of a few years, raise—*breed*—
from the common stocks of different parts of the
kingdom, at this day, distinct varieties, very nearly
resembling the several distinct breeds, above enumerated: the size of the carcase, and the highly improved qualities of the flesh and wool, in some cases,
excepted. But when we consider how many centuries may have assisted in molding those breeds to
soils, climatures and established practices, and how
much ingenuity and expense have, of late years,
been bestowed, on some of them, we can no longer
doubt the practicability of such an undertaking*.
And the short question—if they were not raised by
selection from the native stock, as the different varieties of cultivated grains, and the different species
of cultivated herbage, have been raised—" from
whence came they?" can scarcely fail to convince
every man, that, by such means, they were actually
formed.

What the Reporters themselves say, in their
Chapter " Enclosures" (Rep. 215. Rev. 167.) is sufficient to show the impracticability of changing the
established qualities of common stocks : of course,
that they must necessarily have descended, nearly in
their present states, from a distant period, which may
not, now, be possible to ascertain. If this were a
place to deal in conjectures, one might say—most
probably, from the time when the select flocks of the
itinerant shepherds became intermixed on common
pastures.

On the *management* of sheep, in Cumberland, we
have the following concise, yet intelligent account.

P. 247. " *The management of sheep,* over all this
county, is very similar : through the summer, the
whole flock is depastured on the commons, and range
at large without any person to look after them. In
November,

---

* An instance, in point, is mentioned in the Durham Report.
See p. 154, aforegoing.

November, the whole are gathered together and salved * ; the old sheep are turned again upon the common, but the hogs are kept in the old enclosures, some part of which has been kept uneaten, to support them through the winter : on the approach of snow, the old sheep are brought to the enclosures, or to some part of the common adjoining, and are daily foddered with hay while the storm continues. Those who have not a sufficiency of enclosed ground for wintering their hogs, take wintering for them in those parts of the low country where they do not breed sheep ; the price 2 *s.* per head, to have hay in bad weather.

" In Eskdale and Mitredale, they formerly kept their hogs in the house all winter on hay, and drove them to water once a day ; but this practice is now laid aside, and they winter them upon the enclosed grounds, which are previously kept fresh for that purpose. They give no hay to their sheep here, which are a good deal of the *Herdwick blood.*" Beside, the climature on the south-west margin, and open to the sea air, is no doubt milder in winter, than it is in the interior, and on the north-eastern margin, of these mountains.

" * The salve is composed of butter and tar, in the proportion of sixteen pounds of the former to four quarts of the latter. This quantity will salve forty sheep."

WESTMORELAND.

THE distinct NATURAL DISTRICTS of this county are few.

The valley or district of Appleby,—including the fertile lands in the neighbourhood of Penrith, and the limestone heights on its western banks,—comprizes the principal extent of valuable lands in the county.

The slatestone mountains of Westmoreland make a part of those of Cumberland, already noticed.

The Morelands of this county, northward of the valley of the Beloe, near Brough, are naturally inseparable from those of Durham, &c. (see p. 128.) as those, to the southward of that line of separation, are from the western Morelands of Yorkshire; hereafter, to be noticed.

The valley or district of Kendal, therefore, is the only, other, natural division of the county to be spoken of, here. And this is ill defined; unless we include in it the two vallies of the Kent and the Lone (which are only partially separated, by a narrow ridge of limestone, of which they both partake) and follow them to the environs of Lancaster: by which an extensive and valuable district, is aptly formed; the plan of management at least, being, I believe, similar, throughout.

Of these districts, MY OWN INFORMATION has arisen, in travelling deliberately across the county, in different directions; with a tablet in hand, to retain whatever—of a natural, or an economical, discription—met my observation:—in repeatedly passing

ing between Lancaster and Penrith, by Burton, Kendal and Shap; in going from Kendal, by Ambleside, to Keswick; from Ambleside to Penrith, by Ulleswater; from Penrith by Appleby and Brough, into Yorkshire; and from Yorkshire, by Kirby Lonesdale, to Kendal.

The DISTRICT of APPLEBY. The immediate valley of Appleby rises out of the district of Carlisle; accompanying the Eden, from the neighbourhood of Penrith, to that of Kirby Stephen:—a distance of more than twenty miles; Appleby being situated near the midway between the two extremes. The valley is of considerable but uneven width. Its western banks take the surface, and general appearance, of a range of chalk hills, or of wavey limestone heights, which in reality they are. The eastern side of the valley is more broken; showing some extraordinary precipices of rock. The soil of this valley is various; but is mostly, I believe, fertile; though perhaps not equal in fertility to that of the Emont, which forms the northwest quarter of the district; and on the verge of which the town of Penrith is situated. This rich tract of land accompanies the Emont, from the lake of Ulleswater, to its junction with the Eden, at the foot of the valley of Appleby; where the two vallies, or broad lines of fertile lands, unite; the northern point of the limestone heights of Orton being locked in between them: thus forming a passage of country, which, though girt with mountains on every side except the north, may be classed among the most fertile, and (some allowance for its climature apart) most habitable districts in the kingdom.

The DISTRICT of KENDAL. This, too, is a well soiled passage, and partly calcareous. But its style of surface differs entirely from that of the district of Appleby. It is broken, to a degree of ruggedness. Even

Even its valley lands are set with hillocks; and their lofty banks, especially in the Kendal quarter, are strictly alpine. The valley of the Lone, in the neighbourhood of Kirby-Lonsdale, is of a tamer mold, and contains much sound, deep-soiled grazing land, of a superior quality: while in the valley of the Kent, below Kendal, we find arable lands of great fertility; and in a productive state of management.

" GENERAL VIEW

OF THE

AGRICULTURE

OF THE

COUNTY OF WESTMORELAND;

WITH

OBSERVATIONS FOR THE MEANS OF ITS IMPROVEMENT.

DRAWN UP FOR THE CONSIDERATION OF

THE BOARD OF AGRICULTURE AND INTERNAL IMPROVEMENT.

By Mr. A. PRINGLE,

OF BALENCRIEFF."

WITH

" PRELIMINARY OBSERVATIONS

BY

The BISHOP of LLANDAFF."

OF the QUALIFICATIONS of the REPORTER (proper) in this case, I am not so fortunate as to possess the smallest knowledge; saving that which is furnished by the internal evidence of his Report. By his name, and *designation*, I conclude he is of Scotland.

Respecting

Respecting Mr. PRINGLE's MODE of SURVEY, I
am equally at a loss; excepting so much as may be
gathered, from the following remark on " Houses of
Proprietors," p. 300. " From the short residence
the Author of this Report made in Westmoreland, he
cannot pretend even to enumerate the various seats
of the great proprietors throughout the county, and
the neat snug boxes belonging to gentlemen of moderate fortune, that adorn the banks of its beautiful
lakes;" and excepting what appears in the concluding
paragraphs of the Report. But whether these are
from the pen of the Reporter, or the Reportee, is not
quite evident. Whoever *wrote* them, they were
doubtlessly *printed*, under the immediate superintend-
ence of the latter. They are as follow:

P. 360. " Such are the reflections and observations
that occurred in a Survey of the state of the stock and
husbandry in the county of Westmoreland, made in
the months of October and November 1793, at the
request of the newly established Board of Agriculture.
What success has attended the attempt to place this
important matter in a just light, others will judge;
but it will be doing no more than justice to admit,
that no pains have been spared in the execution of
this task, which others might have performed with
more ability, but not with greater alacrity or zeal.

" It is impossible to conclude this Report, without
mentioning to the Board the very flattering manner
in which the person commissioned by them to make
this Survey, was received by all ranks and descriptions
of persons in the county of Westmoreland. Every
possible aid was given by the two respectable Members of the Board resident in the county. The other
individuals who assisted him, are too numerous to be
discriminated; but the Writer of this Paper will ever
remember their very polite attention with gratitude,
and his short residence in that part of the kingdom
with peculiar feelings of pleasure and respect.

" What gratitude is due to HIM, who first called
the

the attention of the nation to its most important interests, and whose unremitted efforts are directed to promote the good of his country! How well does He deserve, and what a sure road has He chosen to immortal fame, that will survive the ravages of time, and smile at the fleeting celebrity of martial achievements!" Oh! charming! charming! This, most assuredly, means not HIM, but ME!

Prefixed to this Report is a miniature MAP, by Mr. Bailey: on the same judicious principles as that of Cumberland; excepting that the different species of soils and substrata are not defined by dotted lines. The letters, however, show, with sufficient intelligence, their relative situations; and the mode of engraving distinguishes the mountains from the cultivated lands.

SUBJECT THE FIRST.

NATURAL ECONOMY.

EXTENT. The BISHOP of LLANDAFF, whose extraordinary acquirements are universally known, and whose principal residence is within this county, has condescended to employ his wonted ingenuity, to ascertain its extent with superior accuracy,—by the following method.

P. 280. "The County of Westmoreland was surveyed in 1768, and a map of it, upon a scale of an inch to a mile, was engraved by THOMAS JEFFREYS, geographer to His MAJESTY, 1770. It appears from this map, that the greatest breadth of the county, from its southern boundary, near Burton, to its northern one, near Penrith in Cumberland, is thirty-two miles; and that its greatest length, from east to west, is forty miles.

"I covered this map very exactly with fine writing paper, except the estuary near Millthrope and Windermere

dermere Lake; I then cut out a slip of the paper of
an inch in breadth, and of ten inches in length, and
weighed it accurately: from another part of the same
paper I cut another slip, two inches in breadth and
five in length, and found it to be precisely of the
same weight as the first slip; and hence, as the surfaces of the two slips were equal, we may recollect
that the paper was of an uniform thickness. The
area of each of these slips was ten square inches, and
consequently covered a space on the map equal to
ten square miles; I then weighed the whole of the
paper which had covered the map, and by comparing
the weight of the whole with the weight of what had
covered ten square miles, I found the number of
square miles in the whole to be 844; now there are
640 statute acres in a square mile, and consequently
540,160 acres in the whole county."

His Lordship, then continues,—" I measured this
map in the ordinary way, by resolving it into triangles, and found its area to be equal to 636 square
miles, or 407,040 statute acres."

This difference between the two methods, being
nearly equal to one fourth of the larger quantity, or
one third of the smaller, cannot well be reconciled
with strict accuracy of calculation: seeing that both
methods proceed on scientific principles.

The reader, however, is relieved, in a great measure, from this embarrassment, by the following statements, from Templeman and Zimmerman; which I
take the opportunity of inserting, here; as I may
have occasion to refer to them, in the course of the
present work.

P. 281. " TEMPLEMAN, in his Survey of the Globe,
makes the area of the county of Westmoreland equal
to 633 square miles, and consequently, according to
him, it contains 405,120 acres. The medium of these
three different estimates (though I am most disposed
to rely on the first) is 450,772.

" Professor ZIMMERMAN, in his Political Survey of
Europe,

Europe, estimates England and Wales at 54,112 square miles, amounting to 34,631,680 statute acres. TEMPLEMAN, in the work above-mentioned, says, that England and Wales contain 49,450 square miles, or 31,648,000 statute acres; the mean of these two gives 33,139,840 statute acres for the whole surface of England and Wales; and hence the county of Westmoreland may, in superficial content, be esteemed a seventy-third part of England and Wales."

ELEVATION and SURFACE *. P. 296. " The county in general is so mountainous and hilly, that a great proportion of it must for ever remain undisturbed by the plough. Between these mountains there are several very pleasant and fertile vallies, that want only trees and hedge-rows to be truly beautiful."

CLIMATURE. P. 296. " The climate of this county, as may be expected from its vicinity to the Western Ocean, over which the south-west winds blow for eight months of the year, and bring the exhalations to descend in rain on the mountains, is remarkably moist. The quantity of rain that falls in the west part, in a year, has been ascertained by rain-gages, kept at Kendall, and on the banks of Windermere. In the wet year, 1792, it amounted to 83 inches. In ordinary years, it amounts to 45 or 50 inches, the lowest of which is 20 inches above the medium quantity that falls in Europe. The air, however, is pure and healthful, the winters rather long and severe. In the winter 1791—92, 36l. were paid for cutting only a horse-track through the snow, upon less than ten miles of the road from Shap to Kendall." I insert these, as probable facts, though no names, or authorities, appear. Dr. Watson's residence is on the banks of Windermere.

WATERS. P. 298. " Of the numerous streams that rush

---

* Where no name is mentioned, the extracts are taken from the body of the Report.

rush from the mountains, and water the vallies beneath, there are only three that preserve their names to the ocean. The Eden, which springs in Mallerstang, and having received in its course the Eamont and the Lowther, and many little rivulets, enters Cumberland, and running the whole length of that county, empties itself into the Solway Firth below Carlisle. The Kent rises in Kentmere, washes the vale of Kendall, and loses itself in the estuary near Milthrope, the only sea-port in the county. The third is the Lon, or Lune, which has its source in Ravenstonedale, and flows through the vale (dale) to which it gives its name, till it enters the county of Lancaster, below Kirkby Lonsdale.

" Betwixt the mountains several extensive lakes are formed."

P. 298. " The rivers and lakes abound with many different kinds of fish, great part of which is now carried to Lancaster and Liverpool."

SOILS.—P. 296. " The most prevailing soil in Westmoreland, is a dry gravelly mold; sand and hazel-mold appear in various parts, but chiefly in the E. and N.; clay is found on a few farms towards the Eden, and eastern mountains, and a heavy moist soil on others in the N. parts of the county. Peat moss makes its appearance, in small patches, in many of the vales, (vallies or dales) and abounds on the tops of several high mountains, which, however, are in general covered with a dry soil, upon a hard blue rock, provincially called *rag*. The soil that lies upon a limestone bottom, is uniformly esteemed the best."

FOSSILS and MINERALS.—P. 297. " Notwithstanding its mountainous surface, no valuable mines have yet been discovered in Westmoreland. Some trifling veins of lead ore have been found in the eastern mountains: coal is wrought only in the S. E. extremity of the county, and in the neighbourhood of Shap, where a bastard or crow coal is got.

" Limestone,

" Limestone, in almost inexhaustible abundance, is to be found in most parts of the county, except among the western hills, which afford an excellent kind of blue slates, well known over almost all England.

" Gypsum is got at Acron-bank, near Kirkby Thore, and a few other places: it is used for laying floors, but not at all, as a manure.

" Free-stone is found in the eastern parts of the county, and at Hutton-roofe, about ten miles from Kendall.

" On the river Kent, about three miles below Kendall, a vein of beautiful marble was discovered, about four years ago, in the lands of DANIEL WILSON, Esq. of Dallam Tower, by some workmen who were building a barn, and the main quarry has been opened on the estate of that gentleman. It has lately been found on the opposite side of the river, in the property of —— STRICKLAND, Esq. of Syzergh."

SUBJECT THE SECOND.

POLITICAL ECONOMY.

STATE of APPROPRIATION. On this subject, the BISHOP of LANDAFF makes the following remarks.— P. 281. " In 1689, when a bounty was first granted on the exportation of corn, one-third part of the land in England and Wales, or about eleven millions of acres, was supposed to lie in uncultivated commons; if this was then a just proportion between the cultivated and waste parts of the kingdom, we may safely conclude, that much above one-third part of Westmoreland was then waste land; as it is evident, from a bare view of the county, that few, if any counties in England have, in proportion to their whole extent, so much uncultivated land as this has. The many enclosure-

enclosures which have taken place, during the last hundred years, have lessened, in some degree, the waste land of the whole kingdom; but no enclosures of much consequence have taken place in Westmoreland. Instead of one-third, I am disposed to conjecture that three-fourth parts of Westmoreland consist of uncultivated land:"—adding, in p. 283 (after some " conjectural arguments" have been employed to support " this conjecture")—" But whether the uncultivated land in Westmoreland be equal to three-fourths, or one-half of the whole, it cannot be questioned, that there is so much of it, as to render its improvement a matter not only of individual concern, but of national importance."

Moreover, in p. 283, his Lordship thus speaks of the *improvement* of waste lands.—" The uncultivated lands in Westmoreland are of various sorts, with respect to soil and situation, and capable of different sorts of improvement. Some of them consist of extensive commons in low situations, and are of an excellent soil; these might be improved by enclosures, without any risk of loss by the undertaking. Others constitute extensive mountainous districts, called by the natives *fells* and *moors;* the soil of these is, generally speaking, an hazel mold. In its natural state, it produces little else than a coarse benty grass, heath, and fern; or, in the language of the country, *ling* and *brackens.* Many of these fells are, in their present state, of so little value, that the liberty of keeping ten sheep on them may be hired for sixpence a year. Supposing six acres to be sufficient for the maintenance of ten sheep, the rent of such land is a penny an acre; and the price of the fee simple of it, at twenty-four years purchase, 2*s.* Whilst there is an acre of such waste improvable land in Great Britain, it may be hoped, that, when the Legislature shall turn its attention to the subject, no inhabitant of the island will be driven, by distress, to seek a subsistence in Africa or America."

In

In the " Conclusion" of the *Report*, we find lengthened remarks, on the wastes of Westmoreland. But
they are mostly of a general nature ; and many of
them wild as the mountains about which they are
professed to be made. The writer of them, however,
touches on local circumstances, and strenuously recommends (p. 353)—" Some immediate alteration in
their state ; whether by division, or by sale" (?) : in
order to rescue them from " their present deplorable
state."—But let us reserve our judgement, concerning
those *deplorable wastes*, until we have heard something more about them.

STATE of SOCIETY.—*Provisions.*—Less than a century ago, I apprehend, the ensuing statement was
applicable to the whole of the northern department
of England ; some of its larger towns only excepted.—
P. 337.—" Fifty years ago the price of butcher-
meat at Martinmas was from $1\frac{1}{4}d.$ to $2d.$ a pound in
Burton market, and eighty beasts were sometimes
slaughtered in a day, and bought to be salted for
winter provisions. From that time, except a few at
Christmas and at Easter, no cattle were killed there
till they were fattened upon the pastures in summer.
Farmers, in those days, seldom ate any butcher-meat ;
they lived on bread and butter, and what other little
matters the farm afforded."

" Now (the writer continues) laborers generally
breakfast on that very ancient food pottage, with the
help of a little cheese and bread ; they dine on
butcher-meat and potatoes, or pudding ; and sup on
potatoes, or pottage, or bread and cheese. The
bread generally eaten in the county is made from
oatmeal."

On the *prices* of provisions, Mr. Pringle has entered into particulars. They are, of course, the
produce of inquiry, and may not be strictly accurate.
I nevertheless copy them, as they nearly agree with
those of Cumberland, registered aforegoing ; and,
together, they may serve to convey a general idea of
                                                    the

the cost of living, in this cheapest quarter of the kingdom, in 1793.

P. 338. " The difference in the price of provisions in a county so small as Westmoreland, cannot be very great. They are, however, somewhat cheaper in the north and east parts than they are in the south parts, which are more within the reach of the markets of Lancaster and Liverpool. Beef in Kendall market, in the month of October 1793, was sold at 3d. or 4d. a pound, and, a choice cut at 4½d.; in spring it often rises to 6d. a pound. Mutton, which in spring often rises to 7d. a pound, was sold at 3d. 3½d. or 4d. Pork was sold at 3d. or 4d. As all the bull calves are carried to market, veal is for the most part cheaper than the other kinds of butcher-meat, and yet in spring it is sometimes sold as high as 5d. a pound. Potatoes brought 1s. 4d. a bushel, or 5s. 6d. or 6s. a load; in spring they are often sold at nearly the double of these prices. Oatmeal is bought in some places by a measure of sixteen quarts, at a price which fluctuates from 1s. 4d. to 2s. 6d.; in others by a peck of 20 quarts, which in summer 1793 was worth 3s. Butter was sold from 7d. to 9d. a pound; in winter the price seldom rises above 11d.; a stone of 16 lbs. of 20 ounces, costs 11s. 6d. and a firkin of 56 lbs. neat, from 30s. to 35s. Cheese in the country costs 3d. a pound, and new milk 1d. a quart, which in Kendall is contracted for all the year at 1½d.

" A turkey costs 3s. 4d. or 5s. according to its size; a goose 1s. 6d. or 2s. or when sold by weight 3d. a pound; a hen from 7d. to 10d. and a chicken from 4d. to 8d. Eggs fluctuate in their price from 2½d. to 6d. or even to 9d. a dozen. Ducks are sold from 1s. 4d. to 2s. a pair; teal at 4d. a piece; woodcocks at 4s. or 5s. a brace, and pigeons from 4s. to 6s. a dozen.

" Salmon catched in the Lune is sold from 4d. to 8d. a pound; that which is brought from Carlisle,
from

from 3*d.* to 1*s.* 2*d.*   Char are sold at about 7*s.* a dozen ; trouts at 4*d.* a pound ; mussels at 2*d.* or 3*d* a quart ; flounders from 1*d.* to 6*d.* a piece ; eels at 2*d.* a pound ; and rabbits, without the skins, at 1*s.* the pair.   Honey in the comb costs 1*s.* a pound."

Fuel.—P 339.—" The eastern parts of the county are supplied with coal from Stainmore, Blackburton, and Ingleton, in Yorkshire, but in other parts the most common fuel is peat."

Manufactures.—P. 342.—" The manufactures of Westmoreland are not of much greater importance than its commerce.   They consist chiefly of coarse woollen cloth, called *Kendall Cottons*, properly, it is said *coatings**, gunpowder, stockings, silk and worsted, waistcoat pieces, flannels, and tanned leather."

Commerce.   P. 342.—" The commerce of Westmoreland is not yet so extensive as to have any sensible effect upon its agriculture.   Its exports are coarse woollen cloth, manufactured at Kendall, stockings, slates, tanned hides, gunpowder, hoops, charcoal, hams, wool, sheep, and cattle.   Its imports are chiefly merchant goods, wheat, oats, with a little barley, cattle and sheep.

" Milthrope is a very trifling port, and the only one in the county."

LOCAL TAXES.—*Poor Rate.*—Respecting this growing charge on landed property, the BISHOP of LAN DAFF (in argument, concerning the quantity of waste land, see p. 212.) has favored us with the following statement.

P. 282.—" It appears, by the return made by the overseers of the poor to the House of Commons, that the sum raised by assessment in all the parishes and townships of the county, at a medium of three years, ending in 1785, amounted to 5757 *l.*   The town of Kendall, including Kirkland, is the only large town
in

* Rather, I conceive, from COTTWM,—*Welch,* for a sort of coarse woollen cloth.

in the county; it is found, by an actual survey made this year, to contain 8089 inhabitants, having experienced an increase of 518 inhabitants since the year 1784; of the present number, 143, or about one fifty-sixth part of the whole, are *paupers* living in the work-house. The poor-rates of this town amounted, according to the same return, to 1125*l.* a year; this sum being subducted from the annual amount of all the poor-rates in the county, leaves 4632*l.* for the sum raised from all the estates in the county, exclusive of Kendall. From particular inquiries in various parishes, I am of opinion, that the poor-rates do not, in this county, exceed a shilling in the pound in the actual rental of all the lands."—And the REPORTER corroborates this statement, with these remarks, p. 343.—" The poor-rates in the parish of Kendall are 3*s.* 8*d.* in the pound of the actual rent, which is very near four times the average of the rate throughout the county. Were it not unfair to draw a general conclusion from one example, it might be inferred that the poor are most numerous in manufacturing counties and towns."

Tithes. P. 305. " In some parts of Westmoreland, tithes are taken in kind; in some, each farmer has an opportunity of taking his own tithes; in others, the land is tithe free, or pays a small prescription in lieu of tithes."

PUBLIC WORKS and INSTITUTIONS.—*Canals.* P. 340 " There is not at present any canal in the county; but one of great magnitude has been projected from Wigan to Kendall. It is now executing, and when finished, by introducing the coal of Lancashire into the heart of Westmoreland, will be of the greatest service to its manufactures and agriculture."

Markets. P. 341. " There are weekly markets at eight different towns in Westmoreland; but the only one of any note, is held at Kendall. The next in point of consequence is held at Appleby, the county town."

P. 345. " London is not much indebted to this county

county for its articles of consumption. The little it receives from hence consists chiefly of butter, bacon, hams, and excellent blue slates, which form a cover for some of the best houses in the capital. It is probable that, after being fattened in the southern counties, some of its cattle and sheep reach Smithfield market."

Fairs. That of Brough is of high note, in the North of England, for the purchase of Scotch cattle. The Reporter says, p. 316, "Ten thousand Scotch cattle are annually sold at Brough-hill fair in the end of September. Though numbers of these are carried off by drovers to the south of England, and many are brought by graziers from other counties, great quantities remain in Westmoreland."

SUBJECT THE THIRD.

RURAL ECONOMY.

DIVISION THE FIRST.

TENANTED ESTATES; their IMPROVE-MENT and MANAGEMENT.

ESTATES.—*Sizes* of Estates. P. 299. " A large proportion of the county of Westmoreland is possessed by a yeomanry, who occupy small estates of their own, from 10*l.* to 50*l.* a year. The remainder consists of larger estates belonging to noblemen and gentlemen, several of whom are resident in the county, and take the management into their own hands. Others entrust the care of their affairs, in a great measure, to stewards."

Tenures. P. 299. " The larger estates in Westmoreland are commonly freehold, and the small tenements, mentioned in the last Section, are generally held

held under the lord of the manor by *customary tenure*, which differs but little from that by *copyhold*, or copy of *court roll*. In some manors the tenant pays only a heriot, and fine certain, on death of the lord or tenant ; in others the fine is arbitrary, on death or purchase. On customary estates, the wood is generally claimed by the lord of the manor." And, in speaking on " Obstacles to Improvement," p. 344, the Reporter says—" the most material of these, are customary tenures, where the fines are arbitrary, or according to the improved value of the estate ; where the wood is the property of the lord, and where a lease for longer than three years is not valid without his consent."

IMPROVEMENT of Estates.—And, first, on improving *commons*, and other *open pastures*.

In the chapter, " Wastes," the subjoined observations are scattered.— P. 320. " The *wastes* in this county are very extensive and *valuable*. They are depastured chiefly with stocks of sheep, which are managed in nearly the same way, whether the ground be in common, or in severalty."—P. 321. " In addition to all these sheep, numerous herds of black cattle are likewise to be seen upon the commons:"—that is to say, upon these *valuable wastes* (see p. 214, aforegoing). Again, p. 321. " On stinted pastures, it is very ordinary to hire out the right of keeping both cattle and sheep. A summer's grass for an ox, or for ten sheep, on Forest Hall, and Mosley common, is lett at 4*s*. ; on a part of Troutbeck common, where no sheep are allowed to feed, an ox may be kept for 3*s*. 6*d*. and on another part of the same common, *an ox or ten sheep may remain all the year for sixpence*."

In these facts, we may no doubt see cause for improvement. It is to be observed, however, that the very low prices given for the agistment of stock in the stinted pastures, chiefly show that the *summer pastures* of Westmoreland are out of proportion to its *wintering grounds ;* and that the unstinted pastures, or

commons,

commons, are *not overstocked**.   For, if they were,
higher prices would be given for preserved pasturage.
But what man would give even sixpence, for an ox or
ten sheep, when he can have them depastured, free of
cost, nearer home, and perhaps more eligibly, than
on the stinted pasture above-mentioned;—the qualities of which the reader is left to conjecture.

The obvious and great improvement of landed
estates, in these mountains, is to increase the quantity of arable lands, and hay grounds; by the appropriation and inclosure of the lower lands,—for straw,
turnips, cultivated herbage, and watered hay grounds.
If, by the same law which shall authorise the inclosure
of the culturable grounds, the higher inarable lands
were placed under suitable regulations; and parochial
or " town flocks," and perhaps " town herds," similar
to those of the chalk hills of the SOUTHERN COUNTIES,
established,—the principles of improvement, in the
present state of property among those mountains,
might, I conceive, be deemed nearly perfect.   Or if,
under a law or laws of appropriation, the smaller
owners were to be recompensed for their rights of
commonage, on the lower grounds, with *arable lands*
and inclosed pasturage for *cattle*, and the higher
grounds allotted to large proprietors,—to be employed
as private *sheepwalks*, similar to those of the Cheviot
hills, the improvement might approach still nearer to
perfection.

Reclaiming wild lands.   On *sodburning*, I copy the
Reporter's observations; as they probably contain the
prevailing opinion of the country, respecting this
powerful remedy.—P. 322. " The operation of paring
and burning is much practised in Westmoreland, both
in improving moor lands, and in reclaiming rough
pastures, that have been allowed to return almost to
a state

* A strong evidence of this position is registered in the CUMBER-
LAND Report, Section *Sheep.*

a state of nature. It produces excellent crops at first, but the effect is diminished every repetition, and farmers are too apt to exhaust the land by repeated crops of oats without any manure."

EXECUTIVE MANAGEMENT OF ESTATES. On the *Tenancy* of Westmoreland, all that we collect, from the present Report, is comprised in the paragraph which follows.—P. 305. "The mode of farming is nearly the same throughout the county; and the course of crops is often pointed out to the farmer in his lease, which is generally for seven or nine years, sometimes only for five or three years, at others for fourteen, and in a few instances for twenty-one years. Some principal land-owners grant no leases."

Covenants.—P. 301. "The expenses of repairs are for the most part defrayed by the landlord."

Rent.—P. 304. "The rent of the land varies with its situation and fertility. In all situations, and of all qualities, it has increased greatly in its value within these few years. This may be owing partly to the advance in the price of its productions, and partly to improvements in the art of farming. At Shap, Ambleside, and in Troutbeck, the best hay-meadows are lett at about 50s. the customary acre *. Near towns, the rent of the best fields to be mowed may be, at a medium, rather above 3l. per acre. At Kirkby-Stephen and Appleby they are not quite so valuable. Near Kendall, Burton, and Milthrope, some fields are lett at 4l.; and at Kirkby-Lonsdale there are few which fetch above 5l. Lands of inferior kinds may be hired for pasture at all varieties of price. In Ravenstondale, where no tithes are paid, and where the land derives no part of its value from its situation, there are between 2000 and 3000 acres enclosed; four-fifths of these are lett from 4s. to 11s.
the

* Of 6½ yards to a perch: about an acre and three-eighths, statute measure.

the statute acre, and the remaining fifth from 20*s.* to
40*s.*"

These rents, which are high (notwithstanding the
size of the acre) considering the recluseness of the
situation, are accounted for, in the foregoing remarks ;
as they pretty evidently arise out of the small proportion of cultivated lands, compared with untilled
pasture grounds.

DIVISION THE SECOND.

WOODLANDS.

ON this branch of rural economics, the BISHOP of
LANDAFF has bestowed an ample share of attention.
It is a subject on which Doctor Watson has employed his thoughts, at different times. I am well
informed, I believe, that, several years ago, he was
so fully convinced of the accumulating value of
woodlands, that he determined to purchase young
woods,—to fence them securely,—and leave them to
their natural propensities ; as a provision for his
younger children ;—without being aware, perhaps,
that some considerable part of the profits of timber
woods arises from judicious thinnings ; and by relieving, from time to time, such promising young trees,
as are most fit to stand for a crop of timber.

From his Lordship's acquaintance with the subject,
added to his residing in a woodland part of Westmoreland, as well as from his extensive practice as a
planter, there, I indulged myself with the hope of
finding much valuable information, in the preliminary
observations that are now before me. And I have
not been wholly disappointed. Among much local
intelligence, I find many ingenious remarks; with
some speculative thoughts that are new to me.

P. 288. " In some parts of Westmoreland, considerable portions of land are covered with coppices,
con-

consisting principally of oak, ash, alder, birch, and
hazel. These underwoods are usually cut down
every sixteenth year; the uses to which they are
applied are chiefly two, hoops and charcoal. The
hoops are sold in the wood, at 5*l.* a thousand; they
are generally manufactured in the country, and sent
by sea to Liverpool; the charcoal is sent to the iron
furnaces in the neighbourhood. The value of a
statute acre of coppice wood of sixteen year's growth,
is variable, from 10*l.* to 15*l.*; and if it consists altogether of oak, its price may amount to twenty
guineas, 6*l.* for the charcoal, and 15*l.* for the bark; it
being the custom here to peel the bolls, and all the
branches of the oak, which are equal to the thickness
of a man's thumb."

In continuation, his Lordship remarks.—" It is an
extraordinary thing to see any trees left to stand for
timber in these underwoods, the high price of bark
being a temptation to cut the whole down. Fine
saplings, from nine to twelve inches in circumference,
at five feet from the ground, and with bark as splendid
as polished silver, are felled by the unfeeling proprietor with as little regret as if they were thorns or
briars."

But we are not informed, respecting the soil and
situation, where those young sapling oaks are felled.
Are they adapted to the growth of timber? If they
are, and it can be foreseen that timber will pay better
than coppice wood, then, in a private light, ought the
entire ground to be appropriated to timber; and,
instead of one hundred and fifty, more than four times
that number of standards an acre, should be left,—IN
THE SUSSEX MANNER.

Offering *general* remarks and calculations, on this
subject, might be said to be, at best, spending time
unprofitably; and may be productive of much evil,
when undertaken by men of acknowledged talents
and great authority; as will presently be shown.
The proper management of woods, the advancement
and

and progressive value of their produce, the most profitable state of growth, and the most suitable application, depend on the *given* soil, substratum, and climature, aad the market to which the produce can be sent with the greatest profit.

In alpine districts,—in Devonshire, in Wales, and in Westmoreland,—woodlands are mostly confined to the sides of vallies or other steep surfaces. The highest parts of the hills,---being generally thin of soil and exposed to cutting blasts,---produce even coppice wood of a stunted growth: while in the middle regions, coppice wood thrives with luxuriance. But, there, timber trees are forbid to flourish. At twenty or thirty years growth, their tops often begin to wither, and frequently before they are half a century old, they are seen in a state of decay: while on the lower hangs, and at the feet of the slopes, timber trees of size, and of luxuriant growth, are found.

Hence, it is the practice of judicious managers, in such situations, and in districts where coppice wood and timber are both of them in demand, to keep the upper parts entirely in coppiced, the lower wholely in timber: a practice that I am desirous to impress on the minds of the woodmen of Westmoreland.

If the larger proprietors of Westmoreland, stimulated by a laudable regard for the future prosperity of the island, are emulous to supply it with ship timber, in time to come,---be it their's to propagate the *larch*, not the *oak*, for that purpose. It may, I think, be safely averred, that, unless on the lower slopes of steep narrow dells in which neither the plough nor the sithe can operate with due effect, and excepting perhaps a few cold lands in the valley of Appleby, there ought not to be an oak, of sufficient size to be used in building ships of magnitude, in the country. Every acre of land within it, which is capable of maturing such an oak (except as before excepted) should be applied, for reasons above suggested, to the purposes of agriculture.

It

It makes no part of my present views to enter, on ordinary occasions, upon general topics, and speculative discussions. But as I cannot hope, in exploring the barren tracks I am now traversing, to meet frequently with men of Doctor Watson's compass of mind, I am willing to pay every attention to the suggestions he has thrown out.

The subject of ship timber, for the future navy of England, is of so much interest, and so connected with rural concerns, that any light which may be thrown upon it, cannot be indifferent to my readers. I therefore register, here, the liberal proposals contained in the subjoined extracts, with great readiness.

P. 290. " It is a general opinion in this, and, I believe, in other countries, that it is more profitable to fell oak wood at 50 or 60 years growth, than to let it stand for navy timber to 80 or 100. According to the price which is now paid for that commodity, either by the Navy Board, or the East-India Company, I believe the opinion to be founded in truth. The following observations contain the reason for this belief.

" If profit is considered, every tree of every kind ought to be cut down, and sold, when the annual increase in value of the tree, by its growth, is less than the annual interest of the money it would sell for *: this being admitted, we have only to inquire into the annual increase in the value of oaks of different ages."

In prosecuting this inquiry, the Bishop of Llandaff quotes Mr. MARSHAM's paper, formerly published in the Philosophical Transactions : a paper which, ingenious and well intended as it doubtlessly was, has been, I fear, the cause of considerable injury.—The site of Mr. Marsham's plantations (I speak from my own

* Together with the annual value of the land it grows upon :— of more consideration, perhaps, than the interest of the money. *Rev.*

own knowledge of it) is of a peculiar nature: namely, a weak sandy soil, resting upon deep rich clay, which is singularly affected by the oak:---consequently, for the growth of which, lands of that description are pre-eminently suited; while, for the purposes of agriculture, they are of very inferior value. Hence, the PROFITS of PLANTING were, *in that case,* very great, when compared with those of AGRICULTURE. And, in consequence of Mr. M's fair statements, and the misguided encouragement of well-meaning but ill-informed men, millions of oaks, probably, have been planted, on sites of an *opposite description!*---on lands whose surface soils were profitably employed in agriculture, and whose substrata are ungenial to the growth of trees; especially oaks: thousands of acres of valuable lands having thus been laid waste; or diverted from their natural, and most profitable use.

But even on Mr. Marsham's site, and of course with Mr. Marsham's market, young oaks were found to be the most profitable. That superior planter, speaking from the result of his experience, says--- " I have fixed upon thirty shillings as the value of trees which should be cut down: if they are cut sooner or later, the proprietor will be a loser."

The Bishop of Llandaff's remarks on this result show that his Lordship has paid considerable attention to the subject.

P. 291. " It must not be supposed, however, that great precision can attend this observation; since particular soils, or the greater or less thriving condition of the wood, may render it useful to cut down trees before they are worth 30s. or to let them stand a while longer. It ought to be remarked also, that large trees sell for more per foot than small ones do, yet the usual increase of price, is not a compensation to the proprietor for letting his timber stand to a great age. This may be made out from the following experiment:

" On the 27th October, 1792, I measured, at six feet

feet from the ground, the circumference of a very
fine oak, of eighty-two years growth, from the time
of its being planted, and found it to be 107 inches:
on the same day of the month, in 1793, it measured 108 inches.—There is not one oak in fifty
(at the age of this) which gains an inch in circumference in one year. The length of the boll of this
tree was about 18 feet; it contained about 84 feet of
timber, and was worth at 3*s*. a foot, 12*l*. 12*s*. It
gained in one year very little more than a foot and
one half of timber, at 4*s*. 6*d*. in value; but the interest
of 12*l*. 12*s*. at 4*l*. per cent. amounts in one year, to
above twice the value of the increase, even of this
tree, which is a singularly thriving one."—And here,
likewise, is to be added the rental value of the land;
whether for agricultural produce, or for a crop of
young timber or coppice wood.

The Bishop continues, p. 292, " I have been the
more particular on this subject, from a public consideration. Many men are alarmed, lest our posterity should experience a scarcity of oak timber for
the use of the Navy; and various means of increasing
its quantity have been recommended with great judgment. In addition to these means, the making a
much greater than the ordinary increase of price on
timber of a large scantling, might be not improperly
submitted to the consideration of those who are concerned in the business. If the Navy Board would
give 8*l*. or 9*l*. a load for timber trees, containing 100
cubic feet or upwards, instead of 4*l*. or 5*l*. every man
in the kingdom would have a reasonable motive for
letting his timber stand till it became of a size fit for
the use of the Navy; whereas, according to the present price, it is every man's interest to cut it down
sooner."

Having had many opportunities of deliberately
observing the state of growth, and the decay, of timber
trees, and having already ventured to publish my
opinion, respecting the proper ages of felling different
species

species (in MIDLAND COUNTIES, Minute 149) I will confine my remarks, in this place, to the suggestion of the Bishop of Llandaff, relating to the advance of price for oak timber, for the use of the navy.

Supposing Government were, now, to issue an order to that effect, let us consider in what manner it would operate. To the few who have, at present, upon their estates trees of the size proposed, it would be highly advantageous. In those who have trees which are approaching that size, and which, in ten, fifteen, or twenty years, would be able to claim that advance of price, it might be an eligible speculation to let them stand. But would it be prudent, in the proprietors of younger timber, to play so high a game? We need not hesitate in asserting that, *even on oak land*, it requires a hundred and fifty years, or upward, to grow oaks, in number, to a hundred cubical feet, a tree. That above-mentioned was, doubtlessly, " a singularly thriving one." Suppose a man to be possessed of an unentailed estate, stocked with oak timber of fifty to a hundred years growth,---would it be right, even in a man so circumstanced, to look forward, for himself and his successors, fifty or a hundred years, in expectation of a high price, without any other certainty of reaping it, than an order, or a law, which, in any sitting of Council, or session of Parliament, might be annulled?

If oak timber, in quantity, and of a size equal to a hundred, or even eighty, cubical feet, each tree, will hereafter be necessary to the salvation of the country,---let not Government depend on individuals for a supply. A supply that requires several generations of men---with different, perhaps opposite, views, propensities, opinions, or wants---to bring it to the required market!

Much of the land on which oak timber has heretofore been raised, is become too valuable---too *necessary*---for the uses of agriculture, to be employed, again, in the growth of timber. Nevertheless, there

is

is land, as has been shown, which is peculiarly adapted to the growth of the oak; yet is of inferior value to husbandry. Let Government purchase lands of that description,—already stocked with timber, where such is to be had,—or to be seeded with acorns, if at present unwooded; and, in this plain and obvious manner, provide, with certainty, a continual supply of oak timber, for the British navy,—with the least injury, possible, to the supply of human sustenance.

Let it not be said that the plan here suggested, would become abortive, through a want of due execution : as that would be a libel on Government *. A very small portion of the organization and discipline, by which ship timber is preserved, *in the state of manufacture*, would be sufficient, not only to preserve, but to train it, *in the state of growth*.

I cannot allow myself to quit the Bishop of Llandaff's remarks on Woodland produce, without copying the concluding passage. It is fraught with interesting information, which may, hereafter, be productive of practical advantage; in the way already suggested, in page 133.

P. 293. "May I be permitted to hazard another conjecture, respecting the use to which coppices might be applied, without injuring either the quantity or the quality of the charcoal obtained from them? Pit coal yields, by distillation, about a twenty-fourth part of its weight, of a thick tenacious oil, resembling tar. All sorts of wood yield a similar oil by the same process : I do not know whether the oil from wood be of an inferior or of a superior quality to that from pit coal; but I suspect it to be fitter for cordage, &c.

In

---

* Yet there are who bring this as an objection against the most obviously profitable plans of improvement :—judging, no doubt, other men's exertions and integrity by their own. But the exertions and integrity of the Commissioners of Public Accounts may happily put a stop to such treasonable insinuations.

In the ordinary way of making charcoal, the whole of this oil is dispersed in the form of smoke : may it not deserve to be inquired, whether this oil might not be saved with profit ? The process which is used in America, for extracting tar from the pine tree, is little different from that by which charcoal is made in England. Whether the quantity of oil which might be obtained from a pit of wood, when converted into charcoal, would exceed in value the expense of procuring it, can only be decided by experiment. The reader may form some guess at the quantity, from the following statement : the black part of guiacum wood yields a tenth, the sappy part a thirteenth part of its weight, of thick black oil. Sassafras wood, oak, ash, alder, birch, &c. give by distillation (and making charcoal is a species of distillation), from a twenty-fourth to a twelfth part of their respective weights, of this oil. The difference in quantity arises from a diversity in the texture, age, and dryness of the woods. I suppose that a cord of coppice wood would weigh a ton, and that four cords would make one dozen of sacks of charcoal, and that wood of this sort would yield a twentieth part of its weight of oil : on these suppositions, there is dissipated in making one dozen of charcoal 448lbs. of oil, or one ton in every five dozen."

PLANTATIONS.—P. 319. " The Bishop of LANDAFF has planted, on some high ground near Ambleside, above an hundred acres with oak, ash, elm, beech, sycamore, Scotch fir, and larch. He is doubtful whether the climate be not too cold for any sort of wood except the fir and larch ; the other kinds, after seven years growth, are alive, but stunted ; they shoot a little in the spring, but that shoot perishes, as to its greatest part, in the winter. Some of them have been cut down, but the new shoots do not promise well. The firs and larches, but especially the larches, thrive as well as he could wish."

DIVISION

DIVISION THE THIRD.

AGRICULTURE.

FARMS.—*Sizes.*—P. 302. " Farms, in general, are so small, that it is rare to meet with one of 100*l.* a year of rent, though there are some of even 200*l.* or 250*l.* a year."

Homesteads.—P. 300. " The lands of the *statesmen* and farmers in this county lie so intermixed, that their habitations and offices, which are often built together in little straggling villages, must of necessity be very inconvenient for farming purposes ; but convenience has been little studied, even on those farms whose fields lie unmixed. The principal structure is a barn, which, at the same time that it has a stable and cow-house underneath, is frequently large enough to contain the whole crop of both corn and hay, so that it is rare to see a stack of either."

Farm Cottages.—P. 301. " There are very few mere cottages in the county; the labourer and mechanic generally reside in a small farm-house, and occupy more or less land."

OCCUPIERS.—Mr. Pringle's remarks, on this head, are creditable to him, as a man of observation and reflection ; and as a writer possessing liberal sentiments.

P. 302. " It might be useful to know what proportion of the lands in the county is possessed by that numerous and respectable yeomanry already mentioned as occupying small estates of their own, from 10*l.* or 20*l.* to 50*l.* a year. These men, in contradistinction to farmers, or those who hire the land they occupy, are usually denominated *statesmen.* They live poorly, and labour hard ; and some of them, particularly in the vicinity of Kendall, in the intervals of labour from agricultural avocations, busy
themselves

themselves in weaving stuffs for the manufacturers of that town. The consciousness of their independence renders them impatient of oppression or insult, but they are gentle and obliging when treated by their superiors with kindness and respect. This class of men is daily decreasing. The turnpike-roads have brought the manners of the capital to this extremity of the kingdom. The simplicity of ancient times is gone. Finer clothes, better dwellings, and more expensive viands, are now sought after by all. This change of manners, combined with other circumstances which have taken place within the last forty years, has compelled many a *statesman* to sell his property, and reduced him to the necessity of working as a labourer in those fields, which, perhaps, he and his ancestors had for many generations cultivated as their own. It is difficult to contemplate this change without regret; but considering the matter on the scale of national utility, it may be questioned whether the agriculture of the county will not be improved as the landed property of it becomes less divided."

PLAN OF MANAGEMENT.—What is entitled to notice, on this head, in the Report under consideration, relates to the *succession of crops*. To this subject Mr. Pringle has paid more than ordinary attention. The general practice of the county he describes in the following circumstantial, yet compendious, manner.

P. 310. When a field of grass is overgrown with moss, which commonly happens in seven or ten years, it is broken up with the plough in the beginning of March, and sown, about the 1st of April, with oats, at the rate of seven and one-half Winchester bushels upon the customary acre of 6,760 square yards. The crop is reaped about the middle of September, and 60 bushels are reckoned a tolerably good return.

" *Second Crop.*—The land is ploughed for the second

cond crop as soon after Candlemas as the weather will
permit, and 80 or 100 cart-loads of stable-yard dung
are laid upon the acre.   It is ploughed again in
April, and sown with four bushels of barley or bigg.
The harvest is earlier than that of the oats, and 54
bushels are reckoned a good crop.   Some farmers
plough three times for barley, but it is the general
practice that is here described.

   " *Third Crop.*—After the barley, the land is ploughed in April, and eight bushels of oats per acre are immediately sown upon it.   The harvest is commonly
in September, and the crop is usually as good as
the first was.

   " This is the most ordinary succession of crops,
though it is sometimes broken through by taking two
crops of oats before the barley, which, in that case,
is followed by another of oats.   The land is then left
to itself, and the first year it produces a light crop of
hay, of bad quality.   In the third year the crop is at
the best with regard to both quantity and quality.
In seven, or in ten years, it is again mossed over, and
is again ploughed up to undergo a similar treatment."

   Some exceptions to this prevailing plan of management are enumerated, and remarked upon.   But nothing of interest arises in the discussion.

   In the " Conclusion" of the Report, this subject is
again adverted to.—P. 350 —" It is the general opinion of farmers in Westmoreland, that their lands are
better suited for grass than for bearing crops of corn,
and they are ploughed for three or four years, not
with an expectation that the corn will be more profitable than the grass, but in order to renovate them for
grass, and to destroy the moss, which in a few years
over-runs all their ley grounds: but there are some
who are persuaded, that the neat profits of the three
or four years the lands are under crop, usually exceed
the profits of any other three or four years while the
same lands lie in grass, and they think that their fertility for the production of either grass or corn, would
                                                  be

be injured by ploughing for a longer term, or after shorter intervals of rest."

Proposals, for the improvement of the established practice, succeed. But still we find nothing that is new or interesting. The turnip husbandry, with cultivated herbage, if properly pursued, could scarcely fail to become a beneficial change for the stubble-grass practice. Nevertheless, seeing the high rents that are paid for land, we may safely conclude they are not unproductive, under the existing management; which prevails, or recently prevailed, along the western coast, from the Firth of Solway, to the estuary of the Merey *.

WORK PEOPLE. P. 333.— "Labor is dearer in Westmoreland than it is in almost any of the counties either to the north or south of it. This probably is owing to the great number of small landholders, or *statesmen* above-mentioned, who doing the work upon their own estates, with their own hands and those of their families, are perhaps disinclined to labor for other people."

In p. 303, the *uncivil* treatment of the female servants of Westmoreland, is thus feelingly reported:— " It is painful to one, who has in his composition the smallest spark of knight-errantry, to behold the beautiful servant maids of this county toiling in the severe labors of the field. They drive the harrows, or the ploughs, when they are drawn by three or four horses; nay, it is not uncommon to see, sweating at the dung-cart, a girl, whose elegant features, and delicate nicely-proportioned limbs, seemingly but ill accord with such rough employment." What must have been Mr. *Pringle's* feelings, to have seen those elegant nymphs —loaded by unfeeling swains—carrying the dung on their own fair backs to the field† !

WORKING

---

* And see the ensuing article, *Cultivated herbage.*

† See WEST of ENGLAND, Art. *Winnowing.*

WORKING ANIMALS.—P. 331. " There being only one person in Westmoreland who uses ox teams, it may be justly inferred, that the general opinion of farmers in the county is in favor of horses. The writer of this Report has not such information upon the subject, as to be able to draw the desired comparison between these useful animals."

On IMPLEMENTS, I find nothing that particularly claims notice. One-horse carts are in use.

MANURE.—*Lime.* P. 323. " It is sometime laid upon the land when it is in tillage, but for the most part it is spread upon the surface of grass fields; and it has been found to sweeten such as are coarse and bent, amazingly.

Compost—P. 324. " Much attention is paid to the making of compost dunghills in many parts of Westmoreland. They are most commonly spread upon grass, and experience has shown, that they at once improve its quality, and check for years the progress of the moss. One hundred cart-loads of earth, rakings of the roads, mud, or rotten leaves, and fifty of dung, carefully mixed with 300 Winchester bushels of lime, are laid upon three acres with great advantage."

CULTIVATED HERBAGE.—P. 315. " A prejudice against the artificial grasses prevails so generally over all the county, that it may be almost literally said, they are never sown. When the land has produced a few crops of corn, and it is judged that the moss is quite destroyed, it is left to itself; and such is the humidity of the climate, and so strong is the vegetation of weeds and natural grasses, that the very first crop has, by actual experiment, been found to produce 120 stones of hay per acre, weighed from the field."

Here, we have a convincing proof of the effect of climature: as well as an evidence in favor of the Westmoreland husbandry. And, in p. 346, a still stronger evidence is given.—" In many counties of England the land is sown with grass-seeds, and left to
lie

lie for some years, with a view to refresh and enable it to bear crops of corn; but in Westmoreland it is ploughed and sown with corn in order to prepare it for grass. When it hath been cropped for three years, and it is judged that the soil is sufficiently reduced, and that the moss is quite destroyed, the land is left to itself, to grass over. The first crop of hay is never either weighty or good in quality; the second is generally very superior in both these respects to the first, and so favourable are the climate and the soil to the growth of grass, that the third crop is often so abundant as to be lett for two or three pounds per acre, and of a quality so excellent, that in several places cattle are fattened upon it in winter for the markets of Lancaster and Liverpool."

The Reporter's observations on these facts are as follow:—" But even these best crops, are far inferior in point of value to those, that would be produced by the same fields, were their natural aptitude to grow grass directed to the production of clover and ryegrass. The prejudice that prevails almost universally in Westmoreland against these artificial plants, is a great obstacle to the improvement of the husbandry of the county, and must be overcome before the arable lands can be brought to that degree of cultivation of which they are susceptible."

It is far from my intention to convey that the Westmoreland practice is incapable of improvement. I have, nevertheless, thought it right to register, here, the interesting facts which Mr. Pringle has reported.

GRASS LAND.—*Hay Grounds.*—P. 314. " Every occupier of land, whether *statesman* or *farmer*, having it in his power to keep any number of cattle, through the months of summer, upon *joisted* fields where they may be kept at a cheap rate, or upon commons, where they may be kept almost for nothing, it is a principal object with him to provide for them plenty of winter food. Hence his attention is chiefly directed to his crop of hay."—And, p. 315, " as every person who expects

expects to have occasion for hay, hires a field to supply him with that commodity, it is not often that hay is sold in large quantities; and it is still seldomer that the quantity raised upon an acre is exactly ascertained. When sold, it may bring from 4*d.* to 6*d.* a stone in winter and spring, or from 4*s.* to 5*s.* a cubic yard."

HORSES.—P. 330. " As there is but a small portion of the county under crop, the horses are not numerous, nor has any considerable attempt been made to improve the breed of these useful animals. They are small, not exceeding fourteen hands and a half in height, are said to be hardy, but they are neither strong nor handsome."

P. 321. " A few ponies of the Scotch breed are reared upon the commons; but the practice not being general, it need not be dilated upon."

P. 317. " Horses are grazed among fattening cattle for 3*s.* 6*d.* a week. Young horses are kept from Michaelmas to 5th March on the inferior kinds of land, and have straw given them in bad weather for 2*s.* a week."

CATTLE.—*Breed.*—P. 326. " The attention that was formerly paid to the breed of *black* * cattle has rather diminished of late years. They are long-horned, very much resemble the Lancashire breed, and when kept to a proper age, grow to a great size."

Store Cattle. P. 321. " A few of these are of the breed of the county, and the rest are Scotch, either bought at Brough-hill fair in the end of September, and wintered on the low grounds and in the straw-yard, or purchased in the spring from drovers, who fetch them from Galloway and Dumbarton. In autumn, they are either sold to the south-country drovers, or wintered and fattened in the county."—

And

* How aukwardly that epithet is applied to the gayly colored cattle of Westmoreland !

And, p. 317.—" They are wintered on the coarse pastures, and in the straw-yard: in May following the young ones are sent to the commons; and those of an age proper for feeding are put upon the best grounds, and are ready for the shambles in October."

Dairy Produce.—P. 327.—" Cows in the country are kept for the sake of making butter, of which great quantities, of an excellent quality, are sent yearly to the London market in firkins of 56lbs. net.'

Sheep.—*Breed.*—P. 327.—" The breed of sheep, kept on the mountains and commons of Westmoreland, is either native or a cross with Scotch rams. No attempt has yet been made to improve either the carcass or the fleece. They are horned, dark or grey faced, thick pelted, with coarse, strong, hairy wool." P. 328.—" The wool is worth, on an average of years in time of peace, 5d. a pound. Part of it is sold to the manufacturers of Kendall, and part of it to those at Bradford, and other places in Yorkshire. The ewes are said to bear the best wool; and on an average of a flock six fleeces weigh a stone."

P 328.—" *Silverdale Breed.*—Silverdale, a small district in the neighbourhood of Milthrope, gives its name to the breed of sheep in this part of the county. The soil is good, and on a limestone stratum, and a branch of the sea is nearly contiguous to it. They are horned, white faced, and close woolled*. They are said to be native, and are much superior to the common sort, in regard both to fleece and carcass. At the sale of a farmer's stock, in October 1793, the lambs of this breed brought 10s. 7d. a-piece, the dinmonds 17s. 1d. and the ewes at the age of three years and a half. 17s. 6d. or 17s. 8d. In the townships of Burton and Holme, where this breed is kept, five sheep at an average yield a stone of wool, which is worth

* *Dorsetshire* sheep, *bred,* it is probable, in *Westmoreland!*

worth 8*d.* a pound. At a medium of the whole parish of Burton for eight years, from 1772 to 1779 inclusive, it required six fleeces to weigh a stone.

"It is not unusual for the proprietor to be owner of the sheep upon the farm. In this case the farmer is to be considered as little better than a shepherd. The flock is valued at the time of his entry, and again at his removal, and the difference between these valuations is settled in money."—In the manner, it would seem, of the Herdwick flocks. See p. 199, aforegoing.

Management.—P. 320.—"In winter, all the sheep are brought down to the enclosed fields, except the wedders, which, being thought able to endure the severity of any storm or fall of snow, are left to shift for themselves upon the wastes, where they remain till they are four years and a half old, when they are sold from 9*s.* to 13*s.* a head. Having dropped their lambs, the ewes, in the end of April, are sent back to the wastes, where the whole flock pastures indiscriminately without an attendant. The lambs are sometimes suffered to wean themselves; at others, the teats of the ewe are fastened up to her udder by a plaister of coarse paper and pitch."—And, further,—"Great numbers of Scotch hogs and dinmonds are annually bought at Stagshawbank fair in the month of June, and *grazed* on the *wastes* of this county. On some they are found to answer very badly; on others they thrive well, and are ready for the grazier a year earlier than those of the native breed."

P. 327. The whole flock upon a farm is herded together, which is different from the practice in those countries where sheep-farming is thought to be the best understood.

"Those store-masters who have not upon their own farms pastures sufficient for the wintering of their young sheep, send them to the low grounds (?) from the

the 1st November to 6th April, and pay 2s. a-head for those that return. They are so subject to the *black-water (sickness,* or *middling-ill),* that, at an average, ten out of an hundred die before Christmas. After that, being very hardy, they seldom die, and never of that disease."

We are informed, however, in p. 355,—" It has been computed, that one-third of all the sheep in Westmoreland died in 1792. Great calamities are often exaggerated, though no doubt the loss must have been prodigious when it was estimated so high." —But of what malady is not mentioned.

Salving.—P. 328.—" In October, or the beginning of November, the whole flock is salved so heavily, that a gallon of tar and 16lbs. of butter are expended upon thirty-five sheep. A man may be hired for this work at 1s. 8d. a-day, in which time he will not salve above ten or a dozen; or he will undertake to salve them at 2d. a-head. The whole expense is about sixpence a-piece. (?) It has been repeatedly tried to substitute tobacco-liquor for the butter and tar, but it is generally imagined that the wool is better for the sheep having been salved. Near Kirkby-Stephen, this operation is performed with oil and tallow, at an expense of 4d. a-head."

RABBITS.—P. 332.—" A few rabbits are kept in the neighbourhood of Brough and Orton, and there is a small warren in Ravenstondale, but it is rare to see them in any other part of Westmoreland."

SWINE.—Of the *Breed* and *Management* of this species of farm stock, we are not informed, in this Report. The only information contained in the section " Hogs," relates to " *Westmoreland hams:*"—a general name, under which hams that are cured in the northwest of England, and the southwest of Scotland, are sent to the London market.

In the practice of Westmoreland, proper, as here set forth, I find, however, nothing of superior excellence.

lence. I will, nevertheless, insert it. It nearly agrees with the Yorkshire practice.

P. 331.—" The hams are first rubbed very hard, generally with bay-salt; by some they are covered close up, by others they are left on a stone bench to allow the brine to run off. At the end of five days they are again rubbed as hard as they were at first, with salt of the same sort, mixed with rather more than an ounce of saltpetre to a ham. Having lain about a week, either on a stone bench, or in hogsheads amongst the brine, they are hung up by some in the chimney amidst the smoke, whether of peats or coals; by others, in places where no smoke ever reaches them. If not sold sooner, they are suffered to remain there till the weather becomes warm. They are packed in hogsheads with straw or oatmeal seeds, and sent to London, Lancaster, and Liverpool, in such quantities as to form one of the principal branches of export from the county.

" In 1792, neat hams of 16 or 18 lbs. weight were sold as high as $5\frac{1}{2}d.$ per pound when green; when cured, in 1793, they were sold at $7\frac{1}{2}d.$ a-pound. It has been found by experiment that hams lose twenty per cent. of their weight in the curing."

POULTRY.—P. 332.—" Considerable quantities of geese, ducks, and common dunghill fowls are reared in Westmoreland. The two last are generally disposed of in the market towns in the county, or carried to Lancaster; but great numbers of the first are sold to drovers from Yorkshire." Probably, for the manufacturing towns, in the West Riding.

LANCASHIRE.

LANCASHIRE.

THE entire NATURAL DISTRICTS of this county are few. The boundaries of *counties*, as has been said, seldom have any coincidence with the outlines of nature.

The more northern parts of Lancashire agree, in surface, soil, and substrata, with the southern margin of Westmoreland, and the sea-coast of Cumberland. While the banks of the Mersey, which bound the county, on the south, are by natural distinguishments, as well as by locality, similar to the southern margin of the same river :—together forming the VALE of WARRINGTON; which, by agricultural, as well as by natural, affinity, belongs to the western, *not* to the NORTHERN DEPARTMENT.

The most obvious natural division of Lancashire is into moreland, and cultivated country. And a natural subdivision of the latter (the two extremities already noticed excepted) is into the sandilands and the rushlands of Lancashire. The southeast quarter of the county is a broken, mountain-skirt country; the neighbourhood of Manchester abounding, in a singular manner, with morasses.

MY KNOWLEDGE, of these several parts of the county under consideration, has been gained in crossing them, in various directions; and halting, occasionally, to examine such passages as most attracted my notice.

Formerly,

Formerly, I entered the county by Blackstone-Edge, in the way to Rochdale; near which I stopped some time:—thence to Manchester; whose environs I examined:—leaving the county by the Stockport road.

In September 1792, I approached it, by the great western road, from the north:—proceeding by Lancaster, to Preston; where I stopped to look round me:—thence to Manchester, by Chorley; and from Manchester, by the canal, toward Chester.

In July 1798, I entered the county, at Warrington: proceeding on the great western road, by Wigan and Chorley, to Preston, and Lancaster. And, the following year, I travelled nearly the same road; deviating, only, between Wigan and Preston; at this time, taking the more western line.

Finally, in July 1800, I entered it, at Liverpool; and passed through the seacoast quarter, by Ormskirk and Rufford, to Preston.

OF the CULTIVATED LANDS, there are only the two passages already mentioned, that require particular notice : namely, the *sandy lands* that occupy the sea coast, and the *rush lands* which lie between those and the moreland skirts.

It may be remarked, however, in this place, that the whole of the cultivated lands, between the skirts of the morelands and the sea,— in some parts not less than fifteen or twenty miles in width,---partake much of the vale character, both in elevation and surface.

The cold *rush lands* commence about the midway between Lancaster and Garstang. Northward of that, the substrata are chiefly, I believe, pebbles, or rocks of different qualities, giving sound, warm, corn lands : wheat land of superior fertility ; and forwarder, by some weeks, than the adjacent lands which lie more to the south. In 1798, wheat was nearly ripe the first of August ; being there almost as forward, that year, as in Middlesex.

The

The rushlands continue, southward, to near Wigan. They are broken, however, into two distinct passages; by the valley of the Ribble, and the rich and beautiful environs of Preston. To the north of these, the cold lands extend, I believe, to near the sea-shore; being, in that part, some eight or ten miles in width; forming what is called " the Filde." But to the south of the Ribble, they are cut off by the sandy soils; which, in that part, occupy the sea coast: the river, or brook, Douglas,—being the boundary between them.

The soils of these cool rushy lands appear to vary with the surface. The swells are the most productive. The dips, too, are of a warmer nature, than the flat lands, of a middle elevation, on which rushes abound in so remarkable a manner, as to occupy, in some places, half the surface; which is rendered thereby nearly as useless, to agriculture, as if it were covered with rocks, or did not exist. The soil of these rushy grounds is a well textured loam; lying mostly on a deep earthy base: thus bearing a resemblance to the cool lands of Northumberland and Durham. But, in Lancashire, the soil is deeper, and of a more loamy nature, and the subsoil is more absorbent: yet it is sufficiently retentive of moisture, to give an ungenial coolness to the soil. In some places, I have observed gravel, mixed with the substratum; in others pebbles; in others sand, gravel, and earth, as is commonly seen in mountain-skirt situations: and in one instance, sand and clay, seam over seam. But these instances occurred chiefly among the swells and dips toward the feet of the morelands.—In the line between Eccleston and Preston, (more particularly,) I saw some extent of red soil, incumbent on a red base: similar to the red lands of Nottinghamshire, the Midland Counties, Gloucestershire, and Devonshire; the substrata being there, as elsewhere, spread upon the surface, as " Marl."

The *sandy lands* lie between the estuaries of the Ribble

Ribble and the Mersey; reaching westward to the sea, and shooting eastward, by Newton, toward Manchester. The soil, though uniformly, I believe, of a sandy absorbent nature, varies in color, according to the different modes of formation (having in some parts a dark moorish appearance) and the substrata on which it rests. The prevailing base appears to be a red sand rock: in some places, a reddish sandy grout; this part of Lancashire being, in reality, a continuation of the rich sandy lands of Cheshire; the vale of Warrington and its banks enjoying a superior degree of fertility.

On these sandy lands, are chiefly raised, the long famed Lancashire potatoes; whose cultivation forms a favorite theme of the Lancashire Report: the Surveyor's place of residence being in this part of the county.

The MORELANDS of LANCASHIRE are separated into two divisions, by the VALLEY of the RIBBLE; which divides the county into two nearly equal parts.

The *northern division* of the morelands is insulated: being cut off from the western morelands of Yorkshire, by Craven and a flat of weaker lands which intervene between Craven and Lonsdale: the latter being their northern boundary. The cultivated lands of Lancashire embrace them, on the west.

The *southern division* of the morelands of Lancashire is attached to the SOUTHERN MOUNTAINS, which will hereafter come under notice.

" GENERAL VIEW

OF THE

AGRICULTURE

OF THE

COUNTY OF LANCASTER;

WITH

OBSERVATIONS FOR THE MEANS OF ITS IMPROVEMENT.

DRAWN UP FOR THE CONSIDERATION OF

THE BOARD OF AGRICULTURE AND INTERNAL IMPROVEMENT.

FROM THE COMMUNICATIONS OF

Mr. JOHN HOLT,

Of WALTON, near LIVERPOOL.

And the additional Remarks of several respectable Gentlemen and Farmers in the County.

1795."

THE ORIGINAL REPORT was signed by JOHN HOLT, as the *Author* of it. Why the Board, or its President, should undertake the reprinted Edition (after having declared, in a standing advertisement, " that the Board does not consider itself responsible for any fact or observation contained in the Reports thus reprinted,")—may be difficult to guess; unless it were to display superior skill in—*Editorship!*

Mr. HOLT, however, being honored with the name of SURVEYOR, it will be proper to endeavor to estimate his QUALIFICATIONS, not merely as Surveyor, but as Author of the original Report; most of which is reprinted in the volume under review. Mr. H. is ·evidently in earnest, and desirous to promote the

the welfare of his country, as far as he is able : an amiable disposition which, I doubt not, induced him to comply with the solicitations of the Board.

Judging from what appears in the Lancashire Report, compared with the standard qualifications, defined in the introduction to this volume, the Lancashire Surveyor, and original Reporter, cannot be said to possess, in a sufficient degree, either of the three acquirements of a capable Reporter of rural concerns. Of the dairy, it is true, Mr. Holt appears to have some practical knowledge. Of Pigs, too, he speaks as a practical man. In the potatoe culture he is an adept. And his knowledge, of gooseberries and tulips, shows that had his abilities been otherwise fortunately directed, he might have done honor to the discernment of the Board, in appointing him their Surveyor.

Mr. Holt's MODE of SURVEY appears to have been merely that of an inexperienced tourist. He very prudently, however, took with him a neighbour (Mr. James Balmer) " a good judge of cattle."

Respecting the GENTLEMEN and FARMERS, announced in the title page, suffice it to say—that, with fewer cooks the broth might have been the better. Even the original Report was loaded with note upon note ; and, *to these being now added*—more sportings in speculation, and wanderings from the point, with pro-and-con arguments equally far from the truth,—and the whole hustled together in strange confusion, without index, table of contents, or running title to assist the reader,—the time, patience, and labor required for the due understanding of the contents of the mass, for separating the wholesome grains from the chaff and weeds among which they have been ingeniously involved, and finally arranging them intelligibly, so as to render them profitable to the public,—have been found greater and more irksome than all the pains bestowed on the four preceding Reports.

Among

Among the ANNOTATORS to the reprinted edition, however, there are three who are entitled to honorable consideration: namely, Mr. ECCLESTON, a gentleman well known as an active promoter of rural improvements; Mr. BAILEY, likewise of high character as a country gentleman; and Mr. HENRY HARPER, a spirited farmer—of Bank Hall, near Liverpool—possessing genius of a superior cast; but wanting sufficient judgment, on some occasions, to controul it. He not unfrequently appears more in the character of an amateur, than in that of a professional husbandman, practising on a large scale. The agricultural public, nevertheless, have to regret his loss.

The Lancashire Report, like that of the county of Durham, is ornamented, or intended to be ornamented, with a MAP of many colors,—laid on by straight lines!—as if the first hint for this style of map-making had been furnished by the American flag. The colors of the impression affixed to the copy of the original Report, in my possession, are still pretty strong. But that which precedes the reprinted edition, now before me, is blank! and of course rendered ridiculous by the references on its margin.

SUBJECT THE FIRST.

NATURAL ECONOMY.

EXTENT.—P. 1. " The dimensions of the county are as follows*.—Its greatest length 74 miles; breadth 44½ miles.—Its circumference (crossing the Ribble,

at

" * Calculated upon this occasion by Mr. William Yates, who surveyed and published a map of the county of Lancaster in the year 1786."

at Hesketh bank) 342 miles; containing 1,765 square miles, and 1,129,600 statute acres."

SURFACE, SOIL, and SUBSOIL.—P. 8. "The features of this county are, in many places, strongly marked; towards the north they are bold and picturesque, diversified with alpine mountains and fertile *vales*. The north-east part of the county, Blackburn, Clithero, Haslingden, &c. is rugged, interspersed with many rivulets, with a thin stratum of upper soil; the southern part more softened, and the plains are more fertilized: along the sea coast, the land is chiefly flat, and has the appearance, in many places, as if formerly covered by the ocean." Again; "The greatest proportion of that district, which lies between the Ribble and the Mersey, has for its superficies a sandy loam, well adapted to the production of almost every vegetable that has yet been brought under cultivation, and that to a degree which renders it impossible to estimate the advantage which might be obtained, by improved and superior management. The substratum of this soil is generally the red rock, or clay marle, an admirable sandy loam, perhaps one of the most desirable soils that can be found, equally well adapted to the production of every vegetable. In this district there is little or no gravelly soil, no chalk or flint, no stony land, and very little obdurate clay."—And, p. 10. "Moor lands which are in a state of nature, and produce heath, and other wild plants, are of various qualities; very extensive indeed, and much more so than might have been expected in a county so populous, and consequently where lands must be so valuable. These are distinctions, not necessary perhaps, on this occasion, to particularize more minutely, than by observing that the *vales* are in general fertile, but have less of that fertility as they approach nearer to the higher lands."

CLIMATURE.—After an erroneous statement, concerning the mountains of Lancashire, and some
fanciful

fanciful remarks on the effects of its climature, we are told, p. 2,—" Snow continues but a short space of time upon the ground, owing to the maritime situation of the county. The prevailing winds of this county are the West and N. W. winds, which produce a mildness of climate, and salubrity of air and atmosphere, unknown in most districts so far advanced to the north."—And, in p. 3,—" The neighbourhood of the Atlantic ocean, and the elevation of its mountain boundary, certainly render this county more subject to wet weather than most in the kingdom."

In corroboration of this assertion, we are furnished with registers of the quantity of rain which fell, during nine years, in two distant parts of the county. I insert them as valuable facts in the Meteorology of this island :— relying on the authorities mentioned, for their accuracy. p. 4.

Perpendicular

Perpendicular Height of the RAIN that has fallen at Lancaster, during the last Nine Years; distinguishing each Month and Year in Inches and Lines. By DR. CAMPBELL, of Lancaster.

Years.	1784.		1785.		1786.		1787.		1788.		1789.		1790.		1791.		1792.	
Months.	In.	Lin.	In.	Lin.	In.	Lin.	In.	Lin.	In.	Lin.	In.	Lin.	In.	Lin.	In.	Lin.	In.	Lin.
January -	2	8¼	2	6	2	6	1	7½	2	10	4	5	5	11	5	10	3	2
February -	2	3¾	0	6⅓	1	1	5	0	2	1	4	11	1	2¼	3	1¾	3	0
March - - -	2	7½	0	1	0	11	3	7⅓	1	10	0	8⅓	0	8	2	2	5	9
April - -	3	0	1	8	0	4½	1	3½	2	7½	4	3¾	1	3½	4	3	5	9½
May - - -	3	0	1	6	1	8	1	4¼	1	1	4	1½	2	1	2	4½	5	0
June - -	5	9	1	0½	1	10	3	6¼	2	0⅓	5	2½	4	0	0	10½	3	10
July - - -	3	0	2	1½	2	9½	7	0	6	5	5	7¾	7	6	3	6	5	1½
August - -	5	0	10	4	5	0	7	0	2	0¾	0	5½	3	10⅓	6	2	8	6
September -	2	7	5	6	7	11	2	0	3	7¼	4	1¾	5	5	1	9½	9	4
October - -	0	8	5	9	1	6	9	9	2	1½	6	6	2	9	3	10	4	3
November -	3	0	4	6	3	0	4	5¼	1	9¾	4	1	4	6⅓	6	6	4	0
December -	1	6	1	2	3	8	4	5	0	10⅓	6	6	7	4	5	7½	8	1
Total -	35	1½	36	9⅓	32	3	51	0¼	29	4½	51	0¼	46	6½	46	0¾	65	10

N. B.—A line is the twelfth part of an inch.

Perpendicular hight of RAIN that has fallen at Liverpool from the year 1784 to the year 1792 inclusive. By MR. WILLIAM HUTCHINSON, late Dock-master.

1784.	1785.	1786.	1787.	1788.	1789.	1790.	1791.	1792.
36¼ In.	26¼ In.	26½ In.	37¼ In	24⅝ In.	48¼ In.	42¾ In.	45⅜ In.	54¼ In.

P. 65—

P. 65.—" The time of reaping wheat *from* August *to* September."

WATERS.—P. 10.—" The great advantages which this county possesses, both from its having such a range of sea-coast, and also from the numerous streams and rivers it is possessed of (not forgetting the lakes of Windermere and Coniston-water) need hardly be dwelt upon, being so extremely obvious. It may be sufficient to remark, that without those advantages, neither the manufactures of the county, nor the sea and inland fisheries, a matter of no inconsiderable moment to the inhabitants, could be carried on to the same extent." If nothing of wisdom, how much of truth, is couched in the latter part of these Remarks.

FOSSILS.—P. 11. " Lancashire has some local advantages, which have been the cause of rendering the county so famous for its manufactures. These in a great measure depend upon two most material articles, coals and water; the former of which lie in immense beds towards the southern and middle part, and the various rivers, &c. which, together with the springs, in so many places intersect the county, have conjointly had no small effect upon the agriculture of this district, as will be seen hereafter. The north and north-east districts produce limestone in abundance, but no calcareous matter except marle is found towards the south; a small quantity of limestone pebble upon the banks of the river Mersey is also to be excepted. In the township of Halewood, near Liverpool, lime-stone is found and got at different depths, but in small quantities.

" Coals have not been found, as it is said, farther north in the county than Chorley and Colne. The next bed of that useful article, after a long space, appears again in immense quantities at Whitehaven and Newcastle-upon-Tyne. The cannel (a species of coal resembling black marble) lies chiefly at Haigh, near Wigan, and occupies a space, as it is said, of about four miles square.   " Near

"Near Leigh is found lime of a peculiar quality, which resists the effects of water, and is therefore applied to the construction of cisterns to hold water, and mortar for building under water. Also at Ardwick, near Manchester, not many years ago has been discovered a lime of similar, by some it is said of superior, quality. The *tarras*-cistern at Drury-lane house is of this *lime*."

P. 12. " Besides coal, this county also produces stone, of various denominations. Near Lancaster (upon the common) is an extensive quarry of excellent *free-stone*, which admits of a fine *polish*. The county town (Lancaster) is built wholly of this stone, and, for its neatness, is excelled by few towns in the kingdom. Flaggs and grey slates are dug up at Holland, near Wigan. Blue slates are got in large quantities in the mountains, called Conistone and Telberthwaite fells, near Hawkshead, of which many are exported. They are chiefly divided into three classes, viz. London, country, and *tom* slate, which are valued in a due proportion: London are the best, &c. The best scythe-stones are obtained at Rainford, and well wrought on the spot. Iron ore, in large quantities, is obtained near Lindle, between Ulverstone and Dalton, in Low Furness. Copper mines in the North have been worked, but without much success."

SUBJECT THE SECOND.

POLITICAL ECONOMY.

STATE of APPROPRIATION.—P. 86. " In this county there are large tracts of waste land, not less than one hundred and eight thousand five hundred acres, according to Mr. Yates's statement, who took the pains to calculate the number for this particular purpose. —He makes the lands, under the denomination of moss, or fen lands, to be twenty-six thousand

five

five hundred acres. Moors, marshes, and commons, to amount to eighty-two thousand acres. Why seek out distant countries to cultivate, whilst so much remains to be done at home?"—P. 87. " There are many thousand acres capable of being cultivated, and made into either arable, pasture, or meadow land, of a very good quality, provided those wastes were inclosed, divided, and improved ; and, to effect this, there is neither want of inclination or spirit amongst the inhabitants. But there is a want of a general inclosure bill to facilitate that troublesome business, and render it more expeditious and less expensive."

P. 43. " There are but few open or common fields at this time remaining."

STATE OF SOCIETY.—*Provisions.*—In the section, " Crops commonly cultivated," we find a Lancashire *bill of fare.*—P. 56. " The grain principally cultivated is oats, which, when ground to meal, is the food of the labouring class, particularly in the northern and eastern borders of the county ; it is made into bread-cakes, of which there are various kinds, prepared by fermentation with sour leaven; others without leaven, and rolled very thin ; also water, boiled and thickened with meal into porridge; and this, eaten with sweet * or butter-milk. Small-beer sweetened with treacle, or treacle only, was in many families, about forty years ago, both the breakfast and supper meal. The general use of tea, especially among the females, has lessened the use of meal at breakfast ; and the influx of wealth has induced numbers to indulge, upon many occasions, with the wheaten loaf †.

P. 183. " Butchers meat, like other articles in this county,

" * Sweet milk is a provincial term, in contradistinction to the butter-milk, which in this country is sour, and therefore sometimes called sour milk."

† For other remarks on the simple diet of the lower classes of Lancashire, see the subsequent section, *Dairy.*

county, varies in price. It is generally dearest towards the south and south-east, many cattle being driven from the northern part to supply those districts; but still, it is there generally more than a penny per pound under the London market-price. Corn, at Liverpool, is always above the London price, nearly one shilling per bushel, as appears by the returns published."—P. 184. " In estimating the prices of meat, due regard should be paid to the qualities of the meat, different values of the different joints of meat of the same quality, and the different seasons of the year—veal being generally cheapest when beef and mutton are the dearest.

" In the year 1793, the prices of beef might be from 3d. to 5d. per lb.; mutton from 3d. to 6d.; and veal from 3d. to 6d. per lb."

Fuel.—P. 185. " Coals in general abound, and are cheap, insomuch that a small family may supply itself with fuel for about 30 shillings per annum. No wood consumed, but the refuse of ship-carpenters, and other workers in wood. Peat from the different mosses, is an article of fuel in the vicinity of those places, but seldom without the addition of some coals. Faggots, which were formerly an article of consumption among the bakers of sea-biscuit, and other bread in Liverpool, has for some years been discontinued ; coal is preferred, and by experience find it more advantageous."

Employments.—The relation which the employments of *Agriculture* and *Manufactures* bear to each other being here discussed at some length, and this being a proper place in which to endeavor to collect just ideas of their connexion, I am willing to lay in such materials from the Lancashire Report, as will, with others that may fall under my notice in prosecuting my present work, assist in forming a rational and just conception, concerning this unsettled point in political economy.

P. 207.

P. 207. " Manufactures have been carried on to a very considerable extent in Lancashire.

" The cotton, silk, and wool, through all their branches, from the raw material ; and these leading articles include a number of subordinate branches or trades, *e. g.* spinners, bleachers, weavers, dyers, printers, and tool-makers for the different artists, which, if separately enumerated, would in the aggregate extend to an amazing amount.

" There are also manufactories of hats, stockings, pins, needles, nails, small wares, tobacco and tobacco-pipes, snuff, earthen-ware, English porcelain ; clocks and watches, and tools for the artists in these two branches, not only for the neighbourhood but for all the world ; long bows, steel bows, paper, &c.

" There are large works for the smelting of iron and copper, of casting plate-glass, and the fabrication of blown glass ; the process of making white lead, lamp-black, vitriolic acid, and fossil alkali, the refining of sugar, &c."

P. 209. " The good or bad effects which manufactures may have had upon agriculture, is an important question, which merits much attention ; the answers to which, in some letters, have been concise, and discharge by one single word, *e. g.* one answer has been " advantageous ;" another answer " injurious ;" but without either argument or proofs to support these laconic assertions.

" The more extensive answers, however, shall be faithfully stated.

" Manufactures have wrought a change in the agriculture of the county ; the growth of grain is annually and gradually on the decrease. The importation from foreign countries is, of course, upon the advance ; the diminished state of cultivation is one cause of this, and the increasing population is another ; and by the joint operation of these two, the importation of grain and flour, used chiefly in this
county,

county, is almost incredible." And, p. 210, " The advance of wages, and the preference given to the manufacturing employment, by laborers in general, where they may work by the piece, and under cover, have induced many to forsake the spade for the shuttle, and have embarrassed the farmers, by the scarcity of workmen, and of course advanced the price of labour.

" The poor rates fall, with equal burden, upon the farmer, as upon the master manufacturer; and the manufacturers encourage settlers, and consequently increase the number of paupers.

" The water is sometimes so damaged by dye-houses, and other works, erected upon rivers, as to be rendered not wholesome to the cattle, and destructive to fish. The heat necessary for the business of printing debilitates the strongest constitutions.— Damps from obstructed water; pestilential air from crowded rooms;—effluvia from acids and different preparations;—down from cotton; all operate as pestilences to the human constitution.

" On the other hand, the advantages that have been held forth, have been an increase of population; as that which constitutes the riches and strength of a country.

" Increase of the value of lands, and also of provisions. The farmer particularly has an advance on the price of his cheese, his butter, his fatted cattle, his milk; also straw, which, in 1790, sold at the advanced price of 8*d.* per stone in the spring at Liverpool; dearer, probably, than ever was known, even in the London market. Hay is little dearer than thirty years ago, except on extraordinary occasions;— hay is, at present about 8½*d.* per stone, owing to a slight crop;—thirty years ago 6*d.* per stone.

" Capitals, labour, ingenuity, and attention are in this county diverted from agriculture."

Yet the agriculture of this very county was singled out, by the Board, to make the first impression on
the

the public mind—and astonish " the three estates of parliament"—with their important collection of local knowledge, for the improvement of British agriculture.

Let us listen again.—Note, p. 211.—" The following are the observations of a practical farmer upon this important subject.—' From various circumstances it evidently appears, that trade is injurious to agriculture, and in the end to landed property, unless it could be restricted; for whenever a stagnation in trade happens, the poor rates rise, and the land pays for it. Poor rates and other taxes in West Houghton have amounted this year to 16s. in the pound. Corn is not so much grown, for though the farmer can get in his grain, he cannot raise hands but at an enormous price to reap it: if mowing corn were more practised, it would be better.'

" Another farmer says, ' Never inquire about the cultivation of land, or its produce, within ten or twelve miles of Manchester; the people know nothing about it: speak of spinning-jennies, and mules, and carding machines, they will talk for days with you.'

" There are people about Ashton that give 6l. for a summer's grass for horses to work carding engines, and will give from 12l. to 15l. for hay and after-grass, that they may not be troubled with cultivating land to hinder them, as they say. If land were attended to, and improved, for ten to fifteen miles round Manchester, as it is in Derbyshire, the lower parts of Yorkshire, Nottinghamshire, &c. it would be as productive as any land in any part of England; for it all inclines to marl, and is naturally a strong soil, not only fit to carry manure of any kind, but hold it for a sufficient time."

And again,—p. 212.—" There needs little to prove the importance of manufactories in a national view; and their effect upon agriculture, theoretically speaking, seem immense, in as much as they form the best and

and most certain markets :—But, practically speaking, they are baneful to agriculture.

" The immediate wages to be obtained in the manufactories rob agriculture of its most valuable supporters ;—the yeoman and the laborer are both tempted from the plough ;—all competition is precluded.—Who will work for 1*s.* 6*d.* or 2*s.* a day at a ditch, when he can get 3*s.* 6*d.* or 5*s.* a day in a cotton work, and be drunk four days out of seven ?—But their most destructive effect are the increase of the poor rates. In winter many hands are turned out of employment, who must be supported by parish rates ; the laborer at cotton must, when sick, or ill, or aged, be supported by taxes levied upon agriculture.— Manufactories encourage settlers of all descriptions.— Above 5000 Irish were settled at Manchester in the year 1787, and I am told that number was afterwards doubled.—The poor laws in this circumstance are extremely defective."—And, finally, p. 213, " Another evil arising from manufactories is, the propagation of vice, insubordination, and diseases.—What else can arise from the multitude of people of all descriptions pent up in printing-houses, from which it is necessary to exclude all exterior air, and to keep up an artificial heat, which must of course debilitate the strongest constitutions ?—Add to this, effluvia from acids, paints, minerals, and charcoal."

LOCAL TAXES.—*Poor Rates.*—P. 22. " Poor rates are at Liverpool 2*s.* 6*d. per* lb. ; at Walton 12*d. per* lb. ; at Manchester 6*s. per* lb. at a highly-valued rental, but taxed at only half value, they are therefore at 3*s. per* lb. on the rental ; at Bolton 6*s.* a late assessment, but would be 4*s.* of full and present value ; Rochdale about 4*s.* ; at West Houghton 16*s.* the pound ; Ashton 5*s. per annum ;* Oldham 5*s. per annum* on the full rental."

P. 214.—" Whatever may be the state of the poor, they are most liberally provided for, not only by legal assessments, but liberal contributions—when particular seasons,

seasons, or calamitous circumstances, may call forth the humanity of those who, on such occasions, give without sparing. Yet, with all the aid of large assessments, and liberal contributions, it is truly lamentable to witness such appearance of poverty, exemplified in nakedness, dirtiness, and the different garbs which indicate distress. There are mendicants of all ages and sexes, but more particularly in the country villages; the exerted police of well-governed towns restrains these wanderers.

"In brief, it may be asserted, that from appearances, the *state of the poor* is not so comfortable as might be wished; and yet from the sums levied and contributed, if properly applied, their situation might be meliorated.

"Friendly societies seem the guides which point out radical cures for the existing evils. When a man once gets into the habit of *laying up* in store, however small the capital, he feels a satisfaction which stimulates exertions to increase his stock; and that pride of independence which ensues from an enjoyment of the acquisition of his well-deserved, however hard-earned substance, render his meals sweet, his family regular, clean, and decent, and his spirits cheered by the fruits of his own labors. Friendly societies have been the means of causing all this among many of their members; they are numerous in this county; they are increasing, and ought to be encoraged."

These remarks, on the state and melioration of the poor of Lancashire, are creditable to the head and heart that dictated them.

Tithe.—P. 22.—"The tythes are in many places collected, one *eleventh* of the corn—the hay is frequently converted, five shillings *per* acre for old meadows, six shillings *per* acre for first year's clover (acre large measure)."

PUBLIC WORKS.—*Canals.*—P. 197.—"The Sankey canal was the first inland navigation in the kingdom, and was opened in the year 1756; after which the Duke of Bridgewater's canal; and then the Leeds canal, as far as Wigan, were completed. The canal from Kendal, through Lancaster, to Westhoughton, is a great undertaking, ten miles of which are already completed. The Bolton canal, already begun, the Rochdale canal intended, with the navigable rivers Mersey, Douglass, Ribble, Wyre, and Loyne, render the carriage of heavy articles, through the internal parts of the county, more easy and less expensive, than where such chanels of conveyance are not found. They have no small effects upon the agriculture of the county, in conveying dung, lime, and other articles, into parts whither, without their assistance, they could hardly have been transmitted; as also upon the manufactures, by the conveyance of coal and raw materials, the gross weight of which would have been too expensive upon carriage by land."

P. 196.—" In granting new bills for cutting navigable canals, care should be taken by the legislature, that lime or manure be carried upon low terms. The introduction of wealth, in consequence of superior cultivation, by the means of manures, &c. will introduce the carriage of more bulky articles, and soon repay the proprietors the trifling indulgence. A gentleman observed, that, as a certain portion of land was lost to the community, either for tillage or pasture, by cutting canals, care ought to be taken in the banks to preserve as much grass as possible, by burying the rubbish under ground, and applying the best soil to cover the surface of the banks; trifling as such an object may be, as canals are daily increasing, the amount, in the issue, would be something, and would repay to the public a sum sufficient for the general attention requisite."—Beside the stability which the banks would receive, by a covering of sward.

Roads.—On this subject, we have a valuable section;—in which the *Surveyor's* good sense has an opportunity of showing itself. Here, Mr. H. appears

to

to have a practical knowledge of his subject. But his remarks are, in the reprinted Report, so confounded with those of some other person, that it is difficult to recognize them, without referring to the original Report. I therefore keep them separate, here.

P. 186. " Mr. Yates* observes, that there is a greater length of roads in this cownty, in proportion to its extent, than in any other county in the kingdom."

In proof of this assertion Mr. H. adduces two remarkable instances (p. 186): " the parish of Goosnargh contains 3703 acres, and the length of the roads in that parish is nearly forty miles, besides three miles of bridle road, and three miles of road repaired by certain individuals.

" The township of Walton, near Liverpool, which only contains 1988 statute acres, has a public road two miles and a half in length; parochial roads, eleven miles two furlongs, besides occupation roads."

Of the *materials* of the roads of Lancashire, Mr. Holt gives the following account.—P. 186. " In the northern and north-eastern parts of the county, materials for making roads are found upon the spot, the lime stone, which, when broken, binds together, and makes an excellent road; but in the midland and southern parts, the materials, except what the rivers afford, are brought from the Welsh and Scotch coasts, and at considerable expense.

" These are *Boulder stones*, and they are not broken, but paved. The whole expense of which is from 1 s. 2 d. to 2 s. *per* square yard, according to the distance of the materials to be carried. Two quarries of pebbles have lately been discovered. Copper scoria or slag, from two works, Ravenhead and Liverpool, have been successfully tried. This articles makes an excellent side road to the pavements, and is preferred

to

* Who had previously surveyed the county, as a mapist.

to pavements both by the horseman and drivers of carriages.

" Great exertions have been made of late years, at very considerable expense*, to improve the roads , the effects of which are very apparent, both upon those which are public and parochial."

The *paved roads*, I rather think, are confined to the southern, and do not extend into the midland, parts of the county. They mostly belong, I believe, to the sandyland districts. In travelling, northward, from Warrington, the pavements, of the two branches or divaricating lines of the great road, terminate near Chorley and Eccleston. And, in going from Liverpool to Preston, the paved road, I think, ends on entering the rush lands, near Rufford.

P. 188. " With respect to *improvements,* an ingenious gentleman † observed, that the tolls in general ought either to be raised, or the number of bars increased, in order that the public at large might contribute a proper quota, for their ease in travelling, by the improved state of the road, and the farmer, &c. of course eased; and candour must allow, that the facility, expedition, and security of travelling over the roads, in their present state, is worth more than double the money paid for this convenience. Some method should be devised to ease the laborer, and lay the burden upon the traveller. The tenant has frequently been charged with an unexpected tax, amounting to 4 or 5 s. in the pound, upon a short lease, when a fine has been levied; and though, in the issue, this class receives as great benefit as any other, still some method should be devised to ease those

" * So great, that at the time when Mr. Yates took his survey, about ten years since, the average paid through the county, was not less than eighteenpence in the pound."

† In the *original Report,* the following note is appended, p. 64.—
" J. B. Bailey, Esq.—we are deprived of this gentleman's promised communications, on account of indisposition."

those contingent possessors, by more heavily taxing the travelling stranger.

" Under this head, the indulgence shown to the mail coaches in their exemption from tolls, merits reprehension.

" In the first place, the object is too trifling and mean, for the interference of Government. It is also an encroachment upon private property, and upon a capital, the interest of which was expected to be paid upon the credit of certain tolls, with an accumulating surplus, to repair the damage done to the roads by the passing of these carriages—and with the remaining portion, to liquidate the principal advanced to accommodate the public in the execution of these undertakings *. But here is a check upon these spirited endeavours by encroachment. If the price at present paid for the carriage of the mail be not sufficient, it should be increased by an addition taken from the common stock."

Further, p. 189. " What is here objected to, is the infringement upon private property. And if these tolls were not allowed, they would be charged at last upon the passenger, upon whom they ought certainly to fall.

" But again, the tolls allowed to be taken from this species of carriages, if they were even extended to the mail coaches, are not sufficient for the damage done by them, in proportion to the rates paid, and the damage done by other carriages to the roads.

" The weight of a mail coach, loaded with passengers and parcels, may be near two tons, the heavy coach nearly three tons.

" The effects of four horses, scampering and pulling with all their might, are very injurious to the roads; for, after the stones have been nearly displaced

by

" * Mail coaches prevent much travelling post—consequently injure the toll-bars more ways than one."

by this exertion of the horse-feet (very different to the effect of a road-horse), followed by a heavy carriage, supported and dragged upon four narrow wheels, every obstruction is displaced by the violence of the motion. The slow pace of a waggon, moving upon a nine-inch surface, or a heavy-loaded cart, under two or three tons burden, upon six-inch wheels, makes a comparison strongly in favour of these carriages.

"Again, the tolls arising from many turnpikes are very insufficient to maintain the roads. The township of Walton, at the present juncture, is meeting the trustees of the public road, which runs through that district, with not a less sum than four hundred and thirty pounds, besides statute labor, upon a length of two miles and a half; whilst the same township is burdened with other roads of the length of eleven miles two furlongs and a half, as before observed.

"All the townships through which this turnpike passes are, at present, contributing their aid, and that to a degree in some places not a little burdensome to both tenant and freeholders; of which the township of Aintree is a strong example."

Thus far Mr. HOLT.

What follows appears to have been taken from the promised paper of Mr. BAILEY (see note, p. 263): some of whose remarks are highly valuable; while others are more of a speculative, than a practical nature. The subjoined extracts, however, will sufficiently prove the great attention which Mr. B. has paid to this very important subject of Political Economy.

Materials.—P. 187. "Pavements are the most expensive, and most disagreeable of all roads, but we have no other material that will stand heavy cartage.

"Near Warrington, Mr. Kerfoot, who undertook the management of the Prescot and Manchester turnpikes, has made admirable roads with the copper slag.

"Mr. Holt, who is surveyor for one parish, made an attempt

attempt with copper slag, but it is difficult to get the slag sufficiently broken."

Again, p. 190. "The properest roads for this part of the county, particularly the neighbourhood of Manchester and Liverpool, and all the coal district, would be roads similar to those of France and Flanders: a pavement in the centre, made of large fragments of granite (which might be imported from Scotland, at no great expense) on each side of this pavement should be a gravel road, of the best material the country could afford, and made of sufficient breadth, and kept in such good repair as to induce all light carriages to prefer it to the pavement in the centre: I prevailed upon the surveyor of this township to make an experiment of backing up a high pavement with copper slag (scoriæ) some years ago, and to cover it with the loose sandy rock of the country. It is now the best part of the turnpike.

" In addition to the above, it may be necessary to state that from the vast increase of carriage in this county, and the general use of waggons, carts, &c. with *excessive weights*, it is become almost impossible, by any means, and at any expense, to support the public roads. The climate is wet, the soil soft, the stone and gravel found in the county are not hard or lasting, and the only materials that have strength and durability are the paving stones imported from the coasts of Wales, at the heavy price of six shillings per ton. Some of the turnpike roads in the neighbourhood of Manchester, paved with these stones, cost from 1500*l*. to 2000*l*. per mile."!

The *Form* of Roads.—P. 188. "An ingenious road-maker in the neighboured of Warrington, has of late exploded the common *convex* form, and adopted that of *one-inclined plane;* the inclination just sufficient to throw off occasional water. By this alteration he finds that a road becomes more durable; for when it is convex, all heavy carriages use the centre of it, and keep in the same track; therefore the centre

is

is soon destroyed, and the sides seldom used: but when a road has only one small inclination, the whole surface is used, for, in this case, you will seldom see two carriages take the same line."

Applied to *narrow lanes,* and narrow roads, in general, these remarks are justly founded. The surface, however, of a RECLINING ROAD should not be *plane,* but *convex:* should perfectly resemble either side of a well formed barrel road. It would be nearly as improper to form a wide public road with two inclined planes—to resemble the flat roof of a building—as a narrow SINGLE ROAD, with " one inclined plane;"—which, even when first formed, is less capable of throwing off rain water, from its lower skirts, than a surface that partakes of the convex or barrel form. And further, although the wear of a reclining road is more even than that of a narrow barrel, yet the body, or middle part, will ever be more worn than the margins. Hence, a *plane* surface soon becomes *concave;* and, consequently, retains the waters of rains, on its lower side. Therefore, whenever a single road has been worn down to a plain surface, or regularly inclining plane, it requires a fresh covering over the middle parts, to round it,—to raise it, again, into the semi-convex, or half-barrel form.

For analytical remarks, on the forms of roads, with an explanatory diagram, see TREATISE on LANDED PROPERTY, 4to edit. p. 281: or the ABSTRACT, p. 311.

The following suggestions concerning the *placing* of *toll gates,* on turnpike roads,—a subject that has seldom been *publicly* agitated,—are particularly entitled to attention.

P. 187. " The town of Liverpool is a great enemy to turnpikes. There are only three toll-gates within eight miles of it, none within four.

" Commercial and manufacturing towns have *a system* of throwing every possible burden upon the land.

" The

" The toll-bars here, as well as in other parts, from private views and interest, are improperly placed— should they not in each act, be placed in the most advantageous situations for the benefit of the road by strangers, commissioners appointed for that purpose, and private interest totally be laid aside ? Most of the great towns have had sufficient interest to place the toll-bars at some miles distance from them. The toll-bar on the road to the south from Liverpool is placed at 5 miles distance from the town. Would it not be a fair clause in the general act of parliament, when the inhabitants of a town object to a bar being placed near to the town, that they should engage to keep in repair the road from the town to the bar (which is in general the most expensive part of the whole) without receiving the least benefit from the money collected? The distance the bars are placed from the great towns in this county, is almost the sole cause of the wretched condition of the turnpike roads."

Mr. BAILEY,—after exposing the iniquity of suffering *broad wheels*, with *convex fellies*, to bear *heavy weights*, and pay *low tolls!*—and after pointing out the folly of dragging heavy carriages over the summits of hills, while the easy and obvious levels of the subjacent vallies are overlooked,—concludes his valuable communication respecting roads, with the following well conceived suggestion.

P. 196. " As turnpike bills have been usually too much considered as *private* bills (though none are of more *public* concern) the committees of the House of Commons have usually done little more than confirm the agreements of the meetings previously held in the country, in which personal and local interests frequently supersede a due consideration of general benefit. The experience which these committees have had on various occasions of this selfish spirit, has produced some very salutary orders relating to bills for making turnpike roads."

" To

" To enable these committees more accurately to judge of the propriety of future applications for making new or *amending old* turnpike acts, I would suggest another standing rule and order; viz.

" ' That, together with the estimate of expense, and the account of the money subscribed (as ordered by the 3d rule) there be delivered to the committee an exact plan of the proposed road, on a scale of   to a mile, showing its connection with the neighbouring towns; together with an accurate *section* of the whole line of road.' "

Markets.—P. 198.—" *There are said to be* twenty-six market-towns in the county, which are supposed sufficient for the inhabitants, because in every little village or hamlet of houses, there are retailers of the different articles, which are of daily consumption, in great abundance. The two large towns, Manchester and Liverpool, have each two market days every week; but of late years, butchers meat, garden-stuff, and a number of the necessary articles of life, are exposed to sale, and may be purchased any day in the week, Sundays excepted."

In p. 206, Major Atherton says,—" I have heard it confidently asserted that this district (the counties of Lancaster and Chester) do not supply the consumption for more than six weeks in the year, and that the county of Lancaster in particular, does not grow more grain than would feed or be consumed in it in two weeks."!

" *Whence the Markets are supplied.*"—P. 184.— " The principal fatting districts in this county are from Claughton to Hornby, a rich pasture there called the Holmes, and from thence through that fertile vale as far as Kirkby Lonsdale; also some gentlemen's parks, and private inclosures, but the whole of these amount to a mere trifle, compared to the consumption requisite. The deficiency is made up from the counties of Westmoreland, Durham, Yorkshire, Lincolnshire, Derbyshire, and Shropshire; the principality

principality of Wales, the kingdoms of Ireland and Scotland, are also applied to, to supply the county of Lancaster with beef and mutton. The county itself furnishes a very small proportion of the bread and meat actually consumed there. Nay, the poultry and the pigeons are supplied from distant parts. Besides what comes from the Filde (the only district in the county which, with a few trifling exceptions, has any surplus of stock) the Liverpool market has supplies from Cheshire, Wales, Isle of Man, Scotland, and Ireland. Manchester also receives great supplies from Cheshire, Derbyshire, Lincolnshire, and even Nottinghamshire. Eggs of course must be purchased, and come from the same quarters, and some at a greater distance, packed up in casks. Some come even from Kendall, and Penrith*."

SUBJECT THE THIRD.

RURAL ECONOMY.

DIVISION THE FIRST.

TENANTED ESTATES ; their IMPROVE-MENT and MANAGEMENT.

PRESENT STATE of PROPERTY.—*Sizes* of *Estates.* P. 13.—" Since the introduction of manufactures, property

---

" * Some of the eggs sold at Manchester are packed up with layers of straw between every row of eggs, about ten thousand in one cart. The man brings two carts, and comes every fortnight during the season that a sufficient number can be collected; which is chiefly done by women who travel the country with mugs and other articles, which they exchange for eggs in Cumberland, &c. There are two or more higglers (*qu.* egglers?) who follow this practice, besides the old man who gave the information above, and who was counting them out to the hucksters. Few eggs are broken by the carriage. The man is four days upon the road. It seems the collectors of the eggs are paid 6 *d.* per hundred for collection."

property has become more minutely divided. But there remain proprietors who still hold very extensive possessions."

Tenures.—P. 14. " The tenures are chiefly freehold. There are some copyhold."—A literal extract.

IMPROVEMENT of ESTATES. *Superintendents.*— P. 14. " Estates are principally under the direction of stewards and bailiffs. A few individuals have attended personally to the improvement of their own lands; and having executed their work in a superior manner, without doubt have found their account in the superior profit derived from such exertions."— P. 24.—" Upon the estate of that intelligent landlord, Mr. Bayley, of Hope, whenever a tenant wishes for the whole of his farm, or any particular field, to be improved, by draining, marling, liming, dunging, or laying down to grass in a superior manner, the landlord takes the field into his own possession, during the process; and, when completed, returns it again to the tenant, with an advanced rent of ten *per cent.* upon the capital laid out upon the improvements ; by which steps Mr Bayley has advanced the rental of his estate, since the year 1768, very considerably— his tenants are thriving, and getting money."

Reclaiming watery Lands.—P. 88 —Mr. Wilkinson of Castle Head, " by turning the course of some brooks, has recovered lands from the sea; by which the flux of the tide, in the space of about eight years, has raised the lands near six feet; so that, after the water is kept in narrower bounds, by the opening of a new channel, the tide alone does the work."

But, somewhat remissly, the Reporter, be who he may, has not informed the Board where this improvement was effected; in what muddy creek or narrow estuary it took place:—nor what neat advantage, after all expenses paid, accrued from it. The latter, however, we may presume was considerable; as on the success of his first experiment, Mr. W. it appears,

was

was inclined to risk fifty thousand pounds in the prosecution of a larger work: namely, that of covering the Lancaster and Millthorp, the Ulverstone, and the Duddon sands, in like manner: and thereby gaining 38,710 acres of land,—estimated at more than a million and a half of money: and this, by merely diverting the channels of the Kent and other rivers or brooks which now pass downward, through these sands, to the sea,—at the comparatively inconsiderable expense of two hundred thousand pounds.

An increase of productive territory is among the first objects of an island that is unable to feed its inhabitants; and most especially of the county of Lancaster, for reasons that appear, above. It would therefore be unpardonable to check a spirit of enterprize (no matter whether actuated by public or private motives) which might lead to so desirable an end. But when it is considered that nothing tends more to damp that virtuous flame, than a ruinous miscarriage, it becomes a public duty to endeavor to prevent a circumstance so mischievous, not only in its immediate effect, but in its consequences, from taking place.

The sites of the proposed improvements being at present frequented by travellers, when the tide is out, as public roads between places situated on opposite sides of them, they may be considered in this general view, as *naked sands*. And judging from the fatal accidents that happen to passengers crossing these sands, we may conclude that the tide, at its height, covers them several feet deep with water. Hence, a quantity of alluvious matter, sufficient to cover 38,710 acres, some—if not several—feet deep, on a par, will be required to effect the projected improvement.—For no embankments, against tides and tempests, are intended!—only—" when the sea had nearly embanked itself, it might be found convenient to raise sand banks a few feet high, in order to keep off high spring tides." P. 91.

From

From whence, we may be allowed to ask, are the materials, requisite to the accomplishment of this immense work, to arise? If the estuaries, and the margins of the bay, here intended to be filled up, or raised above the overflowings of ordinary tides, were situated at the mouth of the Humber, or that of the Severn, the project might be feasible, would be. I doubt not, in a great measure practicable; and, in a course of years, a valuable addition to the territory of the island might be acquired.

Those two rivers having, century after century. flowed through a great extent of rich and cultivated vale lands, their estuaries are become store rooms of suspendible soil; which being agitated by the rushing in of the tides, and these impelled forward, so as to form the eagre and the boar of those two rivers,—their channels, at high water, may be said to be filled with liquid mud.—Hence, the extraordinary improvements that are made on the banks of the Humber, and its branches, by " warping :" a subject that will be noticed in reviewing the next Report.

But the actual situation of the estuaries and margins, now under view, is the reverse. Most of the brooks, which empty into them, are mere mountain torrents;—forming, perhaps, beds of *stones* and *gravel*, but affording few *suspendible particles,* suitable to the formation of fertile soil. The Kent is the only stream that passes through any extent of cultivated vale lands : and this is proposed to be led away from the site of improvement : the riches which it may bring along with it, in times of floods, being generously intended to be given to the estuary of the Lone !

Hence, it necessarily follows, that the almost only alluvious matter, by which this extent of territory is proposed to be created, is that already lodged in the estuary of the Kent (in which, it is probable, Mr. Wilkinson's improvement was effected); and, with this, the tide, when not counteracted, might be able,

in

in time, to form a few hundred acres of valuable marsh land.

Reclaiming Morass, or *Moss Land*.—P. 94. " In the parish of Eccles, is a large tract of moss land called Chat Moss, lying between the township of Worsley and the navigable river Irwell, containing some thousand acres ; and on the south side the river is another piece of land called Trafford Moss, which adjoins to the park of John Trafford, Esq. and contains about 500 statute acres."—P. 95. " In the year 1793, Mr. Wakefield, and Mr. Roscoe of Liverpool, undertook the improvement of these lands, and a contract was entered into with the proprietor, Mr. Trafford, for a lease of them for a term of years under a yearly rent."

Those efforts of improvement were of course in their infancy, in June 1795. And although some accounts of these and other attempts are here given, I should not have felt myself justified (even if any thing new or excellent had *seemed* to arise from them) in copying after what may, in this particular, be literally termed a *vague report*.—Laying railways upon the unstable moss, on which to draw materials for its improvement, is well entitled to notice.

A circumstantial account of the improvement of moss lands which, I understand, have been going on, in Lancashire, since that time, analytically arranged in the progressive order of practice, and in such a manner as to render every part distinct, and clearly to be understood,—could not fail of being highly valuable.

EXECUTIVE MANAGEMENT of ESTATES. *Tenancy.*
—P. 14. " *Leases on lives* have been more frequent formerly, than at present ; but the practice for granting leases for lives is not entirely discontinued."

P. 22. " Many farms are held by leases on three lives*, on which a fine has been paid, and a small annual

---

* " When a lease is granted for three fresh lives, on an average the term lasts upwards of 50 *years*." (?)

annual rent reserved; and sometimes an addition of
boon services ; which last system seems much on the
decline. These leases are generally estimated at
about *fourteen years purchase.* The, *leases* upon years
are, from seven, eleven, to fourteen; but chiefly
seven."

The following remarks (by whom does not appear)
on the *operation* of *life leases*, corresponding with what
I have observed in the WEST of ENGLAND, I copy
them, at length,—tautological and slovenly as they
are !

P. 26. " Leases upon lives only act as checks to
improvements ; they are, in general, only beneficial
to the first purchaser, who secures an income on three
lives, for fourteen years purchase—the fee simple of
which would have required double the sum. The
successors, elevated by possessing an estate under a
small annual quit rent, instead of full rent, *live up to
the height,* as the phrase is, and are but ill-prepared
to renew the lease, or pay the fine required when a
life drops. The lease, through inability of the tenant
to renew, or some other cause, is suffered to run out,
under the uncertainty of life, and the lands (there being no provision made by covenants to prevent it) are
harassed and abused to such a degree, as to require a
length of time to restore them.

" Theory and practice, it must be confessed, are
perpetually at variance, as well in Agriculture as
many other pursuits. It might at first sight appear,
that the custom of granting leases for three lives (a
tenure that gives such probable security to a tenant)
would excite a degree of spirit of improvement
amongst the holders of these tenures. Experience
however proves the contrary fact—For leaseholds
upon lives are generally under the most wretched cultivation.

" Easy rents may have produced a careless indolence, and hence an aversion to enterprize. The
landlord having but little interest in such estates, and
less

less power over such tenants, is himself checked from
any spirit of improvement upon such contingent property. Those proprietors who look a little towards
the welfare of posterity, are come to a resolution of
running these tenures out, and, of course, the tenants
are not behind in exhausting and every way impo-
verishing the land.

" The ancient custom of granting leases for three
lives is beginning to disappear : It should seem probable that this tenure, which grants so much security
to the tenant, would naturally excite a liberal and
enterprising spirit of husbandry : fact however proves
the reverse of the proposition ; the ancient leasehold
estates being almost universally in a wretched state of
cultivation, beyond all comparison less productive
than those held upon shorter tenures. Easy rents,
secure possession, and good land, have lulled the leaseholders into a careless indolence, an aversion to enterprize, which have been productive of much ill to
themselves and their connections, and, above all, to
the public ; much ill has accrued to the leaseholders
from the power of borrowing money upon this ideal
species of property.—These observations hold good to
the custom of half rent and half fine. Upon such
tenures the immediate landlord can have no induce-
ment to advance money for the amelioration of his
estate, and but little interest and less power either
to prevent his land being exhausted by wretched husbandry, or to oblige his tenants to keep upon their
farms a due proportion of stock. Whoever will take
the trouble of examining the estates of this county
held upon three lives, will find the arable worn out
by a perpetual succession of exhausting crops, and
the grass little more than a collection of rushes and
beggary, the whole unditched, undrained, and un-
manured. Landlords have at length become sensible to their own interests, and are suffering their
leases to run out, which, though a wise policy, is
destructive in its immediate effects : in fact, the
country

country is at this time suffering extremely in consequence.

" Modern leases upon land in high condition are from seven to eleven years;—upon improveable land fourteen to twenty-one:—But landlords in this county will never adopt the system of granting *long leases* free *from all restrictions*, such as are recommended by the surveyors for the West-Riding of York.—To recommend such a system to a manufacturing county would be absurd.

" The first purchaser of leaseholds is generally a sensible industrious man, who understands his business, and attends to it. His successors are often both ignorant and idle, but their tenure is secure, and they cannot be disturbed in their possessions by any thing but their own folly; this often induces them either to harass their estate themselves, or let them off at rack rent to some poor devil, without any capital or means of procuring one.

" I know that the contrary may be, and often is the case, and that the abuse of a good custom is no argument against the custom itself: but I also know that there are no poorer or more wretched people in the county than the occupants of leasehold estates, and that the sons and grandsons of most of the original leaseholders are not to be found upon such estates —A middle man is the devil—all the world knows the consequence of this custom in Ireland—*the little lords* of this country are in the same predicament."

Covenants.—P. 23. " Usual covenants are, the landlord to repair buildings, the tenant carting the materials. The tenants severally to discharge all taxes, serve all offices, and all the duties charged upon the farm.

" Tenants are restrained, by covenant, to the quantity allowed to plow, sometimes to one-third, sometimes to one-fourth, of the whole; and also, of late, to the number of crops to be taken at one breaking up of the ground—sometimes to four crops; and sometimes only three are allowed. Tenants are restrained,

strained, by covenant, from sowing wheat upon bean stubble, or any other stubble from which a crop has been taken the same year. The tenants, by covenant, restrained from paring or burning, except moss lands.

" The tenants sometimes restrained, by covenant, from selling either hay or straw, but are bound to consume the whole upon the premises.

" The tenants, by covenant, restrained from selling off their stock till the close of the year, at the expiration of their term, that the greater quantity of dung may be raised from the produce consumed.

" The tenants allowed to take off three-fourths of the wheat growing upon the premises at the expiration of a lease. The succeeding tenant to have the remaining quarter.

" A succeeding tenant to have permission, after Candlemas, at the expiration of a lease, to occupy certain portions of the outbuildings, by clauses founded for the accommodation of his horses, hay, &c. necessary for the spring feeding, on the new tenant entering upon his farm."—" Covenants in some to pay the rent the day the tenant enters upon the premises. This covenant for the security of the landlord, but not exacted except on emergencies."

Time of *Removal.* P. 23. " The time of entering upon the lands is Candlemas; and on the buildings, May-day."

Rent. P. 22.—" The rent of lands is very variable in the different parts of the county, from ten shillings to ten pounds *per annum*, the large acre, of eight yards to the rod; the latter enormous sum, being frequently paid in the vicinity of large towns, for particular accommodation. The price paid by the farmer is from ten shillings for some barren lands, up to twenty, thirty, forty, and some (but not many) as high as eighty shilling *per* acre *per annum* (large measure)":—which is somewhat more than two acres and one tenth, statute measure.

DIVISION

WOODLANDS.

PAGE 84. " There are no natural woods of any consequence to merit attention. The plantations are in general intended as embellishments for gentlemen's seats, cover for game, or shelter from the blast, rather than with a view of supplying the country with timber, and preventing importation.

" Towards the coast it is with great difficulty that wood of any kind can be raised: the tops of the trees, hedges, and even the corn in the fields (in general) bend towards the east, as if shrinking from the western gale, brought over the Atlantic ocean; yet, near the shore at Formby Hall, several acres of land have been planted with forest and fruit-trees, which are in so flourishing a state as to afford general encouragement to the inhabitants of the sea-coast, to fence against the wintry blast, and to raise wholesome fruits for their tables."—And, in p. 85, Mr. Formby's method is more particularly mentioned.—" On the sea-coast there are some acres of land planted with forest-trees, which are flourishing and ornamental to the country. They were originally placed in holes (with a mixture of sea-slutch and broken pieces of turf at their roots) four inches beneath the surface of the ground; *and sods were raised round them, to guard their tender shoots* from the wintry blast. Its violence is least injurious to the sycamore, the ash, the alder, fir, and platanus.—This observation is communicated by the Reverend Mr. Formby, of Formby, who has succeeded in raising plantations so near the sea, that it was hardly thought practicable till he effected it."

In a note, p. 44, we find the following method of
preventing

preventing cattle from browzing unguarded young trees and hedges.—" The hair from a raw hide, with all the impurities adhering, if laid in small quantities, near the roots of the thorn, have been found sufficient security from the teeth of cattle. The cows will not approach near hedges thus defended."

DIVISION THE THIRD.

AGRICULTURE.

FARMS. *Sizes.*—P. 19.—" In most townships * there is one farm, still distinguished by the name of the Old Hall, or Manor House (the residence formerly of the great proprietor of that district) which is of larger extent than any of the adjoining or neighbouring farms. Few of these farms, however, exceed 600 statute acres: many do not extend to the amount of 200. But the more general size of farms is from 50, 40, 30, down to 20 acres a-piece; or even so much only as will keep a horse or cow only; or one of these, as is most convenient."

This passage, I have pleasure in observing, is written in the best style of agricultural Report. It appears in the original, and is probably Mr. Holt's.

Homesteads.—P. 16.—" Farms of sixty pounds a year, in Lancashire, have offices frequently as large as would be thought to suffice, in other counties, for farms of three or four hundred *per ann.* where it is the custom to stack their corn, which is not the general practice in Lancashire."

OCCUPIERS.—P. 13.—" The yeomanry, formerly numerous and respectable, have greatly diminished of late, but are not yet extinct: the great wealth which

" * The parishes of Lancashire are again subdivided into townships."

which has in many instances been so rapidly acquired by some of their neighbours, and probably heretofore dependants, has offered sufficient temptation to venture their property in trade, in order that they might keep pace with these fortunate adventurers.

" Not only the yeomanry, but almost all the farmers, who have raised fortunes by agriculture, place their children in the manufacturing line.—The farmers in this county mostly spring from the industrious class of laborers, who, having saved by great economy a sum of money, enter upon small farms, and afterwards, in proportion to the increase of their capitals, take larger concerns." --Nevertheless, we are told, p. 19, that notwithstanding " farmers in general are charged with being stupid, obstinate, and attached to old customs. In this county they do not *altogether* merit these harsh accusations."—Admitting this, however, we cannot reasonably expect from the farmers of Lancashire, if they really are what they are here represented to be, much valuable information for the improvement, or accurate cultivation, of the rest of the kingdom. We will not, however, condemn them unheard; but take the evidence of their practice; as their general character may have suffered by the too great modesty of the Reporter.

PLAN of MANAGEMENT.—On due examination, however, the following accounts, I find, are not calculated to remove the impressions of the last.

P. 71. " Although there is a mixture of arable and grass land, yet the latter must greatly preponderate, and *that* to such a degree, *that* it has been frequently asserted, *that* the corn raised in Lancashire would not support the inhabitants more than three months in the year; so that the easiest way of obtaining corn, until the county is improved, is to purchase it at other markets.

" The lands in the immediate vicinity of the great towns are chiefly employed in pasturage; at a remoter distance, in pasturage and meadow, immense quantities

quantities of hay being requisite for the number of horses and cows kept therein. Near some places, such as Bolton, besides the demand for lands under hay and grass, a great number of acres are occupied as bleaching grounds; and throughout the whole of the county there are, in different places, many acres of rich land, covered with yarn, or cloth, under various operations.

" These several causes have had a tendency to change the system of the agriculture of the county, and to convert the arable grounds into grass lands; and this system of management seems yearly increasing, even in those parts which were formerly considered as the corn districts; such as that fertile soil under the denomination of the Filde, a tract of land from the north of the Ribble along the coast as far as Cockersands, to the turnpike road on the east.

" At this period, (1795) the diminution of arable land is likely to become a serious calamity to the nation at large. The conversion of arable land into grass in this county may be imputed to seven causes. —1st. The enormous and immoderate wages to be obtained in the manufactories, which has wrested the arm of industry from the plough.—2d. The consequent increase of the poor rates, because the manufactories do not support their own poor; and the manufacturers, if out of employment, when sick, or infirm, or aged, are supported by *taxes levied upon agriculture.*—3d. By all capitals being invested in the working cotton instead of raising corn.—4th. To the very absurd rotation of crops used throughout the county.—5th. To the barbarous custom of keeping the same land too long under the plough.—6th. To an opinion, originating in the consequence of the two last reasons, that grass is more valuable than corn. Good grass probably may, but not such grass as is to be found through a great part of this district.— And, 7th. To the exaction of tythes in kind." And, p. 72.—" Pasture lands are, in general, most miserably

ably laid down, they being in many places left to nature, to supply the ground with whatever seeds remained in the earth, or came from other quarters, carried by the winds or other accidental causes; and in the Filde particularly the lands have, on many occasions, been so exhausted by repeated plowings, that they are rendered incapable of yielding any useful herbage; seeds that have hitherto been tried upon these lands have sickened and died away, and some have not even vegetated; and the surface remains covered with weeds of various kinds, for a succession of years."

What a plan of management is this, to be first brought forward, as a specimen! What a stumble at the threshold!

WORK PEOPLE.—P. 179.—" The price paid for different kinds of labor, varies more in this county, than probably in any other in the kingdom. An ingenious correspondent observes, ' that the rate of wages is in proportion to the distance of townships from the seats of manufacturers; *e. g.* at Chorley the wages of a common laborer 3*s.* with ale; at Euxton 2*s.* or 2*s.* 6*d.*; at Eccleston 1*s.* 6*d.* or 2*s.*; at Mawdsley and Bispham, I am told you may get them in harvest time, for 1*s.* 2*d.* and 1*s.* 4*d.*; in Wrightington the price of labor was lower two years ago, than the last mentioned sum, and does not now exceed it.'

" Under this head it may not be improper to give the following statement of different prices of labor, &c. at two periods; taken by the surveyor after a residence of thirty years in a village where no manufactory has yet been introduced—namely, *Walton,* near *Liverpool.*"

A comparative

A comparative Price of Labour, and other Articles, in the course of thirty years, taken April 1791.

	In the year 1761.				In the year 1791.		
	£.	s.	d.		£.	s.	d.
Head-man servant wages per ann. -	6	10	0	—	9	9	0
Maid servant - -	3	0	0	—	4	10	0
Masons and carpenters, per day	0	1	2	—	0	2	2
Laborers wages -	0	0	10	1s. 6d. 1792,	0	1	8*

WORKING ANIMALS. P. 172. " Oxen have been made use of formerly, but always upon a contracted scale. Horses at present are universally preferred for husbandry business. The paved roads of this district do not agree with the feet of oxen."

IMPLEMENTS. This section, though of considerable length, affords nothing of public utility; one new and valuable instrument excepted. Whether it is the invention of Mr. ECCLESTON does not clearly appear. Whoever conceived the thought is entitled to public gratulation.

P. 33.—" Another instrument has been lately introduced, which Mr. Eccleston, with propriety, calls the *miner ;* which is a plough-share fixed in a strong beam, without mold-boards, and drawn by four or more horses, and follows in the furrow the plough has just made, and, without turning up the substratum, penetrates into, and loosens the soil, from 8 to 12 inches deeper than the plough had before gone."

For the purpose of loosening a firm earthy subsoil, tolerably free from obstructions, and thereby forming a receptacle for superfluous moisture in a wet season, this implement (which is not particularly described) appears

" * And an attempt to raise them in the spring of 1793 to 2s. per day ; but the calamities, which came on at that period, produced a great change, and every effort was made to procure employment for the industrious."

appears to be well calculated; and, in that respect at least, may answer the end of deep plowing,—without the attendent evil of mixing the crude substratum with the fertilized soil.

As a preparation, for sowing the seeds of woodland plants, or for planting out seedlings, the operation of this instrument could scarcely fail of being valuable.

Six or seven pages of this Report are filled with descriptions and remarks on *thrashing machines,*—in Lancashire! where they had been, at the time of reporting, but just introduced; and were no doubt objects of *curiosity.* Descriptions of the " Spinning Jennies" of Lancashire might have been more in place, in the Lancashire Report.

MANURE. *Town Manures.*—P. 127. " Besides the dung got from the farm-yards, there are great quantities raised by the cowkeepers and stablekeepers in the large towns. At Liverpool horse-dung sells at about 5s. 6d. *per* ton, cow-dung from 4s. 6d. to 5s. 6d. *per* ton, butchers'-dung 6s. *per* ton, the ashes mixed with privies, scraping of the streets, &c. under the denomination of night soil. about 2s. 1d. *per* ton *
Liverpool also occasionally has the dregs of blubber from the whale fishery after boiling the oil, which mixed with soil, is a rich manure, but not lasting. Soap ashes also, if put upon old lays, have been found very advantageous, and very durable in pastures, but not so durable either on ploughed land or in meadows †."

P. 21. " It was in the memory of a worthy and experienced farmer ‡, who only died the present year, that the first load of night-soil brought from Liverpool towards the north was by his father; who was
paid

" * At Manchester, cow and horse dung are about 1s. *per* ton higher."

" † Quantity 40 to 50 ton *per* acre, from 8s. to 10s. *per* ton at Liverpool."

" ‡ Mr. John Harper, late of Bank Hall."

paid for carting the same the price that heretofore had been paid for carting away this nuisance, and throwing it into the river Mersey."

Marl.—P. 111. " Marl is the great article of fertilization, and the foundation of the improvements in the agriculture of this county; and this earth, or fossil, is fortunately wanting but in few places. There are several kinds of this article, valuable in proportion to the intrinsic quality of each, or the calcareous matter which it contains, or the nature of soil to which it is applied. To the stiff clay lands, the blue or reddish slate marl, full of calcareous earth, is more beneficial; but to the light sand lands, the strong clay marl is more genial."

Again, P. 120. " Marl is the foundation of all improvements in the agriculture of this county; and here the husbandmen of Lancashire and Cheshire may afford an useful lesson to the rest of the kingdom: so well are they convinced of the necessity of attending to this primary object, that neither labor nor expense deter them from the most vigorous application of it. There are several varieties of this fossil manure valuable in proportion to its intrinsic qualities, or the nature of the land to which it is to be applied. Shell marl or (and) slate marl are more desirable in the stiffer and more clayey districts, inasmuch as they contain a large proportion both of calcareous matter and of sand—clay marl in an inverse ratio more genial to a light and sandy district, as in both these circumstances the natural defects of the soil are in some measure obviated."

But still we are left in the dark respecting the intrinsic qualities of these several species of marls. In p. 124, however, we find an analysis of four specimens, out of one pit. These afford, on a par, about twenty grains of " calx"—calcareous earth, forty grains of " flinty sand," and forty grains of " clay and silicious earth." But, yet, as to the contexture,

texture, color, &c. &c. of this species of Lancashire marl, we remain uninformed.

The description of "marl" which I have commonly seen, in Lancashire, has every appearance of the red clays of the midland counties, Glocestershire, and East Devonshire, which, in those districts, as has been intimated, have long been set upon grounds, under the name of marl; although they contain but an inconsiderable portion of calcareous matter. Whether the analyzed specimens, above-mentioned, were of a similar description, but of a better quality, does not appear*. Indeed, throughout this lengthened article, to which a whole sheet of letter press is appropriated, there is a want of intelligibleness. Being the production of different pens, and interspersed with desultory matter, without regard to perspicuity of arrangement, its contents are difficult to be understood, and are of course in a great measure unprofitable, in their chaotic state. Nevertheless, involved in a mass of words, I perceive some ideas, in the Lancashire Report, which,—notwithstanding the ample detail I have formerly given of the practice of marling in NORFOLK, and although the Lancashire practice appears to be no more than a variety of the CHESHIRE method, that may hereafter come under consideration,—are worth selecting, and arranging in their natural order.

Marl Pits.—In a country where fossil manure forms the base of the lands to be manured, and where the situation of the pit can be *chosen*, the following hints may be useful.

P. 115. " The first and grand object is the disposition of the pits. Thousands of acres, I can safely say, are wasted, and in many places the land worse than before. (?) It ought to be a standing rule not to suffer a pit to be made, unless it could be laid dry, which

---

* Or, quere, was it of " the blue or reddish slate marl," above mentioned?

which I verily believe may be done in three fourth
parts of the county." Again, p. 117. " It is no
small consideration where to fix the pit, from whence
the marl is to be obtained to most advantage, provided there be a choice; and when there is, the following considerations should be weighed; of destroying
the least land ; of affording the least length of carriage,
which is the heaviest part of the expense; of affording
the least draught, by going down hill, if possible;
that the water stagnating in the pit afterwards may
not be injurious to the land; and of rendering the
least damage to the lands in future."

Many of those ideas are evidently the result of
practice. Duly qualified they may be rendered valuable. But, to gain a downhill carriage, the pit
must be formed on rising ground; where, " the water
stagnating in the pit afterward," has an opportunity
of doing the most mischief to the lands below it. I
have seen many instances of injury being done by old
marl pits, so situated; and certainly " it ought to be
a standing rule" (where it can be observed) " not to
suffer a pit to be made, unless it can be laid dry."
Thus, in those two passages, evidently written by
different persons, and detached from each other, we
find something like rational guidance.

Working the *Pits*. This is done in the Norfolk
manner.—P. 117.—" Marl is got by falling it in
large clods ; this method is expeditious, but requires
great caution, and is frequently attended with danger;
the piece intended to be fallen is undermined, and
loosened at each side, by being cut through; long
piles are then driven in at the top, and sometimes
water is required to insinuate itself into the interstices
which the poles have made. The clod falls with such
violence as to break the mass imto pieces "

State of the *Land*, to receive it.—P. 113.—" Long
experience has sufficiently proved the propriety of
the general practice of the county; which is, to lay
the marl upon grass lands—the older the better; the
                                             sward

sward and grass united causes a fermentation and putrefaction, which seems necessary to produce a proper effect."—P. 121.—" The general experience of this country has proved to a demonstration the propriety of its universal practice, *viz.* to lay it upon grass land which is intended to be broke up the ensuing spring."

The *season* of Marling.—P. 121.—" The general rule is to begin marling about May or June, in short when spring seedings are over, continuing as opportunity serves throughout the summer months; it is not, however, unusual to take a crop of hay before the marling is begun."

The *quantity* set on. P. 113. " The quantity laid on is from two to three, or three and a half, cubic roods (rods) of 64 yards to every statute acre." P. 121. " The general custom is to lay upon the great Cheshire acre, of eight yards to the rood, from three to seven roods, of sixty-four square yards each. From four to five roods may be considered the average quantity to the acre (one Cheshire acre contains two acres and eighteen perches and a half of the statute measure) more and less are frequently applied, but the quantity ought indisputably to be in proportion to the quality of the soil and quality of the fossil."— In p. 123, a Contributor says—" in 1790 I marled it at the rate of seven roods and a half per acre—the expense was very great, as I carted the marl near a mile and a quarter."—Nevertheless, somebody says, p. 113,—" It is reckoned a much better practice to have the marlings repeated, with a gentle covering, than a strong thick coat of marl, which is intended to last a number of years."

This being as it may, the above quantities may be deemed enormous. I have seen a grass field so thickly covered, that, in approaching it, it had the appearance of a red-soiled fallow, fresh ploughed.

Reading the first paragraph as it was probably intended to be written—" from two to three or three and

and a half roods, of sixty-four cubical yards each, to
every statute acre," and taking three rods as the
medium quantity, the number of cubic yards set
upon a statute acre is nearly two hundred ; which
cannot be reckoned at much less than three hundred
middling cart loads, an acre. Indeed, we are told,
p. 119, " two cubical yards of marl make about three
loads."—In Norfolk, the quantity set on varies from
forty, to beneath ten loads an acre.

Spreading Marl.—P. 113. " The marl should
partake both of one summer's sun, and one winter's
frosts, at least. After being exposed to the effects of
the weather, in large lumps, it begins to fall, or melt ;
the particles appear unctuous and soapy, and the
quality of the substance seems quite changed from
its original state. Then, in the ensuing spring, it
should be divided (the parts now separate with ease,)
and equally distributed upon every part of the surface,
this is, with facility, effected by harrows, &c. after
which it is usually ploughed under."—P. 122.—
Marl is spread immediately after carting, but left in
a rough lumpy form, that it may be exposed as much
as possible to the vicissitudes of the seasons ; if it
contains a large proportion of clay it will remain for
many weeks, perhaps months, in large unwieldy
lumps, though in general the rains of the latter end
of autumn, and the succeeding frosts of winter reduces
it into the form of an unctuous but friable material,
the further dispersion of which is easily effected with
clotting beetles, spades, or harrows ; this dispersion
however ought not to be attempted till a week or a
fortnight before ploughing, as the most beneficial
effects are produced by alternate rains and frosts."

The *expense* of marling, in Lancashire, is estimated
at a very low rate, by the load.—In Norfolk, the
estimated expense of marling, with twenty-five loads,
an acre, and the distance of carriage 120 rods, is forty
shillings ; or nineteenpence, each load : whereas, in
Lancashire, where ten times that quantity is set on,
the

the expense, " within the distance of 60 rods, on the average" is only " about eight pounds an acre," (p. 113.) : which is not eightpence, a load, for team work and manual labor. But the distances of carriage, the unsettled dimensions of the Lancashire rod and the Lancashire acre*, and the confusion of tongues in the Lancashire Report, may serve, in some sort, to reconcile this otherwise unaccountable difference.

On the whole, the disparity, in regard to QUANTITY, between the Lancashire and the Norfolk practices, is the most striking. Yet these established practices are equally the result of long experience, and *may* be nearly right : that is to say,—the lands of Lancashire may *possibly* require, of Lancashire marl, ten times the quantity, which the lands of Norfolk require of the marl of Norfolk.

This being as it may, I think, we may safely con- clude—as I have elsewhere done—that nothing but experience, with a given marl and a given soil, can point out the proper quantity†.

Sea Slutch. P. 126.—" Sea slutch, from the Ribble and Wyre, is, in some places adjacent, made use of as a substitute for marl, to which it is reckoned equal, but in general not so durable ‡. It is frequently used as a substratum for fruit trees at Formby. The quantity is a load to each tree ; its effects are won- derful. This practice, however, may not prove bene- ficial where the soil is dense. At Rossal in the Filde, where there is no marl, after a stratum of strong clay under the soil, they pass through a sand with can- kered

---

* P. 230. " The rod, in Lancashire, is of no less than six different lengths, in different parts of the county : namely, the statute or 5½ yards, 6, 6½, 7, 7½, and eight yards, to the rod, pole, or perch."

† Mention is more than once made of *burning marl*, for manure. But nothing of sufficient authenticity, for extraction, is made out.

" ‡ Mr. Standen, steward to Bold Fleetwood Hesketh, Esq. says, more durable than marl."

kered veins, next a sand with sky-blue veins, with thin shells like barnacles, called in the provincial phrase hen-fish; and this proves a good substitute for marl. Sea slutch, particularly at Weston, a village in Cheshire, near Frodsham, is found to be much more fertilizing and more permanent than marl, I mean that part of a salt marsh which has been grassed over for a few years; for that which is overflowed daily contains more sand, and is less enriching. I do not think that all the manures in use in the kingdom combined, could have a better effect either upon arable or grass land, than the above-mentioned soil has. This manure, where the plough is not immoderately used, will last thirty years. It is used in much the same manner and quantity as marl."—A hint this, to salt-marsh occupiers.

Lime P. 128. " Lime is the best manure for grass lands, either laid on by itself or in compost, if used in *sufficient* quantities. In a farm of a cold clay soil, after draining near twenty years, the *lime* was laid on the sward in *May* and *June* to the amount of two hundred bushels on a *statute* acre ; the lands have not been ploughed, but have yielded the *finest grass* for hay and pasture, and yet appear to be in a state of improvement. The use of lime as a manure has nearly superceded that of *marl*. Immense quantities of lime-stone are brought by the rivers and canals from *Wales*."

How does this accord with the two extracts that stand at the head of the article, *Marl?*—p. 286.—Whether they are all from the same pen does not appear. But that they are all literal extracts, from the same book, is certain.

POTATOES. This being the only cultivated crop, *in husbandry,* in the culture of which Lancashire can claim the smallest right of setting an example to the rest of the kingdom, I will carefully collect every scrap I can find on the subject.

General

General Account.—P. 57.—" Lancashire was the
first county in this kingdom in which the potatoe was
grown : and as it is able at this day to boast a superior
cultivation in that important article, in which it still
stands unrivalled, it may be requisite to descend to
particulars in regard to the management of that crop :
1. A sward, or fresh lay, is desirable, but not always
to be obtained. Good crops have been frequently
raised from lands exhausted. The ground being previously cleaned by ploughings, and planted (if the
ground can be got into condition) in April, in drills *
about 3 feet distance, and from 12 to 9 inches
asunder, in each drill, the sets † placed immediately
upon long dung from the yard, &c.; but dung from
the great towns produces a wonderful effect upon
lands not formerly accustomed to that article ; and it
is supposed, will generally enrich twice as far, with
equal effect, as the manure formerly used from the
farm-yard, &c. This is experienced in the lands
bordering upon the canals. The great quantity of
corn, and different kinds of provender, given to cattle
kept in towns, must tend to enrich the quality of the
                                                    dung,

" * I am confident that this method of planting either the early
or late potatoe, is not so productive as that of setting them in beds
of five feet wide, and covering them, when the shoots begin to appear, with mould dug from a trench between the beds. This is the
general mode in the neighbourhood of Frodsham, in Cheshire,
where the planters of this most valuable root have tried all possible
methods, for many years, and are generally allowed to produce a
greater crop on a given quantity of land, than any other people in
the kingdom.—*T. Wright.*"

" † The surveyor has made some experiments to ascertain the
best mode of cutting the sets; for, if the potatoe be set whole,
putrefaction does not always ensue; and a set of a large size, to
a certain degree, is better than a small one. The best method he
has yet discovered, is taking off the sprout, or nose end, and the um-
bilical, or tail end, of the potatoe, leaving the middle entirely for
the set; the worst method of cutting the potatoe, as has been
proved, is cutting the potatoe down the middle, from nose to tail
end ; a practice but too common."—There is much good sense in
these remarks. *Rev.*

dung, which depends upon the food taken, whether of man or beast.

" 2. Although April be the prime season for producing a crop of good potatoes for the table, because this vegetable requires a certain portion of time, to acquire that degree of maturity, which renders it peculiarly mellow and farinaceous, yet it is frequently planted as late as May, or even June; and yet produces abundant crops, but not of the same matured quality, as those planted at a more early season.

" 3. The apprehension of frosts (by which, if the tops are caught, after breaking the surface, they pine and sicken, and the hopes of the husbandman are blasted,) sometimes operate against planting at this early season ; yet good planters risque the chance of frosts, in order to obtain superior quality.

" 4. The crops are kept clean from weeds by the plough, first by turning a furrow, left for that purpose, towards the young plants, as soon as they appear; and afterwards by turning the same furrow back from each side of the drill, and which is sometimes, if very foul, harrowed by a small triangular harrow, running through each drill. After the weeds have been so exposed, the furrow is turned back again, and sometimes the same plough, or a double-wristed one, runs up each drill once more; besides the destruction of weeds, the soil, by these operations, is loosened, exposed to the sun and air, which contributes greatly to improve the crop.

" 5. There are various kinds of seeds in use.—The ox-noble, and cluster potatoe are planted for the cattle* ; the pink-eye, and a variety of others, with
different

" * Of the cluster potatoe, the surveyor had an opportunity of viewing the produce of a crop, lying upon the surface of the ground, after being just taken up, belonging to Colonel Mordaunt, of Halsall, in this county. He, and an intelligent farmer, were both of opinion, that they never saw so large a crop; and yet, as they were informed, raised without dung."

" The

different kinds of kidney-potatoes for the table. The old winter red, as it is sometimes called, ought to be mentioned for its peculiar goodness in the spring, when other kinds have lost their flavor; this potatoe is then in its best perfection; it has another quality, that of never having been known to curl. There are also great varieties of early potatoes, and great attention is paid to raising new sorts of the best qualities from seeds, of what is called the crabs, or apples, which grow upon the stems. Mr. G. Green observes, that after many experiments he invariably found that the watery potatoe (of which there are great varieties) have fallen far short of the purpose intended. That he has several times, both through necessity as well as for the sake of experiment, given the ox-noble to milch-cows, after the more farinaceous sort, *e. g.* the pink-eye, when the decrease of both milk and butter has been evident in a very short space, and the beasts themselves seemed much dissatisfied with the change.

" 6. Great attention is paid to changing the seed occasionally, to prevent the curl*, the practice of obtaining

" The cluster, or conglomerated, or Suffolk (for so it is called by Mr. Howard, who first introduced it to notice) was cultivated in this county 25 years ago (a) from sets left by that gentleman with the Society for the Promotion of Arts and Commerce.

" Vide *Dossie's Memoirs*, vol. X. It has since been produced from seed, and, though much improved in shape, retains the red color and saccharine taste."

" * The surveyor had the honour of receiving a premium from the Society for the Promotion of Arts and Commerce, in the year 1789, for a letter on the Lancashire method of preventing the curl. He has the pleasure to observe, that the fact seems to be confirmed, from the general opinion and practice of the county; nor did he observe a single diseased potatoe in the whole of his survey—the crops were universally luxuriant. This thought is improved upon by Mr. Thomas Wright, gardener to John Fazakerley, Esq. Prescot, who has sent some favourite plants which had caught the disease of curl, to the moss lands, which change of lands he expected would effect a cure."

" (a) By the Rev. Mr. Heathcote, rector of Walton, and Mr. William Haliday, Anfield."

obtaining fresh seed from Scotland (as was the custom a few years ago), is not now so frequent; a change from the moss lands, and *vice versa*, being generally sufficient. A change of land is also desirable, but not always practicable: crops have been successfully taken, for a succession of years, from the same land.

" 7. The produce of a crop is, on a medium, from 2 to 3 hundred measures, or bushels*, the statute acre. The early potatoes are generally planted in beds, in rows about 8 inches distant, and the sets 4 or 5 inches separate, because the early potatoes, being of a less size, require a smaller space; but the advanced price these early crops obtain at market, render them a profitable article to the cultivator †; who, besides reaping a profit from this early produce, has his ground prepared for another crop the same season. Mr. Waring, steward to the Earl of Derby, gave to Major Atherton the following account of the produce of one acre of indifferent land at Knowsley.

" 1793—700 bushels of potatoes, pink-eyes.

"1794—92 bushels of wheat, 70 lb. to the bushel, sold

" * By a bushel of potatoes is generally meant 90lb. before they are cleaned."

" † Mr. Eccleston took the surveyor to view a piece of ground, 30 perches (8 yards to the perch) the early potatoes raised upon which had been sold for 30*l.* in the present year 1793; after which a crop of turnips had been grown, which, at 6*d. per* bushel, were worth 50*l. per* acre; after which the same land was to be copped with wheat.

" *Remark on this Fact.*

" The gross amount of the account of the potatoes appears to be great, that of 20*s. per* rod of 8 yards; but if all expenses of sets, and preparing the land, and getting them up, and afterwards marketing them at the different markets, Liverpool, Manchester, &c. were deducted, it is a query but the outgoings would be considerably more than the gross amount given, although the land must be perfectly well prepared for the turnips; but the account given of the turnips, at the rate of 2000 bushels of thirty-six quarts or ninety-pounds *per* bushel, is more by 800 bushels *per* acre than ever I knew or heard of for either large or small lot, either by hoeing, or any other advantage to be taken.—*Mr. Harper.*"

sold at 7s. 6d. per bushel. 3 months later they would have fetched 10s. 6d. per bushel, cone wheat. Mr. Waring says, the live crops were equal to the fee simple of the land. He is confident that *marl would have produced* 20 *bushels more wheat.* The markets of Manchester, Oldham, Rochdale, and the neighbourhood, are supplied with great quantities, not only from Warrington, but as far as from Rufford, Scarsbrick, &c.

" Upon the same ground, from which a crop has already been taken, the early seed potatoes are in some places afterwards planted; which, after being got up about November, are immediately cut up into sets, and preserved in oat shells *, or saw-dust, where they remain till March, when they are planted, after having had one spit taken off, and planted with another, of a length sufficient to appear above ground in the space of a week.

" But the most approved method is, to cut the sets, and put them on a room-floor, where a strong current of air can be introduced at pleasure, the sets laid thinner, viz. about 2 lays in depth, and covered with the like materials, (shells or saw-dust) about 2 inches thick: this screens them from the winter frosts, and keeps them moderately warm, causing them to vegetate; but at the same time admits air to strengthen them, and harden their shoots, which the cultivators improve by opening the doors and windows on every opportunity afforded by mild soft weather: they frequently examine them, and when the shoots are sprung an inch and a half, or two inches, they carefully remove one half of their covering, with a wooden rake, or with the hands, taking care not to disturb, or break, the shoots. Light is requisite as well as air, to strengthen and establish the shoots; on which account a green-house has the advantage of a room, but a room answers very well with a good window

" * Vulgarly called meal shudes."

window or two in it, and if to the sun still better.—
In this manner they suffer them to remain till the
planting season, giving them all the air possible by
the doors and windows, when it can be done with
safety from frost: by this method the shoots at the
top become green, leaves are sprung, and are moderately hardy. They then plant them in rows, in
the usual method, by a setting-stick, and carefully
rake up the cavities made by the setting-stick; by
this method they are enabled to bear a little frost
without injury. The earliest potatoe is the superfine
white kidney *; from this sort, upon the same ground,
have been raised four crops; having sets from the
repository ready to put in as soon as the other were
taken up; and a fifth crop is sometimes raised from
the same lands, the same year, of transplanted winter
lettuce. The first crop had the advantage of a
covering in frosty nights.

" The above excellent information was communicated by J. Blundell, Ormskirk, and has hitherto
been known only amongst a very few farmers.

" 8. The manner of taking them up varies. The
three-pronged fork is in general use—the soil turned
over, the weeds picked out, the potatoes gathered
and separated, according to their size, by the same
person. Another practice is, for a strong man to
take a three-pronged fork, but crooked (the same
which is generally used to pull dung out of the cart)
which he strikes down between every root, and pulls
it over, laying the roots bare, which are taken up by
two children that follow. Another practice is to
turn a furrow from the potatoes, with a Rotherham
plough, and then with another plough, furnished only
with a share, to turn up the potatoes, which are
afterwards gathered.

" After

" * The early potatoe is a distinct species, (?) of which there are
yet great varieties."

" After the potatoes are gathered, and sufficiently dried, they are put together in heaps, in the shape of the roof of a building, covered closely with straw, which should be drawn straight, and to meet from each side in a point at the top, about six inches in thickness, and then covered with mould, closely compacted together, by frequent applications of the spade; after which Mr. Eccleston makes holes in the mould, at the sides and tops of these repositories, as deep as the straw, and about three yards distant, to permit the air, which, he says, visibly arises from the fermentation, to escape: after the fermentation has ceased, the holes are closed to prevent the effects of frosts or rain.

" 9. The utility of the application of potatoes to feeding stock, is sufficiently known, but not sufficiently practised. Converting the produce into immediate cash, by taking it to market, is a stronger temptation than waiting the more tedious process of purchasing stock, and fattening the cattle; but a source of improvement to the land, and consequently of superior profit in the issue, is by this means done away.

" 10. From the amazing quantities consumed by stock, it may not be amiss to mention the manner of boiling, &c. which is almost universally by steam, in a large hamper, or tub, perforated at the bottom, and placed over the water: in this way they are readier for use than by being immerged in water; after which they are given either warm or cold, mixed with chaff, bran, hay-seeds, barley, or oatmeal.

" The method of boiling potatoes by steam, has been adopted by some for culinary purposes as an improvement, thinking by this process they must imbibe less water from their not being immerged in the substance. But immersion in water causes the discharge of a certain matter, which the steam alone is incapable of doing, and by detaining of which the flavour of this root is injured. The cottager understands

stands this kind of cookery: having poured off the water, he evaporates the moisture by replacing the vessel in which the potatoe was boiled, once more over the fire. Potatoes do not admit being put into a vessel of boiling water like greens. If America*, whence this choice vegetable was first imported, had yielded nothing else to the researches of the European, the present generation would have reason to be thankful for the acquisition, and to be grateful to the planters in Lancashire, for their spirited attention to the cultivation of this excellent root."

Growing potatoes in *Hillocks.*—Section " Cottages,"—N. p. 18.—" Where the cottager has a small garden, the following mode of laying potatoes may be of particular use to him:

" From every eye in each potatoe-set, will proceed different stems; which when they are about nine inches above the surface of the ground, should be spread out in a circular form, bent down, and covered all over (but just the ends) with earth. The following rude sketch (quite useless) may probably render it more intelligible: a pit of earth nine inches diameter, about one foot deep, dunged, then covered with a little mould, upon which is deposited the potatoe whole, that is uncut. From this set may arise several stems, which when of length sufficient, then the stems bent down thus (the several stems radiating from the center): and from the stems thus covered a few inches deep, and rounded up in the shape of a mole-hill, new fibres will strike, take root, and potatoes be produced in large quantities.

" This

" * A note in a common-place book that I wrote several years ago, informs me, that John Hawkins, a dealer in slaves, got in 1565 the first potatoes for ship provisions from the inhabitants of Santa Fé, in New Spain; he introduced the root into Ireland, whence it was farther propagated through all the northern parts of Europe.

" *An old method of cooking potatoes.*—Boil and let them grow cold, then eat them, mixed with oil, vinegar, and pepper.—*Parkinson's Herbal.*"

" This mode may be useful to the cottager, as the practice requires but little dung, some additional labor; but as the pits may be varied, the same ground may be repeatedly and repeatedly planted."

On *early* Potatoes; from the section " Climate." P. 6. " It may be worthy of remark, that there is a general strife betwixt the Kirkdale and Wallasey gardeners, who can produce the first early potatoe at Liverpool market. They generally succeed both on the same day. In the year 1790 the Cheshire gardener had, however, the start by nearly a whole week.

EARLY POTATOES.

1766.	June 7,	20 lb. sold for 5 *d.* and 6 *d.* per lb.
1767.	June 6,	3 lb. sold for 14 *d.* in the whole.
1768.	May 14,	8 lb. sold for 4 *s.* 8 *d.*
1769.	May 13,	2 lb. sold for 1 *s.*
1770.	May 23,	2 lb. for 3 *s.*
1771.	May 18,	½ lb. for 1 *s.*
1772.	May 13,	1 lb. for 2 *s.* 6 *d.*

N. B.—From this period the early potatoes have been regularly sold for 2 *s.* 6 *d.* per lb. when first brought to market.

" After this period the Register was extended to the following articles; namely,

	ASPARAGUS.	POTATOES.	GOOSEBERRIES.
1773.	April 10.	April 7.	May 5.
1774.	3.	30.	9.
1775.	1.	19.	April 26.
1776.	6.	17.	May 2.
1777.	4.	24.	12.
1778.	11.	25.	9.
1779.	March 27.	3.	April 10.
1780.	April 15.	20.	May 6.
1781.	March 31.	14.	April 21.
			1782.

1782.	May 4.	May 11.	May 18.
1783.	April 12.	1.	April 30.
1784.	May 8.	17.	May 22.
1785.	April 23.	14.	18.
1786.	22.	13.	10.
1787.	March 28.	April 11.	April 28.
1788.	April 19.	May 11.	May 7.
1789.	18.	9.	9.
1790.	3.	April 3.	April 24.
1791.	9.	16.	23.
1792.	7.	25.	25.
1793.	May 1.	May 11.	May 18.
1794.	April 15.	April 13.	April 18.

"From the above Register it appears, that the difference between an early and late spring is not less than six weeks; *e. g.*

	ASPARAGUS.	POTATOES.	GOOSEBERRIES.
1789.	March 27.	April 3.	April 10.
1784.	May 8.	May 17.	May 22.

" From this Register may also be traced, the improved cultivation of the early potatoe upon common ground: but the potatoe at present may be truly said to be raised the whole year throughout, by the new method of heating the stoves with steam. Mr. Butler, gardener to the Earl of Derby, at his seat at Knowsley, has practised this some time; and Mr. Collins, late his lordship's gardener, who has ground near Liverpool, had, under glasses, forced by the heat of steam, Christmas, 1794, nearly, as he calculated, one cwt. of potatoes, ready to take up. But he observed, that the process by steam was too expensive to afford any profit at the price they were usually sold.

"It will at this day scarcely be credited, that when potatoes began to be brought to market so early as June, the gardeners were under the necessity of
bringing

bringing the stems adhering to the potatoes, for without this no purchaser could be obtained.

" A gentleman who has been particularly attentive to this subject, observed that, in this northern district, autumnal seeds require to be committed to the earth one fortnight at least earlier than is recommended by Mawe, in his Kalendar."

On the *Curl*, in Potatoes. In the chapter "Mosses," p. 101. " By a change of his potatoe sets from this moss, to his old inclosed lands, Mr. Chorley preserves his crops from the *curl.*—His sets are become famous on that account, and readily purchased for the purpose of planting by his neighbours.

" It is with regret we add, that the curl is a general complaint this year (1795); that there is greater appearance of this disease amongst the potatoe crops than have been observed for some years past.—Recourse must at last be had to the seed, for renewal ;—bulbous roots, it has been found by experience, decay after a certain number of years—' Ranunculus in ' twenty-five, anemone in fifteen, and hyacinths in ' twenty-six years*.' After which period, no arts and pains can preserve them, though a change of soil in the mean time is useful. It is proper however to remark, that the curl may be prevented from spreading, by taking away any plants the instant they seem to be affected with that disease. This important discovery ought to be known as generally as possible.—The question was put to Mr. Chorley ; and he answered, that his crops appeared clear, nor did the surveyor observe any infection."

The *effect* of Potatoes, *on Land*. From the section, "Fallowing," p. 49. " Upon the system of green crops preceding wheat, by way of saving one year's rent, and the labor of fallowing, the potatoe crop should seem to claim a superiority ; both from the dung

* "See Madox's Florist's Directory, p. 91."

dung given, and the clean state into which, under good management, the land is brought. Yet the neatest farmers seem at present not very partial to this mode of agriculture. They say the succeeding crop of wheat is more feeble and worse fed; and the bad effects of these two, potatoes and wheat in succession, are evident upon successive crops for years afterward."

For other remarks on potatoes, see the subsequent section, ' SWINE.'

CULTIVATED HERBAGE.—After mentioning, in a desultory way, various methods of converting arable lands to grass grounds (but none of them new, or particularly eligible) we are informed, p 75, that " Another method is, to manure land very well for early potatoes, which ought to be off the land in June, July, or August at latest, and sowing grass seeds and white clover, without any corn; the hay ought to stand until the hay seeds are pretty well ripened the subsequent year, and the eddish or after-grass to be well manured as soon as the hay is carted off." And, in a note, p. 73,—" some fields have been laid down to pasture, with grass-seeds only, without any corn, and have been found to succeed. There is said to be an evident superiority in lands thus treated, although twenty years ago: but the experiments have been few."

On *making Clover Hay*, p. 75. " *Mr. Eccleston's mode*.—The clover is collected together into small sheaves, and kept straight; then twisted together, in the top part, to admit the sheaf to stand upon its butt, or bottom end, when spread out, in the same manner that horse-beans have been frequently treated; and if these little bundles are not thrown down by the winds, they will resist more rain, if it should fall, than when lying on the surface of the ground; and if the weather be fine, having more surface exposed and open, the clover will cure the faster."—This method, which is well adapted to the moist climature of

of Lancashire, is not peculiar to Mr. E. nor to that
county. I have seen it practised in Yorkshire, for
some length of time. If ray-grass is mixed with
clover, it is loosely tied with bands of the former, and
set up in "gaits," (single sheaves) in the manner of
oats and barley.

GRASS LAND. In the section "*Climate,*" p. 3, it
is remarked—" these frequent rains, however, have
the effect of rendering Lancashire one of the most
productive and certain grass-land districts in the
island. The soil is peculiarly adapted to grass, and
the climate uncommonly favorable for that production."

To destroy Rushes.—P. 52. " If the land be full of
rushes, by only taking a single crop of oats in the
following manner; by plowing one furrow with a
good dressing of dung, harrowed in, upon which the
crop of oats, with grass seed only: by which the
rushes are destroyed, but the grass roots are preserved,
and the grass meliorated by exposing the soil to the
air and sun, by turning it once over." This I insert
as a hint to experimentalists.

The following interesting experiment, on *manuring
hay ground,* was made by the ingenious Mr. HENRY
HARPER.

P. 130. " The following experiments of different
kinds of manure will show the difference of both quantity and the quality of produce on the different kinds
of land on my farm, on which I manured half an acre
of eight yards to the rod with every kind of the following manures; and when made into hay, as nearly
all alike as possible, I weighed one average square
rod from every lot.

" Lot the 1st.—Horse, cow, and butchers dung,
all mixed together, of each about an equal quantity,
which lay in that state about two months, and then
turned it over, and let it lie eight or ten days, and
then put it on the land before it had done fermenting,
and spread it immediately. This was set on in September

tember 1793.—The produce 3 stone 15 pound per rod, at 20 pounds to the stone.

" Lot the 2d.—Horse and cow dung, mixed and turned over the same as Lot the 1st, and set and spread on the land at the same time.—Produce 3 stone 14 pound per rod.

" Lot the 3d.—Horse dung, turned over and set on the land the same as Lot the 1st.—Produce 3 stone 13 pound 8 ounces per rod.

" Lot the 4th.—Cow dung, turned over and set on the land the same as Lot the 1st.—Produce 3 stone 13 pound 8 ounces per rod.

" Lot the 5th.—Night-soil, coal-ashes, and cleaning of the streets, and about 40 measures of lime to every ton weight, and turned over while the lime was in its floury state, and not suffered to run to mortar, for then it is of little benefit ; one part of this was set on in September 1793, the other part the middle of March 1794, but no difference in the crop to be perceived.—Produce 3 stone 13 pound per rod.

" Lot the 6th.—Night-soil, coal-ashes, and cleaning of streets, set on the land in the same manner and times as Lot the 5th, and no difference in the cropping part.—Produce 3 stone 2 pounds 8 ounces per rod.

" Lot the 7th.—Marl fresh got, and mixed with an equal quantity of horse and cow dung, and lay about three months and then turned over, and lay a month and then turned over again, and put on the land in six or eight days, and at the same different times as the two last lots, but no difference in the cropping —Produce 3 stone 8 pound 12 ounces per rod.

" Lot the 8th.—Water from a reservoir that all the urine from the stables, cow-houses, and all drainings from the dunghills, farm-yard, hog-styes, and all the waste water from the house runs into, and is carried on the land in a watering-cart made on purpose that holds four hundred gallons ; and the water was put

on

on the land in April, about 12,000 gallons to the acre
of 8 yards to the rod, and again in May 12,000 more.
—Produce 3 stone 5 pound per rod.

" Lot the 9th.—Blubber, the offal of whale-oil,
mixed with soil, and set on the land the 1st of April
1794.—Produce 3.stone 2 pound 8 ounces per rod.

"Lot the 10th.—Soot, sowed on the land the middle
of April 1794.—Produce 3 stone 1 pound per rod.

"Lot the 11th.—Plaster of Paris (gypsum) sowed on
the land in April, the weather then showery and
favourable for it.—Produce 2 stone 2 pound per rod.

" Let the 12th.—No manure at all.—Produce 2
stone 2 pound per rod : so much for gypsum, that has
been made such account of.

"Lot the 13th.— Soap-ashes or muck, set on in
March 1794.—Produce 2 stone 10 pound per rod.

"Lot the 14th.—Lime, set on in March, clean by
itself.—Produce 2 stone 8 pound per rod.

" An improvement by way of experiment upon Lots
the 1st, 2d, 3d, 4th, and 5th, water from the reservoir
put on these lots the beginning of May 1794, at the
rate of 12,000 gallons per acre.—Produce 4 stone
8 pound per rod."

P. 134. " Now these lots are all in one field, which
is old meadow land all of one quality, the soil 11
inches deep, and a strong loam betwixt sand and clay
with a reddish cast, and is what I call fox-land; and
under the soil is a black loam sand six inches deep,
and then marl of four yards deep, and bottoms on a
red sand.

" This field is not to be considered as a poor worn-
out field, but has been regularly manured every
third year."

P. 136. " Now, to try the quality of all the lots, I
put a small handful from every lot in a dry clean
place, where there was little or no grass, and they
were laid promiscuously down, and regularly marked
and numbered, to avoid mistake. And I had for the
experiment six horses up in the stable, all well fed
with

with clover fresh cut : and I turned one out, and let
him go of himself amongst the lots promiscuously,
and when he got amongst them, some he smelled at,
and others he tasted (there were 19 different lots);
the first lot that he settled at was No. 8, and he eat
it all clean up ; and he then sauntered about as before, and got to lot the 5th, and eat it all clean up ;
and then sauntered as before, and got to lot the 7th,
and eat it all clean up ; he then sauntered as before
he had done, and smelled, and tasted, and went off
from amongst them. I then put him up, and turned
another out, which did exactly in the same manner
as the first had done.—*N. B.* And he then fixed
upon the same lots as the first horse had done, which
were immediately taken away with care, so as not to
disturb the horse, which through the whole of the lots
were always replaced with the same kind of hay ;
and out of the whole six horses there was little or no
variation, for the next horse that came out always
fixed on the same lots as the last had eaten up, after
being replaced.---And he then fixed upon lot 8, as
the first horse had done, and eat it all clean up ; and
then upon another of the same ; and continued till he
had eaten four out of the five, and then went off from
amongst them.   I then put him up, and turned another out, and he did as the others had done, and fixed
upon the first lot, No. 8, and eat it all clean up ; and
then to lots the third and fourth, which he eat all up,
and then sauntered off.   I then put him up, and turned another out, which did exactly the same as the
others had done, and fixed upon lot the 2d, and eat
it up ; and then he fixed upon lot the 11th, and eat
it up ; and then he fixed upon lot the 6th, and eat it
up ; and he then went off.   And I put him up, and
turned another out, which did exactly the same as
the others had done ; and he fixed upon the last experimental lot, and eat it all up ; and then to lot the
13th, and eat it all up ; and then to lot the 14th, and
eat it all up ; and he then went off.   And I put him
up,

up, and then turned the last horse out, which did exactly the same as the others had done, and just tasted of lot the 12th; but the 9th and 10th lots still remained. and never a horse out of the number of six tasted of them, only smelled at them. And I then turned them all out together, and they made to where the lots had been, and eat up the remains of lot the 12th; but they all went off and left the 9th and 10th lots unnoticed.

"And I still let them remain in their places till the cows came up in the evening, and never a cow, out of thirty, tasted of them (9th and 10th lots); they smelled, and even bellowed and roared, and scraped with their feet, and flung it about with their horns.

"Now I will leave it to every reader to judge for himself, which of the lots were of the best quality, and the most nutritive; for myself, I prefer those that were eaten the first."

On *stacking Hay.* P. 76. " In making hay-stacks, besides a chimney in the stack, by a basket placed in the middle, and drawn up by a cord, in order to suffer the air, generated by heating, to escape, and to prevent the stack taking fire, as mentioned in the " Survey of Middlesex," Mr. Eccleston cuts gutters in the ground, lengthways, and covers them across in that place whereon a stack is to be built. Through these trenches, in different directions, the outward air may enter, pass through, then ascend the aperture left in the stack; and this continued circulation takes away the generated heat or foul air, which, if confined together without any vent, might produce damage to the hay, or worse effects; and, by these useful precautions, he is enabled to collect his hay together at a more early period, and in a more juicy state; by which good practice, time is saved, and the quality of the hay improved."

This is an accurate and valuable thought; which, in a moist climate, may be very useful. An annotator,

tor, however, seems to think otherwise. His words are—" When hay is *properly prepared* to be put together in a stack or rick, a chimney ought never to be made; it is a great evil, never to be adopted but when there is absolute danger of the rick taking fire. Rather let an ox-feeder in North Wilts be consulted in the art of hay-making, than a farmer in Lancashire.— *T. W.*" Or rather let either of them be consulted in his own country.

"GARDENS and ORCHARDS." *Gardens.* P. 81. " The *horticulture* of this county is in many instances superior to its *agriculture :*" and finding the Surveyor at home, it would be ill bred not to listen to him, with attention, in his own walk. "The mechanic is generally furnished with a small patch of ground adjoining his cottage ; and from this little spot is extracted not only health, but derived pleasure, and which may not a little contribute to sobriety ; intemperance not unfrequently proceeding from want of recreation to fill up a vacant hour. This small space is devoted to nurturing his young seedlings, trimming his more matured plants, contemplating new varieties, in expectation of honours through the medium of gained premiums. Thus starting at intervals from his more toilsome labours, the mechanic finds his stagnating fluids put in motion, and his lungs refreshed with the fragrant breeze, whilst he has been thus raising new flowers of the auricula, carnation, polyanthus, or pink, of the most approved qualities in their several kinds, and which, after being raised here, have been dispersed over the whole kingdom.

" Not only flowers but fruit have been objects of their attention. The best gooseberries now under cultivation had their origin in the county of Lancaster ; and to promote this spirit, meetings are annually appointed at different places, at which are public exhibitions of different kinds of flowers and fruits, and premiums adjudged. These meetings are encouraged by master tradesmen and gentlemen of the

the county, as tending to promote a spirit which may occassionally be diverted into a more important channel.

" At these meetings, gooseberries have been produced which have weighed singly 15 dwts. 10 grains, e. g. *Lomax's Victory**. *Woodward's Smith** has weighed 17 dwts. ; and the *Royal Sovereign**, grown by George Cooke of Ashton, near Preston, at a meeting held 1794, weighed 17 dwts. 18 grains.

" A single gooseberry-tree, the Manchester rough red, in a garden belonging to Mr. J. Sykes, in Gate-acre, in the year 1792 yielded twenty-one quarts of fruit in their green state, when they sold at 3 *d.* per quart. The whole quantity weighed twenty-eight pounds avoirdupois†. The space this tree occupied was three yards, and allowing an equal space to walk round, and supposing an acre of eight yards to the rod planted with the same kind of trees, and producing the same quantity of fruit, and sold at the same price, the produce would amount to 426 *l.* 16 *s.*"

Orchards.—P. 83. " Except the orchard on the banks of the Irwell," (a new garden orchard planted in the Kentish manner) " in the township of Barton, containing about sixty-four statute acres, there (are) no orchards worthy (of) notice.—There is no cyder made in the county. The importation of apples from the cyder countries, and even from America, has of late been very considerable."

HORSES.—P. 169. " A great number of horses have of late years been bred, owing to the advanced price

" * Names of gooseberries."

" † To ascertain the weight of this fruit in different states of its growth, the surveyor made the following experiments upon the Manchester red gooseberry.—1794, May 3, one ale quart weighed 18½ ounces troy.—July 25, again from the same tree 20 ounces.—July 15, 21½ ounces.—July 29, 22 ounces.—August 4, 21½ ounces.—*N. B.* He has to regret that he did not number the fruit."(!)

price they have generally fetched at market; but proper attention in the choice of either the brood mares, or stallions, has not been paid." Nevertheless, in the same section, p. 172, it is stated, in strong terms, that "there has certainly been a degree of attention paid to the breed of horses at least, for this half century past, in this county. An attentive observer on this head remarked, that within the space of thirty years, horses have doubled their value in real goodness of quality."

We are not, however, so fortunate as to be able to find, in this Report, any thing of a practical nature, relating to the manner in which this great and rapid improvement has been effected. Indeed, there is nothing in this section, though it fills some pages, that is entitled to particular notice; excepting Mr. Eccleston's suggestion, p. 170, " that a yearly tax be laid upon stallions of five times the sum they receive for serving each mare, for the season; it would prevent the use of the inferior sort of stallions, which only serve to procreate those of small value which are nearly useless, with which almost every part of the kingdom abounds."

This might lessen, in some degree, the present number of stallions; but I do not perceive how it would particularly " prevent the use of the inferior sort:" as the lower the leap, the less the tax. The principle of the plan appears to me to be wrong. A uniform and high annual tax on stallions, as twenty guineas each, could scarcely fail to lessen the number of the inferior sort; as a half-guinea horse could not pay the tax, and remunerate his keeper. Beside, a high tax on stallions, and, in consequence, a high price for covering, would prevent many rips, unfit to produce their kind, from being put to the horse. Under such a regulation, not only *better*, but *fewer* horses would be bred. Viewing the matter in this light, it might be good policy to encrease the tax to fifty, or even a hundred, guineas, each stallion.

CATTLE.

CATTLE.—*Breed.*—P. 143.—" The Lancashire long-horned cattle are known all over the kingdom, and found in almost every part of the county, the prime stock of which is bred in the Filde, whither the purchasers from different parts of the kingdom have usually resorted; but applications have not of late been so frequent as formerly. The breed having been almost *entirely neglected,* the pail is become the material object; and as it is an established fact, that animals calculated for speedy fattening are seldom if ever prime milkers, good points of shape and make are less attended to than the milk vein.

" Some years ago, the Lancashire breeders suffered those of the more southern counties, as Leicestershire, Warwickshire, &c. to pick and purchase their best stock. Thus the northern breeders lessened the value of their own remainder: and the others made improvements upon that which they had obtained from them on the new principles laid down by Mr. Bakewell, and adopted by Mr. Fowler of Oxfordshire, and others. Nothing valuable is now brought southwardly, out of the more northern counties, once so famous for breeding stock.

" Amongst the cow-keepers all varieties are found; they change so frequently, that when a cow, likely to be useful, and at the point of dropping calf, is brought to the market, they purchase it, without paying much regard either to the species or country."

On the *management* of cattle, I perceive nothing of general information, or local utility; excepting what is contained in the subjoined passage, p. 166.— Before concluding this article, it may be proper to observe, that a college of Roman Catholics residing at Stony Hurst, near Clithero, in this county, *keep* their horned cattle within doors, and *fed* them upon boiled vegetables; amongst which were included all sorts of weeds, dock, nettles, &c. It is well known that on many parts of the continent they feed their
cattle

cattle on the leaves of trees.—What a resource here opens for the attentive and skilful agriculturist!"— Ha! ha! ha! The English Agriculturist is doubtlessly here meant,—*by the Editor!*

I well remember, those two hobbies, being *in*, and hard ridden, for some time! For even Mr. Harper, we are given to understand, prepared soup for his cows. Indeed, in Lancashire, where every man may be said to have a coal pit at his door, such expedients may be worth a thought. Moreover, in a dearth of food, for cattle, the leaves of trees, green in summer, or preserved in faggots, for winter fodder, might save a few from starving.

The *dairy* is the main object, and a principal source of produce, in the husbandry of Lancashire.

Milk is there a considerable article of sale: especially about Manchester, and at Liverpool.

P. 149. " The Cows kept in the neighbourhood of Liverpool, and within the compass of six miles, are, after supplying the family, principally for the purpose of furnishing the Liverpool market with milk* and butter†. There is milk, it is true, brought to town‡ from a considerable greater distance (10 miles) but the general distance seems no more than what is above stated. In the town of Liverpool alone, there are a considerable number of cows kept, to the amount

---

" * A few farmers there are that do not carry their milk 'o market, but dispose of it at home."

" † Butter-milk is an article of food throughout the greatest part of this county. When made into porridge, and thickened with a little oatmeal, and sweetened with treacle, it becomes an agreeable, nourishing, wholesome, and cheap food: the sweet, mixed with the acid of the milk, makes it very pleasant; mixed with water it is rendered a good beverage at meals, cool, refreshing, and quenching in summer. It is sometimes mixed with butter, and thus used to potatoes."

" ‡ The conveyance of milk has of late years been in wooden vessels in carts, instead of the backs of horses, as formerly. One horse can convey a greater quantity in a cart, with more ease, than on

amount of 5 or 600. A single field, for an outlet in the day-time, is procured at a very advanced rate; but the principal food is hay, and grains from the breweries.—In the town of Manchester, at the present juncture, there are not more than six cows kept within the precincts of the town, for the supply of its inhabitants. There comes a quantity every day by the Duke's canal.

" Those who are supposed to follow the best system of management, with a proper capital, seldom keep the same cow more than one calf, except some particular favorite. They are purchased at the time of calving, and the calf is immediately sold to feeders for the market, and who keep cows for that purpose, and dispose of their milk, and procure a livelihood that way. The cows, when they fail of yielding a certain quantity of milk (about 6 quarts per day) are, if in proper condition, disposed of to the butcher."

P. 151. " The Liverpool cowkeeper does not aim at making butter; his system is, to sell milk and cream; but in the summer season, when milk flows into the town from many quarters, a market sufficient to take off the whole may not always be found, and then he is under the necessity of churning it, and making butter, or disposing of it in cheese, or some other way; but the consumption of milk and cream is universal; and to these two articles his greatest attention is directed.

" A good cow should give daily 12 quarts, and the price of cream is generally 14d. per quart; new

on his back, besides affording more comfortable accommodations to the good woman, who also can carry along with her milk some little garden-stuff, according to the season of the year; and there are but few milk-carriers that do not take a few greens, &c. from their gardens, which they can dispose of amongst their customers, whilst they are selling off their milk. Of late these milk-carts have been covered with painted canvas upon hoops, affording a very good screen from the severity of the weather."

new milk 2*d. per* quart, and inferior milk 1*d. per* quart*. A cow stands the keeper in about 1*s.* per day, for food, attention, &c. so that with contingencies, and losses that frequently happen to the stock, there is but barely a living profit† left to a business, which requires much attention, and not a little skill in purchase and management."

P. 154. " The system at Manchester is nearly the same as at Liverpool. It does not, however, appear, that so many cows are kept within that town, it being supplied by a whole circle of surrounding country; whereas Liverpool has only half the quantity of land, from its maritime situation. The price of labor too, about Manchester, is such, that the milk passes through the hands of retailers, who buy it wholesale from the farmers,—who carry it generally upon horses, and whose servant, upon discharging his load, can immediately return and become useful at home."

Lactometer.—P. 160. " A lactometer, to try the different qualities of milk, has been invented by Mr. Dicas, mathematical-instrument-maker, in Liverpool, and patentee of a neat, simple, and accurate instrument to try the strength of spirituous liquors and worts.

" This lactometer ascertains the richness of milk, from its specific gravity, compared with water, by its degree of warmth taken by a standard thermometer, on comparing its specific quality with its warmth: on a scale constructed for this particular purpose, and by which, if the principle be right, may be discovered

not

" * Dearer at Manchester market a trifle; probably the quality may be superior."

" † In calculations we too frequently find that no allowance is made for contingencies, or falling off of quantity. Twelve quarts *per* day is the prime milking quantity ; and though some cows may have given more at the first, these kind of stock more rapidly fall off in quantity, whilst, at the same time, the quality was of less value, in proportion to the excess of quantity."

not only the qualities of the milk of different cows, pastures, foods, as turnips, potatoes, grains, &c. but also probably which may be the best milk, or best pastures for butter, and which for cheese. This instrument, however, is yet in its infancy."—This is a very ingenious instrument, which may not, even yet, be sufficiently matured.

P. 163. " *Instances wherein the* LACTOMETER *may be useful.*

" In discovering what breed of cattle are most advantageous.

" What food in the winter season, whether carrots, turnips, potatoes, &c. are best.

" What the effects of different pastures may be.

" How far particular farms are best adapted to making butter or cheese.

" How far the inconvenience of large cheeses in some dairies being too rich to stand, may be prevented, by discovering when this redundancy of richness exists in the milk.

" And in fixing a standard for the sale of this useful article of life.

" A standard for skimmed milk may readily be fixed by saying what strength the common saleable skimmed milk shall be by the lactometer."—" From a number of experiments and observations, the common saleable skimmed milk in Liverpool is from 52 to 64 of strength, and that of new milk from 70 to 80."

Butter.—P. 155.—" The practice of managing the milk for butter in this county, might be of service, if followed in other places. Except in the county of Chester, it should seem (as the surveyor understands) peculiar to this district. The mode is, dividing the milk into two parts ; the first drawn, being set apart for family use, after being skimmed; the cream of which goes into vessels appropriated to receive it; as also the whole of the second, or last, drawn milk, provincially

provincially called *afterings* *; these two being mixed together, are stirred, but not a great depth, to prevent the bad effects of foul air accumulating on the surface: and kept, according to the season of the year, exposed to the fire, to bring on fermentation and sourness; which is accelerated by that which may remain in the pores of the vessels; to prepare this fermentation, they are not scalded, except after having contracted some taint: and then to accelerate it (the quicker it is the better) the vessels are sometimes rinsed out with sour butter milk; in which state the milk is ready for the churn; and, in consequence of this treatment, more butter is obtained, and of a better quality, than if the milk was churned sweet. And the butter-milk, as it is called, after the butter is extracted, instead of being given to the hogs, as is generally the practice in many counties, becomes, under this process, an excellent food for man, both wholesome, and pleasant, as before-mentioned. This is the sort of butter-milk which, it has been remarked, is necessary for such laboring poor as live on potatoes."

P. 153. " The average milk of Mr. Harper's stock is seven quarts of milk per day the year through; although some prime cows in their full perfection, and in the height of grass, may yield when fresh calved eighteen, twenty-four, or even thirty quarts, of milk in a day; but this superabundance is but of short duration.—From every twelve quarts of milk is produced one pound of butter, of 18 oz. to the lb."

Mr. Wakefield of Brook Farm, near Liverpool, in a course of experiments, on a large scale, concerning the process of churning, found that—(p. 158.) " A short-horned cow, upon an average of twelve months, yields nine quarts of milk per day, and 4½ lb. of butter per week.   "A Lan-

---

" * About one half from each cow, each meal; but the quantity taken first in some measure depends upon the consumption of milk in the family."

" A Lancashire long-horn yields eight quarts of new milk per day, and four pounds of butter per week for twelve months." And p. 159. " Upon his farm at Aughton Mr. G. Green observes, that the average milk by his cows has been nine quarts of milk by the short-horn, and seven quarts of milk per day by the long-horn cows; and of butter eight pounds per week by the former, and seven pounds per week by the latter. This quantity is three pounds per week more than either Mr. Wakefield's or Mr. Harper's cows yield, which are equal in quantity, namely each 4 lb. per week. The two farms are about equal distances from Liverpool, e. g. Bank Hall, two miles north west. —Brook Farm two miles south east."—What nonsense—to be gravely commented on,—and published!

On the whole of this evidence* we may conclude that Lancashire cows, in the environs of Liverpool, yield, on a par, from seven to eight quarts of milk, one day with another, the year round; and that the par produce of butter, from that quantity of milk, is four pounds, a week,—or two hundred and eight pounds, a year, or season;—which is only sixteen pounds short of four firkins of 56 lb. each: whereas, in the dairy districts of Yorkshire, three firkins are reckoned a full produce. But the Liverpool cows are mostly or wholely in their prime; and are *forced*, all the year.

P. 35. " A churn has been lately introduced, which seems very useful for its neatness, cleanliness, and economy (as it occasions the less waste of milk). The churn, or vessel, instead of being round, has four corners, and the milk is put in motion by turning a handle, upon which are fixed boards which move horizontally in the manner of a reel within side the vessel, by which the operation of churning is something

---

* Which, however, is by no means—quite satisfactory: as neither the " quart" nor the " pound" is sufficiently defined.

thing easier, and the work expedited."—The containing vessel being *square* (if I understand the loose description) renders this a *new variety*.

Mention is also made of a " *milk cistern* formed out of a black close-grained stone, somewhat similar to black marble," p. 154.

Cheese.—P. 145. " There is much cheese made in this county, and also of excellent quality; in many respects equal to the Cheshire, in some superior. The cheese made in the vicinity of Leigh, Newborough, &c. for its mildness and rich flavour, always bears an advanced price at market; and it is somewhat remarkable that the very best dairy (as is usually reckoned) is the very worst land; the soil not being above two or three inches deep."—Again, p. 148. " The land round Leigh is chiefly barren, being ebb of soil and clay under, which makes it cold and wet. A few years since some of the farmers, encoraged by the high price of corn, marled and ploughed their farms, which had been grazed time immemorial; the consequence was, the plough soon wore them out, and left them poorer than ever. The grass that came was coarse and dry, and the cheese made off these ploughed farms of an inferior quality, which had like to have brought the whole into disrepute. But since the plough was laid by, the pastures have come about, and the cheese made upon them begins to fetch as much at market as the others do."

On *cheese making*, all we find in this Report is contained in " a Letter to the Surveyor on the Subject of Leigh Cheese : " and, in this, only one passage demands particular notice, here. In Cheshire we must look for general information respecting the mysteries of this art.

P. 147. " The curd is broke down, and, when separated from the whey, is put into a cheese vat, and pressed very dry, and after that broken very small, by squeezing it with the hands; the new curd used is mixed with about half its quantity of yesterday's, day's, and which has been kept for that purpose, and a part of this new curd is put by for to-morrow, if it can be spared; if not, all to-morrow's is put by to mix with new, as convenience suits, for the best cheese is always made with part old curds. Some mix the old and the new together, after both have been worked very small: others put the old curds in the middle of the cheese: either of which ways will do very well, as I have often noticed. When the curds have been thus mixed, and well pressed and closed with the hands in a cheese-vat, till they become one solid lump, it is put into a press."

Some speculative remarks, however, on *toasting cheese* may serve to agitate the most mysterious part of the art: namely that of "putting the milk together."

P. 148. "The cheese is mild; and when toasted it keeps all its butter within it, which makes it eat soft and rich. This property of its mixing together when hot, is said to be owing to its being put together cool when made, for this makes the curd mild and tender, and likewise the cheese, so that its more solid particles, when heated, are easily separated, and the whole so loosed and broken, that room is made for the butter, which adheres to the small particles of cheese, and forms one pulpous consistence. Not so when the cheese is overheated in making, for then more of the butter runs out, and the curd is faster bound together than before; and when toasting, the parts are loosened, the butter is run out, and the remainder of the cheese is left hard and dry."

SWINE.—P. 174. "Pork is not an article of great consumption with any class of people in this county. The application of the best and most farinaceous kinds of potatoe being chiefly for the food of man, the refuse alone, and the coarser kinds, such as ox-noble, champion, and Surinam *, are given to the cows, horses,

" * It is supposed most of these coarse kinds have been raised from the

horses, and poultry, and to the hogs which may be
kept on the farm, which seldom amount to above
four.

"The idea of hogs being numerous in a potatoe
country is very natural; but the fact is not so: few are
bred here, and those few that are kept are bought
from itinerant drovers from Shropshire, Yorkshire,
Cheshire, &c. Pork does not seem to be a favorite
food with any class of people in this county, though
more is used than formerly. In short, the potatoes
generally grown by the lower people are of the best
farinaceous kinds, which they are particularly nice in,
and consume in their families, or sell to advantage in
the market. Some gentlemen and farmers, who grow
the ox-noble and other coarser potatoes, use them in
general for cows, horses, and poultry, scarcely any
one keeping more than three or four hogs, which,
however, are kept in good condition, and in some
degree fatted with the help of potatoes, but are fatted
off at last with damaged ship's wheat, India corn, &c.
which can often be procured upon reasonable terms
from the *corn warehouses*. Boat loads of ox-noble
potatoes are brought to Liverpool from Cheshire,
which are bought up for the use of cattle, &c.

"The stock of swine are in general purchased
from herdsmen who travel about the country, and
who bring them from Cheshire, Shropshire, Wales,
and Ireland." All this in one breath! What a
jumble of ideas and waste of words.

A "Lancashire Hog," however, has at length
made its appearance. It can certainly claim high
descent: being half blood to the *wild boar:* as if
tame pigs were not *savage* enough, without that vilest
admixture. Cadishness is a cardinal virtue in a farm
hog.

P. 175. "Pigs" (says the Surveyor) " should
during

the seeds of the Surinam, and of which they are only varieties;
indeed they bear strong resemblance to the Surinam, in leaf."

during the stage of their growth, be regularly turned out to graze, where there is a conveniency. This, besides the advantage of grass, which is nutritious and helps digestion, by the fresh air and exercise, causes a disposition to take their rest, and sleep after a meal, contributes to their cleanliness, and renders their flesh of superior flavor."

SHEEP.—*Breed.* P. 166. " This is not a sheep district, therefore they cannot be any where numerous in the county.—There are flocks (but flock is an undeterminate number) it is true of half-starved creatures upon the mountains, but in such proportion, that Mr. Eccleston is of opinion that there is not a single shepherd, properly so called, in the whole county.

" Those which are kept upon the feeding districts are bred in Scotland, and purchased by the Westmoreland farmer from thence at a year old, and afterwards by the Lancashire grazier from Westmoreland at four years old, fatted and sold for slaughtering.

" There is a singular custom prevails in the northern part of the county, and which is universal amongst the mountains and waste lands, which is as follows: Whenever a tenant enters upon a farm upon which *there is a heavy-bred flock of sheep,* that the sheep are separated and sorted; viz. the wethers aged, ewes, one year old (provincially hogs) two years old (twinters) and then valued at certain but different prices ; and the tenant by covenant in his lease to leave an equal number of each sort upon his farm when he quits, or to pay the value in money, according to the deficiency which may appear in each sort ; but if proved, on stating a balance, that it is in favour of the tenant ; he either paid for the overplus number, or his landlord takes them at a proper valuation.

" The sheep are generally delivered to the coming-on tenant about Martinmas." *   P. 168.

---

* In alpine districts, where the value of farms depends mostly on mountain stock, and where tenants of property are difficult to be
met

P. 168. " There is also a breed called the Warton,
or Silve -dale cragg sheep, which is much esteemed
for the fine flavor of its flesh, fineness of its wool,
and tendency to fatten. They pasture upon very
rocky lime-stone land. Their wool commonly sells
at about twelve shillings per stone, of 14lb." See
WESTMORELAND, p. 238, aforegoing.

P. 167. " There are but few sheep kept in the
southern part of the county, except those purchased
in distant parts, by the butchers, and kept a few
weeks on grass for their own convenience—or, by a
few gentlemen." In travelling through the cultivated
districts of Lancashire, scarcely a sheep is seen: excepting a few Scotch wedders.

RABBITS.—P. 175. " There are some lands along
the coast, employed as rabbit-warrens."

DECOYS.—P. 10. " It is believed, that the only
decoy pond is at Orford, the seat of John Black-
burne, Esq."

POULTRY.—P. 176. " The Filde is the principal
district in this county which keeps a surplus stock of
poultry. Poulterers also collect the chief part of
what is brought to the Ormskirk market on Thurs-
day, from the cottagers and farmers, and retail them
out again at the Liverpool market on Saturday.

" On Martin Mere, are turned a number of flocks
of geese, on a certain day, brought from different
parts of the county. These flocks are so marked, as
again to be known. Upon this Mere they continue
till about Michaelmas, and on this water they can
find sufficient of food for their sustenance from the
different grasses, aquatics, fishes, and insects. The
proprietor of the water claims half of the stock that
remains alive for their summer's keep." BEES.

met with, it appears to be judicious in proprietors to provide sheep
for their farms; as, otherwise, they might frequently be under-
stocked, through a want of sufficient capital, in their occupiers;
and their prosperity, in consequence, be liable to be interrupted.
See p. 199.

BEES.—The following fact is worth registering. P. 178. " An accident happening to a hive of bees, belonging to Thomas Dugdale, of Walton, 1794, the honey was taken, and after being cleared from the combs was weighed, which amounted to the astonishing quantity of 18 lb. in the space of twenty-one days after swarming."

THE incidental observations that have spontaneously risen, in appreciating the merits of this extraordinary production, supercede the utility of any RETROSPECTIVE REMARKS which could be offered upon it, here.

YORKSHIRE.

THE face of this extensive county is strongly featured; and abounds in well defined NATURAL DISTRICTS*.

In pursuing the several districts of Yorkshire, geographically, from those of Lancashire, see p. 245, the first we enter is CRAVEN;—a singular passage of country; beset on every side with eminencies; excepting where the Ribble and the Aire have their outlets:—the former into Lancashire, the latter into the central parts of Yorkshire.

To the eastward of Craven, rise the WESTERN MORELANDS;—and, at their southern skirts, lie the MANUFACTURING DISTRICTS of Yorkshire;—which are bordered, on the southeast, by the LIMESTONE LANDS of WEST YORKSHIRE†.

On

* Having already offered an analytic view of this county, according to its natural districts, in "The RURAL ECONOMY of YORKSHIRE," it may seem unnecessary to go over the ground a second time. But having been occasionally led across the county, in different directions, since that work was written, and thereby improved my knowledge of its several parts, and it being my wish to render my present work entire, I have deemed it better to pursue the general plan laid down, than to refer, in this or any other instance, to my former publications; unless to corroborate, or farther explain, what I may have occasion to advance in this. I forbear, however, in the present case, to particularize the routes that I have at different times taken across this county. I have traversed it in almost every direction.

† The last being an *agricultural*—rather than a *manufacturing*—passage, and bearing a distinguishing natural character, I separate it as a natural district.

On the east of the three last mentioned districts, the VALE of YORK extends;—from the marshes of Yorkshire and North Lincolnshire, nearly to the county of Durham;—where it unites with the VALE of STOCKTON:—and attached to this is the NORTHERN SEA-COAST of Yorkshire; situated between the British ocean and the EASTERN MORELANDS; which are embraced, on the west and north, by the vales of York and Stockton.

On the southern skirts of those morelands, and on the eastern margin of the vale of York, are situated the LIMESTONE LANDS of EAST YORKSHIRE;—which inclose, on the north, the west, and the southwest, the VALE of PICKERING;—on the southeast of which rise the WOLDS of YORKSHIRE; and, between these and the sea, lies HOLDERNESS.

Finally, to the west of the manufacturing districts, are situated the SOUTHERN MOUNTAINS of Yorkshire, Lancashire, Cheshire, Staffordshire, and Derbyshire.

THE BOARD of AGRICULTURE, in the prosecution of their plan, divided this county into three distinct Surveyorships, according with its RIDINGS; each of which is the subject of a separate REPORT.

THE WEST RIDING OF

YORKSHIRE.

TO this division of the county belong, wholely, or in considerable part, four of the NATURAL DISTRICTS, above enumerated: namely, Craven, the western morelands, the manufacturing districts, and the limestone lands of West Yorkshire.

CRAVEN. Its situation has been mentioned. Its outline is most irregular: being given by the bases of the hills which nearly surround it, and the vallies

that

that branch out of it. Concerning the limits of Craven, *popular*, (if any precise limits are assigned it) I have no information*. The *natural* district, to which I have assigned this name, extends from Settle, at the northwestern extremity, to Keighley, on the southeast; and from the skirts of the western morelands of Yorkshire, to those of the northern morelands of Lancashire; including the valley of the Ribble to whence it enters between the two divisions of the Lancashire hills. It includes, of course, a small part of the county of Lancaster. Its extent would be difficult to ascertain, or even to estimate near the truth. I will suppose it to contain a hundred and fifty square miles.

The surface of Craven is very uneven; in some parts, beautifully varied. Near the banks of the Aire and the Ribble, both of which pass through it, there is much low vale land. But the prevailing characteristic is upland; some of it of considerable elevation. Yet the soil is mostly of a productive quality. Much of it is sound limestone land. Some of the higher swells are of a cooler clayey nature. The whole country may be said to be covered with grass, and full of livestock :—mostly cattle; but many sheep are observable, on the limestone heights. The lower lands are mowing and grazing grounds. Together, a very valuable passage of country.

The WESTERN MORELANDS. The limit of this tract of black heathy mountain, on the north, has been

---

* Excepting what is contained in the following vague account of it, by "a gentleman in that neighbourhood," App. p. 51. "The extent of the vale of Skipton cannot be accurately ascertained; indeed, a very small part bears that name, being generally included in the vale (valley) of the river Aire which extends from Leeds, in a north-west direction, to the source of the river, about thirty-five miles, is upon the average about a mile broad, in some places more, yet not so much (I think) as to add a quarter to the average."—Are we to understand, from this, that Craven commences at Leeds!

been mentioned, p. 128, aforegoing. Its boundary, on the south, is formed by the manufacturing district,—and by the valley of the Aire;—by which it is cut off from the more southern mountains. On the northwest, this main link of the mountains of England extends into Westmoreland; where it joins the shistus Alps of Cumberland, &c. The boundary on the west and southwest, is formed by Lonsdale, Craven, and the plain before-mentioned, which connects them; except where the line of low grounds is broken by the narrow ridge of limestone, above Giggleswick. On the east, these morelands shelve down to the cultivated lands which form the western bank of the vale of York.

The elevation of these wild lands is very considerable; especially on their more western confines; but they are in no part, I believe, equal in loftiness to the Cumbrian mountains. Their surface in general is tame,—merely swelling; except on the western margin, which is much broken, and strongly featured; and except where their sides are furrowed, by dells or wider vallies. In the northwest quarter, they are severed, nearly to their summit, by the vallies of the Swale and the Ure (still, provincially, and no doubt anciently, "Yor") which open into the vale of York:—the latter, named Wensleydale, being of considerable width, and containing an extent of valuable cultivated lands.

The MANUFACTURING DISTRICTS of Yorkshire. This large portion of the West Riding is well defined. On its north, the western morelands,—on its south, the sandy lands of Nottinghamshire,—on its west, the southern mountains,—and on its east, the limestone lands of West Yorkshire—are situated. Its length from north to south, may be estimated at forty miles, and its mean width, at twenty miles; together giving an area of eight hundred square miles.

This

This area naturally separates into two divisions :—the northern, which is occupied by the woolen manufacture ; and the southern, in which the different branches of the iron manufacture are carried on. The former, unless on the banks of the principal rivers, as in the neighbourhoods of Leeds and Wakefield, is naturally a mean, mountain-skirt country. The latter, on the contrary, is one of the most habitable parts of the island :—the surface well turned, well soiled, and well wooded ; a clean, productive, charming country ; though, here and there, it is disfigured by manufactures. Nothing, however, of that squalidness and apparent penury, which obtrudes itself in the northern division, is here observable.

The LIMESTONE LANDS of WEST YORKSHIRE. This fine tract of country extends from Doncaster to Wetherby : a distance of thirty miles. The width, however, is narrow, and very irregular. The manufacturing district forms its western—the vale of York its eastern—boundary. The surface is much varied ; rising in some parts to heights of a mean elevation. But it mostly enjoys a better climature ; and, in many parts, a deep fertile soil, on a sound calcareous base ; forming arable land of the first value ;—capable of maturing the most valuable productions of this island. The liquorice grounds of Pontefract are situated within this district.

" GENERAL

" GENERAL VIEW

OF THE

AGRICULTURE

OF THE

WEST RIDING OF YORKSHIRE.

SURVEYED BY

Messrs. RENNIE, BROWN, and SHIRREFF, 1793.

WITH

OBSERVATIONS ON THE MEANS OF ITS IMPROVEMENT,

AND

ADDITIONAL INFORMATION SINCE RECEIVED.

DRAWN UP FOR THE CONSIDERATION OF

THE BOARD OF AGRICULTURE AND INTERNAL
IMPROVEMENT.

By ROBERT BROWN,

FARMER AT MARKLE, NEAR HADDINGTON,

SCOTLAND.

1799."

THE ACQUIREMENTS of the above-named SUR-
VEYORS,—as *Agriculturists*,—rank high among the
qualifications of the Board's Reporters : each of
them, I believe, being a considerable occupier, in the
county of East Lothian ; a highly cultivated district,
in the South of Scotland.

From Mr. RENNIE I am happy in saying I received civilities, about the time that the Survey under
notice was taken ; and had great satisfaction in
accompanying Mr R. in walking over his farm ;
which,

which, as far as the judgement could determine, at that season of the year, the twentieth of November, appeared to be conducted in an exemplary manner.

Of Mr. BROWN, the ostensible AUTHOR of the REPORT, I can only judge from his work : from which it is abundantly evident that Mr. Brown is an ARABLE FARMER of a superior class.—As a WRITER, too, Mr. B. evinces sufficient ability,—had he been more patient in study, and less ready to write,—to have furnished a masterly Report.

Respecting the MODE of SURVEY, Mr. B. has been amply explicit: having not only furnished us with the Surveyor's ROUTE : but with an abstract of their JOURNAL. By this it appears (in Appendix, page 1.) that he and his colleagues commenced their "Survey, at Boroughbridge, on the 24th of October, 1793." And, by a SKETCH of their route, given by dotted lines between the places which they visited, they proceeded from thence to Copgrove (Mr. H. Duncomb's), Knaresborough, Harrowgate, Ripley, Settle, Sedbergh, Skipton, Otley, Leeds, Bradford, Halifax, Pontefract, Bretton Hall (Col. Beaumont's), Barnsley, Penniston, Sheffield, Rotherham, Wentworth House (Earl Fitzwilliam's), Park Hill (Mr. M. A. Taylor's), Bawtry, Doncaster, Thorn, Snaith, Ferrybridge, Scarthingwell Hall (Lord Hawke's), Selby, Sherborne, Tadcaster, Harewood (Lord Harewood's), Wetherby : and made excursions to York, and to Ripon. The time spent in those journies does not appear. No dates are given ; either in the reprinted—or the original Report.

In looking over their Journal, or, as it is styled— " a selection of the principal articles contained in the Journal"—the reader must be disappointed in regard to its intelligence. It reads more like the Journal of hasty *Travellers*, than of *public Surveyors*. Unless in some few instances, their mode of gaining information appears to have been that of posting from place to place, generally from town to town, often from one manufacturing

manufacturing town to another, *there* to make enquiries after the state of Agriculture, and other country concerns.

For instances:—App. p. 12. " Arrived at Leeds." (Respecting the line of country between Otley and Leeds—not one remark.)   " The following are the most accurate accounts we could procure of the state of husbandry near Leeds."

P 15. " Arrived at Halifax—the whole country from Bradford to this place, being almost a continued village; roads bad ever since we left Leeds, and materials very scarce."

P. 19. " From Wakefield to Pontefract, the soil is much drier, and corn fields more numerous. Passed a large common field, which appeared in very bad order. Arrived at Pontefract, and met with a number of intelligent farmers, from whom we received much information."

From those and innumerable other instances, it is evident, that the principal part of the information gained was collected by them, in the character of ENQUIRING TOURISTS*. For the reader is told, p. 247. " When we entered upon the business of surveying the husbandry of the West Riding, we were totally unacquainted with the practices and customs of the district."

It is to be remarked, however, that Messrs. Rennie, Brown, and Shirreff, in whatever related to the arable management of the district, were less liable to be imposed upon, than men who might want their superior knowledge of the subject. It is true, that, in passing between town and town, the nature of the soil is sometimes, yet by no means generally, noticed:—But respecting the *substrata*, which may frequently be detected in travelling, and the *turn of surface* which may always be seen (by day light) scarsely a remark
occurs :—

---

* See the QUALIFICATIONS of a REPORTER,—in the INTRODUCTION.

occurs:—although every arable farmer must know that the value of land, for agricultural purposes, depends on these, rather than on the specific quality of the soil.

The following is Mr. Brown's *official account* of the tour. Introd. p. iv. " Under the authority of the Board, my friends, Messrs. Rennie, and Sherriff, and I, surveyed the West Riding of Yorkshire; and, during our progress, scarce a difference of opinion occurred respecting the matters which underwent our examination. We remained about five weeks in the district, and, during that time, used every means in our power to gain an intimate knowledge of the different modes in which husbandry was carried on, as well as the general and local impediments to its improvement."

Regarding the reprinted Report, now under Review, Mr. B. informs us, p. vii. " When the Board signified their desire, that we should undertake the task of preparing the work for re-publication, application was immediately made to almost every person, who had formerly favored us with intelligence, and they were particalarly requested to point out any errors in the original copy respecting facts, which we considered as of the utmost importance. In consequence of these applications, a good deal of additional information was received, which is incorporated with the text, where it did not militate against the sentiments formed in our progress. The copies, returned to the Board with marginal remarks, were also consulted; and every thing favorable or unfavorable to our opinions has been inserted, either in the body of the Work, in the Appendix, or by way of Notes. In some cases the latter were so hostile, that we have thought it necessary to follow them with suitable answers."

Mr. Brown concludes his Introduction in a way which every reader will approve; if not admire. P. xi. " We trust that our observations will be can-
didly

didly considered, and that unintentional defects will be forgiven. We are not conscious of having misrepresented a single fact, or of having offered an opinion, which, to the best of our judgement, would prove disadvantageous to the public. Others might have executed the work with greater ability, but we must be pardoned for declaring that few could have been more anxious to present to the Board a Report, which would communicate a faithful account of the present state of Husbandry in the district, and at the same time describe the obstacles to improvement, and how they might be removed."

The ANNOTATORS, and other CONTRIBUTORS, to the West Riding Report, are numerous. The original having been circulated with singular industry, and containing many positions that were *new* to the gentlemen and farmers of the district, their remarks are almost endless;—and Mr. Brown's answers to them are neither few, nor short.

Those notes and answers are inserted at the ends of chapters;—an arrangement which renders them troublesome to be referred to; and to refer from the notes, to the text, is still more irksome to the reader, (and hard labor to a Reviewer!); who may have twenty or thirty pages to go over, in search of a diminutive *d, e,* or *f !* Had the page of the text preceded the note which belongs to it, this aukwardness would have been avoided. The other contributions are either inserted, as quotations, in the body of the Work, or appear as Appendices.

Of the CONTRIBUTORS some are anonymous, and many have used their initials, only. Among those who stand conspicuously forward are—

Mr. PAYNE of Frickley, near Doncaster; whose remarks are generally interesting and valuable; excepting when his judgement is borne away by his liberality and goodness of heart.

Mr. STOCKDALE of Knaresborough is a large contributor:

tributor: he appearing to have taken uncommon pains to assist the Surveyors.

Mr. DAY of Doncaster is also a contributor: and the late

LORD HAWKE has furnished a valuable paper.

Among the more frequent ANNOTATORS are— Mr. YORKE,—Mr. FOX,—and a *Yorkshire farmer*,— who complains of the haughtiness and insolence of *laborers*, without seeming to be aware of his own, when he speaks of *landlords*.

SUBJECT THE FIRST.

NATURAL ECONOMY.

ON this subject, the Reporter's remarks are brief.

ELEVATION and SURFACE.—P. 5.—" The face of the country is strongly irregular. In the western and northern divisions a considerable portion is hilly and mountainous; though in these situations it is intersected with numerous vales, (vallies) carrying grass of the richest quality; but the middle and eastern parts are generally level, having no more eminences than what serve to variegate the prospect."

CLIMATURE. P. 4.—" As the Riding is of great extent, and contains large tracts both of mountainous and low land, the climate, of course, varies much. Upon the whole, however, it is moderate and healthy, except near the banks of the Ouse, where, from lowness of situation, damps and fogs sometimes prevail. The harvest over the greatest part of the district is comparatively early, commencing usually before the middle of August, and, backward seasons excepted, is finished by the end of September; but, in the western parts, it is at least a fortnight later than about Pontefract and Doncaster. The average gauge of rain,

rain, at Sheffield, is 33 inches in a year, which is about a medium betwixt what falls in Lancashire, and on the eastern coast."—On whose authority these particulars were inserted is not mentioned.

WATERS. P. 6. " The West Riding is remarkable for the number of its great and navigable rivers: 1st, The Ouse which takes this name a few miles above York, being formerly called the Eure*, and in its course to the Humber receives all the other rivers that run through the district. 2dly, The Don, which is navigable nearly to Sheffield, and of great advantage to the trade of that neighbourhood. Over this river, betwixt Snaith and Thorn, there is a wooden bridge which turns upon a pivot, and affords a passage for the numerous shipping employed in the inland trade. 3dly, The Calder, which flows along the borders between this Riding and Lancashire, and running in an eastern direction falls into the Aire, fives miles below Wakefield. 4thly, The Aire a large river issuing from the mountain Penigent; which, with the aid of canals, is navigable to Leeds, Bradford, and Skipton. 5thly, The Wharfe which has its rise at the foot of the Craven hills, and after a course of more than 50 miles across the Riding, keeping for a great way an equal distance of 10 miles from the Aire, discharges itself into the Ouse. Besides these principal rivers there are many of lesser importance."

It is proper to remark, here, that the river Aire rises in Craven, or out of its immediate banks, and the Wharfe, several miles to the North of Penigant. And I cannot refrain from observing, farther, that a mistake which might have been avoided at so small an expense of time and labor as that of casting the eye over a map of the county under survey, naturally impresses on the mind of the reader a degree of diffidence

---

* YORK. The provincial name (as has been said above) of that river is " Yor ;" and it probably gave name to the ancient City of York. Thus,—Yor-wych, Yorwick, Yorrick, York. *Rev.*

dence respecting points that required more care and attention to settle.

SOIL. P. 5. " The nature and quality of the soil, in this extensive district, differs materially. There are all sorts, from the deep strong clay and rich fertile loam, to the meanest peat earth; and probably it contains all the different varieties that are to be found in the island. Vicinity to great towns, and superior culture have, no doubt, rendered a considerable part fertile and productive that was originally barren; but a large proportion of the district is of a quality naturally favourable to the purposes of good husbandry, and, under a proper system of management, will amply repay the farmer for whatever trouble and expense he bestows on its cultivation."

SUBSTRATA. Of these, no mention is made, in the chapter " Geographical State," &c. But, in the section " Tillage," we find some notice of them.— P. 80.—" The arable soils of this Riding, as referring to cultivation, may be considered as comprehending all the varieties which prevail in Britain, but the prevailing quality (keeping off the moors) is loam, the value of which is in a great measure regulated by the subsoil, upon which it is incumbent; limestone land, or in other words, where the surface lies upon a limestone bottom, is also very prevalent, and a great part of that large tract of ground adjoining to the river Ouse, is of a clayey tenacious nature, holding water like a cup, very difficult to manage, but, under the hands of skilful cultivators, capable of carrying the most luxuriant crops."

MINERALS.—P. 5.—" There are numerous mines of coal, lime, ironstone, and lead, and some copper, in this district, which have been wrought for ages past, and may, in some places, be said to be inexhaustible. At Grassington" (in Wharf Dale) " the lead mines are numerous and valuable, but they are now wrought with less advantage than formerly, owing to the want of a fresh level, which can only be
done

done by the Duke of Devonshire who is Lord of the
manor. We believe his Grace formerly took one
seventh for his dues, but of late, in fresh bargains, he
demands one fifth."

SUBJECT THE SECOND.

POLITICAL ECONOMY.

STATE of APPROPRIATION. To this important
subject, the surveyors have paid much attention. It
appears to have been one of a few standing subjects
of enquiry. I find it brought forward, in various
parts of the volume.

STATE

App. p. 73. " STATE of the WASTE LANDS in Yorkshire, calculated by MR. TUKE, Junior.

	Capable of cultivation, or of being converted into Pasture.	Incapable of being improved except by planting.	Total.
Waste lands in the *North Riding*.	Acres.	Acres.	Acres.
The Western moor lands — —	150,000	76,940	226,940
Eastern ditto — —	60,000	136,625	196,625
Detached moors, or waste, in the country — —	18,435		18,435
Total —	228,435	213,565	442,000
Waste lands in the *West Riding*			
The high moors — —	200,000	140,272	340,272
Detached moors, or waste, in the country — —	65,000		65,000
Total —	265,000	140,272	405,272
Waste lands in the *East Riding*			
Detached moors, or waste, in the country — —	2,000		2,000

In the North Riding — 442,000
West Riding — 405,272
East Riding — 2,000

Total waste lands in
Yorkshire — 849,272"

P. 131. " The waste lands, in this district, are very extensive, amounting, according to Mr. Tuke's calculation, to two hundred and sixty-five thousand acres, which are capable of cultivation*, and one hundred and forty thousand acres, which are incapable of improvement, except by planting; being rather more than one-fourth of the whole lands of the district. If we add to these the common fields, which are also extensive and susceptible of as much improvement as the wastes, it will at once appear how much remains to be done, before the cultivation of the district can be pronounced finished or perfected."

In the chapter—" Obstacles to Improvement"— we find the following strong reasons urged, for a *general law* of *Appropriation.* P. 248. " Under the first head, we beg leave to state the present situation of a considerable part of the Riding, occupied as common field, and of much larger tracts lying in a state of absolute waste. From the want of a general bill, these grounds cannot be divided, or held in severalty, without the proprietors incurring a vast expense by applications to the Legislature, which, in many cases, from the obstinacy and caprice of individuals, is not even practicable. We account it as demonstrable as any proposition in Euclid, that no real improvement can take place on the common fields and wastes, without a previous division; and it is nearly as certain, that without a general law being passed at once for the whole kingdom, their division, according to the present system, will never be accomplished."

On this devoutly to be wished for measure, Mr. PAYNE, in his own manner observes,—App. N. p. 14.— " But what would become of the *poor* but *honest* attorney,

---

" * Great part of which, call loudly for improvement by the plough and the spade; may the call be obeyed, lest we *fight,* and *weave,* and *hammer,* till we have not bread to eat.   *W. P.*"

attorney, officers of parliament, and a long train
of &c. &c. who obtain a *decent* livelihood from the
trifling fees of every individual inclosure bill—all these
of infinite use to the community, and must be encouraged whether the wastes be enclosed or not. The
waste lands, in the dribbling difficult way they are at
present inclosed, will cost the country upwards of
twenty millions to these gentry &c. which on a *general*
inclosure bill would be done for less than *one*."—And
in a letter, inserted in the Appendix, Mr. P. enters,
analytically, into the subject.—App. P. 58. " The obstacles to the improvement and inclosures of waste
lands, in many places, amount nearly to a *pro-
hibition;* viz.—1st, The tithes, the dislike of which,
with the freeholders, &c. makes a very difficult commutation, the absolute condition of their concurrence.
2dly, Manorial claims and powers. 3dly, The heavy
expense and trouble of obtaining acts in the legislature.
To which may be added, the caprice, *partial* interest,
and disinclination to all improvement of some of the
claimants in many cases. All these obstacles might
be much lessened by a law, specifying and *explaining*
the claims, and *limiting* the *powers* of tithe and
manorial proprietors, in such manner, that *their
simple opposition* should not hang *in terrorem* over the
very threshold of every such inclosure; and also
facilitating and *encouraging* such applications to the
legislature; perhaps a general act of inclosure upon
a good plan might be a wise and seasonable measure
to liberate the *active improvers* from the torpid do-
minion of indolence and stupidity; however the government can scarcely do wrong in this matter,
except by *suffering* the *wastes* to remain as they
are.

" Entirely owing to one or all of the obstacles I
have mentioned, very few indeed of inclosing bills have
passed these twenty years, in the whole district comprised between the towns I mentioned above, (347,)
notwithstanding the value of the lands, and the great
scarcity

scarcity and smallness of farms; in the few instances that have occurred, their beneficial consequences to the stock of public industry and produce have been conspicuous."—Again, in p. 134.—" There are great tracts of waste land in this neighbourhood; I may extend this remark to the whole county : lands now utterly lost to the community, even in this rich and populous Riding; and be it mentioned to the utter disgrace of every thing in the country, that after a long period of years, in which this island has depended ou foreigners for a part of its necessary consumption, these lands are still waste; they are a complete nuisance to every occupier, who has the misfortune to border upon them."—And, in a note (signed W. P.) p. 110.—" Inclosures ought to have been promoted by all the might of the legislature, and if more of this is not speedily done, by removing all impediments to so necessary and natural a work, *famine* and misery of all kinds will inevitably be the consequence; a just and merited punishment for our neglect of the domestic cultivation of our own *bread plant*, and a foolish predilection for the culture. of the foreign sugar cane."

On perfecting the appropriation of *common fields*, and thereby facilitating their division and inclosure, we find, in the chapter " Waste and unimproved Lands" some sensible remarks emanating from the same extraordinary mind.—P. 133.—" Upon this article, Mr. Payne at Frickley says, ' A considerable proportion of the arable land is uninclosed, to the great obstruction of agricultural improvement; the advantages of inclosing are numerous and important. The liberal occupier of *inclosed* land, whose mind is actively improved in the employment and increase of his produce, with whom innovation has no fault, but when it is useless, this man on *inclosed* land has not the *vis inertiæ* of his stupid neighbour to contend with him, before he can commence any alteration in his management, that he is clearly convinced will be to his

his advantage; he is completely master of his land, which, in its open state, is scarcely *half his own.* This is strongly evident in the cultivation of turnips, or other vegetables for the winter consumption of cattle; they are constantly cultivated in inclosures, when they are never thought of in the open fields in some parts; and I know no township in this Riding, except that of Wath upon Derne, where the turnips are cultivated in any degree of perfection in open fields. At that place, they have long been wisely unanimous on the management of their common fields, and in selling the whole turnip crop, by a valuation, to a person engaging to stock them entirely with sheep on the land: but even *there* they cannot apply their own produce to the improvement of their *own* stock, nor have they it in their power to vary their management by the introduction of any grasses for more than one crop in their rotation; both essential articles, when the improvement of live stock, particularly sheep, is in contemplation; this argument for inclosure might be very amply dilated on, were I writing a treatise instead of a letter.'"

STATE of SOCIETY.—*Provisions.*—P. 209.—" It is unnecessary to give a statement of prices of provisions during the time we remained in the district, as, from the fluctuation of markets, no light would thereby be thrown upon the value of produce. We may only hint, that the cheapest article of provisions was poultry, the cause of which we attribute to the taste of the inhabitants, who very judiciously give a preference to well fed beef and mutton, which is furnished them in the greatest perfection."—The epicures of the West Riding will, doubtlessly, think kindly of Mr. B. for this hint.

Manufactures. The following observations (by whom, we are not told) are valuable. P. 226.— " Hints, respecting manufacturers residing in the country, who are occasionally employed in cultivating the soil.

" The

" The few observations which the writer is able to furnish upon this chapter, will be confined to such manufacturers as are employed in the making of woolen and worsted goods, exposed to sale in the different market-towns of Leeds, Wakefield, Huddersfield, Halifax, and Bradford, in the West Riding of the county of York; and which consist of broad and narrow cloths, shalloons, callimancoes, and the various worsted articles, which the industry and ingenuity of the persons employed have diversified and improved; and in considering the question, it is the writer's opinion, that those manufacturers have many advantages by residing in the country. For,

" 1st, They enjoy a more uncontaminated air, which, as the employment of the clothiers is not the most cleanly, will conduce to their health.

" 2dly, The country affords them a more open exposure of their manufacture to the sun, which is necessary in different stages of their work.

" 3dly, In general, the villages, where the manufacturers are resident, are nearer to, and more cheaply supplied with coals; an article, not only necessary to the comfort of their families, but also to enable them to carry on their trade.

" 4thly, Another advantage attending a country residence, is the many springs of good wholesome water for the supply of their families and their dyehouses; for it is to be observed, that every clothier dyes his own wool, unless colours are required of uncommon brilliancy.

" 5thly, Another advantage is, that by being thus disposed in villages, the manufacturers are nearer to the fulling mills, with which the different rivers are occupied; and it is this dispersion which has occasioned so many fulling mills to be erected, to the great advantage of the owners of the different falls upon the rivers, which otherwise would have been almost useless.

6thly,

" 6thly, The manufacturer of cloth in particular, requires roomy buildings, which are obtained upon much lower rents in the country than in towns.

" 7thly, From the bulkiness of the raw materials, and upon various other accounts, a horse is almost necessary to enable a clothier to carry on his trade; and as land at a distance from large towns, is cheaper generally than near them, the manufacturer in the country can better keep so useful an animal.

" 8thly, To do this, and also to maintain a cow, which is one of the first comforts and chief supports of the infant part of his family, the country affords him a much cheaper, and better opportunity; and as both hay and straw are wanted for the animals, the manufacturer, partly of necessity, occasionally becomes employed in the cultivation of the soil, and it is no uncommon thing to see, in a manufacturing farm, which ought not to exceed (and seldom does) 16 acres, great attention, judgment, and spirit, in cultivation. Certain it is, that by manufacturers residing in the country, and occasionally employing themselves in cultivating the soil, the barren commons of these parts, a great many whereof have been lately inclosed and divided, have been made productive to a degree, which no regular farmer could have made it their interest to have attempted. By thus becoming the cultivator of land, the manufacturer is enabled to raise poultry, and keep a pig, and, recustomed to cut his own corn, he becomes acquainted with the sickle, which he is called forth frequently to use in the harvest of the country, where more corn is grown, and where there are fewer hands to get it in.

" Lastly, By living in the country there is less temptation to vice; and by occupying a small parcel of land, a life of labour is diversified, and consequently relieved."

Those sensible remarks, after what has been observed of the manufactures of Lancashire, naturally
give

give rise to a comparison between the cotton and the woolen manufactures; in which the latter appears with many and high advantages :---and, fortunately for the lasting welfare of the country, it is a *native*, is rooted in the soil—depends on indigenous produce; —the former, on far fetched materials,---the produce of distant climes. It is painful to relate, however, that many of the advantages, above enumerated, are now decreasing. Invention has done too much. Machinery is drawing spinners of wool, as of cotton, into the pestilential lazarets of manufacturers !

Mr. Payne, in a letter already mentioned, speaks dispassionately, and justly, on the manufacture of foreign materials.—App. p 54. " I shall principally confine my replies to your inquiries to the parish in which I reside, Frickley cum Clayton, and the extensive and populous one adjoining it northward, South Kirkby. Yet these answers will, I believe, *generally* apply to the whole tract of country lying between the market-towns of Doncaster, Rotherham, Pontefract, Barnsley, and Thorne ; in divers parts of which district I have resided, and practised agriculture, as a freeholder; not having been without the means and inclination of acquiring some intelligence in many departments of its rural economy. As a true friend to the solid prosperity of my country, I am a sincere well wisher to its agriculture, as the only sound basis of its real and permanent interest ; and though I do not wish manufacture in general to be depreciated, yet I am convinced, that if a considerable portion of the public industry and capital which for some years past has been applied to the manufacture of foreign materials, had instead thereof, been employed in the cultivation of our extensive wastes, the profits on the *whole* of such employment to the *public* would have been immensely superior."

LOCAL TAXES. *Poor Rates.* On this head, Mr. Brown writes at some length. The subject is new to him. He is, of course, feelingly alive to the folly and unjustness

unjustness of the English poor laws. In Mr. B's remarks, however, I find nothing of novelty or peculiar excellence; except the following suggestion; which to me is new, and is certainly ingenious. How far it may be practicable, I will not pretend to say. I copy it with great pleasure, as a hint to those whom it may—must 'ere long, I conceive—more immedi ately concern.

P. 27. " Perhaps the best mode of supporting the distressed, would be a law obliging every householder to contribute a certain part of his income toward the support of those who stood in need of public relief; the sum to be optional, and the contributor when in distress to draw from the fund in proportion to his monthly, quarterly, or annual payment: to this fund might be added a permanent tax upon landed property, say 5 *l.* per cent. upon rents, in lieu of the present rates, as there is no reason why the possessors of land should get entirely free of a burden which has affected them for near two centuries. Our object is to prevent an increase of the rates, and to throw the charge of supporting the poor upon the public at large, not to emancipate landed property altogether. This plan, upon the whole, is something similar to those of the friendly societies, (which cannot be too much encouraged,) and if established in every parish, and the funds administered by a committee of contributors annually chosen, would prevent these peculations so grievously complained of under the present system, and in a great measure, put public charity or assistance on its proper basis. We throw out this hint, forbearing to enlarge upon it, under the hope it will be taken up by others more versant in such affairs."

Tithes.—P. 22. "This is an important article, which well deserves the minutest consideration of the Board of Agriculture. For reasons to be afterwards mentioned, we decline investigating the consequences attending the payment of tithes whether they are considered as a

part

part of the tenant's rent, operating in direct proportion to his industry or abilities, or as a tax originally imposed for certain purposes, which circumstances have now totally changed. That it may be seen that the suppression of what we formerly said against the payment of tithes, either by an annual valuation, or by an exaction in kind, does not proceed from any change of principle, or alteration of sentiments, we subjoin an extract of a letter from Sir John Sinclair respecting this part of our survey, which we are authorised to publish in our own vindication.

" In drawing up this work, there is only one restric-
" tion, which I wish to impose upon you ; it relates
" to the payment of tithes, a subject of great delicacy
" and importance, which regards only the sister king-
" dom, consequently it is a point with which we
" North Britons have no particular occasion to inter-
" fere. I wish, therefore, that in your Report, any
" particular discussion of that subject may be
" avoided."

" After the restriction thus laid upon us respecting this article, it would be improper to say more than that the real interest of the country is concerned in having tithes regulated as soon as possible.

" In a moral point of view, every well disposed person must lament that the collection of a tax, originally designed for the support of religion, should now be the means of creating disrespect for its ministers. There are no arguments necessary to prove, that where the clergyman differs with his parishioners upon this subject, the usefulness of his office is totally frustrated ; which makes not only the practice, but even the profession of religion be disregarded."

On *searching* the ORIGINAL REPORT,—for there is no other way of *finding* any thing in the works of the Board,—I have discovered three passages, in different parts of the body of the Report, and several in the Appendix, relating to tithes. The first, p. 18, is the legitimate article, stating in plain—and appropriate—
terms,

terms, the existing modes of COLLECTING tithes, in the West Riding of Yorkshire. In the second, p. 46, within the chapter "Obstacles to Improvements," the Reporter goes out of his way to *prove*, what has long been considered as *self-evident :* namely, that tithes taken in kind, or paid for by valuation immediately before harvest, are not only OBSTACLES to IMPROVEMENT, but a TAX upon INDUSTRY ; or as the Reporters have put it,—not only " a tenth of the natural produce of the earth, but also a tenth of the superior cultivation, and additional manure bestowed upon the land, and more than a tenth of the farmer's industry, merit, and abilities."—In the third, p. 54, chapter " Improvements suggested," the COMMUTATION of tithes is proposed; and two schemes for that purpose offered. But, to my mind, neither of them appears to be entitled to public attention. They are equally ill founded. Neither of them gives sufficient security to the clergy. The suppression of these was therefore perfectly right.

The passage first mentioned was probably suppressed by mistake. It stands thus:—O. R. p. 18. " In some parts the small tithes are only drawn in kind, and a modus is taken in lieu of the great ones. In other parts it is the custom for the tithe owners, to send a person before harvest to value the tithes in the parish, and afterwards to deliver an estimate of their value to the farmer ; giving him the alternative of paying that sum (which for various reasons is generally agreed to) or having the tithes drawn in kind."

In the reprinted Report, beside the passage first above quoted, we meet with other remarks on tithes. In speaking of the old grass lands of Craven, &c. Mr. Brown says, p. 115. " But before any of these rich fields can be broke up, the tithe system must undergo a change, as it would be a notable affair for a tithe-holder to have a tenth of the weighty crops they would produce. From respectable authority we learned, that the payment of tithes, was in a great
measure

measure the cause of laying these fields totally in grass, and that this tax continues to operate as a prohibitory restriction against breaking them up."

To show that Mr. Brown bears no ill will against the English clergy, though of another church, I copy, with peculiar satisfaction, the following passage, p. 254. " The next thing we have to state as an obstacle to improvement, is the payment of tithes in kind. We shall here only remark, that the clergy in general are favourable to a commutation, being sensible, that in many instances the payment of this tax in kind, is detrimental to their interest. While the rough hardy collector insists for his full tenth, the quiet good natured clergyman, who studies ' if it be possible, to live in peace with all men,' is imposed upon in many respects. In short, the payment of tithes is a tax upon industry, for it operates in direct proportion to the merit and abilities of the farmer ; and England is almost the only country in Europe, where they are rigorously exacted."

In the Appendix, p. 53, in a letter from a gentleman of the neighbourhood of Skipton, are the subjoined remarks on tithes.—" Tithes are generally collected in kind, and are very reluctantly and ill paid. Since the introduction of grazing into the country, they are reduced in an astonishing degree; the lands which are most profitable to the occupier, are least, or indeed not at all so to the clergyman ;—he must either submit to this, or involve himself in a tedious and expensive law-suit, for agistment tithe, perhaps against an obstinate and powerful combination of the farmers and land-owners. It is the opinion of the most intelligent people here, that the present mode of collecting tithes is one principle cause of the high price of corn. Large quantities are continued in grass, which would be ploughed to advantage, if a certain and general commutation for tithes could be established."

And, finally, Mr. Payne, in the close of his letter,

says,—App. p. 59. " Tithes are drawn in kind here, and generally over this district; yet there are some instances of payment in money by annual agreement, &c. If genuine christianity, if agricultural prosperity; if domestic peace, and smiling plenty, be for the public good; then it will be for the public good to have the tithes commuted, and their very name abolished for ever."

PUBLIC WORKS.—*Inland Navigations.*—See *Waters*, p. 337.

Roads. These appear to have engaged a principal share of the Surveyor's attention, in travelling.

App. p. 15.—Bradford to Halifax.—" Observed most of the roads provided with a foot-path, paved with free stones, which is a most useful measure; but strange to tell, every person upon horseback uses the foot paths."—And, in the body of the work, p. 214, Mr. B. gives the West Riding credit for " an attention to the comfort of foot passengers that is very laudable."—The fact is these flag pavements were formed for HORSE PATHS, not foot paths. Before carriage roads were formed of hard materials, these horse paths were common in the north of England, and, necessarily, on the sides of public lanes, in every deep soiled district of the kingdom;—for the use of pack horses and travellers on horseback, in the winter season; when clayey lanes were otherwise impassable. Where broad stones were not to be procured narrow causeways of pebbles were the packways. Remnants of them are still seen in different parts of England.

App. p. 18.—" The road from Halifax to Wakefield was in most shocking condition, and the heaviest stage we have travelled. Observed the materials are of bad quality, and that to render them harder, a great part of them are burnt before they are laid on the road; also that clay was burnt into a kind of brick, and used likewise for repairing the roads. Want of proper materials is a local disadvantage, for which the road surveyors never can be blamed. They seemed

seemed however, to us, to be carrying on repairs upon bad principles : instead of filling up the old ruts, which were very deep, and levelling the surface, a new covering was laid on indiscriminately, which will never bed firmly, or consolidate in any situation." This folly is not confined to the western parts of Yorkshire.

The section " Roads," in the body of this Report, fills several pages. But the remarks they contain are mostly of a speculative nature. The subjoined passage, nevertheless, is full of good sense, and entitled to especial notice.

P. 216.—" It is absurd to have the statute labor of the whole kingdom regulated by one general law, seeing that, in some districts, from the nature of the ground and scarcity of materials, the expence of repairing them, is more than double what it is in others. We would therefore recommend an alteration of the law in those respects, that the tax should be levied in an equal and just way, by a parochial or county rate upon all persons, in direct proportion to the benefit they received from the roads; and that coaches, chaises, and saddle-horses, kept by landed gentlemen and others, should pay, which are at present totally exempted. If this rate was made to rise or fall according to the good or bad condition of the roads, we entertain the hopes, that the whole roads in the island would soon be in a comfortable state of repair, and consequently the facility and pleasure of travelling, greatly increased."

The West Yorkshire—as the Lancashire—Report condemns, in severe terms, the regulations respecting mail coaches being exempt from tolls ; and broad wheeled waggons, with convex fellies being suffered to carry enormous weights, at a low rate of tollage.

Markets.—P. 222. " A very considerable corn market is held at Knaresborough, where dealers from the western parts of the Riding attend, and purchase from the farmers in that neighbourhood. A great
part

part of this is resold at Skipton market in Craven, and carried still farther westward, where corn is scarce, and gives employment to a number of people who are concerned in this traffic."

On *weights* and *measures*, the Reporter might be said to have given us a bushel of argument, in which it would be difficult to find a single grain of useful information, that has not passed the scales, again and again.

On the *corn laws*, too, he has bestowed considerable attention :—with how much profit, I will not presume to determine. It is a subject that requires more thought than most men who write upon it seem to be aware of.

On *societies* of *agriculture* we meet with a suggestion which, to me, is *new*. How far it may be applicable, I leave to gentlemen, clergy, and others, to settle!

P. 236. " In constituting agricultural societies, we are far from recommending an intermixture of proprietors and farmers together. It is absolutely necessary, for many obvious reasons, they should be separate. Without dwelling upon these, it may only be said, that, in presence of his landlord, the farmer is too ready to be diffident, and will not propose his opinions in that free and unrestrained manner he would do, if only amongst the company of his brethren and equals. We heard of the Sheffield society, where gentlemen, clergy, and farmers, met promiscuously; the consequence of which was, that the latterr were in a manner prohibited from mentioning improvements, in case they should be a watch-word for the one to increase the rent, and the other to raise the rate of tithes."

A note which is published on this passage will not render it more palatable to the gentlemen of the West Riding; nor add to the reputation of the Board's Reports.

SUBJECT THE THIRD.

RURAL ECONOMY.

DIVISION THE FIRST.

TENANTED ESTATES; their IMPROVE-MENT and MANAGEMENT.

ESTATES. *Sizes* of *Estates.* P. 7. "A considerable part of the West Riding is possessed by small proprietors, and this respectable class of men, who generally farm their own lands, are as numerous in this district as in any other part of the kingdom. They are useful members of the state; they are attentive in the management and cultivation of their lands; and they form an important link in the chain of political society. There are likewise a great number of extensive proprietors, such as the Duke of Norfolk, Earl Fitzwilliam, &c. whose annual income it is unnecessary, and at the same time it would be improper, to state."—P. 8.—"A good deal of land likewise belongs to the Archbishop, Colleges, Deans, Prebends, and other church dignitaries; and the inferior clergy, in consequence of inclosure bills, are accumulating landed property every year."

Tenures. P. 8. "The greatest part of the Riding is freehold property, which is evident from the astonishing number of free-holders residing in it, the number of copy-holders, or those who hold by a copy of court-roll, is also considerable."

IMPROVEMENT of ESTATES. On this the most important subject of Rural Economicks, in as much as it forms the basis of good husbandry, we find very little valuable matter, in the West Riding Report.

On the *reclaiming* of *wild lands,* and other rough grounds, it contains a few remarks that may be useful

ful. Mr. STOCKDALE,—in speaking of the improvement of Knaresborough forest,—after having mentioned the rapid increase of produce raised from it, by poor cottagers and other small owners, while the large allotments of great proprietors remained "scarsely effectually ringfenced,"—makes the following sensible remarks.

P. 138.—" Many impediments prevented their activity; first, what was to be done must be committed to the care of servants, or agents; secondly, the extravagance of wages, by reason of the want of inhabitants; and above all, the impossibility of letting large tracts as farms, where it must be a series of years before any returns could be expected, or even provision obtained for their working horses. These obstacles operated to a total neglect, or desertion; and in consequence, large tracts indeed at this hour are in their wild uncultivated state.

" If I may be allowed to offer my sentiments how to turn these tracts to better advantage, I should advise building a number of cottages, with suitable small out-buildings, and laying to each not more than 10 acres of land; tempt individuals by suffering them to live rent-free for the first seven years, but obliging them to break up two acres annually, till the whole was improved; then fix a reasonable rent, and add 10 acres more for the same term, and conditions; and so proceed gradually, till the whole of such part, as would admit of cultivation, was gone through. The land thus improved, would be considered by the inhabitants as the work of their own creation, and nothing but cruel treatment by their landlords would drive them away. In a few years population would improve, and that once locally obtained, every other difficulty would vanish."

Great attention would be required, and many inconveniencies would doubtlessly attend on the prosecution of the proposed plan. But if it were to be coupled with the linen manufacture, which, I believe,

prevails

prevails in that neighbourhood, considerable benefits might arise.

Paring and *Burning.*—P. 148.—" Our information on this head, was various and contradictory. In some places, the practice is prohibited, unless with the consent of the proprietors. In others, it is deemed the best method for breaking up all grass grounds, and is not supposed to waste the soil in any shape."

On *Cottages*, see the ensuing section, FARMS.

EXECUTIVE MANAGEMENT of landed estates.— *Managers.*—P. 7. " Few of the large proprietors reside upon their estates, at least for a considerable part of the year, and the management of them is mostly devolved on their stewards, who, from being early trained to business, are generally intelligent, active, and industrious men."

Tenancy.—P. 30.—" The greatest part of the land in this district is not occupied under the guarantee of a lease, the occupiers being generally bound to remove upon a warning of six months. Where leases are granted, their duration is from 3 to 21 years; but three-fourths of the land is possessed from year to year, and this practice, which to us seems destructive of good farming, is upon the increase, although the Duke of Norfolk and several other proprietors, much to their honor and profit, act otherwise. The duty we owe to the public, from the office entrusted to us, renders it necessary that we should describe the ruinous consequences accompanying the want of leases, and how absurd it is to expect that the ground will be improved by persons who may be turned out of their possessions, whenever the proprietor, or more properly speaking the steward appointed to manage his estate is disposed, by caprice, whim, enmity, or interested motives, to give them a warning of removal*." In

* In the " Introduction," p. vi, it is thus written—" To us, it would seem as incongruous to tye a man's legs together, and then order

In the Reporter's arguments on this subject, though of some length, and reiterated, I find, nothing (in this his section, on " Leases") that can claim particular attention.   The beneficial operation of leases has been so frequently shown, and is, I flatter myself, so well understood by land proprietors, in England, as not to require any extraordinary strength of argument to *enforce* it.   We have no law, in England, to *oblige* land owners to grant leases;—not even for the good of the community.   It therefore becomes individuals to crave—rather than to demand—them.

Let us hear Mr. Payne, on this subject.   His language differs widely from that of the Report.   App. p. 57.—" Few leases are granted, and I rather think few are asked for; the nature of the covenants between landlord and tenant, has a general reference to law and custom, which secure to the landlord quiet entry on due notice, with recovery of damages if any be done to the farm; and to the tenant, on quitting, a fair valuation of his property and labor, in the ground; as fallows, crops, manure, &c. &c. being parts of his *stock* in *trade*.   It is an article essential to a good and spirited agriculture, and which cannot be too much insisted on, that the farmer be scrupulously allowed, on quitting his farm, a fully and fairly appraised valuation of his *stock* in *trade*.   It forms a security and bond of entire confidence, equally to landlord and tenant, a security which sets all leases, parchments, bonds, and seals at defiance; it secures to the landlord the payment of his just demands, with a certain improvement of his estate: and to the tenant an easy mind, under the application of his ingenuity, industry, and cash, to the prospect of increasing his produce, and ameliorating his farm.   I wish this matter was more attended to; I have seen many painful deviations

order him to run, as to suppose, that improvements are to be made by a farmer, without the security of a lease."

deviations from justice in this respect, to the great injury of the *cause*. An act of the legislature might probably extend this *real* benefit, and promote the improvement of the lands already inclosed, more than *millions* expended in the way of premium."

On this sound basis, every species of tenancy requires to be founded. No lease can be deemed sufficient that does not bear upon it. But Mr. P's Philanthropy has not borne him out, here, in its wonted manner. For even admitting that, as to *pecuniary* matters, a tenant would be safe under the protection of such a law or regulation; yet his COMFORTS and PROSPECTS in LIFE, might still be at stake, were he liable to be removed at a short notice. To secure these, some *term* is absolutely necessary; to allow him time to look round him, and exercise his judgment, in choosing a fresh situation; as well as to make a variety of arrangements which every man possessed of extensive personal property (as a large occupier *ought* to be) and numerous connexions, has to plan and execute,—before he can wind up his existing concerns, remove, and resettle himself in business. Beside, a man who has the spirit, the skill, and the perseverance requisite to successful improvements, has a personal gratification in reaping, with his own hands, the benefit of his exertions,—independent of the profit that may arise therefrom. In *six months*, scarsely one of those desireable ends can be fully accomplished. But in *three years*, the whole (excepting some remnants of improvement, for which he ought in course to be remunerated) may, under ordinary circumstances, be compleated.

These and other considerations led me, some twenty years ago, to turn my mind towards framing a new species of tenancy, on those premises. And, I trust, my endeavors have been sufficiently successful to become extensively—if not generally—beneficial to TENANTS, PROPRIETORS, and the PUBLIC. For in a matter in which these three distinct interests are severally

verally concerned, it is essentially requisite that they should be jointly considered. See TREATISE on LANDED PROPERTY, or the abstract, on the MANAGEMENT of LANDED ESTATES,—article *Tenancy;* or *Form* of *Lease.*

Covenants. The ordinary covenants of West Yorkshire are seen in the lease of Earl Fitzwilliam; the substance of which is given in the following words, p. 41.—" The tenant covenants to keep all the buildings and fences in repair; to pay all parliamentary and parish taxes; not to plough up grass land without consent of the landlord; not to take more than three crops of corn before a fallow; to lay 12 cart-loads of dung upon every acre so fallowed; not to sell any hay, straw, or other fodder from off the premises, but eat and consume the same thereupon; to spread all the manure arising from the premises upon some part thereof, and leave the last year's manure thereupon. The landlord covenants to allow the tenant, on quitting his farm, which is by the custom of the country at Candlemas, what two indifferent persons shall deem reasonable for what is generally called full tillage, and half tillage, being for the rent and assessments of his fallow ground, the ploughing and managing the same; the lime, manure, or other tillage laid thereon; the seed sown thereupon; the sowing and harrowing thereof; also for the sowing, harrowing, manuring, and managing any turnip fallow, which he may leave unsown; also for any clover seed sown on the premises, and harrowing and rolling in of such seed; and for every other matter and thing done and performed in a husbandry-like manner on such fallow lands, in the two last years of the terms; also for the last year's manure left upon the premises; and for any manure and tillage laid upon the grass land."

The Reporter's Remarks on those covenants run thus:—P. 41.—" The primary error of the Yorkshire husbandry consists in not giving the tenant a security of possession for a reasonable time; and the second, and

and no less important error, arises from the restrictions imposed during the time he occupies his farm, which prevents him from changing his management, or of adapting his crops to the nature of the soil he possesses. Agriculture is a living science, which is progressively improving, consequently what may be esteemed a good course of cropping at one time, may, from experience and observation, be afterwards found defective and erroneous.

" That particular covenants in a lease are obstacles to improvements cannot be disputed ; for the very nature of a covenant supposes that the practice to be regulated by it had arrived at its *ne plus ultra*, and could not be mended."

After amusing himself, for some time, with those and other ingenious arguments, the Reporter had nearly closed this his first dissertation, on " Covenants," with much good sense and moderation, in the following terms :—p. 44. " We are ready to admit that general rules of management are very proper in leases, such as, to keep the farm in good order, to consume all the straw raised upon it, and to sell no dung. These restrictions we will allow ; and every good farmer will follow them whether he is bound to do so or not. Nay, we will go farther—If leases of a proper duration were granted, it is very reasonable that the property of the landlord should be protected by restricting clauses for the 3 years previous to their expiration." Unfortunately, however, for his credit, as an arable farmer, he adds—" But after all, it will be found that no clause can be inserted, besides the general ones already mentioned, that will serve to enhance the value of the land, except obliging the farmer, to leave a proportional quantity of such land in grass at the expiration of the lease, and specifying the manner in which that land is to be sown down. Other clauses serve only to distress the farmer, but will never promote the interest of the landlord." How, farmer ! no wheat to be sown, for the incoming
tenant

tenant and the community? no turnips, for spring feedage of farm stock, after Candlemas? nor ground duly prepared for spring corn and sown grasses?—to enable the landlord to procure a suitable tenant, and such a tenant, to prosecute his labors, for the benefit of himself and the public, without interruption, as if no removal had taken place?

The Reporter's second lecture on leases commences in chapter the seventh, entitled "Obstacles to Improvement;" wherein he gives, p. 254, "an extract of a letter from a worthy friend in the West Riding;" setting forth a hard case, no doubt. But all the letter writer complains of is a breach of faith, or, in other words, a *breach of covenant*, by the manager of an estate; who, after encoraging him " to go on with spirited management, and assuring him that no advantage should be taken thereof," sent a " land doctor," who " charges so much per pound for valuing, and the more he advances, the more he receives;" and who, valuing the improvements made subsequent to the promise, raised his rent, accordingly. Acts, like this, naturally point out to tenants the necessity of *legal promises*.

But what engages most of the Reporter's attention, in this part of his work, p. 256, is the covenant or restriction against " subsetting, underletting, or assigning over, the lease to a third person, at the pleasure of the lessee, or tenant"!—To borrow his own phraseology—" it gives us always pain to notice," a man of natural and acquired abilities wasting his time and bestowing his talent, unprofitably. This attack on the rights of proprietors can be excused, only, by the Reporter's want of experience in the management of landed property. He could not have been aware, at the time he wrote, that, on every well managed estate, the proper CHOICE of TENANTS is a matter of the very first consideration. On this one point, its prosperity may be said to turn. The writer, I am certain, will, on reflection, immediately

see

see the propriety of such a conduct; and, knight-errant as he is, in the cause of tenants, he assuredly would not advise a man of bad moral character, desiring a farm, but without capital, skill, or industry to manage it properly,—to repair to a proprietor, having one to let, and insist upon taking possession of it (at a fair rent)—*without his, the proprietor's consent.*

But if such a man should offer an improving, un-restricted tenant a full—or somewhat more than a full—value for his improvements, he has no counter interest, like that of the proprietor, to dissuade him from accepting the offer. For, taking care to receive his money, before he assign over and part with pos-session, he has for ever done with the farm; and with the tenant whom he has forced upon it;—of course, *against the proprietor's consent.*

The transaction closed, the spirited improving tenant, with his pocket full of money, and another farm in view, takes it on an improving lease, and pro-ceeds to meliorate its condition;—in hopes of another good offer.—While the tenant, with whom he has saddled his former landlord, is committing acts of rascality and ruin: and thereby reducing the farm, of which he has been iniquitously put in possession, to a state, perhaps, tenfold worse than that in which it lay at the time it was let, to the former WELL CHOSEN TENANT;—*provided he had been prudently restricted from subsetting without consent.*

In all the leases which I have had occasion to examine, the restriction which the Reporter so flatly objects to, runs in these words, or in words of the like import;—" shall not underlet, or assign over, the whole or any part thereof, without licence in writing, from the said lessor his heirs or assigns."—And we may safely say—no lessor, heir, or assign, possessed of common sense and ordinary uprightness of cha-racter, would withhold his licence, in any of the cases which the Reporter has ingeniously imagined;—pro-vided a proper tenant,—a *sufficient substitute*—were offered.

offered. I acknowledge, with concern, that there are estates under foolish and profane management; and had the Reporter, in his zeal, cautioned his brethern against trusting their alls, on estates under such management, he would have deserved well, not only of tenants, but of the community.

The third attack which the West Riding Reporter makes on English leases, we find in a chapter entitled " Means of Improvement;" in which he explains himself deliberately, and intelligibly, concerning that species of contract, entered into by a landlord and his tenant, which is termed a lease!

P. 265. " Our ideas of a lease are, that it is a mere bargain betwixt landlord and tenant, wherein the former, for a valuable consideration, to be paid annually, conveys over to the latter, all his right in the premises (!) for a specified number of years, and that during their currency, it ought to be left to the wisdom and abilities of the farmer, to manage the land in such a manner as he may think most proper for enabling him to make good his engagements to the landlord. If leases were granted upon these principles, a great deal of unnecessary trouble would be saved to both parties, improvements would increase with rapidity, and the peace, comfort, and happiness of that useful body of men, the *farmers*, would be materially promoted."

The writer then enumerates some ordinary clauses, or covenants:—prudently, however, leaving that of " subsetting" to be *understood*, and proposing one which improves his former position, p. 361:—as, by it, he allows the tenant to agree, not only to leave, at the expiration of the term, " one fourth of the farm in grass, at least three years old;" but " likewise a sixth part of the remainder, *as fallow*, to the incoming tenant." If by this expression be meant— *in a state of clean fallow*, the incoming tenant would not want land for spring corn and ley herbage. But still

still the farm would be left destitute of wheat, and of spring feedage.

If, however, the writer had here finished his dissertations concerning this subject, he would probably have left more favorable impressions on the minds of his readers, than after " more last words"—in addenda to Chap. 4. " Mode of Occupation :"— where, after combating an objection made by Mr. Donaldson, author of " The present State of Husbandry, in Great Britain," against the remarks of the West Riding Surveyors, in the original Report, he thus proceeds—p. 290 ;—" If we had wished to answer this unprovoked attack, in the manner it deserved, we could easily have refuted Mr. Donaldson with words, extracted from his own book. As for instance, he says, p. 232, same volume, ' That the Legislature, the Board of Agriculture, and the proprietors of the country, may adopt what measures in their wisdom may appear proper to improve the national territory ; but unless they go to the root of the evil ; unless they adopt such measures, as will tend to place the British farmer in a more comfortable situation, and more on a footing with merchants and manufacturers, the object will not be attained.' Now what do we say more? Is not the whole scope and intention of our Report to place the farmer in the comfortable and independent state recommended by Mr. Donaldson ? The merchant and manufacturer certainly lies under no restriction in the management of their affairs. They may carry on trade in the manner which will return them the greatest profit, or manufacture such commodities as the market requires. We contended for similar liberty being given to the farmer, and decidedly join Mr. Donaldson in thinking that unless it is granted, the national territory will not be improved to its greatest height."

Now, is it possible for a man of the Reporter's extent of mind, not to perceive the wide difference which exists between the profession of the farmer,

and

and that of the manufacturer! And the unalterable
relation which they severally have in society! The
raw materials of the manufacturer are *his own :* he
may burn, destroy, waste, or work them up, in any
way he will.   But those of the farmer—of a tenant—
are his *landlord's!* He has only the *use* of them, during the term of his occupation; and is obliged, by
the general law or constitution of his country, to
return them, at the end of his term, " without waste,"
to their owner.   Yet strange, but true, to tell, the
Reporter is indignant against the proprietors of West
Yorkshire,—for restricting their old grass lands from
being broken up,—at their tenant's pleasure!!—Or,
in other words, (well understood by manufacturers)
for refusing to receive damaged unsaleable goods, in
return for those of a good quality entrusted to their
care.   Take the following taunt as a specimen.
P. 40. " In other leases we saw, the tenants were
expressly prohibited from breaking up all grass lands
that have lain 6 years, which renders the situation of
the pasture and meadow fields as immutable as the
laws of Media and Persia were of old."—Until, let us
add, their *owners*, for a suitable consideration, *consent*
to their being broken up*.

IF IT were required, in this place, to speak, *gene-*
rally, on the subject of TENANCY, and the COVENANTS
of LEASES, we might say,—if all tenants were strictly
honest, nicely honorable, covenants to bind them
would be useless. If, in the nature of their profession, they had no other object in view, than the advancement of husbandry, and the improvements of
the country, covenants might, in truth, be injurious
and

* I say nothing of the numerous objections of ANNOTATORS,
against those foreign doctrines; nor of the *powerful* answers that
are annexed to them, by the Reporter. I am weary with combating the TEXT. But if it should be that I have fought a good
fight, I shall not regret the attention I have thought requisite to
bestow upon it.

and improper. But such a sublime theory of things rural being altogether imaginary, it behoves the proprietors of tenantable lands, whose interests are not always precisely the same as that of their tenants, to institute some rational and practical regulations, to secure their property from spoil, by those tenants who may prefer their own interest to that of their landlord. In England, I much fear, where there is one to improve, there are three to deteriorate.

Regarding covenants to regulate a tenant's plan of management, much depends upon the state of husbandry, in the given district. In a country like East Lothian, which is, or rather has been, rising from an abject state of culture, to a superior style of management, under the laudable exertions of men of liberal minds and integrity, it would have been ill judged in proprietors, to have trammelled such tenants with restrictive clauses; unless toward the expiry of their leases. But, in the West Riding of Yorkshire, or in any other district where agriculture is below par, yet in a degree stationary, and where the generality of tenants require a stimulus to improvements, covenants, to teach such tenants the way they ought to go, so as to bring up their practice to a level with that of the best managed districts of the island, could scarcely be injurious to either of the three interests concerned in the agriculture of the country. Hence, we may add, the covenants of management, throughout the kingdom, should keep pace with the state of agriculture, in its best managed districts. And, under the triennial form of tenancy, such a plan of progressive improvement may be practised.

Even the West Riding Reporter is an advocate for this principle of management;—in other words, is a friend to restrictive, if not to compulsory, covenants.

Thus, p. 98. "In order that drilling of turnips and horse hoeing may be generally practised, we presume that no method could be more effectually taken, than for proprietors to refuse taking broad-cast ones

as

as a fallow crop. It is a mock upon fallow, to consider some of the crops we examined as such ; and we are confident, that unless a very great expense is laid out, a broad-cast crop will never allow the ground to be cleaned in a manner equal to where they are horse and hand hoed." This is in the true spirit of dictatorial management. If the above, and several others, of the Reporter's favorite practices were urged, in a similar way, by the proprietors of the West Riding of Yorkshire, their country, I doubt not, would thereby be greatly profited. Because there are many absurd and injurious clauses inserted in leases, through the ignorance of those who are entrusted with the important charge of framing them, let not this be produced in argument against the GENERAL PRINCIPLE of REGULATIVE COVENANTS, in LEASES.

Rent.—P. 20. " It is difficult for us to say what may be the real rent of land. We could not with propriety, push the farmer upon this point, when he was ignorant what use we were to make of his answer; and even where we got sufficient information of what was paid the landlord, we found there was a long train of public burthens, over and above, which could not be easily ascertained. There is, in the first place, the land tax, which is uniformly paid by the tenant, and generally amounts to 1s. per pound upon the real rent. 2dly, The tithes which are levied in so many various ways, that it is impossible to say what proportion they bear to the pound rent, much depending upon the actual state of the farm, and not a little upon the character and disposition of the drawer. Upon arable lands, where they are annually valued, the payment of money may be from 5s. to 8s. per acre, in some cases more. 3dly, The roads, the expense of which to the tenant is about 7*l.* per cent. upon the rent. 4thly, The poor rates, for which no fixed sum can be set down. The lowest we heard of was 18d. in the pound; and the highest 8s. ; but from the very nature of the tax they are

are continually fluctuating, and since our survey was made are greatly increased. 5thly, The church and constable dues, which are about 1s. in the pound.—From all these things it may be supposed, that in many places the sums payable by the farmer to the church, the public, and the poor, are nearly as great as the nominal rent paid to the landlord."

Those remarks tend to lessen our surprise at the excessively high rents that we hear of being given for lands, in Scotland,—where there are few or none of those additional payments. Therefore, according to the above statement, forty shillings, an acre, in England, is nearly equivalent to four pounds, in Scotland.

What follows the above extract will make an Englishman smile.—"It will appear surprising to many, that rents are higher for grass fields than for those under the plough. This is however actually the case."—And the writer proceeds to account for it. But of this under GRASS LAND, or perennial herbage.

The time of entry—upon the *lands*—Candlemas—to the *house*—Mayday:—(p. 39.)

The times of receiving rents.—" Whitsuntide and Martinmas;"---(p. 40.)

DIVISION THE SECOND.

WOODLANDS.

THERE is nothing in this Report, sufficiently intelligent or instructive, on " Woods and Plantations,' to engage particular notice.

AGRICULTURE.

FARMS.—*Sizes.*—P. 16. "The majority of farms are comparatively small, and few are of that size as would be considered in other parts of the kingdom as large ones. Upon the arable lands we heard of none exceeding 400 statute acres, and for one of that extent there are a dozen not fifty acres. In the grass division of the county they are still smaller, and we often heard the occupier of a hundred acres of ground styled a great farmer."—P. 18. "With regard to the question, whether large or small farms are generally best managed? we apprehend very few words will suffice. Who keeps good horses, and feeds them well? Who makes the completest fallow, takes the deepest furrow, and ploughs best? Who has the greatest number of hands, and sufficient strength for catching the proper season, by which the crop upon the best of grounds is often regulated? Who purchases the most manure, and raises the weightiest crops? We believe, in general, these questions must be answered in favor of the large farmer."

Plans of Farms.—P. 9. "The farm houses and offices are, in most cases, very inconveniently situated, being generally crowded into villages or townships, and not placed on the lands the farmer has to cultivate."

Homesteads.—After describing Lord Hawke's farm offices, the Reporter explains his own ideas of a homestead. But I perceive nothing that requires to be noticed, here, excepting what relates to

Cottages.—P. 11. "A row of cottages for farm servants, should be built at a little distance, say a hundred yards, from the suite of offices."—Again, p. 13. "We venture to recommend, that proper houses should be built for farm servants, contiguous

to

to every homestead. This will not only promote the welfare and happiness of that class of men, by giving them an opportunity of settling in life, which is not at present an easy matter, but will also be highly beneficial to the farmer himself, as he will at all times have people within his own bounds, for carrying on his labor; and have them of that description, that are generally esteemed most regular and careful."

But, in these, as in other parts of his Report, on *Agriculture,* the Reporter's desire for the didactic has led him to transplant East Lothian ideas into West Yorkshire; without having duly considered, whether the existing circumstances of the situation will permit them to take root. When the large farms of East Lothian were first laid out, and new farmsteads erected, it might be perfectly proper to build rows of cottages in their respective neighbourhoods. The habitations of the " acre men" and " run-rig tenants;" who, I apprehend, previously occupied the lands, were probably of turf—" Feal and Divot"—and were taken down, after a stated time, for manure for their lands; and fresh ones raised in their stead :—a practice which is still prevalent, in some parts of Scotland.

But in England,—where not only most farm houses, but almost all the cottages of *farm laborers,* have been, for ages, what they are at present,—many of them having gardens, and some of them orchards, attached to them,—such a procedure, as the Reporter recommends, would be improper; there being, in most districts, enow of these permanently fixed habitations, for the reception of married farm laborers.

OCCUPIERS.—P. 16. " Various causes might be assigned for land in the West Riding being occupied in such small portions. Manufactures being carried on to such extent has naturally occasioned capitals to be laid out in trade, which, in other counties, would be employed in agriculture; and wherever this is the case the occupiers of the ground will generally be found

found destitute of stock for cultivating the ground in an advantageous manner, and defective of knowledge in the science they practice. We hazard this as a general observation, without applying it to the farmers of the West Riding, many of whom are as enlightened and liberal as any of their profession in the island."

PLAN of MANAGEMENT. In the chapter—" Arable Lands"—Mr. Brown has furnished the Board with a compendious account of the prevailing systems of practice, in different parts of the West Riding.— P. 77. " Before entering upon this chapter, we think it necessary to make some preliminary observations, so as the different systems practised in this extensive district may be easier understood.

1*st*, A great part of the West Riding is exclusively kept in grass, and where this is the case, cultivation by the plough is considered as a secondary object.

" From Ripley, to the western extremity of the Riding, nearly the whole of the good land is kept under the grazing system, and seldom or never ploughed, while corn is raised upon the inferior or moorish soils. During the time we were in that part of the country, we hardly ever saw a plough; and a stack of corn was a great rarity. Upon the higher grounds, there are immense tracts of waste, which are generally common among the contiguous possessors, and pastured by them with cattle and sheep. Some of them are stinted pastures, but the greatest part are under no limitations: the consequences of which are, the grounds are oppressed, the stock upon them starved, and little benefit derived from them by the proprietors.

" 2*dly*, The land in the vicinity of manufacturing towns. The greatest part of the ground is there occupied by persons who do not consider farming as a business, but regard it only as a matter of convenience. The manufacturer has his inclosure, wherein he keeps milch cows for supporting his family,

family, and horses for carrying his goods to market, and bringing back raw materials. This will apply to the most part of the land adjoining to the manufacturing towns; and although much ground is not, in this case, kept under the plough, yet comparatively more corn is raised, than in the division above described.

" 3*dly*, The corn district, or those parts of the Riding where tillage is principally attended to, and grass only considered as the mean of bringing the corn husbandry to perfection.

" If we run an imaginary line from Ripley southward by Leeds, Wakefield, and Barnsley, to Rotherham, we may affirm, that the greatest part eastward of it, till we come to the banks of the Ouse, which separates the West from the East Riding, is principally employed in raising corn. About Boroughbridge, Wetherby, Selby, &c. there is about one half of the fields under the plough. Further south, about Pontefract, Barnsley, and Rotherham, there are two-thirds; and to the eastward of Doncaster, to Thorn and Snaith, three-fourths of the land are managed in a similar way. There is not much waste in this division, but what is in that situation, is capable of great improvement.

" 4*thly*, The common fields. These are scattered over the whole of the last division, but are most numerous in that part of the country to the eastward of the great north road, from Doncaster to Boroughbridge. It is impossible even to guess at the quantity of land under this management. In general, it may be said to be extensive, and from the natural good quality of the soil, and the present imperfect state of culture, great room is afforded for solid and substantial improvement being effected upon all land coming under the description of common field.

5*thly*, The moors. These, besides the large tracts in the first division, lie in the western part of the Riding, and perhaps contain one-eighth of the district.

Upon

Upon them sheep are chiefly bred, and afterwards sold to the graziers in the lower parts of the country. A great part of them is common, which lays the proprietors under the same inconveniences as are already pointed out; and which might easily be remedied, by dividing and ascertaining the proportion which belongs to the respective proprietors."

This might be deemed a luminous—and certainly is a valuable—part of the Report. A provincialist of West Yorkshire might, no doubt, cavil at particulars; but, from my own general knowledge of the country, it is sufficiently near the truth for the information of the Board. And the following passage of the section " Tillage,"—relating to the general state of husbandry, is full of thought and consideration.

P. 79.—" The West Riding cannot be considered as a district where the cultivation of corn is practised in the most approved way, and many circumstances concur to retard its improvement. From the flourishing state of manufactures, capitals are thrown into that line, which in other places would be employed in the cultivation of the soil; and the advantageous markets for disposing of cattle and sheep, induces (induce) the actual farmer to bestow a greater portion of his attention upon the management of his live stock, than upon his corn fields. This observation we make in justice to the farmers of the West Riding, many of whom have their farms in the most perfect condition. Where the case is different, it is but fair to infer, that the above mentioned circumstances have operated to prevent them from being so perfect as their neighbours." Again, p. 225, speaking of " Manufactures."—" A considerable portion of the land is occupied by persons whose chief dependence is upon manufactures. We are not, in this case, to expect the same attention to the minutiæ of farming, as from those who make it their sole occupation. Their minds and capitals are generally fixed upon their

their own business, and land is solely farmed by them as a matter of convenience or amusement."

From the sum of these observations, it is evident, that much useful information, on the management of arable lands, cannot reasonably be expected, from the practice of WEST YORKSHIRE, for the instruction of other districts. It cannot, therefore, be deemed a proper subject of study, for that purpose.

WORKPEOPLE. In the Surveyors' Journal of their tour through the manufacturing district, we meet with this notice, App. p. 23,—" No want of hands in this neighbourhood to cut the crop. In the year 1792, the scarcity was great in the East Riding, but felt here no farther than rising wages."—This shows the use of village manufacturers, to agriculture, in busy seasons. In the East Riding, a corn country, with few manufacturers, the farmers, (especially of the Wolds) depend much upon West Yorkshire, for harvest laborers; and are of course liable to be disappointed of the required supply, by a brisk demand, there, for manufactures.

On *Wages.*—P. 203.—" The West Riding being a great manufacturing district, it may at once be inferred, that labor of all kinds is higher than in those districts where manufactures are not extensively carried on. From the result of our enquiries it appeared, that wages varied considerably, even in the district itself; but, that in most cases they were highest in the neighbourhood of the manufacturing towns, and that for these some years past, they have greatly increased."

I insert the following extract from a paper of Mr. Payne, on the *rate* of *wages*;—not as being quite convinced of the indisputability of Mr. P's arguments; but as they give a peculiar turn to the subject. P. 204. " One word for the laboring peasantry.— Throughout this work, and almost every other of the kind, there seems a kind of complaint of the high rate of wages, in rural labor. Now, as the landlords

can

can speak for themselves, as the clergy can speak for themselves, and as the farmers can either do it, or get others to do it for them, it is but reasonable that the poor laboring peasants should have something said for them. I believe the *fact* is, that the laboring peasantry never had greater difficulties to encounter in the rearing of families, than they have at present, notwithstanding the *apparent* high rate of wages; for, that it is apparent only, will be evident to every attentive observer of the case. During the course of the present century, the landlord has trebled his rent, the clergyman or lay rector, has doubled his tythe, the farmer has increased his property, and maintained his family in conveniences and comforts, at least *decent;* but have not the poor's rates increased enormously, incontrovertibly showing the low condition of the poor." There is certainly too much truth in those suggestions. But, I am afraid, the farm laborers of the present day do not possess the same sort of frugality and forethought, as did those of former times.

In the Reporter's remarks on Mr. P's ideas, he says, p. 207 (what, indeed, he had said before, p. 14, on " Cottages')—" The only way that we know of for making the laborer's wages proportional to the rise or fall on the value of money and provisions, is to pay him in *kind;* that is, with a certain quantity of corn, as parties shall agree, which insures him, at all hazards, a comfortable subsistence, and prevents him from a daily or weekly visitation of the markets. When the laborer is paid in money, it exposes the thoughtless and inattentive to many temptations; whereas, when paid in kind, he cannot raise money to gratify the whim of the moment. In those counties where this mode of payment has been long established, we believe ploughmen and laborers are on the whole better fed, live more comfortably, and rear healthier children, than in those parts, where, from being paid in money, the currency of the article facilitates the expenditure,

expenditure, and prevents him from laying by a stock of provisions for his support, when laid off work by casualties or distress."

I have, already, had occasion to speak on this subject (in p. 51, aforegoing).—In Scotland, this practice appears to be a relick of the customs of less civilized times; when the husbandman *necessarily* paid, not only his laborers, and his pastor, but his landlord, *in kind*. Even that of paying rents, in kind, is still practised in the more remote and recluse parts of Scotland.—And, in England, there was undoubtedly a time, when, through the same necessity, the same practice prevailed.

But admitting that the practice under consideration is still proper in Scotland, and still reconcileable to the habits of its cultivators, does it follow that English agricultors should *return* to what they have formerly found expedient to relinquish?—In some parts of England, especially in its western extreme, a melioration (as it would seem) of that practice is now prevalent; not having, yet, been *there* done away: namely, that of allowing farm laborers bread corn, at a stated price; let its value, at market, be what it may.

Both these practices, viewed in a political light, during a great scarcity of corn, have an evil tendency, and ought to be forbidden. In a time of extreme scarcity, sound policy requires that as small a quantity, as possible, of the article, wanting, should be consumed: and, if it were wholly brought to the public market, or which in effect is the same thing, the whole of it paid for, by the consumers, at the market price, every individual would have an interest, or be compelled by necessity, to spare the scanty supply. But if the farm laborers of Scotland have the same quantity given out to them, and the English laborer can purchase as much for the same money, when the supply is deficient, as when it is plentiful, neither of them is compelled to spare it, in the former case.

" Oh! but the humanity of the thing" (exclaims the

the well meaning philanthropist).—Rather let it be put—" the unwarrantable injustice and cruelty of such a procedure." What claim can those have, whom circumstances have casually bred up as laborers in husbandry, to be lavish of the inadequate public stock, while those whose lot in life has placed them in the ranks of artisans and manufacturers, are starving?

I ask not the farmers of Scotland and the West of England to alter their practices. But the above reflections having spontaneously risen, in pursuing my present undertaking, and appearing to me to develope a political truth of some importance, I have deemed it right to give them a place, here.

On laborers keeping poultry and cows,—see the Section POULTRY.

WORKING ANIMALS.—P. 194. " Very few oxen are wrought in the West Riding; and these only upon the farms of proprietors. We know working of oxen is a popular topic; but, from what we could learn upon this subject, the practice is not likely to become general. From their being almost universally given up, in those places where they were formerly in repute, a suspicion arises, that working them is not attended with profit. Those who object to the use of oxen say, that there is nothing saved by working them, as the difference betwixt the value of a horse and an ox, when unfit for work, is more than compensated by the superior labor of the former when employed. At the same time, it is a business of infinite difficulty, to get persons to work them."

The Reporter then proceeds to argue in favor of horses. But, pretty evidently, without the least practical knowledge of the use of oxen! I cannot allow any man, who has not had *mature experience* of *both*, the right of deciding on their *comparative* merits. All, therefore, I have to do, here, is to collect the practices and opinions of those who have some knowledge of both, in the West Riding of Yorkshire.

In the neighbourhood of Selby,— App. p. 42.
" Ploughs

" Ploughs of the common kind, drawn by two horses are used; but a number of oxen are wrought in the waggons."—Doubtlessly, in the deep roads of that district.

App. p. 45.—" Lord Hawke ploughs with two oxen a-breast, without a driver, and sometimes with horses, but depends principally, and almost entirely on oxen, for his ploughing and harrowing."

Mr. Payne's account; App. p. 57. " The work is almost entirely performed by horses; very little use is made of oxen at present; though where they are employed, they are found to answer very well, and I have no doubt of their superiority over the heavy draft horses in point of *real* utility to the farmer. I have used a pair of oxen several years in harness like that of the horses, working them at the plough and on the road, in every respect as we use our heavy draft horses; and as far as I can judge, they are equal to them for *use*, though the pride of the drivers will never allow it. However, in the stage of fattening them, we are all agreed, that *their beef* is preferable to the *carrion* of an old horse. The advantage to the community of working oxen on farms is beyond dispute, or calculation."

IMPLEMENTS. Respecting the Yorkshire *plow*, Mr. Brown brings forward (on what authority is not mentioned) some interesting particulars, which I had not before met with. P. 51.—" The Rotherham plough has been heard of over the whole island, and was invented by Mr. Joseph Foljambe, of Eastwood, in this Riding, about seventy years ago. Mr. Foljambe got a patent for this plough, which he afterwards sold to Mr. Staneforth, of Firbeck, who at first gave the liberty of using it to the farmers for 2s. 6d. each. Mr. Staneforth afterwards attempting to raise this premium to 7s. or 7s. 6d. the validity of the patent was combated and set aside, on the ground of its not being a new invented plough, but only a plough improved." On its introduction into East Yorkshire, it was called the " Dutch plow."   The

The *Thrashing Mill.* Details of the history, con-struction, and uses of this valuable invention may seem to be entirely out of place, in a Report of the practices of West Yorkshire; as it was barely intro-duced, and of course little understood, in that district, at the time the Surveyors went over it. But as Messrs. Rennie, Brown, and Shirreff were residents in the country of its invention, and possessed mature knowledge of its construction and use, it would be improper to neglect so favorable an opportunity of endeavouring to add to the information already ob-tained on the subject (see p. 64, aforegoing); espe-cially, as the Board's Reports may not afford us another, equally favorable, of making the desired additions.

On the *history* of the thrashing mill, we have the following particulars; which, I think, it is right to insert, entire; though some of them may have appear-ed in the Northumbrian account.

P. 57.—" The first attempt which we know of with certainty, was made by an ingenious gentleman of the county of East-Lothian, Mr. Michael Menzies, who invented a machine that was to go by water, upon the principle of driving a number of flails by a water-wheel, but from the force with which they wrought, it was found the flails were soon broken to pieces, and consequently the invention did not suc-ceed *.

" Another threshing machine was invented about 1758, by Mr. Michael Stirling, a farmer in the parish of Dumblain, Perthshire. This machine was nearly the same as the common mill for dressing flax, being a vertical shaft with four cross arms, inclosed in a cylindrical case, three feet and a half high, and eight feet

* My father, about the year 1755, constructed a horse wheel, to work a range of flails, on a beautifully simple principle. But it was given up for want of due efficiency: and not from any excess of power; as that might surely have been moderated.

feet diameter. Within this case the shaft, with its arms, were turned with considerable velocity by a water-wheel, and the sheaves of corn being let down gradually, through an opening for the purpose, on the top of the box, the grain was beat off by the arms, and pressed with the straw through an opening in the floor, from which it was separated by riddles shaken by the mill, and then cleaned by fanners also turned by it. The great defect of this machine was, that it broke off the ears of barley or wheat, instead of beating out the grain, and was only fit for oats.

" A third species of a threshing mill was attempted by two gentlemen in Northumberland about 1772, viz. Mr. Elderton near Alnwick, and Mr. Smart at Wark, nearly about the same time. The operation was performed in their machine by rubbing instead of beating. The unthreshed corn was carried round between an indented drum, of about six feet diameter, and a number of indented rollers arranged around the circumference of the drum, and pressed towards it by springs, so that when the drum revolved, the grain was rubbed out in passing between it and the rollers. This machine was found, on trial, even more defective than the former, as it not only bruised the grain, but did very little execution, though the Northumberland surveyors, either from inadvertency or mistake, would arrogate to that county the invention of the threshing machine now in use, from which this attempt was obviously different*.

" The late Sir Francis Kinloch of Gilmerton, Bart. having seen the Northumberland machine, attempted to improve it by inclosing the drum in a fluted cover, and

---

" * In a correspondence with those gentlemen on this subject, they authorise us to say, that, from recent information, they are *now* convinced the statement given by them in the Northumberland Survey is defective, *and that they are satisfied the merit of perfecting the machine, as specified in the patent, belongs solely to Mr. Meikle.*
R. B."

and instead of making the drum itself fluted, he fixed on the outside of it four fluted pieces of wood, capable of being raised a little above the circumference of the drum by means of springs underneath, so as to press against the fluted cover, and rub out the grain as the sheaves passed round between them; but, finding that it bruised the grain in the same manner as the Northumberland machine did, he sent it to Mr. Andrew Meikle at Knowmill, in his neighbourhood, in order to have it rectified, if possible.

" Mr. Meikle who, for several years, had been making many trials of different machines for the same purpose, after repeated experiments with Sir Francis' mill, found that it was constructed upon wrong principles, and that beating must be had recourse to, instead of rubbing. He therefore, in 1785, made a working model, turned by water at Knowmill, in which the grain was beat out by the drum, after passing through two plain rollers, which were afterwards altered for two fluted ones*. Mr. George Meikle, son of the former, being at Kilbegie, the residence of Mr. Stein, agreed to erect a machine of this nature for that gentleman, upon condition of Mr. Stein furnishing all the materials, and paying him for the work, *only in case the machine answered the desired purpose.* This was agreed to, and the machine was completed in February 1786, being the first ever made. It was found to work exceedingly well, and the only alteration made from the above mentioned model was, that, instead of plain rollers, fluted ones were substituted.

---

* In a *History* of the Thrashing Mill, should be mentioned the " ENDLESS WEBB" which was in use, to conduct the corn to the beaters, before the invention of fluted rollers, for that purpose. It was formed of about two yards of canvas, or other cloth, with the ends sewed together, and kept on the stretch by two rollers; which being put in motion, the upper part of the cloth, and the corn spread upon it, were impelled forward; the corn being thus exposed to the action of the beaters; but could not be held with the same firmness to receive their strokes, as between fluted rollers. *Rev.*

tuted. In consequence of this successful attempt, a patent for the invention was applied for, which, after a considerable opposition from a person no ways concerned in the invention, was obtained in April 1788."

The *uses* of this machine are now so well known, in every quarter of the kingdom, as not to require to be here enumerated.

And, on its *construction*, I find nothing, noticeable, in the Report under consideration; excepting what relates to its adaption to the WIND, as its moving power.—P. 60. "The expence of horse labor, from the encreased value of the animal, and the charge of his keeping, being an object of great importance, we beg leave to recommend that, upon all sizeable farms, that is to say where two hundred acres, or upwards, of corn are sown, the machine should be wrought by wind, unless where local circumstances afford the conveniency of water, which is always to be preferred. Many persons recommend what they don't practise; but the surveyors of the West Riding are not in this predicament: Upon their farms the machines are all driven by wind, and upon two of them horse machines are annexed, which prevents every inconvenience that might arise during a tract of calm weather.

"Wind machines were, till lately, exposed to dangerous accidents, as the sails could not be shifted when a brisk gale arose, which is often the case in this variable climate. These disagreeable circumstances are now effectually prevented by the inventive genius of Mr. Meikle, and the machine may be managed by any person of the smallest discernment or attention.

"The whole sails can be taken in, or let out in half a minute, as the wind requires, by a person pulling a rope within the house, so that an uniform motion is preserved to the machine, and the danger from sudden squalls prevented.

"Where coals are plenty and cheap, steam may be advantageously used for working the machine. A
respectable

respectable farmer in the county of East Lothian works his machine in this way, and being situated in the neighbourhood of a colliery, is enabled to thresh his grain at a trifling expence."

On the *cost* of these machines, we are told, p. 60,— " A horse machine of the greatest powers, with the appendages of rakes and fanners, may be erected for one hundred pounds, and when wrought by wind, for two hundred pounds independent of the buildings and fixtures which are required. It would be unfair, however, to charge these to the account of the threshing machine, as, even upon a middle sized farm, a greater extent of buildings is required for barn work, when the corn is separated from the straw by the flail, that when the operation is performed by the threshing machine."

I perfectly agree with Mr. Brown and his colleagues, in opinion, that—" as a farmer's capital ought never to be laid out in expensive building, or works of an extraordinary kind, we are humbly of opinion, that the sums necessary for erecting machines, should, in the first instance, be expended by the landlord, and the tenant taken bound to leave them in a *workable condition* at his departure."—p. 62. If a farm is under lease, let the tenant pay six per cent, for the money laid out, during the remainder of his term. A thrashing mill, as a barnfloor, a cider mill, or a hop kiln, may well be considered as part of the homestall : the rent of the premises being of course regulated accordingly.

MANURE.—*Lime.*—P. 154. " Lime is applied to the greatest part of the land in cultivation, and the quantity laid on at one time, is so inconsiderable, that in our humble opinion, it can never produce the intended effect. Whenever we speak against a general practice, we do it with diffidence ; but upon this occasion, we cannot refrain from expressing our dissatisfaction, both with the quantity applied, and the frequent repetition of this article."—P. 155. " We were

were particularly anxious to ascertain the quantity
of lime laid upon an acre, and we found it to be, in
different places, from 1 chalder, or 32 bushels, to 100
bushels.   Some people may use rather more, but from
60 to 70 bushels per acre, may be regarded as an
average ; a quantity very inadequate, in our humble
opinion, to the intended purpose."—P. 161. "A farmer in the West Riding whose opinion we highly
respect, writes us upon this subject in the following
words :

" Lime husbandry was more practised some time
past than at present ; for it is found, that where lands
have been long under the plough, and often dressed
over with it (which has been the general practice for
a century past), it has very little effect.   The old
farmers used no other tillage, till very lately, but what
was made in the farm-yard, and many of them no
other yet, always liming their clay land fallows, and
sowing wheat ; next oats, beans, or broad clover, and
again wheat.   They have thus fallowed and limed,
again and again, for 30 or 40 years together, laying
on at the rate of about 120 bushels of Knottingley
stone-lime upon an acre."

Those (and one which follows) are the principal
facts collected, respecting the lime husbandry of
West Yorkshire.   Yet the article "Lime," in the Report, fills half a sheet :—mostly, with ingenious arguments ; but, in part, with a course of experiments, on
liming lands of different qualities.   But where the
lands are situated, on which those experiments were
made (unless in East Lothian), or what was the quality of the lime employed, we can only conjecture.
These, however, would seem to be matters of no
import ;—for the Reporter's concluding paragraph
renders null and void what he had previously written ;
the facts inserted above excepted.

It is this.—P. 163. " Mr. Peach at Sheffield informed us, that the lime brought from the neighbourhood of Doncaster, would not answer upon his land ;
but

but that 80 or 90 bushels per acre of the Derbyshire lime operated well. This confirms what we have already said relative to the theory of lime being imperfectly understood. Indeed the liming of land being an expensive business; where quantities such as from 2 to 300 bushels are laid on an acre, every person should previously ascertain the qualities of the lime, and consider attentively the nature of the soil upon which the application is to be made."

Bones. These appear to be a favorite manure of the West Riding:—particularly, in the Sheffield quarter of the manufacturing district. Their use may have there been pointed out, by observing the effects of the refuse of the cutlers' workshops.

Immense quantities of bones (as of calcarious waters) are annually suffered to pass away, uselessly; although, by due attention, they might be rendered greatly beneficial to Agriculture and the community. In large towns, great quantities might be collected. Yet I do not remember to have observed any instance, in which it is the established practice to collect and grind them, for the purpose of manure; unless, in and near the metropolis. Bones are composed of calcarious earth, and *other* animal matter. Every particle of them may be said to be conducive to the production of vegetables. If ground down, before their better parts have been extracted by heat, their effect will undoubtedly be found the greatest.

The subjoined extracts contain the valuable parts of the information, on this subject.—P. 153. " Bone dust, or as it is called, *hand tillage*, is used to great extent upon all the fields for twenty miles round Sheffield. Bones of all kinds are gathered with the greatest industry, and are even imported from distant places. They are broke through a mill made for that purpose; are sometimes laid on the ground without any mixture; but it is supposed most advantageous to mix them up with rich earth, into a compost, and when fermentation has taken place, is the proper time

to

to lay them on the ground."—App. p. 22. " Mr,
Hague, one of Mr. Beaumont's tenants, says bones
answer best on the turnip land, 100 bushels of bone,
and four loads of dung, mixed with good earth, is laid
upon a statute acre,"—App. p. 30. " Where the
land is strong, it is clean summer fallowed, and sown
with wheat at Michaelmas; of all the manures that
are used, bone dust is found to have the most effect;
60 bushels applied to the acre, and often bought so
high as 20 d. per bushel,"—App. p. 32. "Mr. Taylor
showed us a mill for breaking bones, which are in
great repute in this neighbourhood, and found to
answer better upon lime-stone land than any other
manure. Sixty bushels are applied to the acre. Has
very little effect the first year, but afterwards operates
for a considerable time—we think 10 or 12 years.
Prime cost at the mill 18 d. per bushel, and the demand greater than can be supplied."

Warping. But by far the most valuable part of the
information,—not only concerning manures, but
every other subject of the West Riding Report, and
that by which, alone, it can confer on other districts,
any important advantage,—relates to the practice of
" Warping;" or improving lands by the mean of
ALLUVION, artificially deposited.

This practice, it is true, especially belongs to the
banks and creeks of estuaries, and the mouths and
banks of large vale rivers, whose channels are lined
with mud, and up which the tide is impelled with
sufficient force to agitate that which is lodged in its
course, and keep it suspended so long as the motion
continues. But this ceasing, the water, by a general
law of nature, deposits the suspended particles,—returns them to the state of mud,—upon the lands to
which they may have been conducted.

It is not the Humber and its branches, alone, that
are capable of affording this extraordinary species of
improvement. The Severn, the Parret, and every
other muddy river, up which the tide rushes with impetuosity,

petuosity, may be able, in particular parts, at least, to produce this beneficial effect. Indeed, all tide rivers, having low flat margins, and containing in their channels the materials of improvement, are proper subjects for experiments. The value of the sediment of land floods is, in some situations, experienced. But this is generally of a sandy lean nature, compared with the rich, saline mud that is, in many instances, brought up from the margins of the sea, or the brackish beds of estuaries. See p. 273.

The surveyors of the West Riding were favored with three papers, on this interesting subject. Two of them are very valuable. The one from Lord HAWKE, the other from Mr. DAY of Doncaster. I place Mr. Day's first, as it contains some account of the origin, and history of this admirable practice :— a recent discovery!!!

P. 166. " Information from Mr. Day of Doncaster concerning the warping of land.

" The practice of warping, in the low part of the West Riding of Yorkshire, I conceive, originated from the tides overflowing the banks of the rivers, and thereby leaving a sediment, which was found to be excellent manure and that the land brought very large crops after being flooded in that manner. Indeed I believe the first trial of warping was made by a small farmer, who had some low land adjoining a certain river called the Dutch river, which was very poor soil, the lowest part of which was levelled with the highest, by the overflowing of some very high tides, which convinced the farmer that he could, by banking the land round, and laying a tunnel through the bank of the river, raise the same, and make it of considerable more value. He therefore applied to the commissioners of sewers for the level of Italfield chase, (being commissioners appointed for draining that part of the country, &c.) to grant him an order
giving

giving him leave to lay a tunnel, a few inches square, through the bank of the said river, for the purpose of warping his land, which was granted him (with a great deal of reluctance, for fear of overflowing the country with water) on his giving a proper security for indemnifying the country against any injury which might happen thereby, which answered his purpose extremely well. But now there are cloughs laid of 6 or 8 feet wide, and drains made of proper dimensions, to convey the water accordingly. I am not certain how long it is since warping came much into practice; but however it is not many years ago; I believe not more than 20 or 25 years or thereabouts.

" As to the expence of warping, it is an impossibility to make any estimate without viewing the situation of the lands to be warped, and the course and distance it will be necessary to carry the warp to such lands, as, 1*st*, The situation of the lands must be considered. 2*dly*, The quantity of land the same drains and cloughs will be sufficient to warp. 3*dly*, The expence of building the cloughs, cutting the drains, embanking the lands, &c. An estimate of which expence being made, then it will be necessary to know the number of acres such cloughs and drains will warp, before any estimate per acre can be made; therefore you will easily conceive the greater quantity of land, the same cloughs and drains will warp, the easier the expence will be per acre. In my opinion there are great quantities of land in the country, which might be warped at so small an expence, as from 4*l*. to 8*l*. per acre, which is nothing in comparison to the advantages which arise from it. I have known land which has been raised in value by warping, from 5*l*. to upwards of 40*l*. and 50*l*. per acre; therefore it is easy to conceive that the greatest advantages arise upon the worst land, and the more porous the soil the better, as the wet filters through, and sooner becomes fit for use.

" The

" The advantages of warping are very great; as, after lands have been properly warped, they are so enriched thereby, that they will bring very large crops for several years afterwards, without any manure; and, when it is necessary, the lands might be warped again, by opening the old drains, which would be done at a very trifling expence, and would bring crops in succession for many years, with very little or no tillage at all, if the lands were kept free from quick grass, and other weeds, which must be the case in all lands where they are properly managed ; besides the drains which are made for the purpose of warping, are the best drains that can be constructed for draining the lands at the time they are not used for warping, which is another very great advantage in low lands.

" As to the disadvantages in warping, I conceive there can be very few, if any, as the land might be warped in the year that it ought to be a summer fallow. Indeed all lands that are warped, ought to be prepared in the spring as fallow lands, so that they are ready to let in the warp by the month of June, as the three succeeding months, are the most proper months in the year for warping, (but they might continue warping longer when it is necessary, therefore the rent is out of the question. The only inconveniences that can arise, in my opinion, are from the blowing up of the cloughs, or breaking of the banks, (which is seldom the case but where there is some neglect in the works,) and thereby overflowing the adjoining lands, and very probably destroying the crops ; but it nevertheless very much enriches the land that it overflows ; however, these circumstances should be guarded against by every cautious engineer.

" Warped land seldom fails of carrying good crops; but oats are most to be depended on the first season. I think warped land is better calculated to grow oats, wheat, and beans, than barley, as the soil by that means

means is so very rich, that barley generally grows too coarse. It never fails growing artificial seeds of all kinds, and is the best of pasture land.

" Land once well warped will last a number of years; but in my opinion where conveniency serves, the best way is to lay on a little warp every time it becomes fallow, which if kept in arable land, would be about every 5 or 6 years, and by that means the farmer would seldom fail of having great crops. In short I know no sort of management so cheap as warping. when properly applied."

" Mr. Day of Doncaster's answers to the queries on his former observations on warping land.

" *Answer to Query* 1*st.* *Warp*, is the sediment left upon the land by flooding the same with tide water. Letting in the water is also called warping, from the sediment which the water leaves behind it, which is called warp. Letting in fresh water, not being tide water, would not be called warping, but flooding the land.

" *Answer to Query* 2*d.* The water being tide water, and coming from the sea or large rivers, is of course brackish, and the warp or sediment it deposits is of the same nature. Fresh water, though very useful upon some land, at proper seasons of the year, would by no means answer the same purpose as water coming from the rivers where the tide flows, as it never could deposit a sufficient sediment, neither would it be of half so rich a nature as what is left by tide water.

" *Answer to Quere* 3*d.* The water does not at all lie stagnate, nor is it unwholesome to the neighbourhood, as it goes off and returns regularly every tide; it only continues a little time, till the greatest part of the sediment has subsided, and then returns through the same drain, clough, or sluice, it came from; or, if convenient, through some other sluice or inlet made for that purpose.

" *Ans*

" *Ans. to Qu. 4th.* The drains are open drains, and cut the same as all other drains, for the purpose of draining lands. The depth of the drain is according to the level of the land, with the river from which you take your warp; and the width agreeable to the quantity of land you mean to warp at one time, and the clough or sluice which communicates with the river.

" *Ans. to Qu. 5th.* June, July, and August, are thought the best months for warping, on account of their generally being the dryest months in the year; they might warp land in any month in the year, when the season is dry, and the fresh water in the river very low. But, if the season is wet, and the rivers full of fresh water, it mixes with the tide, and makes it not half so thick and muddy, and of course hinders it from leaving one half or one fourth the sediment upon the land, it would in a dry season of the year; neither is the water got so readily off the land in wet seasons as dry. Warping land in the spring, can answer no better purpose than summer, as there could be no crop that year, for the warp must lie to soak and dry, before the land can be cultivated to any advantage.

" *Ans. to Qu. 6th.* Warped land is supposed to be the best of land for potatoes, and the most productive.

" *Ans. to Qu. 7th.* The depth of the water upon the land, entirely depends upon the level of the land, and the height of the tide in the river, from whence the water is taken; but, where it can be accomplished, it might be 3 or 4 foot deep or upwards, as the deeper the water, the more sediment is left; but land may be warped with a deal of less water, as it is only letting on more tides, and taking longer time to the work; it does not at all signify whether the water is always kept at the same height or not, only take care that it does not overflow the banks.

" *Ans.*

" *Ans. to Qu. 8th.* Mr. RICHARD JENNINGS of ARMIN, near HOWDEN, was the first person who tried the experiment of warping, about 50 years ago. It was next attempted by a Mr. Farham, steward to ——— Twisleton, Esq. of Rawcliffe, also by a Mr. Mould of Potter Grange, both about 40 years ago; and it has been tried by a great variety of people since that time, to their great advantage.

" *Ans. to Qu. 9th.* What is meant by *warping being found to be excellent tillage ?* is no more than that it is excellent manure, and good for all kinds of land where it can be accomplished.

" *Ans. to Qu. 10th.* Cloughs, what are they? A clough is an inlet cut in the bank of the river, walled on each side with a strong wall and floodgate fixed in the middle, for the purpose of letting in and out the water, and is commonly called a clough or sluice; it is nearly upon the same principle as what are used at water mills."

P. 164. " Observations on Warping Land, transmitted by the Right Honourable Lord Hawke.

" The land to be warped must be banked round against the river. The banks are made of the earth taken on the spot from the land : they must slope six feet ; that is three feet on each side of their top or crown of the bank, for every foot perpendicular of rise : Their top or crown is broader or narrower, according to the impetuosity of the tide, and the weight and quantity of water ; and it extends from two feet to twelve : Their height is regulated by the height, to which the spring tides flow, so as to exclude or let them in at pleasure. In those banks, there are more or fewer openings, according to the size of the ground to be warped, and to the choice of the occupier, but in general they have only two sluices, one called the flood gate to admit, the other called the clough to let off, the water gently ; these are enough for ten or
fifteen

fifteen acres: When the spring tide begins to ebb, the flood gate is opened to admit the tide, the clough having been previously shut by the weight of water brought up the river by the flow of the tide. As the tide ebbs down the river, the weight or pressure of water being taken from the outside of the clough next the river, the tide water that has been previously admitted by the flood gate opens the clough again, and discharges itself slowly but completely through it. The cloughs are so constructed as to let the water run off, between the ebb of the tide admitted, and the flow of the next; and to this point particular attention is paid: The flood gates are placed so high as only to let in the spring tides when opened. They are placed above the level of the common tides.

" Willows are also occasionally planted on the front of the banks to break the force of the tide, and defend the banks by raising the front of them with warp thus collected and accumulated: But these willows must never be planted on the banks, as they would destroy the banks by giving the winds power to shake them.

" The land warped is of every quality; but to be properly warped it must be situated within the reach of the spring tides, and on a level lower than the level of their flow. The land in general is not warped above one year in seven, a year's warping will do for that time.

" The land is as other land, various as to the preference of grain to be sown on it.

" Land has been raised considerably by warping: One field of bad corn-land, good for nothing, was raised in three years fourteen inches: It lay idle for that time that it might be raised by warping, it was sown with beans last year, and promised by appearance a crop of eight quarters. If possible this shall be ascertained as to the quantity threshed.

" The warp consists of the mud and salts deposited by the ebbing tide: Near Howden one tide will

will deposite an inch of mud, and this deposite is more or less according to the distance of the place from the Humber.

" Cherry Cob sands were gained from the Humber by warping: They are supposed to be four yards thick of warp at least: Some of those were ploughed for twelve, fourteen, or sixteen years, before they would grow grass seeds: The greater part is now in feeding land, and makes very fine pastures.

" The land must be in tillage for some considerable time after warping, for six years at least: The land if laid down to grass, and continued in grass, is not warped; for the salts in the mud would infallibly kill the grass seeds.

" When it is proposed to sow the land again with corn, then the land is warped: When they find the grass decline, then they warp and plough it out: As the land varies in quality, so does the time during which it will produce good grass: The land is never fallowed but in the year when it is warped."

TILLAGE.—In a section entitled, " Fallowing defended"—p. 80,—Mr. Brown enters the list of argument, to combat with Mr. KENT; introducing his lengthened debatement with this brief exordium.— " Whether summer fallow is necessary or unnecessarry? is a question lately agitated; and in a respectable work, (the Survey of Norfolk) an attempt has been made to explode this practice, which has long been considered as a most beneficial improvement. The agriculture of Britain being materially interested in the issue of this question, the following answers to the Norfolk surveyor, are submitted to the public." But, as " comparisons are odious"—and censure always painful—I will only remark, here, that Mr. B. is well acquainted with the management of arable lands, Mr. K. with that of landed property.

I must not, however, think of escaping, thus easily, from the adroitness of Mr. B's arguments on fallowing. Mr. B. has done me the honor to notice, in a handsome

handsome manner, what I have said on this subject, in my account of the Yorkshire husbandry. What I think requisite to be said, here, in reply, is, that if Mr. Brown, previously to making his remarks, had read what I have written, in Surrey, in Glocestershire, in the Midland Counties, in the West of England, and in the district of Maidstone, in the Southern Counties,—as well as what I have said in Yorkshire, on this very material point in arable farming,—he would, I am vain enough to think, have been convinced of the propriety of my practice, if not have adopted it, in preference to his own.

Mr. Brown's concluding paragraph is moderate, and judicious. P. 88. " But want of fallows is not the want of the Yorkshire husbandry; in the corn district they prevail to a much greater extent than necessary, and, unless where turnips can be introduced, occasion great drawback upon the farmer's profits. If good land be fallowed properly, can it ever be supposed necessary to repeat it after carrying only wheat and beans ? When this practice is too often repeated, it also loses much of its effects, the superior advantages arising from a first fallow being well known to all farmers; and while we condemn the system that would throw out this beneficial practice altogether, we are decidedly against an unnecessary repetition of it."

WHEAT. P. 95. " This valuable grain is cultivated to a great extent, upon all the low land of the district ; and is sown after fallow or turnips, or clover; sometimes after peas and beans."

Harvesting Wheat.—P. 151. " We are of opinion, a great deal more dung might be accumulated, if the stubbles were cut lower than is presently done. Barley and oats are often cut with the scythe, which so far obviates this argument; but wheat, which is the prevailing crop, is always cut with the sickle.

" From not seeing the crops upon the ground we cannot say with precision what proportion of the

straw

straw might be left. But, from a careful examination of the stubbles, we suppose it at least to be one-third. This not only occasions a great loss of grain, as all the straggling heads are thereby left, but also deprives the farmer of a large portion of home manure, for the dry stubble, left upon the field, will never ferment; it is therefore of no use to enrich the ground, and occasions great inconvenience, when the land is ploughed down afterwards."—Where it is not the practise to mow, "chop," or otherwise collect, wheat stubbles, after harvest, low cutting is more particularly eligible.

BARLEY.—I copy the subjoined passage; as it contains opinions that are new to me; not from a full conviction of their justness. P. 95. "We believe that double the quantity of land is sown with wheat in this Riding, than is sown with barley, and that this preference extends over the greatest part of the island. Barley is a tender grain, easily injured by adverse weather, generally raised at greater expence, and an acre of its straw will not produce half so much dung as that of a crop of wheat upon the same land. It is really surprising, that the price of barley should, in all ages, have been greatly below that of wheat; whereas the latter is generally raised at less expence, while the former, especially upon clay soils, is a most precarious crop."

BEANS. P. 96. "The drilling of beans is now become common in many parts of the island, and we earnestly recommend its adoption upon all lands where the soil is of a proper depth for carrying this plant. They are, on the whole, when drilled and horse-hoed, nearly as valuable, upon clay soils, as turnips are upon those of a different description."—On a merely arable farm, in a situation in which manure can be purchased, the above remarks are perfectly just. But not so where a large number of livestock are necessary to be kept, to maintain the ground in a state of productiveness. There, cabbages, for

for early spring feedage, gain a preference, as a fallow crop, (in due proportion at least) on strong land: especially where old grass lands are not sufficiently abundant.

FLAX.—P. 102. " In the neighbourhood of Selby, a considerable quantity is annually raised, and from the list of the claims given in to the clerk of the peace, for the West Riding, it appeared that the parliamentary bounty was claimed, in the year 1793, for no less a quantity than 59,000 stones."—And, p. 103. " The bounty paid for flax and hemp, grown in the West Riding, for the year 1794, amounted to the sum of 720 *l*. which at 4 *d*. per stone, will make 43,000 stone ; and taking the average of the crop at 30 stone per acre, will give 1440 acres sown ; and from the same calculation there would be, in the year 1795, 1650 acres sown."

I insert those particulars; although we are not told by whom they were furnished. The following remarks, though not of English growth, I readily copy; as flax is a universal crop, throughout Scotland; especially for domestic purposes.

P. 102. " From our own experience (having formerly sown many acres with flax,) we can say with confidence, that, upon a proper soil, no other crop will pay the farmer better than flax ; and if due pains and attention are bestowed upon the pulling, watering and skutching, flax of as good a quality may be produced at home, as what is imported from Holland, or the Baltic.

" The produce of an acre of flax will be from 24 to 40 stone averdupois, after it is clean skutched. This operation is performed by the hand, in the West Riding, there being no mills erected in that part of the country for this purpose. Some of the flax is allowed to stand for seed, which of course renders the flax of less value.

" We have found inferior soils, such as new broken up muirs, as well fitted for raising seed as others of a better

better quality; and they have this advantage, that while the rent is but small, the trouble of weeding them is equally trifling *. Besides, seed and flax ought never to be attempted together; when the former is intended, the ground ought to be sown much thinner, so as the plant may have sufficient air to fill the bolls; whereas, when the flax itself is considered as the object, it ought to be sown much thicker, to prevent it from forking, and becoming coarse; we believe a neglect of these things has contributed to render this valuable and necessary plant, not so profitable as might, from the public support bestowed upon it, have been expected."

TURNIPS. P. 98. " Although the turnip husbandry prevails over a great part of the Riding, yet the proper cultivation of that root is not attended to so carefully as good farming requires. Except by a few individuals, turnips are universally sown broad-cast, and most imperfectly cleaned. We understand that it is not much more than thirty years since they were hoed at all; and that the introduction of this most necessary practice, was principally owing to the indefatigable exertions of that truly patriotic nobleman the late MARQUIS of ROCKINGHAM :"—A fact that is corroborated by Mr. Payne; App. p. 56.—"Turnips are generally sown broadcast; but the expertness of our hoers sufficiently compensates for the want of drilling. That excellent mode of cultivation, the hoeing of turnips, has been practised in this part of the county upwards of thirty years; being introduced about that time into the township of Wath upon Derne, by that excellent cultivator, William Payne of Newhill Grange, my late honored father; as it was to the county, by that truly patriotic nobleman, and benefactor to his country, the late Marquis of Rockingham."

It

---

* This appears to be a valuable hint,

It may here be observed, that the hoing of turnips was introduced into the midland counties, by the Marquis Townshend's sending expert hoers, from Norfolk. These circumstances show with what facility MANUAL OPERATIONS may be propagated upon an estate, by dispersing skilful workmen among its tenantry.

In speaking of the practice of Mr. Latham, near Snaith, the Reporter says, App. p. 38.—" His turnips, although not drilled, are all in rows, about sixteen inches wide, which enables him to hoe them with accuracy. His method to do this, is to give the last furrow very broad, which takes all the seed when harrowed into the furrow, and so gives the field an appearance of regularity. Mr. Latham said this plan was fallen on by accident, which indeed is often the parent of many improvements;—when ploughing one of his fields some years ago, he ordered his servants to finish it that night. There being a feast in the neighbourhood, the ploughmen were anxious to be early at it, and so gave a furrow much broader than usual. When the young plants came up, Mr. Latham was surprised to see them in regular lines, and inquired into the cause of it; which pleased him so well, that he has since continued the practice."

A similar method is now practising in East Yorkshire. It is eligible, in as much as many of the seeds being buried deep, the young plants are less liable to the injuries of a droughty season, than those which are uniformly more superficially rooted. And the crop is more readily set out by inexperienced hoers: or may, in part, be cleaned, with a narrow horse-hoe.

The Surveyors observed with some surprize (as well they might) the method of eating off common field turnips. App. p. 39.—" We saw a large common field of turnips to the eastward of Kellington, which were middling good, but very imperfectly cleaned. At least 40 acres were stocked off at once, and

and cows, bullocks, young cattle, and sheep were feeding indiscriminately."

The Reporter, as has been noticed, p. 367, is an advocate for *drilling turnips.* His only remarks, on the operation, are these: — p. 98.—" When drilled turnips are meant instead of a complete summer fallow, the intervals ought to be at least 32 inches; and, in this way, if due care be taken to use the hand-hoe, the ground will be cleaned in the most perfect manner." —This is a bold assertion.

LIQUORICE. I insert the following account; but do not warrant its *authenticity.* What I have seen of the soil of the liquorice grounds of Pontefract, appears to be a deep, rich, calcarious loam, on limestone;—Hop ground of a superior quality.

P. 107. " We received the following information from Mr. Halley, seedsman and nurseryman at Pontefract, concerning the cultivation of Liquorice. ' The ' soil most proper for liquorice is that of a dead, light, ' sandy loam. It is trenched three feet, well dunged, ' and planted with stocks and runners in the months ' of February and March, on beds of one yard wide, ' thrown up in ridges, with alleys between them, and ' the beds hoed and hand-weeded. The first year a ' crop of onions is taken in the alleys, and the tops of ' the liquorice cut over every year. The ground is ' trenched when the liquorice is taken up, and all the ' fibres cut off. A considerable quantity, more than ' 100 acres, is cultivated in this neighbourhood. It ' is a very precarious plant, often rotten by wetness, ' and also hurt by sharp frosts in the spring and dry ' weather afterwards. Rent of the land upon which ' it is cultivated, about 3*l.* per acre.' "

CULTIVATED HERBAGE.—P. 116.—" The grasses that are cultivated are red clover, when it is to be followed with wheat, and white clover and hay seeds for pasture. Sometimes hay seeds are sown by themselves, and a good deal of Sainfoin is cultivated in the neighbourhood of Tadcaster and Ferrybridge."

GRASS

GRASS LAND, or perennial herbage.—To lands of this description, the Reporter may be said to be a sworn foe;—notwithstanding the first enquiries he made after them—his first impressions—were favorable to them. App. p. 5. " Leaving Grassington we passed through a wide range of uncultivated moors, and arrived at Settle. At this place we saw the finest grass we ever viewed. Indeed the richness of the soil is hardly credible to those who have not seen it, and the possessors were unanimously of opinion, that it is of greater value to them when kept in grass, than when cultivated by the plough." Again, App. p. 9.— " At Gargrave, half way between Settle and Skipton, we saw most excellent fields of grass. It is impossible to say what sorts of seeds had been sown, or whether any had been sown at all; they seemed a mixture of all sorts of hay seeds, but richer grass cannot grow." And, in the body of the Report, p. 116, " As for the old rich pastures about Skipton, Settle, and other places, it is not easy to say what they have originally been sown with. (!) There appears among other grasses, a great quantity of what is called honey-suckle grass, which we suppose to be the same plant sold under the name of *cow-grass* by the London seedsmen. Most of the vale of Skipton has been 50 years in the same situation as at present; and the proprietors do not seem anxious for changing it."

We need no further evidence to convince us that the Reporter, at the time he wrote, was an entire stranger to the nature of this species of landed property;—which is common to every department of *this* kingdom;—namely, rich, deep-soiled grounds, that have been covered with native herbage, for a length of years.

Some of these lands, it is pretty evident, have never been in any other state, from the time they were first reclaimed; although they may be equally well suited, in their natural quality, to the production of arable crops, as of herbage. But it having been found, by experience,

experience, that they could be kept, continually, in a state of highly profitable herbage, without any other labor than that of freeing the surface from obstructions, they have been suffered to remain in that peculiarly profitable state: in which they are, accordingly, let at high prices: not unfrequently at twice the rent of the arable lands, in their neighbourhood. (See p. 369.)

But others, and probably the principal part, of these old grass lands, have formerly been in a state of aration; as appears by the wavey turn of their surfaces. Yet the species of plants, which grow on these, are the same as those of the lands on which no traces of the plow are discernable.—They are the NATIVE PLANTS, belonging to the *soil, substrata, situation*, and *climature*, wherein they NATURALLY INHABIT. For some account of the production of this profitable species of landed property, and Nature's tardy process in generating it, See YORKSHIRE,— Section, *Cultivated Herbage.*

On the *management* of grass land, in the West Riding of Yorkshire, we find nothing to interest; excepting a remarkable instance of practice in *grazing;* communicated by a gentleman in the neighbourhood of Skipton.—App. p. 51.—" It is worthy of notice, as it appears to me of great service to the land, as well as very profitable to the occupier, that most of the principal graziers take all their stock out of some of their best pastures in the beginning of July, and put nothing in them till about Michaelmas, when they are equal or superior to the best fog: indeed they call this, fogging their pastures."—For supplying markets, in early summer and the wane of autumn, a practice of this kind might be found eligible, perhaps, in other districts of rich, sound, absorbent lands.

LIVESTOCK.—P. 178.—" The West Riding being a great grazing district, it might be expected that much attention would be paid to selecting good
breeds

breeds of stock; which, from our observation and information, was not generally the case. Indeed, the
horned cattle and sheep, fed in the district, include
almost all the different varieties reared over the whole
island. This mixture may be attributed to the extent
of the demand, which far exceeds what can be raised
in the district," P, 120.—" The district is neither
able to supply its consumption with lean cattle, nor
sheep, as immense quantities of both are annually
brought from Scotland, and the contiguous northern
counties."

In a communication, by Mr. DAY of Doncaster, "regarding the SIZE of LIVE STOCK," (App. p. 74) Mr. D.
militates against the fashionable folly of great sizes of
cattle and sheep. But *general* observations on this
subject must necessarily be unavailing. The sizes of
those animals should be suited (as Nature ever suits
them) to soils and climatures. That they ought to
be rather below, than above, the given situation, is,
in my mind, evident. And this, perhaps, is all that
Mr. D. is desirous to inculcate. Large domestic animals are generally the offspring of pride, rather than
the means of profit.

HORSES.—P. 194.—" There are not many horses
bred, except in the eastern parts of the Riding. The
size of those employed in the western parts, is generally small; but they are hardy, and capable of great
fatigue. In other parts of the Riding, they are large,
and sufficiently able for any field operations. Those
used in the waggons are strong and well made."

CATTLE.—*Breeds.*—P. 178.—" The horned cattle
of this district may be classed under four different
heads. 1. The short horned kind, which principally
prevail in the east side of the Riding, and are distinguished by the names of the Durham, Holderness, or
Dutch breeds. 2. The long horned or Craven breed,
which are both bred and fed in the western parts, and
also brought from the neighbouring county of Lancashire. These are a hardy sort of cattle, and con-
stitutionally

stitutionally disposed to undergo the vicissitudes of a wet and precarious climate. 3. There is another breed which appears to be a cross between the two already mentioned, and which we esteem the best of all. A great number of milch cows of this sort are kept in Nidderdale and the adjacent country, which are both useful and handsome. They are perhaps not altogether such good milkers, as the Holderness cows, but they are much hardier, and easier maintained. They are, at the same time, sooner made ready for the butcher, and are generally in good order and condition, even when milkod. 4. Beside these, there are immense numbers of Scotch cattle brought into the country, which, after being fed for one year, and sometimes two, are sold to the butcher. Beef of this kind always sells higher in the market, than that of the native breed; and from the extent of population, there is a constant demand for all that can be fed."— App. p. 6.—" At Settle we had an opportunity of seeing a great show of fat cattle of the country breed. They were all long horned, and seeming in shape, skin, and other circumstance, to be nearly the same as the Irish breed. We learned, that of late there had not been the same attention paid as formerly to keep the breed pure, by selecting proper bulls. Be this as it may, the long horned breed of cattle, which prevails over the western part of the island, from the thickness of their skin, and the hardness of their constitutions, are much better calculated to undergo the vicissitudes of this climate, than the short horned breed of the eastern coasts."

Dairy.—App. p. 4. In Nidderdale—" A good deal of butter is likewise salted here for the London market, and a cow pastured upon the low grounds, is computed to yield three firkins of 56lb. each, during the season."

Much is said, p. 179, about keeping cows in the house, during the summer season; but nothing is clearly made out, in its favor, that a *country dairyman*

can

can profit by. By the *milkmen* of *Leeds*, the practice may, nevertheless, be found eligible.

Fatting Cattle. P. 119. " The West Riding may be considered as a great feeding district, and the graziers in general are very expert at their business. Horned cattle of all kinds are here fattened in a complete manner, the best evidence of which is the quality of beef and mutton offered to sale in all the public markets."—P. 120.—" Cattle are generally made, what in many places would be called fat, upon grass, and afterwards finished by stall feeding with turnips, or allowed to run in the small well sheltered closes, and turnips or hay carried thither for their food."

SHEEP.—*Breeds.*—P. 186.—" There are so many kinds of sheep, both bred and fed in this district, and they have been crossed so often, that it cannot be said to possess a distinct breed.

" The sheep bred upon the *moors* in the western part of the Riding, and which, we presume, are the native breed, are horned, light in the fore quarter, and well made for exploring a hilly country, where there is little to feed them, but heath and ling ; these are generally called the Peniston breed, from the name of the market town, where they are sold. When fat they will weigh from 10 lb. to 15 lb. per quarter. They are a hardy kind of sheep, and good thrivers. When brought down, at a proper age, to the pastures in the low parts of the country, they feed as cleverly, and are as rich mutton as need be."— App. p. 25.—" A market for sheep is held at Peniston, and large quantities of those that go by that name, are sold weekly. They are bred on the *moors* to the westward of Peniston, and on those of Cheshire and Derbyshire."—P. 186.—" Upon the waste *commons*, scattered up and down the Riding, the kind of sheep bred, are the most miserable that can be imagined. As they generally belong to poor people, and are mostly in small lots, they never can be improved. This will apply to the whole of the sheep kept

kept upon the commons, that are not stinted; the numbers that are put on beggar and starve the whole stock."

App. p. 5.—In the neighbourhood of Settle,—an *upland* country,—" the sheep bred here are called the Malham breed, and we received favorable accounts of them."

P. 186.—On the *lower lands,* in the southern parts of the Riding, " there are a good many of the flat ribbed, Lincolnshire sheep, which are ugly beyond description."—P. 187. " In many parts of the Riding, a superior attention is now beginning to be paid to this useful animal, by selecting rams of the best properties, and breeds; which it is to be hoped, will be more and more attended to."

Management of Store Sheep.—In a communication from " a farmer of great professional merit," we find the subjoined passage, p. 192.—" A particular friend and neighbour of mine, the year before last, wintered 100 of these ewes in the straw fold, which kept the produce of two threshers down, better than 20 beasts would have done. He gave them a third part of a common cart load of turnips every day, to keep their bodies open, as the straw would otherwise bind them. This winter he has them come up every night of themselves, which shows they like it; they eat the straw very greedily, and goes out of themselves in the morning to an adjoining grass field. This change of food and warm lodging, agrees with them very well to all appearance, the grass having the same good effect as the turnips, and the straw in the night time, more agreeable to their nature than confinement. But the manure being subject to heat the sheep, when too great a quantity is accumulated together, it should be led out of the fold when that happens to be the case. He led out about 150 loads of manure at Christmas, chiefly from this fold, which he says is in as fine a state of fermentation, as any he ever had."

had."—This Report, even at the third or fourth hand, is worthy of attention, by sheep farmers, in some situations.

Fatting Sheep.—P. 186.—" There are great quantities of Scotch sheep from Teviotdale, &c. fed in the country; numbers of ewes are also brought annually from Northumberland, which, after taking their lambs, are fed that season for the butcher. Many two years old of this kind are also fed upon turnips."

The references prefixed to the preceding extracts, on sheep, will show how loosely the information, collected on that subject, is dispersed, in the volume under Review; and perhaps will suggest to the mind of the reader, that some little attention has been employed, in reducing the scattered parts to their natural order; and, of course, to the most intelligible form.

POULTRY. P. 198.—" It is really diverting to read the modern declamations against inclosures, and the increased size of farms. The authors alluded to, take it for granted, that these measures lessen the number of poultry, and that the only way of getting the markets plentifully supplied with that article, is to lessen the size of farms, and to keep the waste lands of the kingdom in their present unproductive state. At this time we shall not enter upon these topics, being convinced that such a discussion is wholly unnecessary. We may only say, that where poor people, laborers or others, get poultry supported at the expense of the farmer, it may be a material object to them, seeing that they are fed by others; but, considering the question, so far as respects public advantage, the breeding and feeding of poultry ought never to be ranked as an object deserving the farmer's attention.

" It might also be a question, whether the benefit said to be derived by poor people is not in many cases imaginary. We have heard, that in some places,

places, (not in the West Riding,) a man would spend a day in going to market to sell a pair of chickens, the value of which did not compensate for the loss of time spent in disposing of them."

This circumstance may equally tend to silence the " declamations" about LABORERS KEEPING COWS, and each having a few pounds of butter to carry to market; as to show the impropriety of their breeding POULTRY, to annoy their neighbours, get habits of idleness, and spend their time unprofitably.

PIGEONS. The following pointed remarks are in the Reporter's best manner; and are highly creditable to him as the farmer's friend.

P. 199. " Whether the farmer has a right to shoot pigeons, when committing depredations on his property, is a question which has been disputed in several parts of Britain. To us it appears clear, that if he has not such a right under the present laws, he ought instantly to be invested with it. Shall a man be banished when he steals a certain part of my property, and hanged when he takes a larger portion, and must I patiently submit to greater depredations, merely because they are committed by a pigeon? What is it to me, whether the owner of the pigeon takes my property with his own hand, or keeps these animals to pigeon me out of it? The law protects me in the one case, and certainly ought, and probably does, protect me in the other also.

" Several attempts have been made in the northern parts of the island, to punish persons who shot pigeons, which in general proved unsuccessful. Some old obsolete laws have, in these cases, been founded upon, which are a disgrace to our statute books. The matter has not as yet, to our knowledge, received a fair investigation, such complaints being usually set aside upon previous points, or dismissed, because the complainer had either no legal right to keep pigeons, or could not identify his property. As for our parts, we we decidedly think, that no man can have a just right to feed his live stock of any kind, upon the grounds of another; and, that where pigeons are kept, the owner should either confine them in the house during seed-time and harvest, or submit to their execution upon the spot, when they are allowed to fly about at large, and destroy the corn of other people at these important seasons."

IMPROVEMENTS,

SUGGESTED BY THE REPORTER.

Mr. Brown appropriates his concluding chapter to the " Means of Improvement, and the measures calculated for that purpose." The following is a summary of the improvements proposed, p. 263.

" 1st, That the nature of the connexion betwixt the landlord and the tenant should be changed, and that leases of a proper duration should be granted.

" 2dly, That the arbitrary and injudicious covenants generally imposed upon the tenantry, should be discontinued, and conditions more favorable to improvements substituted in their stead.

" 3dly, That tithes should be commuted.

" 4thly, That a general bill should be passed by the legislature, for the division of the common fields and waste grounds.

" These are the leading means of improvement; without which no material encouragement can be given to the husbandry of the district. In hopes that the Board of Agriculture will consider them in the same light, we proceed to recommend,

" 5thly, More improved rotations of crops.

" 6thly,

" 6*thly*, Breaking up the old pasture fields, and frequent changes of corn and grass.

" 7*thly*, Drilling and horse-hoeing beans and turnips.

" 8*thly*, Planting the waste lands which are improper for cultivation."

And, toward the close of the chapter, p. 278, Mr. B. enumerates four additional items of improvement: namely,

" 1*st*, It would be no injury to the proprietor, and save much trouble to the tenant, if all public taxes were paid by the former; besides, the tenant is very apt to conceive an idea, that these burthens are not a part of the rent, but that he is paying heavy taxes, while his landlord is free. We confess, that we would not be fond of signing a lease, which obliged us to pay all parliamentary taxes *already imposed, or to be imposed*, which, in the present state of our national finances, might prove a serious business." All this would be very convenient, and save much trouble—to tenants.

" 2*dly*, It would be of material advantage to agriculture, that some alteration was made upon the game laws, and that the privilege of hunting was used in a more lenient way. It really shocks the feelings of a farmer, to notice the injuries committed by a parcel of people mounted on horseback, and galloping like madmen after a poor fox, or an innocent hare." This, too, might be a very pleasant thing—to tenants.

" 3*dly*, It has been suggested to us, that it would be of public advantage, for the Board to take into their own hands, experimental farms in different parts of the country; and, that if this measure was adopted upon every variety of soil, and the management, for which they are naturally disposed, steadily adhered to, real knowledge in husbandry would increase in course, and substantial improvements be rapidly disseminated."

seminated." The Reporter enlarges on this suggestion, as if he believed it to be new !

" 4thly, It would be very conducive to agricultural
improvement, that encouragement was given for increasing the number of farm servants and laborers.
This can only be done by amending the poors' laws,
and by building cottages contiguous to every homestead." This has been spoken to, in p. 370.

On these several topics, particularly the first eight,
the Reporter expatiates at full length; repeating
many of his former arguments, and adducing other
evidence in favor of his positions. But I perceive
nothing that would convey useful information to my
readers.

In a RETROSPECTIVE VIEW of this Report, the
paucity of the materials, collected by the Surveyors,—
and immediately pertaining to the established practice
of the district of Survey,—compared with the size of
the volume,—forms one of its most striking features.
The communications, notes, and answers, fill, it is
true, some considerable portion of it. But the great
body of the work may, with much truth, be said to
be composed of general remarks, that are not peculiarly applicable to the West Riding of Yorkshire;
and that might have been written with nearly equal
propriety, before the Surveyors left East Lothian, as
after their return. Sometimes, it must be allowed,
they grow spontaneously out of the matter of Survey.
But, more frequently, they read as parts, or passages,
of a didactic treatise on rural subjects, rather than of
a report of local practices.

In these observations, however, I do not mean to
convey that Mr. Brown's remarks are generally fri-
volous and of no value. This would be doing an act
of injustice, not only to Mr. B. but to myself;—as I
have repeatedly quoted them, as being appropriate
and valuable. I rather wish to intimate how much
it

it is to be regretted that Mr. B's time and talents were not employed more profitably, than in reporting the state of *agricul'ure,* in a district possessed by *manufacture;*—and in a country in which he was a *stranger.* If Mr. Brown's experience and general knowledge had been fortunately engaged in a Report of the practice of East Lothian,—or in *considerately* composing a general work on the present state of agriculture, in the southern counties of Scotland, I am convinced he would have deserved well of the British public.

NORTH RIDING

YORKSHIRE.

WITHIN this division of the county are included, wholely, or in great part, the following NATURAL DISTRICTS:—namely, the vale of York, the vale of Stockton, the north coast of Yorkshire, the Eastern Morelands, the limestone lands of East Yorkshire, and the vale of Pickering.

The VALE of YORK. This is the first of rivered vales in the island. The waters of the Swale and the Wiske pass down it, from its northern extreme, until they fall into the Humber, at its base; mixing in their way, with the other waters of the county.

It is situated, mostly, within the North Riding; but extends into the West and the East Ridings, toward its southern extreme. Its northern limit is given by the separation of the waters of rains, which fall between the Tees, and the Swale and Wiske; where, owing to the levelness of the surface, in this part, a number of shallow meers, or lakelets, are seen; especially in a wet season :—a circumstance that frequently occurs, where rain waters divide, and take contrary courses.—Its southern boundary is formed by the marshes of Yorkshire and Lincolnshire: the vale of York terminating with the vale lands. Its western limits have been mentioned to be the limestone

stone lands of West Yorkshire; and the line of uplands that form the skirts of the western morelands. —The eastern boundary is less regular; but equally definite; being given by the morelands and limestone heights of East Yorkshire,—and the wold, hills.

Its length, from north to south, is about sixty miles. Its width varies. Its medial breadth may be estimated at sixteen or seventeen miles; and its area, or entire contents, at more than one thousand square miles of valuable territory.

The towns, situated in the area of the vale, are North Allerton, Thirsk, Borough Bridge, . York, Cawood, Selby, Howden, Snaith, Thorn :—On its western margin—Richmond, Bedal, Ripon, Knaresborough, Wetherby, Tadcaster, Doncaster :—On its eastern—Easingwood, Pocklington, Weighton, Cave.

The surface of this extraordinary tract of country is cast in the true vale style. It is sufficiently diversified to give richness and beauty to its appearance; without any thing of steepness, to interrupt the plow and sithe; or any low flat lands that are liable to floods;—unless, on the immediate banks of its rivers and brooks.

Its soils are greatly varied. The upper parts of the vale are mostly occupied, by cool strong lands, varying in color and fertility, from pale cold clay, to rich red loam. Round Borough Bridge, lands of the very first quality,—deep red loam on absorbent rock,—are found. On the margins, as near Ripon and Easingwood, passages of sandy lands of a fertile quality occur. And, in the eastern quarter of the vale, as well as in its more central parts, weak, sandy, heathlands occupy some considerable space. It is small, however, comparatively with the whole extent.

I forbear to say more of the soils of this vale, though I find on my journals many particulars relating to them. But Mr. Tuke having, it may be presumed, gone deliberately over the county, as a Mapist,

Mapist,—if not as a Reporter,—and being, moreover, a professional landsurveyor within the vale; and, particularly, as he has given a detail of its soils, so far as they are included within the North Riding,—his account of them is, of course, much *fuller* than mine.

The VALE of STOCKTON. This valuable natural district has been already adverted to, in examining the Report of the county of DURHAM; in which a considerable portion of this vale is situated :—it being composed of the lower vale lands of Durham, and the district of Cleveland in Yorkshire; which, together, form one homogeneous rivered vale. The Tees, which is the boundary between the two counties, winds through the middle of it.—The lands and their management, however, are similar, or the very same, on both sides of the river.

This vale accompanies the Tees, from the morelands of Durham, &c. in the neighbourhood of Barnard Castle, to its mouth :—an extent of near forty miles. Its width, between the eastern morelands, which bound it to the south, and the rising grounds of Durham, its northern confine, (see p. 126.) is not less than fifteen miles. But its upper part, above Darlington, is narrow. It may, I think, be computed to contain about four hundred square miles *.

The

---

* The upper part—the southwest margin—of this vale imperceptibly unites with the upper part—the northern extreme—of the vale of York; the waters of rains being (as above-mentioned) the only guide to accurate discrimination between them. The swell by which nature has divided them (see p. 414,) is so inconsiderably elevated, as to elude the eye, in a general view of the country :—the soil and its products being the same, on both sides of it. Thus, we have an uninterrupted continuance of wide-spreading vale lands, from the mouth of the Tees, to the estuary of the Humber: a distance of almost a hundred miles. In approaching these sister vales, by the great road from Carlisle, their combined richness, and oceanlike extent, are most striking.

The towns of Barnard Castle, Darlington, Yarm, Stockton and Stokesley, are included in its area. Those of Hartlepool and Gisborough stand on its margins.

The surface of the vale of Stockton is remarkably flat ;—even as a vale district. But the whole, except its water-formed lands, lie well above the level of floods. On the margins of the river, below Stockton, there are marshlands of considerable extent, and great fertility.

The soil of this vale is singularly uniform. Whether on the north—or on the south—side of the river, a light colored clayey loam, of considerable tenacity prevails :—differing, however, in degrees of fertility. Cleveland being situated at the feet of very high and steep cliffs, and these standing to the southward of it, may tend to render its lands in general of a cooler nature, than those which lie on the north side of the river.

The NORTHERN SEA-COAST of Yorkshire is noticeable, only, as occupying a small space in the county which does not properly fall within any of its larger districts. It forms an irregular scroll, which runs between the eastern morelands and the sea.

It may be said to extend from Gisborough to Scarborough. It is separated from the vale of Stockton, on the north, by the hills that run northeastward from Gisborough ; its southern extremity terminating in a narrow point, which unites with the eastern extreme of the vale of Pickering. Its width is most irregular. The lower stages of the morelands reach, in some places, to near the sea.

In the environs of Whitby, there is a rich and interesting, but small, plot of country ; being formed by a dilation of the valley of the Eske. But the more honorable distinguishments, of this mountain-skirt district, are the ports of Whitby and Scarborough ;

borough ; and the manufactories of English allum ;
which, I believe, are peculiar to it.

The EASTERN MORELANDS. These, as has been
noticed, are bounded, on the west, by the vale of
York ; on the east, by the sea-coast district ; on the
north, by the vale of Stockton ; on the south, by the
limestone lands of East Yorkshire.

Their extent, including the cultivated vallies, by
which they are deeply indented, may be estimated at
four or five hundred square miles.

The elevation, of this minor mass of English mountain, is inferior to that of the western division of the
Yorkshire morelands. The surface, also, is tamer ;
and the soil of a meaner quality. In natural economy,
it resembles the morelands of Northumberland and
Durham, rather than those of West Yorkshire.

The soil or covering, of the hills, is mostly the black
vegetable mold of heaths ; and the prevailing subsoil,
a yellow grout : namely, a mixture of infertile clay,
sand and gravel *

The LIMESTONE LANDS of EAST YORKSHIRE.—
These lands, collectively, afford a remarkable passage,
in the geology, or natural economy, of England.
They form a narrow line of uplands, stretching, westward,

---

* Hence, the fortuitous *roads*, which cross this mountain tract,
and off which the black mold has been worn, or washed away,
take a *yellow* appearance ; so as to be seen at a great distance.
And hence, probably, the ancient name of the whole, or a considerable part, of those hills : namely, BLAKE-WAY MOOR :—a term
which has probably been corrupted by writers unacquainted with
the provincial language of the country, into *Blackamoor;* as
" Helmsley Blackamoor." The principal coal pitts, in the western
quarter of these morelands, are called "Blaikah Pitts," and a
house, near them, " Blaikah House :" while a conical hill, in the
eastern quarter, still retains the name of " Blaikah Toppin :"—
these being the most apt, and almost inevitable, contractions of
Blakeway Pitts, Blakeway House, Blakeway Topping. Blakeway
(as Redway and Greenway) is still in use as a sirname.

ward, from near Scarborough, along the feet of the morelands, to the Hambledon hills, which form part of the eastern banks of the vale of York ; there bending, southward, to the extremity of those hills :—where the line returns, eastward, along the Howardian hills, to Malton :—thus forming a bending chain of limestone heights, sixty miles in length; yet, in many places, not more, perhaps, than a mile in width.

The surface of these uplands, especially that of the line first mentioned, is greatly varied, by the channels of the brooks, and minor rivers, which rise in the morelands, and pass through steepsided narrow vallies; formed, as it were, to let them pass into the vale, below.

The soils resemble those of other limestone heights. The lower parts deep and productive—the higher, thinner and less fertile. In general, free-working calcareous loam.

The limestone rocks, of which these hills are in great part composed, are of different textures. Those which rise at the feet of the morelands, are chiefly of a strong firm nature ; consisting of shells and small granules intimately combined ; but of a rough, *stonelike* texture ; as if the masses had undergone a slight degree of chrystalization. In some places, the chrystalizing process appears to have made much greater progress (or—according to the theory of Professor Hutton, and Sir James Hall,—the masses may have enjoyed a warmer embrace); the rocks, there, having acquired a more *marble-like* appearance. But, on the Howardian hills (as far as my examinations have gone) the stones are almost wholly granulous; and of a soft loose texture :—resembling the Bath and Kettering stones. In many—perhaps in most—parts, the limestone rests on a free working grit, or sand stone.

The VALE of PICKERING. This natural district is defined with extraordinary accuracy. It is surrounded by by calcarious hills. The limestone heights, just described, form three-fourths of its outline* : the remaining quarter being filled up with the chalk clifs of the wolds.

Those outlines describe an imperfect oval, whose longer diameter is near thirty-five miles, its shorter, more than ten; its contents (including the lower skirts of the limestone hills) near three hundred square miles.

The general surface of the base of this vale is singularly flat, considering its great extent. It shelves gently, however, from its marginal banks, towards its center; where its two rivers, the Rye and the Derwent, *meet*, and, in times of floods, prove its extraordinary levelness. This general flatness, however, is broken by three headlands that shoot into the area, from the marginal banks; and by some insulated swells that rise within it, and give a variety of surface.

The soils of this, as of most other vale districts, are various. The water-formed lands, near the courses of the rivers, in the low flat base of the vale, especially those that have been formed by the Rye, are of an extraordinarily fertile quality :—rich mud banks, raised with the washings of the cultivated and fertile calcareous soils, which nearly surround them. The low lands, in the eastern parts of the vale,—the wide level of marshy lands, on either side of the Derwent,— are less fertile : while the outer area, toward the feet of the hills, is mostly of a highly valuable quality :— sound, deep loam ; equally productive of corn and herbage : and of considerable width; especially in the Pickering quarter of the vale.

I CANNOT

* In Caermarthenshire, a tract of country which is embraced, in a similar manner, by a belt of limestone, abounds in a singular degree with coals. And other symptoms concur in rendering it probable that coals are deposited beneath the area of this vale. See also p. 27, aforegoing.

I CANNOT allow myself to quit the vale of Pickering, before I have exposed a crime, which the North Riding Report has wantonly committed against it. For, notwithstanding the remarkable *entirety* of this natural district, we find it, there, frittered into parcels!—or, what is worse, spoken of *partially*, under the appellations of "Ryedale," and the "East and West Marishes:"—meaning, by the former, the *mudlands*, and, by the latter, the *marshy lands*, of the vale; leaving undescribed, and unnoticed, the upper grounds,—the true vale lands,—by which it is characterized!

Now, "Rydale" is the name of a weapontake, or hundred, which includes, not only the mud banks in the west end of the vale, but a portion of the limestone heights, together with a large portion of the morelands, within its limits! And the "Marishes" are merely the lower outskirts of the parish of Pickering, (whose extensive limits reach to the center of the vale) and of other parishes, situated in the habitable parts of the vale.

Had not the Reporter previously surveyed the county, for a map, or had he not read *my Report* of it, or had he not adopted the other new names which I have given to its several districts, (together with their relative situations in a map of the county) I should have concluded that he was uninformed, as to the facts above stated, or that he had refused to acknowledge every "innovation" with respect to natural districts and their appropriate appellations.

After having experienced the facilities that arose from the terms—*Western Morelands—Vale of York—Eastern Morelands—Howardian Hills*—(all of them names that had no existence before the Rural Economy of Yorkshire was written*) one would reasonably have

* Previously to that time, the grouse-shooters of the vale of York might speak of the "East Moors," and the "West Moors," as objects

have expected some intimations of gratitude for that
of the *vale of Pickering*. Why did not the Board's
Reporter, in speaking of the two first named districts,
introduce the appellations—"Hang East" and "Hang
West"—(other names of weapontakes) or, in ham-
mering out a partial account of the third, talk of
"Blackamoor"—"Kemp-Swidden"—"Wheeldale"
and "Shunnorhow ;"—as well as of their equals in
propriety—"Ryedale" and the "East and West
Marishes?"

If the *Reporter*, in friendship, or gratitude, gave
way to the childish jealousies of the minor gentlemen
of the west end of the vale*, surely the *Board*, or
whoever had the charge of editing the Report, ought
to have rectified the impropriety.

To resolve an extent of country, into natural districts—with any degree of success—requires much
time, and travelling in the *country ;* as well as a maturity

objects of diversion ; but *Eastern Morelands*, and *Western Morelands*,
as terms of science, were never before used. Nor was *the vale of
York*. Some portion of the upper part of it was formerly known
by the name of "the vale of Mowbray." But the natural district, described aforegoing, had no general appellation assigned it,
had probably never been *seen*, much less defined, before that time.

* Whose mud banks, probably, had not yet shown their heads,
when the district of Pickering was of royal distinction. The
forest laws of England, are principally formed from decisions
recorded in the courts of the forest of Pickering.—MANWOOD,—
Author of "a Treatise and Discourse of the Lawes of the Forrest;"
printed in black letter, in 1598,—says, "whosoever will be learned
in the forrest lawes must diligently studie the assises of the forrest
of Pickring and Lancaster : in which assises there are plentiful
examples and presidents of matters alredie adjudged and tried, yea
almost for every matter that can be spoken of or come in question
touching forrestes. And therefore the assises or iters of Pickring
and Lancaster are, as it were, the bookes of yeeres and termes,
unto the forrest lawes, even as the bookes of yeeres and termes,
that are printed, are unto those that studie the common lawes of
this realme." (p. 16.) The said examples and presidents being
principally taken from the assises of the forest of Pickering.

rity of study and discrimination. Allowing that the
Board had no fit means, within themselves,—*in town,*
—to execute so difficult yet valuable an undertaking,
could it be right, in a public institution, ostensibly set
on foot to throw light on the rural science, to be instrumental in frustrating the endeavors of an individual, in performing so arduous a task?

But leaving these matters to the reflection of those
whom they properly concern, I will here beg leave to
express my gratification, on finding, in the writings
of another, the advantages which arise from giving
due discrimination, and names, to natural districts.
There is a distinctness, and a degree of intelligibleness, in most parts of the North Riding Report, which
are not observable—cannot take place—where large
tracts of country, comprizing districts of dissimilar
natures, are spoken of, in a general way, without
accuracy of discrimination. If, therefore, in going
through the North Riding Report, I should find
occasion to make extracts relating to the vale of
Pickering, *generally,* I shall use its proper name; instead of the jargon of the Report :—if, *partially,* under
the name of "Ryedale," or the "East and West
Marishes," I will substitute for the former, the *mudland quarter,* and for the latter, the *marshland quarter*
of the VALE of PICKERING*

* For a sketch of the vale of Pickering and its adjacent hills, see
the RURAL ECONOMY of YORKSHIRE. Also a sketch of the county :
in which the singularity of its situation more distinctly appears.
Also the sketch affixed to this volume.

"GENERAL

"GENERAL VIEW

OF THE

AGRICULTURE

OF THE

NORTH RIDING OF YORKSHIRE.

DRAWN UP FOR THE CONSIDERATION OF

THE BOARD OF AGRICULTURE AND INTERNAL
IMPROVEMENT.

By JOHN TUKE,

LAND-SURVEYOR.

1800."

OF the QUALIFICATIONS of the REPORTER, in this case, I cannot speak from personal acquaintance. Mr. TUKE, I understand, is not only a land surveyor, but an estate agent, of some considerable practice:—facts to which his Report bears witness. But so far, and no farther, Mr. T's practical knowledge of rural affairs appears to extend. His remarks on Agriculture are those of a man who is conversant with the practice of others, rather than of one who speaks from his own matured experience. His manner of writing is well adapted to the business of Report; to which a land surveyor is professionally habituated. And although Mr. Tuke is said to be a Quaker, little of formality, or stifness, is observable in his style.

Mr.

Mr. T's MODE of SURVEY is not expressed.
Having previously surveyed the county, for a map of
it, he thereby of course acquired a comprehensive
idea of its natural economy; and some evidences
appear, in the course of the work, of his having made
further examinations, as a Reporter. Beside, in the
ordinary pursuits of his profession, his acquaintance
with the district assigned him would necessarily be
considerable; especially with that of the vale of
York, in which Mr. Tuke resides. His Introduction
is dated at " Lingcroft near York."

The CONTRIBUTORS, which *appear* in this reprinted Report, are chiefly ANNOTATORS; who
though not so numerous, as in the West Riding,
exceed in number those of any other of the foregoing
Reports :—a circumstance that shows the attention
which is paid to rural concerns, in this county.

Mr. CLEAVER of Nunnington, in the vale of
Pickering, may claim a preference, whether for the
number or the intelligence of his notes. Mr. C. possesses extensive practical knowledge; both of estate
agency and of agriculture.

The next that claim attention are the long and
labored notes, signed W. S.—in which we find much
ingenuity, and some information. But they savor too
much of the closet. They are evidently the effusions
of a studious mind,—the remarks of a man of reading,—rather than of one possessing much practical
knowledge.

Mr. STEELE, and Mr. SMELLIE also have furnished
numerous remarks; together with several other persons, whom I may have occasion to mention, in examining the volume under Review.

In his Introduction, Mr. Tuke says—" It is here
proper to remark, that free use has been made of the
Rural Economy of Yorkshire, the Survey of my pre-
decessor MARSHALL, but never without acknowledgment, by marking what has been taken from that
work, as quotations." The latter part of this notice,

it

it may be proper to mention, is not quite accurate. There are some unmarked instances, in which my book has evidently been made use of, but, perhaps, inadvertently. The marked quotations I consider as a compliment paid to it. And I trust that Mr. T. and others, the Board's Reporters, will view the quotations which I may occasionally make from their works, in the same light.

SUBJECT THE FIRST.

NATURAL ECONOMY.

ON this subject, the North Riding Report furnishes many materials: some of them claiming notice, here.

EXTENT. The Reporter has given a sort of table of the extents of the several natural districts of the North Riding,—*after* the rural economy of Yorkshire: and distinguished each with the name by which it is " usually known" !—But it is so loaded with error and ingratitude, that I suffer it to sink, with the weight of its sins, into the darksome shade of oblivion.

ELEVATION. In a note, signed W. S. we have an interesting account of the effect of elevation, on cultivated grains.

N. p. 4.—" The highest of these hills" (the eastern morelands) " is about 1444 feet above the level of the tide, an altitude which between latitudes 54° and 55° is greatly above that in which grain of any kind will ripen. I have frequently observed on these hills, that where grain is sown at an elevation of about 600 feet, the crop becomes extremely uncertain; that may be reckoned the greatest height at which wheat will grow, with any chance of repaying the husbandman

bandman for his labor, and there the grain will prove very light, and about a month later in ripening than if sown at the foot of the hills; between that and 800 feet may be reckoned the maximum of elevation for any other grain: between 600 and 800 feet, in backward seasons the produce will be little worth, and sometimes not approach maturity; and in other seasons it may be late in October before the ground may be cleared; and frequently before that period, heavy showers of snow will have fallen, and sometimes while the crop may be still standing, such showers the people who inhabit the dales of these morelands always expect, and in their expectations are rarely deceived, during harvest. But in speaking of these heights, we must not look for mathematical accuracy; aspect and soil will make considerable difference, for which allowances must be made; a sheltered, warm situation may hasten vegetation, and bring a crop to proper maturity at an height greater than the above; or a warm, dry soil, may have the same effect."

CLIMATURE. The subjoined account of the climate of the North Riding is too amusing to be thrown aside among the refuse of the Board's Reports.

P. 5.—" The general character of the climate of the North Riding, like that of all the counties bordering upon the German Ocean, is that of dryness throughout the year, and of peculiar coldness during the first half of it, when the prevailing winds are from the eastern points of the compass; they set in with the regularity of a monsoon about the end of February or beginning of March, and continue with almost uninterrupted drought, and uniform severity till the middle of May, and frequently later; about that time, however, their violence begins to abate, the west winds then entering into conflict with them, but not entirely prevailing over them, till the near approach of July. About the middle of May the west winds will blow for an hour or two in the morning,

ing, to be mastered at that time by the superior powers of the east; in about a month the east wind will only be perceptible for an hour or two in the afternoon, and will then, perhaps, not penetrate the country above twenty or thirty miles; soon after which time it gives way to the more powerful current of the west. The conflict of these two winds is remarkably uniform; their point of contact may be often perceived, and is usually attended with a few drops of rain; during this conflict, and for some time afterwards, while the wind on the surface of the ground is blowing from the west, an opposite current may usually be observed aloft, passing with considerable velocity; to this current in the upper regions, may probably be attributed the almost constant rains that fall on the Western Morelands; the clouds from the Atlantic pushed forward by the westerly winds, which prevail as uniformly throughout the year on the western coast of this island, as the opposite winds prevail on the opposite coast during a great part of it, are there stopped in their course by the powerful resistance of the easterly winds, as well as by the mountains that arrest their progress, and there fall in almost unceasing rains. These easterly winds during the months of March, April, and May, are usually attended by a bright sun in the day time, with sharp frosts during the night, and frequent showers of snow and sleet: the united effects of such contrariety of weather is to parch the surface of the ground, to scorch the tender vegetation of the season, and almost totally to arrest its progress; frosts sometimes occur even in June, cut off that which is farther advanced, and greatly injure the crops: till June vegetation lingers in its progress in the district under survey, unless in sheltered situations, or under other favorable circumstances."

Such a " particular account" of the climate of a newly discovered island, in the southern hemisphere, might read well enough. But when related of any
part

part of England, whose climate is proverbially most uncertain, it is the less credible. Nevertheless, it may serve to convey some *general ideas*, concerning the climature of the North Riding of Yorkshire:— which, however, it is proper to remark here, is not, nor ever was I believe, *quite* so distressing to the husbandman, as we find it represented, above :—though it is allowed to be less rigorous, now, than it was formerly. A moderately backward spring is generally favorable to English agriculture.

But notwithstanding the above cited passage is extracted from the text, or body of the work, I cannot give the ostensible Reporter credit, either for the matter or the manner of it. It is evidently the production of a man of leisure. Mr. Tuke says, in his Introduction, (p. viii.)—" much of the information received" (by circulating the original Report) " has been incorporated with this" (reprinted) " Report." And the above quotation is probably a part of the additional information, so incorporated. It does not appear in the original*.

WATERS.

---

* This spring (1807) would have been sufficient, alone, to have convinced a stranger to the country, that the above relation was altogether imaginary,—merely an ingenious fiction. We have not, speaking with some little latitude, had any easterly winds,— certainly, no severe pinching winds from the east,—even to this time (the close of May). The third week in March, there were two days, and in the last week of April, a few days more, of light winds from that quarter: also, for some days past, the current of air has been from the east; but the weather has been scorching hot! and vegetation unusually rapid! From the North, we have experienced, at different times, severely cold cutting blasts.

My observations have been made at some distance,—namely, about twenty miles,—from the sea coast:—where easterly winds are said to have been, this season, somewhat more prevalent. And it is probable that whoever wrote the account under notice had been accustomed to make his observations near the coast. Applied to the North Riding at large, and to seasons in general, it is unpardonably erroneous, and censurable; as tending to mislead, not usefully to inform, the reader.

WATERS.—P. 24.—" The principal of these is, first, the Ure, which rises near the borders of Westmoreland, and collecting, during it course through the beautifal dale of Wensley, many tributary streams, flows with a very rapid current for many miles within the North Riding. About three miles below Masham, it becomes the boundary of this Riding, dividing it from the West Riding, till it arrives at Ripon; thence it takes a circuit of a few miles into the West Riding, and again becoming the division between the two, so continues as long as it retains its name; this it loses about six miles below Boroughbridge, at the influx of an insignificant stream, that gives to the great river Ure its own name of Ouse, which at last, in its turn, is lost in that of the Humber. The Ouse continues to be the boundary of the North Riding, dividing it from the West Riding, and the Ainsty of the City of York, till its arrival at York, where it entirely quits the North Riding. The Ouse is navigable for vessels of 120 tons as far as York, where the spring tides would rise about twenty inches, if not obstructed by the locks about four miles below, and would be spent about six miles above. The Ure, with the aid of a short canal, is navigable for vessels of about 30 tons as far as Ripon, in the West Riding, where, on account of the rapidity of the stream, all prospect of navigation ceases.

" The Tees rises between the counties of Westmoreland and Durham, beyond the north-west extremity of this Riding, and taking an easterly direction, divides it from the county of Durham through its whole extent, and is navigable for vessels of· thirty tons from the ocean to Yarm, where the spring tides rise seven feet."

SOILS, &c.—P. 9.—" To describe the soils of the extensive *vale of York*, it will be necessary, on account of the great variety of them, and for the sake of accuracy, to traverse the country, and describe the soils in each part.

" The

" The level land near the river Tees consists in general of a rich gravelly loam.

" Upon the high ground on the west side of the road leading from Catterick to Peirse-bridge, the soil is for the most part strong, and generally fertile, but in some places cold and springy : some fine hazel loam is also to be met with.

" On the right of the road leading from Greta-bridge to Catterick, is much fine gravelly soil, with a considerable quantity of clay, and some peat ; and, on the north of Richmond, a mixed loamy soil in most places upon limestone, but in some, upon a freestone most excellent for building.

" On the east side of the road between Catterick and Peirse-bridge, there is some cold thin clay upon what is here called, a moorband*; there is also some gravelly and some clayey loam, part of which is cold and springy.

" About Barton, Melsonby, and Middleton Tyas, the soil is loamy upon limestone. About Halnaby, and from thence in an easterly direction, to the edge of Cleveland, and betwixt the Wiske and the Eastern Morelands, as far south as Borrowby and Thornton-le-moor, the soil for the most part is a cold clay ; though in some places less tenacious soils mixed with considerable quantities of large cobble-stones, or pebbles, of various kinds, are to be met with.

" On the west side of the road betwixt Richmond and Leeming, a good gravelly soil prevails ; towards Hornby, a good gravelly clay ; at Langthorn, a good sandy loam and some peat.

" The land on both sides of the brook which runs from Constable Burton past Bedale, consists for the most part of a rich loam, but in some places intermixed

---

" * This stratum, which is from six inches to a foot thick, is of a ferruginous, ochreous appearance, probably containing much iron, and wherever found is attended with great sterility.—*J. T.*"

termixed with a large quantity of cobble-stones,"
(pebbles) " and coarse gravel.

" The country betwixt the above-mentioned brook
and the West Riding, and on the west side of the
road from Boroughbridge to Leeming, is generally a
turnip soil, though of various qualities, consisting of a
loamy soil upon limestone, a gravelly loam, and a
rich hazel loam; except that in some parts there are
patches of swampy ground, and cold clay land.
That corner of the vale east of Middleton Tyas, and
west of the Wiske, and north of a line drawn from
Scorton to Danby Wiske, is mostly cold and wet,
some of which has a moorband under it; but on the
west side of this tract there is some clayey loam of
pretty good quality, and a little excellent gravelly
loam, which last is chiefly employed as grazing
ground.

" On each bank of the river Swale, and between
that river and the Wiske, and south of Scorton and
Danby Wiske, to the junction of the Ure and Swale,
is a very fertile country; consisting of rich gravelly
loam, and some fine sandy soil, with, in some places,
very good clay soil, of the last of which the country,
for a few miles north of Pickhill, chiefly consists;
nevertheless, there are some patches of cold clay soil,
and also a little peat here and there scattered through
the whole of this part of the district. On the banks
of the Swale are many very rich grazing grounds.

" For a few miles north of Thirsk, there is some
fine rich strong loamy land.

" On the north-west side of Thirsk begins a vein
of sandy soil, which runs betwixt" (near) " the rivers
Swale and Ure until it comes within about ten miles
of York; where leaving the river, it passes York a
few miles to the north, and extends to the river
Derwent; it is in most places four or five miles broad,
and in general leaves only a narrow strip of rich
grazing ground adjoining the rivers Swale and Ure.
About Myton, Brafferton, and Helperby, the sand is
of

of a dark color, and remarkably fertile; but in general this sandy tract is barren and wet, a considerable part of it lying very flat, and on a substratum through which the water cannot drain off. About Shipton and Skelton, fine sandy loam prevails; but on each side of York (south of the sandy tract, and to the boundary of the Riding) is a good strong clay or loamy soil.

" The country between the above-described sandy soil and Hambleton, from Easingwood to Thirsk, is in general a strong retentive clay, in some places full of cobble-stones, with a little good loam upon limestone, some fine sandy soil, and wet springy sand occasionally intermixed. Near the rivulets the soil is in general strong, upon a strong bed of gravel.

" The country betwixt the tract of sandy soil above described and the Howardian hills, is in general level, the soil varying in all degrees from a strong clay to a sand; the clay in some places good, in others poor, thin, and cold: near the Derwent is some fine loamy soil."

P. 16.—" The *Western Morelands* differ materially in their produce from the Eastern Morelands; instead of black ling, we find many of the mountains covered with a fine sweet grass: others with extensive tracts of bent; some produce ling, but it is mostly mixed with a large portion of grass, bent, or rushes. The soil in the lower parts of these moors is a fine loam, in many places rather stiff, upon a hard blue limestone. The bent generally covers a strong soil lying upon grit or freestone rock; the black ling a reddish peat upon a red subsoil, or in many places a loose grit rubble, beneath which is a grit rock.

" Many of the dales which intersect these moors are very fertile, of which Wensleydale may be ranked the foremost, both for extent and fertility; the bottom of it consists of rich grazing grounds, through which the river Ure takes a very serpentine course, forming in many places beautiful cascades. From the bottom of of the valley the hills rise with a moderate slope, though with a very irregular surface, to an amazing height, and are inclosed for a mile or a mile and a half from the river. On the south side of the dale several small dales open into the larger.

" The soil of Wensleydale, on the banks of the river, is generally a rich loamy gravel; on the sides of the hills a good loam, in some places a little stiff, the latter of which upon a limestone is predominant; some clay and peat also occupy a part of them.

" Swaledale is next to Wensleydale in extent, but falls far short of it in beauty, the bottom of it being narrow, and the hills steeper than in Wensleydale, but the soil is in some parts not much inferior in fertility; in the lower parts a rich loam prevails, which is in some places gravelly; on the hill sides a thin loam upon grit, under some places upon limestone; some clay and peat moss are also met with.

" The other dales, though much smaller than those above described, are very similar to them in their soils, and several of those whose streams empty themselves into the river Tees, are very fertile."

FOSSILS.— P. 20.—" A slate somewhat resembling that which is usually called Westmoreland slate, but of a coarser texture, thicker, and of a more purple color, is found in Swaledale; but the use of it does not extend far beyond the place which produces it."

P. 20.—" Marble of various kinds, some much resembling, and others superior, in closeness of texture and distinctness of colours, to that which is worked in Derbyshire, is found in many parts of the calcareous hills of the Western Moreland, but hitherto turned to no other purposes than those of making lime, or repairing the roads; though it is said to have been heretofore raised for other purposes on the banks of the Tees above Romaldkirk*.

P. 21.

" * See Magna Britannia, vol. 6. p. 644."

P. 21. " In the vicinity of the river Greta, and in other places in the north-western extremity of the Riding, large blocks of a light red granite, much resembling that worked up by the antients, is to be found scattered over the face of the country, and in some places also, those of a light grey, but no use is known to have been, or is at this time, made of either.

" Marl is met with in several parts of this Riding, but I do not find that it is at this time made use of, or ever has been, to any considerable extent."

P. 23.—" Gypsum is met with on each side of the river Swale, about Thornton-bridge, lying in veins of several feet in thickness, and in some parts, not more than four feet from the surface of the ground, and that through many hundred acres. It is at present only applied to the use of the plasterers of the neighbourhood, though, were there a demand for it, it lies extremely convenient for conveyance in several directions, and might be procured at a very moderate expense."

P. 18.—"Bilsdale, Brantsdale, and Rosedale," *(Rossdale,)* * "and probably some other of the dales, contain great quantities of iron-stone, though at present no use is made of it; but the vast heaps of iron-slag, and the remains of antient works, prove that much iron must have been made there in former times: nor are the appearances of the hearths where charcoal has been burnt every where scattered over these wooded dales, as well as in some places in the neighbourhood of which wood no longer remains, a less convincing proof that great quantities of charcoal have formerly been demanded in this country, which could have been applied to no other purpose; but at what time these

* Being well designated by an insulated *hill* that rises near its center.

these works have been carried on, no record now remains to shew*."

Minerals. P. 19.—" Veins of copper are supposed to be scattered about in several parts of the Western Morelands and their vicinity; and a search is now making for that metal near Richmond, but with what prospect of profit, is not yet ascertained; ore, however, has already been got there; and some lately (1798) found in a gentleman's garden, very near the bridge in the town, has by an assay, proved to produce about 30 per cent. of metal of a very fine quality.

" A vein of very rich copper ore was worked to great profit for some years at Middleton Tyas, but given up about forty years since, on some supposed disagreement among the proprietors. The clergyman of the parish is said to have received a considerable sum for copper found under the church-yard.

" Upon the Western Moorlands are many lead mines, some of which have been, and others still are, very valuable; coals are also got in various parts of them, but not of better quality than those found in other parts of the Riding."

SUBJECT

" * An inspeximus, dated at York, 26th February, 2d of Edward III. (anno 1328), recites the grant of a meadow in Rosedale, called Baggathwaite, to the nuns of Rosedale, by Robert de Stuteville, which grant bears date at York 16th of August, 11th of John (anno 1209); a confirmation of that grant by Eustachius de Stuteville, excepta tantum modo forgeâ suâ, and also a remission and quit claim of the same Eustachius to the said forge, ita quod eadem forgea penitus amoveatur et nullo hominum unquam reædificetur ad ipsarum monilium danaum seu nocumentum;—Dug. Monast. tom. i. p. 507. Edit. 1655.

" Whence it is evident, that iron has been worked in Rosedale at a very early period; but whether it continued to be wrought in other parts of the dale, on the destruction of this forge, no where appears.—*W. S.*"

SUBJECT THE SECOND.

POLITICAL ECONOMY.

STATE of APPROPRIATION. *Lands unappropriated.* P. 90.—" In the best parts of this Riding, few open or common-fields now remain, nearly the whole having long been inclosed; the moors and mountainous parts still remain in their original state; but such is the spirit for improvement, that were the many obstacles removed that oppose inclosures, no waste lands would long remain neglected, that were capable of cultivation: and even under all the present difficulties, several inclosures, under acts of parliament, have annually taken place. But since this Report was first drawn up, an almost total stop has been put to all improvements, and not more than one or two acts for inclosure in this Riding have been passed in 1797, 1798, and 1799." For the estimated quantity of unappropriated lands, see p. 340, aforegoing.

Mode of Appropriation. P. 201.—" The principal obstacle to the improvement of the moors, is the great expense of obtaining acts of parliament for their inclosure, and the difficulty of settling with the tithe-owners and lords of the manors.

" An instance occurs in a township on the verge of the Eastern Morelands, where two-thirds of the number of freeholders, and considerably more in value, desirous of an inclosure of their commons, amounting to about 800 acres of fine sward land, and about 12,000 acres of high moors, 4000 of which are capable of very great improvement, had agreed with the tithe-owners, and signed a petition to parliament; but the lord of the manor, who possessed very little other property there, being determined to oppose it, the

the business was dropped, from an apprehension of the expense and trouble attending an opposition in parliament.

" An inclosure of open fields, amounting only to about 250 acres, in a township near to the above, was made a few years since; the expense of obtaining the act alone, and without any opposition, cost the proprietors, 370*l**.*"

In a note signed W. SADLER, a detail of an interesting decision, respecting *the rights of stocking common pastures*, is given. The following extracts will sufficiently show the substance of it.—P. 199.—" It has become a prevailing practice, for the occupiers of small farms (some of which occupiers frequently resided in distant townships, and took single fields, which were entitled to common-right) to stock their commons with great numbers of cattle, and without any regard to the smallness of the farms, in respect of which these cattle were turned on.

" This evil of surcharging had increased to an alarming degree, but will now, in a great measure, be crushed, by a late legal decision, of which the following is a statement: At the York Lent Assizes, 1795, an action was tried before judge HEATH and a respectable jury, which had been brought by JOHN BYWELL, who occupied a farm of about 150 acres, entitled to common-right in Thornton Rust, against THOMAS BAINES, who occupied a house and about five acres of land, entitled to common-right in the same township, for surcharging Thornton Rust common."—P. 200.—" The learned judge approved much of the action, and was clear in his opinion, ' that the defence set up was insufficient; that the surcharge had been fully proved; and that comparing the yearly value

---

" * The expense of this act of parliament, viz. 370 *l.* perhaps would have improved the whole of the land inclosed; it would have allowed 1 *l.* 7 *s.* per acre for improvement.—*J. Smeddle.*"

value of each person's farm with the yearly value of all the farms, and then calculating the stock a common would fairly carry, was a proper rule for regulating the common-rights of persons entitled.'—The jury, without hesitation, found a verdict for the plaintiff."

Game Laws.—The Reporter, in speaking of "Obstacles to Improvement," heavily exclaims against the mischiefs committed by city sportsmen; which, however, he probably much over estimates.—P. 334.

—" What I particularly allude to, is the excessive injury done to neighbouring farmers by tradesmen, who, in most considerable towns, keep packs of hounds; and, residing myself in a situation to experience them, I am qualified to speak feelingly upon the subject. Were it possible to form an estimate of the loss suffered in my own neighbourhood, by such trespassers, in breaking down hedges, riding over young wheat, trampling the first year's grass-seeds, damaging the turnips, chacing ewes heavy with lamb, and mixing the several stocks of cattle and sheep, by leaving gates open, and breaking gaps in the fences, he could not state it at less than several hundred pounds a year—and all this for the cruel sport of chacing a hare! This calls for redress; but the agriculturist, as laws and customs at present prevail, has not the means of obtaining it.

" Hares and pheasants, where they abound, are very destructive to the corn in spring, and the turnips in winter; many of the last, being wounded by them, are lost to the farmer, as they rot, unless consumed immediately after receiving the injury.

" To prevent these and other inconveniences, might not the game be made, with advantage to all parties, the property of the occupier of the soil? He now undoubtedly feeds them; and should the owner of the soil wish to reserve a power to hunt, shoot, or course over his estate, he might have it, by its being made
a con-

a condition in the lease or agreement between him and his tenant."

STATE of SOCIETY. *Manufactures.*—P. 313.—
" The linen manufactory in the eastern part of the Riding, and the woollen manufactory" (chiefly of stockings) " in the western part, are, in their present state, rather an advantage to agriculture, without being very prejudicial to the individuals who carry them on, by corrupting their morals, or impairing their health; but instances have already occurred, of serious illnesses having prevailed in some of the cotton-mills;"—recently erected in the North Riding.

LOCAL TAXES. *Poor Rates.* On this subject we meet with some valuable items of information: by whom, does not appear. I do not find them in the original Report. The subjoined extracts contain what is particularly interesting.

P. 50.—" This Riding is favored with various circumstances which ought to operate forcibly in keeping down the expenditure on account of the poor, the most material of which, the general residence of the principal landed proprietors on their estates, and an almost total absence of manufactures, need only be enumerated as adequate to the purpose. Fortunately in this instance, the reasoning appears fully to be borne out by the fact. There is reason to believe that the average of the poor-rates of the Riding are still moderate, compared with those of many other places, notwithstanding a late and great increase brought on by the war; but this addition caused by the war, it is to be hoped will cease, whenever the country is blessed with a return of peace."

P. 52.—" An account of the assessments for the relief of the poor in twenty-two townships in the hundred above referred to," (not named) " in the North Riding of Yorkshire, during thirty-five years, from the year ending April 1758, inclusive, to April 1793; the average being taken in each seven years, extracted from the books of the parish officers of as many townships

ships in the hundred as had books of accounts going
back to the year 1758:

From 1758 inclusive to 1765.	From 1765 to 1772.	From 1772 to 1779.	From 1779 to 1786.	From 1786 to 1793.
L. 176 3 3	L. 214 17 10	L. 338 3 9	L. 449 13 1	L. 627 19 9."

P. 53. " Sum total of the return made by the overseers of the poor of the hundred above referred to, in
the North Riding of the county of York, of the assessments raised for the relief of the poor in their respective townships, in the years 1783, 1784, and 1785, in
pursuance of the act of 26 Geo. III. b. 56.

	Money raised by assessment.	No. of constant poor.	No. of occasional poor.	Expences of journeys and attendance on magistrates.	Expended in entertainments.	Law business, orders, certificates.
1783	L.1202 14 7	188	251	L.21 3 1	L. 7 17 1	L.69 5 7
1784	L.1149 17 10	201	252	L.14 18 3	L. 6 17 1	L.50 1 11
1785	L.1370 8 8	207	240	L.30 5 2	L. 7 15 3	L.88 8 0."

P. 54. " At the period when the above return was
made, (1785) it appeared, that in the above hundred,
the highest rated parish paid under two shillings in the
pound poor-rate, and that five townships had never
yet raised any assessment for the poor, and were entirely exempt from any charge on their account; and
it is a circumstance deserving of much attention,
*that the three market towns in the hundred were much
higher rated than any other parish, and that the rate of
assessment generally increased in proportion to the size
and population of the parish or township; and that the
five townships that had never yet levied a poor-rate, were
among the smallest in the hundred; and also, that the
poor were best attended to, and the least numerous in*
proportion

proportion, in the smallest and least populous townships; strong arguments these, against uniting great districts in the general maintenance of the poor, under the plea of their being better attended to, and maintained at less expence."

Speaking of *Provident Societies,* Mr. Tuke, or some one for him, says, p. 316, "Many of these societies have long been established in the Riding; and their affairs, excepting some few instances of embezzlement, have generally been well conducted. Fifty-one societies have already been enrolled under a late act of parliament; forty-five societies in 1794, three in 1796, and three in 1797; and their number is likely to increase by fresh associations."

The following observations on *free schools* confer, on whomsoever wrote them, very much credit. They appear to have recently found their way into a great assembly. P. 317. "It is an undoubted fact, that of many of these schools (it is believed of a majority of them) in this Riding, *the doors are shut, and the stipends evaporate in the hands of sinecure masters:* the gentry of the Riding are thus put to a great and unnecessary expence and inconvenience, in sending their children to remote schools for their education; and the inferior orders, for whose use these free-schools were more especially founded, suffer an irreparable injury, in being deprived of every means of education. The reign of ignorance in the latter class of society, has been sufficiently long, and the fruits of it have nothing in them commendable: to it may be ascribed much of the licentiousness, and much of the unsettled principles of the times; it is now fitting to counteract these evils, by the practice of an opposite system. Let it be tried what education can do; enable the lower orders to think; place before them the advantages that will arise to themselves, from order, from sobriety, and industry; and having learnt in what their happiness consists, they will not turn their backs upon it."

Tithes.

Tithes.—P. 50. " The greatest part of this Riding is subject to tithes in kind, both rectorial and vicarial; but in many parishes they are compounded for, especially the latter; this mode, however, of provision, fortunately for the clergy and the public, is annually declining, by means of acts for inclosure; while tithes in lay-hands are becoming gradually extinct, by purchases made of the lay-impropriator by the owner of the soil.—Wherever tithes are taken, or liable to be taken in kind, they become the sure cause of strife, frequently of scandal to the church, and of ill-will and hatred to it on the part of those from whom they are exacted; an evil which, in this instance, has a far more extensive range, and a far more injurious tendency, than any dissention between mere individuals, or the lay-impropriator and the occupier of the soil: to the credit, however, of the tithe-owners of this Riding, a rigid mode of exacting them does not generally prevail."

In the chapter, " Obstacles to Improvement," the subject of tithes is re-entered upon, and spoken of, at some length :—calculations being made, to show their operation on the profits of the farmer, to the advantage of the tithe owner. But neither the above extract, nor those strictures, appear in the ORIGINAL REPORT. All that is *there* said of tithes is contained in the following short notice; which, considering Mr. Tuke's *persuasion,* shows his good sense and moderation. O. R. p. 96. " The taking of tithes in kind, or advancing the rent of them as improvements are made, are" (is) " a great obstacle to improvements. Though most of the parishes of this Riding, are liable to tithes in kind, yet there are many which are exempt from them; and where taken in kind, it does not appear that a rigid mode of exacting them is *generally* practised by the tithe owner."

In the reprinted Report, however, this passage is cast afresh, and dilated; until, with the notes upon it, it fills six or seven pages :—whether by Mr. T. or
some

some other hand is not said.   But, from an appending note, signed J. T. the whole, perhaps, is his own. The extracts, subjoined, will show its tendency.

P. 322. " Tithes, by being a tax not only upon the land, but on every exertion of industry or expence laid out in the cultivation of it, operate as a powerful obstacle to improvements in agriculture, and are the cause of much land remaining in a state of unprofitable sward, which, by ploughing, and proper cultivation, might be increased to more than double its present value.   Though in some cases the farmer might, notwithstanding the payment of tythe, improve the land with some profit to himself, yet the reflection that he would, at the same time, increase the interest of the tithe-owner to three or four times its present value, induces him rather to forego his own profit, than thus, at his own expence, increase that of another, with whom, in general, he is not likely to be on the most friendly footing.

" The following calculations will sufficiently shew the oppressive tendency of tithes, and, in the improvement of lands, what a great proportion of the farmer's profit must go to another, who in equity cannot have the least claim to it.

" Suppose a farmer is possessed of ten acres of land, in a state of nature, or nearly so, and of the value of $2s.$ $6d.$ per acre, subject to tithes in kind, which, in the present state of the land, will not be worth more than $3d.$ per acre : this he ploughs out with a view to improvement; the expences and profits of which will be nearly as follows :"

I have already intimated that *complex* calculations, on agricultural subjects, are liable to gross fallacy. The result of those, now under notice, is thus set down.   P. 327. " Thus, it clearly appears, that the farmer's profit for five years, in the improvement and cultivation of ten acres of land subject to tithe in kind, only amounts to $30l.$ $19s.$ $2d.$ while the tithe-owner's profit amounts to $15l.$ $7s.$ $2\frac{1}{4}d.$ and the landlord's lord's rent is only 6*l.* 5*s.* and this where the land is supposed to be already fenced, and not to want draining: if these are necessary, the farmer will for many years be considerably out of pocket, while the tithe-owner will be reaping a profit equal to the above."

PUBLIC WORKS.—*Canals.*—Mr. STEELE, in a well written note (too long to be wholely inserted) impressively recommends a line of inland navigation, between the upper parts of the vale of York, and the collieries of the county of Durham.

I know no instance in which an undertaking of that kind could be set about, with fairer prospects of advantage, to the country, and the undertakers.— Mr. S. truly says, note p. 26, " The prospect of advantages to this country" (the vale of York) " to be derived from such a navigation, far exceeds any thing I am able to describe. Our servants and horses would be beneficially employed at home; less force of both would perform the farming business; and, as observed before, we should have coals of the best quality at a very easy rate. By this conveyance the Durham lead and lime, and Westmoreland blue slate, would pass into this, and adjoining counties, upon moderate terms; and I believe even the city of York, by a junction of the Wiske canal with the Swale, or by some other means, might be supplied with Durham coals at an easier rate than the inhabitants of that city are at present served with that article, and of a quality vastly superior.

" By this navigation, our butter, cheese, and barley, would in return, go up by Darlington and Barnard Castle, into the dales and western country, and there always find a brisk and profitable market. The destruction of our principal roads (some of which, notwithstanding the high tolls, are in an insolvent state), would be prevented, and the public would derive innumerable advantages."—A communication might
thus

thus be easily opened, between the Humber and the Tees.

County Bridges.—P. 304. " Perhaps in no district in the kingdom, of equal extent, are the bridges maintained by the Riding, commonly called county bridges, equally numerous or better attended to ; the nature of the country, covered in great part with lofty mountains, some of them among the most lofty in the island, among which various rivers have their sources, will probably account for both; certainly for their number, and the number probably for the care exerted in their maintenance."—Again, " Their number is supposed to amount to about 130, many of them of great extent, and erected in very danger-ous situations. The Surveyor cannot help pointing out the little circumstance of their being marked with the initials of the Riding (Y. N. R.), in large characters. Where public works are so conducted as to do credit to those who have the direction of them, that credit the directors have a right to receive from the public ; and the public knowing from whom they receive an accommodation, will not fail to acknow-ledge the debt. The mark is moreover highly useful to the magistrates, by pointing out what bridges are under their jurisdiction, and thereby affording the opportunity, through that knowledge, of pointing out any repairs or alterations that may be necessary."

Roads. With this subject the Surveyor is particu-larly conversant. Several of his remarks are worthy of preservation.

P. 296. " The tolls which have hitherto maintained the turnpike-roads, are no longer adequate to their intended purpose, not only on account of the increased price of late universally demanded for labour, but also on account of all that supply of materials being ex-hausted, within a reasonable distance of the roads, which used to be gathered from the surface of the ground, and which was always the cheapest in the

first

first instance, and of the hardest and most durable quality."

P. 297. "The tolls of several of the turnpikes in this Riding have lately been doubled, and all will require a considerable increase when the present acts expire. Few pay an interest upon their debt of 5*l.* per cent.; many of 4*l.* per cent.; and some only 3*l.* per cent.: and it has not occurred to the Surveyor, that the trustees, in any instance, by having paid off their debt, in whole, or in part, have been able to lower the tolls under their direction."

P. 305. "*Guide-posts.*—There appears to have been more attention paid to the fixing of guide-posts in times past, than to keeping them in repair at present: many of them have their arms broken off, or are so defaced as not to be legible, and many more are entirely wanting. Without their assistance, it is very difficult for a stranger to find his way in almost every part of the Riding."

The regulations which permit mail coaches to travel free of tolls does not escape Mr. Tuke's severe censure.

The subjoined remarks on *repairing roads by tenure,* are well entitled to a place, here. P. 298. "In the lower part of the vale of Pickering, the parochial roads are in as bad a state as possible: good materials are scarce in some parts of these districts, but care and attention, much more so in them all. Many of these roads are upon the natural soil, and in winter not passable without great danger and difficulty, if passable at all. No part of England produces worse roads, either turnpike or parochial. This, however, may be in part attributed to many of these roads being repaired by tenure; a system which experience explodes. However adequate it might have been to its ends in former times, when there was little intercourse betwixt place and place, and roads consequently were little frequented or injured, it no longer answers its purpose; and magistrates and passengers
now

now rather suffer a road to become impassable, than compel an individual to repair it, at an expence beyond his means, or amounting to his ruin. This now would be frequently the case; for however extensive the land liable to the repair, might formerly have been, it is, at this time, frequently reduced into a narrow stripe, on each, or at least on one side of the road, perhaps into the little tenement and garth of a cottager. Under these great changes of circumstances, where roads remain liable to repair by prescription, and the individual bound to repair, is unequal to the burden, the law ought to allow some redress; for he cannot perform an impossibility; and it is not desirable that any one should be ruined with performing even what is possible. Without this alteration of the law, many roads will long continue in a state almost impassable." In ordinary cases of this kind, a sum of money paid down, or an annual payment made, to the parish or township, would seem to be the most eligible method of relieving individuals from such disagreeable burdens;—and providing travelable roads for the public.

The following may serve as a valuable hint to the formers of *roads across mountains*. P. 299. "Over the eastern morelands, between Kirby-moorside and Egton, for eleven miles, a road has lately been cut: the earth is taken from the sides of the road, so that the barrel is formed without any of it being thrown upon the crown, but it is laid in heaps on each side of the road, which enables the traveller more easily to trace the line of it during storms of snow, to which this dreary tract is so liable in winter.

" This practice ought to be generally followed upon both the morelands, where snow in winter, and many extensive mosses, render travelling at all times dangerous to such strangers as are under the necessity of traversing them."

SUBJECT THE THIRD.

RURAL ECONOMY.

DIVISION THE FIRST.

LANDED ESTATES; their IMPROVEMENT and MANAGEMENT.

ESTATES and TENURES. *Sizes* of Estates.—P. 28. " The size of estates in this Riding is very variable; about one-third of it is possessed by yeomanry; the remainder of it is divided into estates of various sizes, from 500l. to 17 or 18,000l. per annum; to which last amount a single instance of an estate occurs, though it is thought no other nearly approaches it. Much the largest proportion of the dales of the morelands is in the possession of yeomanry, rarely amounting to 150l. per annum."

Tenures. P. 31.—" The tenure of the country is freehold, with some few instances of copyhold property, and some of leasehold for 1000 or other long term of years, and some instances of leases for three lives, renewable at the fall of every life; these last are chiefly held under the church, or other corporate bodies; are seldom occupied by the lessee, who generally leases the whole estate at the place, but are farmed out again by him to others."

IMPROVING ESTATES.—*Reclaiming Wild Lands.* In the different Reports of the MOUNTAIN DEPARTMENT, it was reasonable to expect that circumstantial accounts of the present state, and the management, of the mountain lands comprised within each county, would have been laid before the public; together with the most successful means of reclaiming them from their wild state. But, hitherto, I have been unable

able to detect much satisfactory evidence, on any one of those three points; excepting what relates to the operation of *sodburning*.

In the Report now under notice, however, many remarks are brought forward, on the general subject of Reclaim :—several of which are deserving of notice.

The first that arrests attention is a paper of Mr. SIMPSON of Saintoft Grange, near Pickering; containing an account of his improvements on a tract of wild lands, situated between the limestone heights and the morelands, of East Yorkshire.

P. 207.—" Entering on the above farm in the year 1787, it was evident that the nature of the mossy herbage, intermixed with patches of ling," (heath) " on even the best of the limestone and sandy soils, indicated paring thin, and burning, as the best husbandry ; so indeed I thought, and so in general acted ; but being a young farmer, and having frequently heard it asserted, ' that to burn soil was to destroy it,' I ploughed out ten acres of the best herbage, and the most free from ling, on the limestone soil, without paring ; I may add, that I had sufficient cause to repent it, for I have not even had one middling crop from it since ; and although laid down with seeds, they have by no means so good an appearance as those sown the same year on similar soils, although I have expended as much lime and manure on this as on any part of the farm.

" It appeared to me likewise, that paring and burning the black moory soil on a good sub-soil, would answer a doubly good purpose ; for by paring tolerably thick and burning, I not only changed the worst and least putrified part of the soil into good ashes, rich in alkaline salts, but, by so doing, I brought the sub-soil within the reach of the plough, and could at pleasure mix it with the remaining black soil, and expose it to the influence of the air.

" I kept

" I kept likewise another object in view, and that was, to begin with a larger proportion of the best and most productive land, and a smaller of the worst, that, by so doing, it might not only pay for its own cultivation and improvement as I proceeded, but that I might get into a better stock of manure."

In giving a detail of his proceedings (which is not sufficiently interesting to be copied at length) Mr. S. says, p. 209,—" One thing in this field deserves remark : about an acre of it, of as good a soil as any of the rest, was not limed; the consequence of which was, that although not perceptible in the turnip crop, it was very much so in the oats, and still more in the grass-seeds; very little white clover was to be seen : and now, although the other parts of the field is a tolerably good herbage, with a few thinly-scattered small branches of ling coming amongst it (owing, I suppose, to its not having been long enough in tillage to destroy all the roots of this hardy plant), *yet* that *part of the field unlimed, is nearly destitute of herbage, and covered with heath.*"

I insert the following remarks of Mr. Simpson, as they may be useful in *agitating* a difficult subject. They are very ingenious.—P. 213.—" The great error into which many, in my recollection, have fallen, in opening out-land for the first time, is the *ploughing out the tough mossy sward without paring and burning**; the consequence is, that for the first four or five years, there is an almost total failure of crop, and, of course, a want of manure for the next succession. This is done under the mistaken idea that, by burning, so much of the soil is almost totally dissipated

----

" * Mr. Simpson's observation perfectly agrees with mine : the best method of making this kind of tilth valuable, is to burn it.— *J. Smeddle.*

" Mr. Simpson is certainly right; paring and burning can never be attended with any bad consequences upon such lands as these. A landlord should never object, under such circumstances.—*W. M.*"

sipated and lost. Now, although we are in want of experiments to make it evident, what greater proportion of vegetable matter is dissipated in suffering combustion with a slow fire, and in contact with earthy matter, than would be dissipated in the same undergoing putrefaction; yet we know, that as all vegetable soils contain more or less of calcareous earth, in its mild state, the subjecting this to the action of fire, must increase its activity as a manure, by bringing it nearer to the state of quick lime, and that the silecious and argillacious parts of the soil are not dissipated in burning."

The REPORTER, in answering a note, adverse to paring and burning, elicits this apt retort.—N. p. 215. " Anonymous seems to conclude, that if land be pared and burnt, corn must be grown thereon. This is not a necessary consequence. If I am going to improve any of these morelands, the first considerations are, what do I want to obtain ?—Improvement of the land.—By what means can I best obtain that !—By producing the largest quantity of food for sheep.— How is this to be obtained ?—By paring and burning, and the use of lime ; and by those means, a larger crop of either turnips or rape may be obtained, than by lime without paring and burning; and the better crop of turnips that is obtained the first year, the better the second year ; and the better the crops of turnips are, the better will the grass be afterwards.— J. T."

P. 218.—" A very capital improvement was made about twenty years since, under the direction of WILLIAM DINSDALE, on a large tract of the moors betwixt Hawkswell and Richmond ; the soil a black turf earth.

" The ling being first burnt off, the land was ploughed in summer, and cross-ploughed in autumn. In spring following, it was limed, and after one more ploughing, sown with turnips, which were eaten off with sheep : these were succeeded by oats, they, by
                                                        a whole

a whole year's fallow; after which, turnips were again sown, which being eaten with sheep, were succeeded by oats and grass-seeds: this new ley continued to be pastured with sheep for two years, and was then ploughed out again for oats.

" A gold medal of the Society for the Encouragement of Arts, Manufactures, and Commerce, was granted for this improvement; for a more particular account of which, see the Transactions of that Society, vol. ii. 1784.

" Since the above improvement was made, several hundred acres of the same tract of moreland have been inclosed and improved in a similar manner."

Mr. Dinsdale, in a note appending to the above passage, says—" A gentleman of Bowes tried, with good success, a method of improving the pasturage of barren moreland. Impressed with the idea, that the poverty of the soil would not repay the expense of cultivating by the plough, he pared and burnt the ling and bent, and mixed the ashes with an equal quantity of lime; these, spread upon the land, he harrowed sufficiently to be mixed with the soil nearest the surface. Upon the land thus prepared, were sown hay-seeds, clover, rib-grass, &c.; these being again harrowed, the produce was equal to his expectation, and afforded useful and good herbage for some years."

Mr. Tuke's concluding remarks corroborate what I have long been advancing.—P. 219.—" The primary object of the cultivation of these moors should not be corn, but food for sheep; the former might sometimes be taken without disadvantage; but two green crops, exclusive of temporary leys, for two or three years, ought to intervene between each crop of corn. By this mode of culture, and the use of large quantities of lime, the land would be in a constant state of improvement, and would be found much more profitable, than when kept exhausted by repeated crops of corn.

" The

" The stock of the improved lands should be principally sheep, as the growth of winter food for them,
and their consumption of it upon the ground, are the
most certain and expeditious means of improving
them."

In a section entitled " Paring and Burning" we
find another series of observations. And, hacknied
as the subject now begins to be, there are a few particulars worthy of selection.

Mr. CLEAVER's remarks on this subject are valuable. Note, p. 229.—" In regard to paring and
burning, I am of opinion, that nothing contributes
more to the improvement of an estate of maiden-soil,
provided the tenant is not permitted to make too free
in cropping it, for his immediate benefit, beyond its
natural course. I have pared and burnt, upon my
different farms, near 1000 acres, and am persuaded,
that there are not many farms that surpass mine, in
the weight of the corn crops, after this process, which
I have practised near thirty years, though I never
ventured to pare it a second time, as very little ashes
would be produced."—Again,—" I recommend the
sods to be as lightly burnt as possible, and not consumed to red ashes. It is best to spread them as
soon as burnt, otherwise the turnips and corn will
grow in patches, and irregular; besides, if a high
wind should come, it may blow all the ashes away
which are in the heaps, although it would not touch
those upon the ground.

" This happened to me some years ago, upon a
farm I have upon the wolds; in a few hours, the
ashes which were in hills unspread, were blown off
the premises, while those which were spread a few
days before, remained unmolested."

Mr. SMEDDLE's observations, also, are well entitled to a place, here.—N. p. 231.—" In my opinion,
it is particularly necessary to spread the ashes as soon
as the heap is burnt; if this be neglected, the inside
of the heap, from the fire dwelling so long in it,
becomes

becomes a hard, red, and useless brick. If it be not convenient to spread the ashes immediately when burned, the heaps may very easily be opened with a spade, in order to cool the ashes. The fire ought to be built upon a turf hearth, in order to prevent the grass roots from being burned, viz. two or three turfs ought to form a bottom for the stack."

The Reporter, p. 230.—" About the south-east corner of the Howardian hills, if the land be strong, it is pared and burnt as early in spring as the weather will permit, then fallowed and limed for turnips : this is found to be the best mode of managment of that soil." Mr. T. then suggests—" After paring and burning, upon all soils, except where too wet, turnips, or rape, for eatage, ought to be sown the first or second year : and it is the best mode to spread the ashes upon the land after it is ploughed, which may be easily performed, by throwing all the sods from the ridges of the lands, till they are ploughed ; after which, the sods must be removed back upon the ridges, to be there burnt. During the burning, the furrows are ploughed, and then the ashes scattered uniformly over the whole : the additional expense is trifling ; the advantages very great."

Now, this I conceive to be *one* of the instances, in which the Reporter has made use of my register, without due acknowledgment. See YORKSHIRE, vol. i. p. 288. ed. 1796.

I insert the subjoined note, signed H. M. M. VAVASOUR, as containing ingenious suggestions that may lead to improvements, in the process of combustion. I mean not, however, in so doing, to attest the theory on which they chiefly rest.---N. p. 231. " In paring and burning land, it is of great importance that the process be so conducted, as to convert the vegetables into charcoal not into ashes. (?) This may be effected, by burning the turf, as soon as dry enough to keep up a slow fire, from which the air should be excluded as much as possible. Vegetables, when burnt

to

to ashes, are reduced to one-twentieth of their original bulk : these ashes consist of unearthy substance, and fixed vegetable alkali. When vegetables are converted into charcoal, they are little, if at all, reduced in bulk. Charcoal consists chiefly of carbone : this substance enters largely into the composition of all plants, and when used as a manure, has been found, by some recent experiments, to possess a highly fertilizing quality." (?)

EXECUTIVE MANAGEMENT OF ESTATES. — *Proprietors.* P. 28.—" Fortunately for the district under survey, the greatest part of the gentlemen of property reside constantly on their estates, and the rest during the greatest part of the year ; many of these occupy considerable tracts of land, are skilful in the management of it, and attentive to introducing the improved practices of other countries, and liberal in the communication of the knowledge of them.

" Perhaps few parts of England can boast of a greater number of gentlemen's seats than such parts of this Riding as are calculated for comfortable residence, nor a more general residence in them. The proprietors of many of these derive their estates from a long line of ancestors settled in this country : the names of BELLASYSE, CAYLEY, CHALONER, CHOLMELEY, CONYERS, CRAYTHORNE, DALTON, DANBY, FAIRFAX, FRANKLAND, GRAHAM, HOTHAM, MAULEVERER, METCALFE, MEYNELL, PERCY, SCROOPE, STAPYLTON, STRANGEWAYS, STRICKLAND, TANCRED, WHARTON, WYVILL, and perhaps some others, are those of persons still proprietors of lands here, all of whom may be traced back as land owners, many of them owners of the estates they still possess, during several centuries, and some of them from a very early period of our history. The good effects of this general residence, is every where visible in the improved state of the country, in the advancement of agriculture, the repair of the roads, the regular administration of justice, the good order, the comfort, and general

general happiness of the people, and prosperity of the country; some estates might be named, and large ones too, that in the course of a few years witness an active management, and a state of improvement, hardly to be paralleled. Resident gentlemen generally attend to the improvement and management of their own estates, and no doubt experience the profit arising from such exertions. Other estates, and the estates of gentlemen not conversant with country affairs, must be left to the care of stewards and bailiffs, on whose integrity and knowledge must the profit of the owner, and the welfare and comfort of the tenant, depend. Not more than eight noblemen—the Marquis of CARMARTHEN, Earls FAUCONBERG, GRANTHAM, BEVERLEY, CARLISLE, Lords DUNDAS, MULGRAVE and BOLTON, have residences in this Riding, though many others have estates in it; the cultivation and improvement of these estates, may generally be estimated according to the length of time their proprietors reside on them. Those which are never visited by their owners, but abandoned to the care of a steward, perhaps a law agent, or other person still less acquainted with the management of land, and resident in London, are, as may naturally be expected, specimens of waste, neglect, barbarism, and poverty : fortunately, however, these examples are not numerous.

" It is a common question to ask, whether the number of the yeomanry increases or diminishes; but so far as respects this Riding, there do not appear sufficient data on which to ground an answer; no contested election for the county has taken place for many years, which might in some degree be the means of ascertaining it. In a country like this, which is merely agricultural, I should suspect them to increase, in consequence of large properties having of late years been sold in parcels, and there being but few instances of gentlemen already possessed of considerable estates, making large purchases."

The

The above intelligent account of proprietors, in the North Riding of Yorkshire, does not appear in the original Report:—nor does it bear on its face any evidence of its being the production of the *ostensible* Reporter. It is more in the manner of W. S.—who, in a note upon it, steps out of his way " to rectify a mistake," which, he asserts, I have committed, in the Rural Economy of Yorkshire, when speaking of " an Estate in the Vale of Pickering."

I confess myself infinitely obliged by the trouble W. S. has given himself on my account (whatever might have been his intention) as it affords me a fair opportunity of claiming a right which, I believe, I am entitled to:—namely, that of having, by timely and true representations, given a happy turn to the proceedings then taking place, on the estate alluded to ; and, thereby, of having been the mean of encreasing the happiness of some thousands, and the respectability of an individual, who, as a landed proprietor, had a right to preeminence, in the county in which he resided, and who, by a happy change of conduct, lived and died in peace and good will, with his numerous tenantry. And doubly happy am I to hear, that he has left behind him a successor, who is judiciously treading the middle line, between the over indulgence, and the too great severity (in the outset) of his immediate predecessors.

The following observation of Mr. Steele, on the happy effects of proprietors' residing on their estates, flow from the heart ;—like the other remarks of this benevolent annotator.—N. p. 33. " For a moment let us consider who are the persons to whom the country in general owes its improvements ? They are gentlemen who (according to the usage of good old times), have the sense and virtue to reside the greatest part of their time in the country upon their estates, chearing the inhabitants with their hospitality, and with the expenditure of most of their annual income amongst them ; and the middle class of men, who

who occupy their own property, and being acquainted with the wants of the country, by their exertions, and patient labors, are continually adding to its beauty and improvement.

" Alas ! in how different a light do we behold too many of the absent great; their persons, nay even names, are very frequently not known upon their extensive estates, which in general are not half cultivated. These great men have nothing of the interest or command upon their own property, that their agents or bailiffs, nay, that the leading farmer of the village is in possession of."

Tenancy.—In the North Riding—as in the West Riding—Report, we meet with numerous remarks, on this subject of controversy—bordering on animosity—among Reporters and Annotators.

The Reporter,—p. *55.*—" In this Riding very few leases are granted, especially by the owners of large estates, or by long established families, the occupiers of the soil being what are usually called *tenants at will,* holding their property by lease for a year; and notwithstanding the supposed precariousness of this tenure, few parts of England can produce a tenantry, who, and whose ancestry, have lived an equal number of years uninterruptedly on their farms; this, however, I do not apprehend in general to be a favorable circumstance for the interests of agriculture, such men, as I have before remarked, not being in general the most enterprising cultivators; but it has a tendency to shew, that permanency of occupation, one of the greatest sources of happiness to the farmer, is not confined to leases alone. Experience nevertheless teaches us, that under some landlords, especially those in straitened circumstances, instances of which must be met with in every country, or where considerable improvements are to be made at the expence of the tenants, it is more advisable to be under greater certainty, though attended with greater rent."

Mr.

Mr. Steele's sentiments, on this subject, will be seen in the following extracts from his notes, in pages 55 and 56.—"To be sure, leases may sometimes induce tenants to advance a few steps towards trifling improvements, principally to answer their own convenience; but that they do not on the whole further the general weal of the country, is my firm opinion; and on my side, I think I have at this day a majority of sensible and disinterested men."—"Leases are sometimes obtained by covert ways and specious pretences; perhaps to answer the views of a wealthy designing steward, whose chief intentions we frequently perceive, are how to obtain and tie up large portions of his unwary lord's estate, to the advancement of himself and friends."---"If the great would wish to improve their large estates, let them above all things endeavour to appoint a land-steward or bailiff of diligence, disinterested integrity, and skill in country business; they may then have the satisfaction of seeing their estates prosper, and avoid the inconvenience of leases."

W. S. in a voluminous note, has taken ample room to prove himself a decided antilease'an. He coincides with Mr. Steele in the idea of leases being the creatures of land stewards, or their superior agents. N. p. 59.—"From observations I have made, it is evident that it is stewards who cry down tenure" (tenancy) "at will, and so highly extol long leases; they have a personal interest in the question; it is their business to extort the greatest possible rent for their employer, and their interest to do it with the least possible trouble to themselves: the influence of good-will and friendship is nothing to them; the comfort of the tenantry occupies little of their thoughts; they live an hundred miles off, or more perhaps; they hear no complaints; they visit not the estates except on a rent-day, and even then, if they be *great men, visit it by a deputy*, who has still less interest in it, or about it. Besides, long leases are favorable to, and en-
corage

corage large occupations: a numerous tenantry is troublesome to stewards; but one great occupier of an estate can easily, through a banker, remit one large draft for his rent, which may save a steward a long journey: this is a strong recommendation. The favorable opinion of long leases which is held by land-stewards, is strongly evinced by looking over the original surveys laid before the Board of Agriculture: where the surveyor is of that description, we seldom fail to witness a pretty warm attack made on tenantry at will, and as warm a panegyric on long leases. In general, the southern surveyors condemn this tenure, who know little of it, except the trouble they experience in receiving northern rents; while it meets with praise from the northern surveyors, who are well acquainted with it."—The West Riding Report must surely have escaped W. S.'s notice. The Reporter is from the northward,—and, pretty evidently, no land steward!—Nevertheless, there may be some truth in W. S's remarks. But, in this, as in other instances, he has *imagined* too much.

In combating the objections of leaseans to annual tenancy, W. S. says—N. p. 57.—" Another argument against this tenure is, that the tenantry must be uneasy under a liability to continual raisement of their rents, and a too frequent practice of it; but this keeps pace with the change, and no greater excess of it prevails than of the former; a much longer term runs than fourteen years on an average, between one raisement and another; an estate is seldom raised more than once in the life-time of the owner, and many landlords make it a principle never to raise a tenant to whom they have let a farm; and some even make an agreement to the purpose, as long as such tenant shall conduct himself as becomes a man and a farmer." These, I fear, are the obsolete rules of the old school. W. S. I believe, knows that the tenants, of one estate at least, in the vale of Pickering, were raised twice or thrice, in half a life time; and the
estate

estate being afterwards sold, many of its tenants were scattered abroad, like chaff before the wind.

In setting forth the many advantages that arise from tenancy at will, W. S. elicits the luminous doctrine, which follows, and with which I close my extracts from his extended note;—p. 58.—" There is another, and far more valuable character which this tenure possesses, which is entirely overlooked—its moral and political tendency is disregarded, or unknown; the tendency it has to make good neighbours, and orderly, virtuous citizens. In no country does there subsist between landlord and tenant, a more friendly intercourse, or more frequent exchange of good offices; this tenure operates like the marriage tie in countries where divorces are obtained with the greatest facility, because, being easily obtained, the good sense of the parties teaches them to bear and forbear, to correct their own faults, and to be lenient towards those of their partners; to live in mutual accommodation, not in mutual opposition; where such is the practice, divorces are never applied for: so it is here with the landlord and tenant; the tenant will not conduct himself in an unbecoming manner, because the consequence would be the loss of a good farm, and a good landlord; the landlord, for still stronger reasons, will not be guilty of vexation or oppression, because his character being forfeited, he would be unable to procure other tenants, than the outcasts from the estates of other people, to the certain ruin of his own;—can there be greater ties upon the conduct of both landlord and tenant? and such ties universally prevail with tenure at will, and are most powerful."

On deliberately weighing the substance of what has been collected from the Reports, of the West and North Ridings, we perceive the arguments of leaseans, and antileaseans, balancing each other; the TRIENNIAL TENANCY being, to my perception at least, supported, in equipoize, between them. And let us
indulge

indulge the hope that, at a time not far distant, it will become the only tie between landlord and tenant; even as matrimony is between husband and wife. For, as I have elsewhere intimated, misunderstandings, which, in six or twelve months, might produce a separation, will, in three years, generally be forgotten, and good harmony be reestablished. It can, therefore, scarsely fail to become, among men of fair character, a perpetual bond:—binding not only individuals, but generations of proprietors and tenants, in lax yet permanent union;—being, in the light kindly held up by W. S. infinitely preferable to " Tenure at Will."

Covenants.—Respecting repairs, the Reporter gives the following account,—p. 36. " The tenant usually stands to all common repairs; he expects to receive the premises in an habitable condition, and in such he is expected to leave them; but where he wishes for considerable repairs or additions to be made during his tenancy, it is not unusual to agree, to stand to a certain proportion of the expenses, an half or third; this is an excellent condition, inasmuch as the tenant being a partaker in the expense, will see that due economy is attended to, and that workmen employed by the day, do not mis-spend their time, when the landlord might not have the power of superintending them himself. Tenants are of course at all times willing to perform whatever carriage-work may be required for repairs; by taking leisure opportunities, they can do it at little or no expense."

In regard to *restrictions*, the Reporters of the West and the North Ridings are in direct opposition. The latter, in proposing " Means of Improvement," goes so far as to form " Scales of Cultivation;"—to show the tenant the road, to improvement. These scales of husbandry, or cultivation, are tables of the succession of crops, which the tenant is to covenant to observe ; one of them being held out as proper for " light"—another for " heavy—soils." These tables, however,

however, only serve to convey, to my mind, that whoever formed them was but a tyro in husbandry. Nevertheless, the reply made to a note of Mr. Smeddle,—in which he says, " a scale of husbandry would check agricultural improvements," — shows that the maker of it was not equally deficient in practical knowledge, as a land steward.—N. p. 339.— " Has not a landlord an equal right with a tenant to expect his property to be secured? Certainly he has; but if he lets his estate to tenants without restrictions, he commits his property to their prudence and honesty: every man of agricultural experience will allow, that the fee-simple value of landed-property may be greatly depreciated by the avarice or injudicious management of its occupier. In the course of my practice, I have seen frequent instances of this kind, and of the landlord's being under the necessity of taking a farm into his own occupation for a few years, to restore it to a proper state of cultivation and fertility. This is always attended with a great expense. How then can an impartial man think that it is wrong for an owner of an estate to lay his tenant under resrictions, when he has suffered so largely by the preceding one? I cannot see the impropriety, as the tenant makes one half of the bargain, and they mutually agree on a general principle of cultivation for a certain number of years.—*J. T.*"

Rent.—On this subject, Mr. Tuke's statement, I take for granted, may be admitted as good evidence. P. 49.—" The average rent of farms of pretty good soil, is from 15 to 21 shillings per acre, in which there may be land rated at from five to 35 shillings per acre: so that the average value of a farm will vary according to its proportion of good and bad land. Some farms of the latter kind may be lett as low as five shillings per acre, and some lett, cheaper at 30*s.*; so great is the inequality of the soil, that nothing accurate on this head can be stated. Near large towns, land for convenience in small parcels, and in the

the aggregate to no great amount, is lett at 3*l*. or 4*l*. per acre."

On the *choice of tenants*, Mr. Smeddle makes the following short, but pertinent, remark.—N. p. 331. " It is singular in the highest degree, that gentlemen do not enquire into the characters of their tenants. If the character of a domestic servant be necessary, that of a farmer must be more so."

DIVISION THE SECOND.

WOODLANDS.

NATURAL WOODS. The *quantity* of woodland, in the North Riding, is *estimated* at 25,500 acres.

Disposal of Timber. P. 186.—" It is the practice in this Riding to sell the falls of wood to professional wood-buyers, who cut up the trees in the woods, according to the purposes for which they are best calculated, and the most valuable." So far the Reporter is pretty right in his statement. The wood-buyers certainly separate the trees that are fit for ship timber, from those that are proper for " country uses:"—and not unfrequently cut off a crooked top, for the use of the ship or boat builder, from a straight stem, which is fit for the house carpenter. But when he says, p. 187,—" All the ship-timber grown in the Riding, is thus cut up in the woods, into shapes ready for the builder to make use of,"—he is certainly wrong. It is not probable that in any part of the Riding such a practice prevails: it being impossible for the woodman to know exactly the wants of the ship builder; unless the latter were to furnish him with molds. The French are said to have lately pursued such a practice; but I have not seen nor heard of any thing resembling it, in the North Riding of Yorkshire. Nevertheless, in

in a country in which the carriage of timber is sometimes equal to the value of the wood itself, in the
place of its growth, such a practice, it would seem,
might be profitably adopted.

PLANTING.—P. 180. "There are two or three considerable nursery-gardens in this Riding, that raise
large quantities of forest-trees, and shrubs, for the
supply of the public ; the proprietors of which contract to plant on an extensive scale, and at reasonable
prices.

"Plantations of a mixture of forest-trees of two
years old, and planted at about four feet distance, are
made, at from three guineas to 4 *l*. per acre, and of
trees of three years old, at from 5 to 6 *l*. per acre;
and all failures replaced for two years succeeding."

P. 189. "FRANCIS CHOLMELEY (Mr. Cholmeley
of Bransby on the Howardian hills) has found that
the timber of the larch is very durable for every purpose* : he has used it for gate-posts, and has had
some of them taken up after having been in the
ground eleven years, which, he says, were as sound
and perfect as when cut out of the tree.

"The plantations already finished have a pretty
large mixture of firs and other trees ; but the larch
being so much more valuable, thriving so well, and
being of such quick growth, he intends, in future,
chiefly to plant it.

"He estimates his planting to cost him not more
than 50*s*. per acre, at the utmost, as he is in the
practice of raising his own plants in the following
manner :

"The

"* As a proof of the durability of larch, some posts made of
small larch trees, not squaring more than three or four inches, were
set in the ground in the spring of 1779, nearly the whole of which
are still standing (1798), and apparently sound ; a rail made of a
small tree, not more than two inches diameter at the small end, has
been in use from the same period, and has still some of the bark
adhering to it : though all sap, and exposed thus to the air and
weather, it is still perfectly sound.—*W. S.*"

" The beds on which the seeds are to be sown, are
dug in the spring, and the larch cones laid upon their
surface; these the sun and winds drying, cause them
to open, and shed a considerable part of their seed;
and the cones are afterwards beaten to get out the
remainder; they are then covered very slightly with
earth, and kept clean weeded. At first, great care is
necessary to keep the birds from them, otherwise they
will pick off the seed from the head of the plants just
peeping above ground.

" The plants are pricked out at one year old; and
he finds it best to transplant them a second time, and
finally plants them out, at four years old, though those
which have been only once removed, answer to be
planted out at three or four years old; but the roots
are not so good as of those which have been twice
transplanted."

DIVISION THE THIRD.

AGRICULTURE.

FARMS.—*Sizes.* P. 47. " In the northern part of
the vale of York, the rental of farms is usually from
100*l.* to 300*l.* per annum; of very few, perhaps, as
low as 40*l.* and some as high as 600*l.*; but further
to the southward, there is a larger proportion of small
farms, some of which are as small as 20*l.* per annum;
with others as high as 200*l.*"

On *Fences* and *Gates*, the Reporter has filled nine
or ten pages of letter press, and two plates; without
adding one useful idea to the stock of information
already recorded, on those subjects.

Homestalls. Nearly the same may be said in regard to farm buildings and cottages; on which, as on
fences and gates, we find more of theoretic contrivance, than of practical instruction The following
remarks,

remarks, however, will serve to corroborate what I have repeatedly suggested, on this subject.

P. 35. " Little can be said in praise of the arrangements either of the farm-houses or offices throughout this district; the old ones appear as if built without plan or contrivance, patched together at various times, as the circumstances of the occupier might happen to require. Their shapeless and inconvenient form and situation, may be accounted for in the practice which formerly prevailed, of the occupier standing to all repairs, unless, perhaps, the landlord might contribute timber, the produce of the farm : where the tenant was architect, regularity or efficiency of plan could not be looked for; and where he was also to be at the expence of the execution, the landlord had hardly any right to interfere in correcting it. Those of a more recent date, are far more commodious and compact, and the plans are daily improving, though not yet arrived at perfection; much more attention is paid than formerly to external accommodation, and some judicious plans of farm-yards may be met with. Instances, however, are not wanting, where flying from one extreme to its opposite, people have built farm-houses and offices upon a scale far too large for the ground occupied with them : this brings on the owner, in the first instance, unnecessary expence, and induces an habit of extravagance in the tenant, which sometimes has proved ruinous to him. In building farm-houses, one year and three quarters rent was formerly held to be about the sum required for a new and complete erection; but now (1798) a much greater sum will be required, on account of the great advance in the articles in building, in labour, and taxes, though this may vary somewhat, according to circumstances ; but economy ought to be observed, as the owner has a right to reasonable interest for his money expended : beyond this it is too much for the occupier to pay."

And the hay-barns of the western morelands are entitled

entitled to notice.—P. 34. " The western dales are remarkable for their hay-barns, which are situated in the centre of every third or fourth field : those barns have always a cow-house at one end, and frequently at both, where their cattle are wintered : by this arrangement, the hay and manure are not carried any great distance ; an important circumstance in these hilly countries. The barn is of particular use during the time of making hay, in a country where the weather is very uncertain, and attended with sudden, frequent, and violent showers."

Regarding the Reporter's *plans* and *elevations* of farm-yards, houses, and cottages, suffice it to say, that they very much resemble other fancy wares of that sort, with which, one would imagine, the market must, by this time, be overstocked. However, while customers continue to be pleased with *any thing pretty on paper*, it may be right, in professional men and artists, to endeavor to gratify their childish desires.

OCCUPIERS.—P. 48. " In those parts of the North Riding which are best cultivated, the farmers form a very respectable class of society ; they are liberal in their sentiments with respect to their profession ; they do not think, that the science of agriculture has arrived at its ultimate perfection ; they are desirous of making improvements, and are ready to adopt any in which there is a reasonable probability of success ; exceptions, however, are not wanting in the more remote and sequestered parts of the Riding, of those who holding different sentiments, and influenced by different habits, are content to jog on in the way of their forefathers."—Again, " For conduct and character, the farmers under survey must deservedly rank high among their fellows in any part of England, they are generally sober, industrious, and orderly ; most of the younger part of them have enjoyed a proper education, and give a suitable one to their children, who, of both sexes, are brought up in habits of industry and economy : such conduct rarely fails meeting its reward ;

ward ; they who merit, and seek it, obtain independence, and every generation, or part of every generation, may be seen stepping forward to a scale in society somewhat beyond the last ; fortunately, this country is purely agricultural, and the inhabitants, solely cultivators of the earth, are endowed with the virtues of their profession, uncontaminated by the neighbourhood or vices of manufactures."

The subsequent remarks, on the AGRICULTURAL PROFESSION, are fraught with good sense, qualified by judgment ; and doubtlessly result from extensive observation—in the country.

P. 76. " It has long been a prevailing opinion, that the produce of the farm should be equal to three rents ; one for the landlord, one for the expences of cultivation, and another for the farmer. This might have been accurate some thirty or forty years since, when improvements were seldom made ; and the system of three crops and a fallow was almost invariably pursued. It is at this time difficult to form an accurate calculation upon the subject, in consequence of the various improvements in agriculture which are taking place, and the various degrees according to which the disposition and purse of the farmer enable him to pursue them. In consequence of this change of system, as well as the great increase of taxes and wages, the land is cultivated at a much greater expence than formerly, and consequently ought to be much more productive to repay the farmer for his time and his skill, and a reasonable interest for his capital. A well-managed farm, two-thirds of which is arable, should not produce less than five rents, and these rarely leave the farmer much more than one rent, for the present maintenance of, and future provision for his family.

" In general, the farmers in this country are apt to begin upon too small a capital ; they are desirous of taking large farms without possessing the means, a great error, which makes many a one poor upon a
large

large farm, who might acquire property upon one that
was smaller. To say what sum a man ought to possess by the acre, is hardly to be attempted ; it must
depend upon the value of the acre, and the mode of
stocking and cultivation adopted ; it may however be
received as a general principle, that he who lays out
the most upon his farm, will reap the largest return
from it, supposing the money be expended with judgment.—That the profits of farming are not too large,
is evident from the few considerable fortunes that are
made by it.—A man of industry may, in the course
of a long life, acquire a competency according to his
rank in society, and if he can have placed several
children during his life-time in a situation similar to
his own, or be enabled to do it at his death, he may
be said to have done much ; more does not often
occur, while such instances are daily met with in every
other profession in life. Should a farmer make such
a fortune, it is in general in consequence of his
uniting some other profession with his farm ; he is a
land-surveyor, a steward, a corn-factor, or has some
other pursuit ; instances of fortunes acquired by such
an union, may frequently be found ; without it, the
industrious, the orderly, the persevering farmer, the
man peculiarly the pride and boast of England, is
not often enabled to quit the path on which he first
entered."

PLAN of MANAGEMENT.—P. 101. " In the vale
of York, one-third of the ground is in tillage, and two-
thirds in grass. This is the common proportion ; but
where there are extensive open-fields, and in some
places where the soil is light, the proportion of tillage
is larger, and may amount to about one-half. On
the western end of the Howardian hills, and from
thence to Thirsk (being chiefly a dairy country), not
more than one-fourth is in tillage ; on the rest of the
Howardian hills, near one-half.

" The vale of Pickering, and the northern part of
the coast, have about one-third in tillage ; the southern
part

part of the coast about one-fourth ; and Cleveland about one-half.

" In the dales upon the eastern moors, only about one-fifth is in tillage ; and in those upon the western moors much less. In Wensleydale, scarce any land is in tillage, except a little of an inferior quality, which lies near the moors, the humidity of the climate among these hills not admitting of tillage, with any prospect of advantage ; but it is favourable to live-stock, from the abundance of grass which it produces. In the dales further north, rather more corn is grown than in Wensleydale ; but the quantity even there, is very small. The inclosed lands in all those dales are chiefly appropriated to meadow ; the lower and bet-ter parts of the moors are mostly stinted pastures, on which the cattle are kept in summer."—I have copied these statements on the word of the Surveyor ; who has had peculiar opportunities of ascertaining, or sufficiently estimating, matters of this nature.

But is it possible that John Tuke, land-surveyor, and author of a map of a county, can have seriously drawn the ensuing conclusion ? I do not find it in the original Report. I am therefore willing to believe that it has been imagined by a man of less obser-vation.

P. 105. " It is a well known fact, that land which produces a luxuriant crop one year, will generally produce a greater the next year, than land of equal quality, and in an equal state of cultivation, the crop on which, by some casual circumstance in the season, seed, or otherwise, has been injured ; it should there-fore seem, that land is more *fertilized* by a large crop than a poor one." Nearly as well, I conceive, might any other Hiberniarian say, that drawing a large sum of money out of a purse *enriches* it more than a small one. The first grand attack of a fresh farmer is generally the potatoe crop ; which, he finds in the end, so fertilizes his land for wheat, that it is thereby (if not of extraordinary quality) rendered infertile, for

several

several years afterward. That a full shady crop tends to make the soil mellow, and *prone* to produce a succeeding crop, is obviously true; but it is certainly rendered the less *able* to throw out and mature another large crop, by the *exhaustion* which the former has necessarily caused. The disciples of Tull will not thank the writer for his *reflections*.

On the *succession* of *crops* we find the following notice, p. 107. " Some farmers in the northern part of the vale of York, have fallows, wheat, beans, or blendings, or early oats, upon *loamy and gravelly soils ;* but a few, with more judgment, upon those soils grow turnips, barley, clover, wheat, and sometimes white peas, instead of the clover ; *also turnips and barley alternately,* the turnips being always eaten off with sheep, and raised, after the first time, without manure, except sometimes a little lime. Upon such soils, in the neighbourhood of Catterick, turnips succeed clover, in the rotation of barley, clover, turnips, and after the first crop, also without manure, they being eaten on the land with sheep as well as the clover, except that the first crop of the last is sometimes mown : both these courses are practised with good success, as by these means *the manure is spared for the grass land."*

The Reporter is so well satisfied with the " course" —second above-mentioned,—namely, " turnips and barley, alternately," that he appends the following note to it ;—" This is an extraordinary course, and worthy of being observed : by calculation, it appears to be more profitable than any other.—*J. T.*" But he does not inform us how long such a *course* can be *continued.* However, in suggesting " Means of Improvement," he renews his recommendation of the alluring practices, above reported.—P. 341. " To obtain a turnip-crop without dung, is a point extremely desirable throughout the Riding, as it is now done in a considerable degree in the northern part of the vale of York ; for, by this great improvement, the
manure

manure of the farm, which is generally entirely consumed for the turnip-crop, is spared for the grass-
land."

Now, are we to understand, by those several statements, that, not only the turnip crops, but the corn
crops, are produced, and the entire routine of aration
carried on, without "the manure of the farm?"
This were, indeed, a "great improvement." How
it can be effected, I leave for the well practised Reporters of the West Riding to explain.

WORKPEOPLE.—In the section, "Poor," Mr.
Tuke gives a just—though it may be thought somewhat flattering—account of the farm workpeople of
the North Riding.

P. 315. "The labouring classes of both sexes, generally set out in life as servants in husbandry. In
this occupation they are liberally paid, and many are
able to save in a few years, sufficient to enable them
to marry, and start as housekeepers, in possession of
the necessary requisites of their situation. While thus
living and occupied, they learn the habits of industry
and economy in the houses of the farmer; for it has
generally been observed, that no people are better
paid, work harder, or are more economically maintained, than the farming servants of this district. To
these early habits, may much of the future comforts
of this class be fairly attributed; nor ought it to be
forgotten, that to the females a very large share of it
is to be ascribed: their industry is not exceeded by
that of the women of any country; equalled by few:
the dairy is entirely theirs; and no trifling labour
attends it: they perform at least half the harvest
work; they labour at that season with the men, and
many of them as well; they weed the corn; they
make the hay; they mould the fields" (spread the
mole hills and dung); "and perform a multitude of
the lesser occupations of husbandry. For so much
out-of-doors labour, it is not a little money that they
earn, which goes a considerable way in maintaining
the

the family; while the labourer's wife, in many other parts, is only occupied *in drinking tea, perhaps, dashed with gin.* At home, when the weather or season of the year does not permit the labours of the field, the women spin flax, or wool, chiefly for the use of the family. For the men, there is constant employment, and high wages; at this time, more work than hands, and higher wages than are requisite."

On the wages of laborers, Mr. T. has been sufficiently particular. But his list has grown out of date. The rise has, of late years, been excessive. The present wages of the vale of Pickering are,—for day laborers, two shillings and sixpence,—for able indoor servants—fifteen to twenty,—on the Wolds,—twenty to twenty-five pounds,—a year.

WORKING ANIMALS.—P. 253. *" Drawing Oxen.* In the western part of this riding, oxen are rarely worked, but in the eastern morelands, the coast, the vale of Pickering, and the Howardian hills, the practice prevails much ; the cattle of those districts being, from their natural strength and hardihood, arising from the nature of the country in which they are, in general, bred, well adapted to that purpose. They are trained to labor at two, or two and a half years old, and are worked until five or six years old; but a few" (say many) "years since, when the demand for cattle was not so great, it was not uncommon for them to be worked several years longer, even to ten years old."

In the section, *" Horses,"* Mr. Tuke enters into the " comparative *expense* and *profit* of oxen and horses, as used in husbandry;" premising his statements with the following just observations.—P. 278. " The use of oxen, as beasts of draught, in the district under survey, having already been noticed, it remains only to draw a comparison between the expences of each, as accurately as the nature of the subject will admit, where no particular attention

tion has been paid to it, or experiments actually made with that view. Under a system already noticed, adopted by some farmers, of cultivating their farms, in whole or in great degree, with young horses, purchased during their growth, and worked till they arrive at maturity, and then sold, the horse-team will be found to prove the most profitable ; but this mode of management can only be of a limited nature, and therefore can weigh little on either side of the question. To farmers who keep blemished, aged, or any horses meant to be worn out upon the farm, the ox-team will have the advantage, and to the public it will be by far the most beneficial."

The result of those statements is all that requires to be inserted here. And I have the less reliance on this, as the Reporter's experience, relating to the subject, does not fully appear. P. 282. " Thus, four horses, working upon a farm, do not appear to leave as much profit, by this last mode of cultivating it, as five oxen would, by the sum of 19*l.* 5*s.* 6*d.* while the former mode of cultivating it by horses, would leave a profit of four guineas in favor of the horses ; the balance, therefore on the whole, is in favor of the oxen, by the sum of 15*l.* 1*s.* 6*d.*"

IMPLEMENTS.—*Wheel Carriages.* The subjoined remarks, incongruous as they may appear, are just. —P. 79. " It is remarkable, that in these dales, (those of the eastern morelands) *waggons* are generally used, because the country is hilly; but in the dales of the western morelands, and the northern part of the vale of York, carts are used for the same reason— so little has reflection and experiment yet determined."—But in the western dales, single horse carts (mountain carriages) are mostly in use.

In speaking of *thrashing mills,* Mr. Tuke says, p. 82. " With these mills, laborers will undertake to thrash and dress oats at 6d. and wheat at 1s. per quarter, the farmer finding horses."

For

For the *breast draining spade*, see the EAST RIDING,
—Sect. *Implements.*
MANURES.—*Lime.* P. 234. " Lime is in general
use, and, when the land has not been long in ploughing, is found to answer very well on all soils, but in-
comparably well upon land first pared and burnt.
It is seldom laid upon grass-land, except in composts."

The Reporter's opinion, on the *effects* of *lime*, appears to have been too hastily drawn, and is too loosely delivered, to be recorded as authority. That lime
has had its day, or rather let it be said, its hey-day, in
Cleveland, is generally believed. But whether the
effects ascribed to it, namely that of " rendering the
land liable to run to mortar in winter, and to bake
much in summer" (p. 234)—is owing to the immediate action of the *lime*, or to the operation, or the
co-operation, of *tillage* (which lime has enabled the
farmers to continue for a length of years, without sufficient intermission of herbage) may remain to be
proved. Many common field lands, in different parts
of the kingdom, of a quality similar to those of
Cleveland, were liable to the same effect, though they
had never been limed.

Sea Wreck. P. 238. " Sea wreck, or sea weed, is
frequently thrown up by the tide on the coast, after
blowing weather, and is often made use of: when it
has been laid some time in heaps, to ferment, it becomes tender, and being strongly impregnated with
salt, is an excellent manure.

" A few instances have occurred in the vicinity of
the sea, of the use of sea-sand as a manure, and always
with the greatest success; a more valuable manure
can scarcely be devised for the districts of Cleveland
and the coast, where the wet adhesive clays want
draining and breaking, and in most parts of which it
might be easily procured: it is, there, probably not
generally used, because it may at all times be had,
and always for nothing, and is therefore too plentiful
to be valued."

Sheepfold.

Sheepfold.—P. 239. "No manure is procured by folding of sheep; that practice not obtaining in any part of the riding."

WHEAT.—*Smut.* I insert the following information on Mr. Tuke's authority.—P. 111. "A farmer in Devonshire made a very valuable discovery a few years ago, of the means by which this disease is propagated, and of the cure for it, which he proved by experiment at Lingcroft, as well as at several other places, to my full satisfaction. As the remedy is perfectly simple, and the use of arsenic is at all times so dangerous, and so many accidents have happened in consequence of it, it is the more desirable that the practice should be known and adopted; nothing more is required, than that the wheat should be thoroughly washed, and in several waters, if it appear necessary. He proved the effect of it in the following manner : he took a small quanty of wheat of my own growth, not entirely free from the disease, then mixing some powder of the smut with two thirds of it, he divided these again into two parts, one of which he washed clean, after which the three samples were sown in three rows in my garden. The result was, that the row of washed corn was perfectly free from smut; the row of smutted corn not washed, was generally smutty; and that which was sown in its original state, had a few smutted ears in it. I have continued this practice ever since, and have not known it fail. Whatever may be the original cause of the complaint the above experiment proves, that it is continued by some portion of the diseased plant adhering to the seed."

OATS.—P. 127. "Much of the oats intended for bread, are purchased by weight, and a sort of standard fixed, which seems to point out the necessary quality for the purpose, much below which they will not answer for the purpose of making oatmeal. These oats are expected to weigh twenty-four stone to the quarter, and many grown on the mudlands of the

vale

vale of Pickering, and that neighbourhood, weigh considerably more : twenty-four stone in some markets are called a quarter, and if they do not weigh that, so much more in measure must be delivered as will make up that weight."

BEANS.—What follows is contained in a note, signed J. T.—I do not select it, for the neatness or perspicuity of the language, but because it points out a convenient method of getting *drill* beans into the ground *early*, in a moist situation, and a wet season. —N. p. 129. " In the marsh lands below Howden, they have an excellent mode of cultivating beans. Previous to sowing, the land is set out in one bout ridges, causing them to roll into the furrow; they are covered by harrowing the land over; weeds are destroyed whilst the beans are small, by harrowing which, also serves for an earthing of the beans, and the intermediate spaces are afterwards ploughed as there is occasion. This is making beans a perfect fallow crop."

FLAX.—P. 160. " By the records of the North Riding, it appears that the following bounties have been paid for the cultivation of this crop, for the last ten years :

		£.	s.	d.
" In the year 1783	-	112	14	2
1784 and 85	-	57	15	2
1786	-	45	8	0
1787 and 88	-	35	16	0
1789	-	18	1	8
1790	-	43	4	8
1791	-	28	5	6
1792	-	17	9	8
1793	-	25	12	6
1794	-	7	0	2."

These sums I insert on Mr. Tuke's authority.

TEASELS (Dipsacus fullonum) —This is an article of field produce, of which I have had no experience. I therefore thank Mr. T. for the information he has furnished,

furnished, respecting it: especially, as he has given it
in my own way. I register it, here, on his word.

P. 166.—" *Soil, and Preparation.*—Teasles will
only answer upon a strong soil: if the land is fresh,
they do not require much manure: they are frequently
sown upon pared and burnt land, as well as upon land
ploughed out of swarth, and also after a winter and
spring fallow.

" *Seed, and Time of Sowing.*—Sow from one to two
pecks of seed per acre, a little before May-day.

" *Culture whilst growing.*—The surface of the ground,
to the depth of about once inch and a half, is turned
over with spades three times, viz. in June, October, and
about Lady-day, at an expense of about 20s. per acre
each time.

" The plants are set out at about a foot distance,
in the first operation.

" *Harvesting, and preparing for Market.*—They are
fit to reap, in the latter end of August, or beginning
of September: this is done by cutting them off with
about nine inches of stalk, and at the expense of 6s.
per thousand bunches; they are then tied up for 5s.
per thousand; each bunch containing ten teasles.

" *Produce.*—Ten packs per acre is a good crop;
each pack containing 1350 bunches.

" *Price.*—From three to five guineas per pack."

In West Yorkshire, this crop, probably, forms an
ordinary article of culture. The teasel is, even yet,
I believe, essentially instrumental to the woolen cloth
manufacture.

POTATOES.—*Disease* of curled tops.—There is much
plausibility in the following remarks on this disease.—
P. 151.—" The circumstance of this disease being
unknown in America, points out the probability of
its originating in a natural degeneracy, the consequence of long cultivation in a climate uncongenial
to the plant, and the want of attention in not recurring
to the native country for a change of seeds; and this
conjecture is much strengthened by the certain fact,
that

that where potatoes for planting have been procured
of late years from America, no alteration is yet known
to have taken place in them, though cultivated for
ten or fifteen years; they continuing during that time
to be as productive as when first introduced, and not
suffering any perceptible change."

Facts, in point, are fully established in the vale of
Pickering. Facts which probably gave rise to the
above-quoted remarks. The descendants of potatoes
imported from New York, about the year 1783, still
remain free from the curl:—while the other varieties,
cultivated in the vale, are more or less liable to it.
But may not much, or the whole, of this difference
arise from the inherent qualities of these several varieties? The "American potatoes" are of a comparatively austere and *earthy* nature;—are devoid of that
smooth mellow texture, and fine farinaceous quality,
which the modern varieties of England mostly possess; and which may render them acceptible, as a
nidus, to the insect which is the probable efficient
cause of the disease.

Cleaning the Crop.—The following well described
method, of ordering the crop, is entitled to attention.
P. 152.—" As soon as the plants begin to make their
appearance above ground, the ridges are harrowed
down, and are suffered to remain in that state about
a week, when the weeds will again begin to appear;
the ridges are then earthed up, and in a week or two
as much of the earth from the sides of them is
ploughed down, as can be done without leaving the
roots too bare; after this, the tops of the ridges are
carefully hand-hoed, and the earth which was ploughed from the ridges is again ploughed to them; if afterwards weeds should grow, they are again hand-hoed
or weeded, after which, the earth is drawn up to the
top of the ridges. The tops of the potatoes having
by this time got to a considerable size, soon overcome
all weeds, and consequently require no further attention till the time of taking up."

BULBOUS

BULBOUS RAPE.—In a note, p. 342,—*Anonymous* remarks, that, " if ruta-baga, turnip-rooted cabbage, &c. are left on the ground till May, the farmer should have a mode pointed out, of getting his land again into the usual course; preparing it for wheat the succeeding autumn, that is, two fallows running, is what few will submit to, and would also throw a part of a field, all that need be devoted to such a crop, into a different course. Buck-wheat was sown this year (1794) after turnip-rooted cabbage, and it answered well."—Mr. Tuke's reply, to those remarks, are judicious.—N. p. 343.—" Ruta-baga may be pulled and dressed in spring, and laid by to be used as wanted: it may this way be preserved until Midsummer; and the land on which it grew is thereby set at liberty to be cropped; but if this practice is not thought fit to be adopted, and the whole field is wished to be kept in the same state of cultivation, that part which had been cropped with ruta-baga, might be sown with buck-wheat and grass-seeds, or with grass-seeds alone, the remainder of the field which was turnips, being supposed to be sown with oats or barley, and grass-seeds: thus the whole field would be kept in a similar state of cultivation."

CULTIVATED HERBAGE.—*Succession.*—P. 171. " Grass-seeds are chiefly sown, with the intention of the land remaining permanently in grass; and this is often done with the second crop of corn after a fallow, when the land is become foul and exhausted; nevertheless, there are several farmers who sow their grass-seed with the first crop after a fallow or turnips, and a few in the midland quarter of the vale of Pickering, who sow them upon a spring fallow, without corn, upon strong land, and find it answer much better than sowing them with corn. There is a very evident superiority in favor of this practice, when compared with the other.

" The method is, to sow the grass-seed as soon in spring as the land can be made fit; the tops of the weeds

weeds which may grow amongst them, are mown off
twice in the course of summer, and the land rolled
after each mowing; by autumn, if the season has
been tolerably favorable, a rich luxuriant pasture is
produced."

Seed. Mr. Steele's directions, for procuring *natural seeds*, are well conceived.—N. p. 172. "After the
land is thoroughly cleaned from noxious weeds, and
properly encoraged for the reception of the seed,
judgment should be exercised in procuring good and
proper hay-seeds to suit the nature of the land intended to be set down.

"If it is up-land, and free from floods, then procure your grass-seeds from the best old up-land pasture, and not from low meadow, liable to be flooded.
If it consists of ings, or low-land adjoining a river,
then refrain from sowing hay-seeds grown on up-land,
and procure your seeds from good low meadows; for
the seeds of up-land hay will not prosper well on low-
land, nor the hay-seeds of water-land upon ground
not liable to be flooded. This remark is of more importance than the generality of farmers conceive.
Sow about eight bushels of hay-seeds and ten pounds
of white clover-seed to an acre. To procure your
hay-seeds, ride into the neighbouring farms, see
which of them has meadow growing that will suit
your purpose; by which means you may obtain your
desire, which is difficult to be done at the seedsman's
shop, or with hostlers at the public inns."—It is proper to add, however, that if it be right to procure the
seeds of herbage, in this manner, the producing crop
should be *weeded,* once or oftener, while growing,—
the hay, when thoroughly dry, be *thrashed* in the *field,*
—and, when circumstance will allow, the *seeds* be *immediately sown.*

Young Leys.—P. 179.—"The best farmers usually
pasture their new-laid ground the first two years, and
that chiefly with sheep; as sheep improve grass-land
more than any other kind of stock, both by their
treading

treading more lightly and uniformly, and by the dung and urine being more regularly dispersed over the land. But the practice of eating them very bare during the first autumn and winter after sowing, and also mowing them the first summer, is too prevalent. Such practices are the ruin of seeds."

Spring Feedage.—In the section " Fallowing," the Reporter says, N. p. 105,—" I have met with two instances, one in Lincolnshire, and the other near York, of rye-grass being sown with the last crop before a fallow, which was eaten during winter and spring, until near Midsummer, and afforded an abundant supply of food during the time; after which it was ploughed up to be fallowed for wheat : this, where the land is clean, and does not require to be winter ploughed, affords a great relief to the farmer for his stock in the spring, and is very profitable."— And further to show his good opinion of the practice, he brings it forward again (p. 342), as a " means of improvement."—As an *expedient,* it may sometimes be eligible; but certainly not, as a *practice.* If land be clean, it ought not to be summer-fallowed ;—if foul, it should be broken up in autumn, that it may receive the melioration of the atmosphere in every season, and be the more effectually cleansed ;—with the loss of only one year's rent.

GRASS LANDS, or perennial herbage. Seeing the large proportion of the cultivated lands of the Riding, which is found in a state of natural herbage (see p. 471), it were but reasonable to expect a superiority in the management, of such lands, prevalent in the district. Yet I find that, on repeatedly reading, or let me say attentively studying, the Board's Report concerning it,—in order to discover what useful information it might contain,—I have not marked a single line for extraction; and I had, now, nearly left the subject unnoticed ;—important as it is, in the rural affairs of North Yorkshire. Lest, however, my readers should suspect that I have passed carelessly over the North Riding

Riding Report, I will mention what the Reporter says, in opening his chapter on " Grass."

P. 168.—" The principal part of the grass-land in the North Riding, consists of old pasture and meadow, which is chiefly appropriated to the dairy. In most parts of this Riding, the dairy is a principal object of the farmer's attention; it is therefore natural to expect, that where grass is so prominent a feature in the cultivation of the district, that such district would excel in the management and improvement of that particular produce; but the reverse is the case with respect to most of the grazing parts of this Riding, and of the vale of York in particular:"—and, there, it is probable, the Reporter's observations had been more particularly made. He speaks, however, of the practice of the dales of the western morelands, as being exemplary. And I can speak to that of the dales of the eastern morelands, and of the vale of Pickering; as being, in the management of *hay grounds*, on a par with, or superior to—that of the kingdom at large;—always excepting the accurate practice of the hay farmers, near the metropolis; who have no other object to engage their attention.

The Reporter's remarks on the high grass-land ridges of the vale of York (p. 168.) show that he had not duly considered the subject he was writing upon: being led, perhaps, by popular ideas, more than by his own observation and judgement. He had not, probably, at the time he wrote, sufficiently examined into the existing state and management of the cow-grounds, and other old grass lands, of the kingdom at large.

HORSES.—*Breed.*—P. 273.—" YORKSHIRE has long been famed for its breed of horses, and particularly this Riding, in almost every part of which, considerable numbers are still bred; the prevailing species of which, are those adapted to the coach and the saddle.

" In

" In the northern part of the vale of York, the breed has got too light in bone, for the use of the farmers, by the introduction of too much of the racing blood ; but the most valuable horses for the saddle, and some coach-horses, are there bred."

P. 274. " Horses constitute a considerable part of the stock of the high parts of the Western Morelands ; the farmers there, generally keep a few Scotch galloways, which they put to stallions of the country, and produce an hardy and very strong race, in proportion to their size, which are chiefly sold into the manufacturing part of the West Riding and Lancashire to be employed in ordinary purposes."

Cutting Colts.—P. 275. " The colts are usually gelded in the spring following, and in summer, are allowed only an inferior pasture ; the next winter, they make their living in the fields, or in the strawyard, except they are intended to work in the spring, which is frequently expected of those of a strong kind : such are rather better kept as the time of labor draws nigh, and are only put to light and easy work, and generally work only half a day at once.

" Some keep their colts a year longer, before the operation is performed, and find that such become the stronger and handsomer horses. The foal always receives a great check by being weaned, which it does not well recover before it gets the fresh pasture of the following summer. The foals which are gelded at one year old, receive a second check, at the very time they should begin to recover from the first ; whereas, at two years old, they appear to be in the best condition for the operation, and recover at least as well as at one year old, and are much improved by the keeping of the preceding year."

Making up for Sale. P. 276.—" The method practised by the farmers, in making up their two-year old colts for sale in autumn, is to give them good grass, and only take them up about a week before the time of sale, in order to reduce their carcase, improve their coats,

coats, and teach them to lead; they are usually sold
with their full tails, to dealers, who afterwards make
them up more according to art. The first business,
is to draw their corner teeth, in order to make three
and four-year old horses have the mouths of those of
five; they also undergo the operations of docking
and nicking; and after having been kept for two or
three months on mashes made of bran, ground oats,
or boiled corn, they are sold to the London dealers,
who, it is said, sell those three or four-year old horses
as if they were five years old; they are then taken
into immediate work, either for the coach or saddle;
and in a few months, many of them are completely
destroyed by this premature and too severe labor.

" This drawing the teeth, is not a fraud practised
upon the London dealers; they know the deception,
and insist upon its being done by the country dealers.
It is requisite to be done some months before the
London dealers finally sell them for use, or the tooth
which denotes a horse to be five years old, would not
be grown; consequently the deception could not
have taken place."

CATTLE.—*Breed.*—P. 247.—" The breed of cattle
throughout the North Riding, is the short-horned,
except towards the western extremity, where some
small long-horned cattle are to be met with, and also
a mixed breed between the two; the natural consequence of bordering on the West Riding and Westmoreland, the countries of the long-horned breed."—
P. 249.—" The cattle of the Western Morelands are
small; in the lower parts of the dales, they are generally of the short-horned kind; but in the higher
situations, near the moors, and on the borders of the
West Riding and Westmoreland, the long-horned
breed prevails; and in consequence of there being
two breeds in the neighbourhood, it is natural that
there should be a considerable number of a mongrel,
or mixed breed, between the two."

Butter

Butter Dairy. P. 170. —" Many dairy farmers think it of material consequence to preserve some of their old pastures in an unimproved state, as the milk produced on them churns with more ease, and the butter keeps better, than if those lands, naturally rich, were improved to their highest state : some have experienced, after their whole farm has been ploughed up, and the land highly manured, particularly where much lime has been laid upon it, great difficulty, both in making and preserving their butter in the warmer months of the year; whereas, before such cultivation, no such difficulty occurred, and their butter was of the best quality."

Grazing Cattle. P. 259.—" The short-horned cows, in consequence of the great quantity of milk they give, when put to feed," (fatten) " part with their milk with greater difficulty; and it is more apt to return, it is thought, when they improve in condition, than in cows of most other breeds: this, without great attention, and good management, causes a wedged," (swelled) " and frequently a ruptured udder, by which many weeks, perhaps a season, may be lost—no trifling object to the grazier. Many remedies are applied, which it is perfectly unnecessary to detail; that which appears most successful, is to bleed the cow, as soon as a suspicion arises that she is likely to suffer any inconvenience from her milk, and to administer an ounce, or more, of saltpetre dissolved in water, daily, for some time. The penetrating nature of this salt is well understood, and the property it has, of preventing the coagulation of milk, and of separating that which is coagulated. Soon after this salt has been taken, the milk will either disperse of its own accord, or be easily drawn off, in a consistence not thicker than water." I have copied this, as it appears to be a *probable* remedy.

Considering Yorkshire as the original source of the short-horned breed of cattle, in this island, and seeing that its most celebrated variety is propagated, in

part,

part, within the North Riding, the chapter under notice may well be deemed deficient in useful intelligence. But the Reporter seems to have depended on his pencil, rather than his pen:—not, however, so much, in delineating the genuine breed of the country, as in depicting mongrels, and far-travelled strangers!

SHEEP.—*Breed.*—P. 260.—" The sheep of the old stock of the northern part of the vale of York, and of Cleveland, generally called Tees-water sheep, are very large, coarse boned, slow feeders, and the wool dry and harsh : they feed" (fat) " to from thirty to forty pounds per quarter*, at three years old ; and a few have been fed above that weight, and produce ten or eleven pounds of wool each †; but of late years, the stocks of very many of the breeders have undergone a great change, and been much improved by the use of rams of the Dishley and Northumberland breed, which have considerably reduced the bone and offal, improved the wool in quality, and the mutton also, which is much finer grained than of the old breed, and fatter, at two years old, than the other at three."

The following intelligent account, of the distinct breeds of sheep in the North Riding, comes timely, to make amends for the want of information in the foregoing chapter.

P. 262. " A few sheep are bred on the higher inclosed lands of the dales in the Western Morelands, which are mostly white-faced, with horns, and of a very different appearance from any others in this county : they seem to be an unmixed breed; they are slow feeders, and will weigh, when three years old,

---

" * Mr. HUTCHINSON, of Smeaton, had a wether some years ago, which weighed above sixty pounds per quarter.—*E. Cleaver.*"

† Some remains of the " mud," or mudland, breed are still observable in the vale of York. But they are a vile degenerate race: widely differing from those which formerly inhabited the Banks of the Tees. *Rev.*

old, and fat, about eighteen or twenty pounds per quarter, and produce about five pounds of dry, harsh and thick-set, but on some sheep, and on some parts of most of the sheep, very fine wool. The whole of this wool is worked up into the hosiery, for which the dales of these Morelands has long been so celebrated; and on it, much of the reputation of this manufacture depends.

" The sheep which are bred upon the heights of the Western Morelands, are horned ; have grey faces and legs, and many of them a black spot on the back of the neck, and wool rather coarse and open. It is usual to sell the wethers of this breed off the moors, when rising four years old, at about 16 s. or 18 s. each, which, when well fed, the ensuing winter and spring, will weigh about sixteen pounds per quarter ; but the principal part of the sheep on the western moors, are short Scots (so called in opposition to a larger breed of Scotch sheep, called long Scots), which are bought about Midsummer, and are usually sold off again in the wane of that summer, or the summer following.

" The breed of sheep on the Eastern Morelands, have horns, and black or mottled faces and legs ; are small, and very hardy, suitable to their pasture, and the climate they inhabit; their wool is open, loose, and coarser than of those bred on the Western Morelands ; they are rather less in size, and sell, when rising four years old, at about 12s. or 14s. each, and, after being well fed, will weigh about fourteen pounds per quarter*.

" The fleeces of the sheep of both the Morelands, average from three to four pounds each ; and much of it being of a very coarse quality, some not much better than goats' hair, and frequently much mixed
with

" * The moor sheep are nearly as good as the soil and climate will admit.—E. Cleaver."

with brown or grey hairs, it does not fetch an higher price than 7s. per stone, of sixteen pounds to the stone.

" Thus has been traced out, three perfectly distinct breeds of sheep in this Riding: the large, white-faced, hornless, long-woolled sheep, variously mixed with crosses of the same breed. and forming several varieties, according to those crosses; this breed occupies all the low-land, rich cultivated tracts of this Riding, and is probably much more numerous than the others.

" The next, an unmixed race, and second, in point of number, are the horned—black, or speckle-faced and legged, coarse and short-woolled sheep: this hardy race possess, exclusively, the summits of all the Morelands; little alteration is likely to take place in this breed; as long as the wilds on which they now range, remain, they will remain. In point of carcase, many of them are well made; and their mutton is not surpassed, when of a proper age, by that of any breed of sheep in the kingdom.

" The third race, by far less numerous than the others, in this Riding, but extending themselves considerably into the adjoining parts of the West Riding, occupy a middle region, the grassy summits of the calcareous hills, and higher inclosed lands of the Western Morelands: these are a pure unmixed race, very different from any others in this part of the kingdom, but not altogether unlike the sheep of the downs in Wiltshire: they have heavy horns; almost always white faces; white and long legs, long neck, and, in general, a thin flat carcase; are a hardy race, and have probably been chiefly encouraged for the sake of their wool, in a country where a local and peculiar manufacture is carried on, to which it is peculiarly adapted." See p. 238.

Management of Sheep —*Salving*, or annointing with tar and grease.—(See YORKSHIRE.)

P. 270. " Though this is the practice of most breeders, yet there are some who do not adopt it, but use, in the place of it, a solution of soap in water, or a decoction of tobacco and broom; and some others do nothing at all."

I insert the subjoined note, signed **W. M.**; as the practice it recommends is new to me. The accidents, that may possibly attend it, will deter some people from following it,—nevertheless, it may, under careful management, be valuable.

N. p. 270. " Salving is comfortable to the animal, and may add weight to the wool, to make amends for the reduction of the price; but it is a practice many people do not like : it is not only tedious, but expensive, and disfigures the sheep. Many people use a solution of mercury" (arsenic) " and soap, and clip their lambs immediately after clipping their ewes, in order to destroy the tick. I have practised it some years with the utmost satisfaction; and it ought to be imitated throughout the kingdom, by all the sheep-breeders. My method is as follows : to every pound of mercury (arsenic) four pounds of sweet soap; boil these in water till dissolved; put the solution into twenty-seven or twenty-eight gallons of water; the quantity must be repeated in proportion to the number of lambs. Put some of the liquor into a large tub, in which two men should dip them up to the neck; then lay them on a creal, or bench, and press out so much of the liquor as they can, which should run into a tub set underneath to receive it. The ticks are all immediately destroyed; the animal, easy and comfortable, thrives well, and till much rain comes to wash off the smell, the fly is entirely kept off; when that is the case, we wash their backs again with the same. The expence of this operation is about 1½d. each."

Disorders of Sheep.—The *Rot*.—The Reporter, p. 271.

p. 271. " In the autumn of the year 1790, I bought
some ewes, which, on the approach of winter, proved
to be rotten, and several died. I had eight of the
worst of the remainder put into a large straw-yard
amongst some beasts, where they got no other food
than straw and water; the former they ate very
freely, and soon improved in their appearance of
health and condition; but one day, by some means
they got into a field adjoining, where they continued
some hours: from some unknown cause, possibly from
the sharpness of the weather, or the grass they had
eaten, some of them were so seized, that two died
before they could be got back again into the straw-
yard, and it was with difficulty that some of the others
walked there, where one of them died a little while
after: all of these, on inspection, proved to be very
rotten; the others continued there till spring, and
were in better condition than those which had remained in the field: they all brought good lambs,
and fatted them well, and were afterwards fed themselves; and when killed, it was sufficiently evident
they had been infected with the complaint, and had
recovered from it."

Foot Rot.—I copy the following recipe, as I have
known a similar preparation successful.—P. 272.
" The most certain remedy for this disorder, which
I have met with, is, two ounces of blue vitriol, two
ounces roach-alum, one ounce verdigrease, and a
quarter of an ounce of corrosive sublimate, all
dissolved in one quart of double-distilled vinegar.
This dropped on to the part affected, and the
sheep's feet being kept dry for a few hours after,
will generally effect a cure, after being repeated a few
times."

Black Water.—P. 272. " There is another disorder
to which lambs are liable in autumn ; it is called the
black-water: it generally attacks those lambs which
are

are in the best condition, and causes a very sudden death.

" For this disorder, I have not heard of any cure to be depended upon ; but it is generally thought, that keeping the lambs in dry stubbles, and particularly where the grass is of a dry nature, is a good preventative."—These ideas accord with my own, respecting this destructive malady. It has long appeared to me to result from a plethora, or over fullness of blood ;—the lustiest of the lambs being its first victims. It usually accompanies the Michaelmas flush of grass. A quantity of extravasated liquid of a dark red, or blackish color, is found in the cavity of the abdomen.—See WEST of ENGLAND, Sect. *Sheep.*

IMPROVEMENTS.

PROPOSED MEANS. In this as in the other Reports (agreeably to the plan of the Board) the *obstacles* to the improvements, of which a district is thought to be capable, are treated of, before the improvements themselves are enumerated, or at all *known* to the reader! The impropriety of such an arrangement is seen in the following extracts;—p. 338. " The removal of the obstacles to improvement, noticed in chapter XVI. forms a considerable part of the means of improvement; but as they are fully treated upon in that place, it is unnecessary to dwell upon them here. What remains to be done, is to point out the objects to which the attention of the land-holder and the farmer ought to be directed; those will come under the following heads, viz.

Improvement

Improvement in estates.

in cultivation and crops.

by draining.

by irrigation.

in fences.

in live stock.

by the establishment of agricultural societies."

Those several heads are touched upon ; and the few particulars of value, that occur in the discussion, have been noticed, in their proper places, aforegoing.

OBSTACLES to IMPROVEMENTS.—P. 321. "The obstacles to improvement in agriculture, though numerous, are either such as are general throughout the kingdom, or, if of a more confined nature, extend to various districts beyond the one under survey ; none are to be mentioned, as peculiar to the North Riding. Of those general obstacles, the following are the principal, viz.

" 1st. Tythes.

" 2d. The want of a general inclosure bill.

" 3d. The want of such an agreement or understanding between the landlord and tenant, as may induce the latter to lay out his money with a reasonable certainty of reaping the benefit of it, or at least not losing the principal, in case of death, or being discharged from his farm.

" 4th. A too frequent want of sufficient capital in those who take farms; and of an agricultural education among farmers in general.

" 5th. The general monopolies of all the produce of the land, which prevail in favor of the manufacturer and the merchant, and (as it is intended at least) in favor of the consumer, in opposition to the interest of the land-owner.

" 6th. The present excessive taxes upon, and the oppressive

oppressive and unreasonable restrictions in, the consumption of salt.

" 7th. The rapid increase of the poor-rates.

" 8th. The undue liberties taken by many in the
pursuit of game." The useful ideas, comprized in
this chapter, also, have been noticed.

UNDER the silly plan of arrangement, with which
the Board's Reporters are trammeled, the same subject is commonly brought three times under discussion : as if the distinct topics of the rural science were
not sufficiently numerous !

THE

EAST RIDING

YORKSHIRE.

THE NATURAL DISTRICTS of YORKSHIRE, which remain to be spoken of, and which are comprised within this fortuitous division of the county, are the Wolds, and Holderness.

The WOLDS of YORKSHIRE. The natural characteristics of these hills are the same as those of the chalk hills of the southern counties :—these being the most northerly mass of chalk, that is found in this island. I have never met with, nor heard of there having been discovered, even a masslet or fragment of this singular fossil, to the north of the Yorkshire Wolds.

In this respect, the northern termination of the chalk hills of England differs from that of their western extreme. Here, they end abruptly in tall steep clifs: —the mass appearing to have been impelled, southward. There, the extremity is more shelving, irregular and broken; as if the matter of which they are formed had been forcibly thrown westward :—fragments being found, scattered, at several miles distance from the body of the hills.

The outlines of the Yorkshire Wolds are irregular. Their extent—measuring from the vale lands of Holderness, to those of the vale of York, and from those of the vale of Pickering, to the non-calcareous lands,

at

at their southern extremity,—cannot, I apprehend, be much less than five hundred square miles.

In elevation, surface, soil and substrata, the Wolds of Yorkshire so perfectly resemble the chalk hills of the southern counties, of Kent, Surrey, Sussex, Hampshire, Wiltshire, and Dorsetshire, that, in a general view, they afford no specific marks of distinction. See the SOUTHERN COUNTIES,—subject *Chalk Hills;* also YORKSHIRE,—subject *Wolds:*---details being, there, respectively given.

The DISTRICT of HOLDERNESS, or the SOUTHERN SEA COAST OF YORKSHIRE. This, as a natural district, is bounded on the north and west, by the Wolds; on the east, by the British ocean; on the south, by the estuary of the Humber. The towns of Bridlington, Driffield, Beverley and Hull, stand near the outline of the district.

The extent of the district of Holderness, between the skirts of the Wold hills, the sea, and the Humber, may be estimated at full four hundred square miles.

The natural characters of this valuable tract of country, whether in regard to elevation, surface, or soil, are those of a true vale district.

" GENERAL VIEW

OF THE

AGRICULTURE

OF THE

EAST RIDING OF YORKSHIRE,

AND THE

AINSTY OF THE CITY OF YORK,

WITH

OBSERVATIONS ON THE MEANS OF ITS IMPROVEMENT.

By ISAAC LEATHAM,

OF BARTON NEAR MALTON, YORKSHIRE.

DRAWN UP FOR THE CONSIDERATION OF

THE BOARD OF AGRICULTURE AND INTERNAL

IMPROVEMENT.

1794."

To the QUALIFICATIONS of the REPORTER, in this instance, I can only, as in the last, speak from information. Mr. LEATHAM, I understand, was bred to the agricultural profession: but set out (not very early in life, I believe) as a land valuer; and had, before he wrote the Report under review, acted as Commissioner under Bills of Inclosure, and been accustomed to be called in, as referee or arbitrator, in country concerns: ---circumstances highly in his favor, as a Reporter of the rural practices, in his neighbourhood. For,

although

although Mr. L's residence, as appears by the title page, is in the North Riding, it is only a few miles distant from the district he undertook to survey.

As to his MODE of SURVEY, as a Reporter to the Board of Agriculture, very little is to be gathered from the Report. Judging from the paucity of materials, the indistinct method by which they are arranged, and the inapt verbosity in which they are frequently involved, one is involuntarily impressed with an idea, that he had not given himself sufficient time to study his subject, maturely, before he sat down to write. Brief as the Report is, it contains more of the Reporter's own opinions, than of the established practice of superior husbandmen, in the East Riding of Yorkshire. *Some* of his opinions, however, are highly valuable; and, so far, the Board were fortunate in having engaged Mr. Leatham as one of their " Surveyors."

The volume under Review being the ORIGINAL REPORT (no reprinted Report having, yet, been published of the East Riding) there are not, in this case, any ANNOTATORS :---the whole appearing to be the production of the Reporter.

SUBJECT THE FIRST.

NATURAL ECONOMY.

ON this subject, nothing of useful information is to be gathered. In a " plan," the Reporter has divided the Riding with the Ainsty of York, into eight districts! ---most of them imaginary,---having neither natural, nor political, distinguishments : and all of them, except the Wolds, and the Ainsty, are nameless ! (even Holderness is not spoken of more than once or twice under that name) : so that it is impossible, in many parts

parts of the Report, to understand which of them is treated of.

The fact is—there are only two natural *descriptions* of lands, within the riding (a small plot of limestone upland near Malton excepted) :—namely, the *Wolds*, and the *vale lands* by which they are surrounded,— except where the sea, for a short distance, washes the feet of their cliffs; and excepting where they are butted upon by the Howardian hills.

Four of the prettily colored plots are situated in —are essential parts of—the VALE of YORK,—reaching to and occupying its very center! Two of them form the vale lands of HOLDERNESS; and the seventh is a part of the VALE of PICKERING, which happens to be included within the East Riding.

These facts, alone, are sufficient to demonstrate the folly of surveying a country, by political divisions, to obtain Agricultural information.

SUBJECT THE SECOND.

POLITICAL ECONOMY.

STATE of APPROPRIATION.---P. 39. " This riding contains very little, if any, of what is generally termed waste land, such as high moors or mountains: the commons vary in extent, from two hundred to two thousand five hundred acres, but the generality contain from three to five hundred, and all of them may be converted into useful land by drains, subdivisions, plantations, and other improvements; some are stinted (as no doubt most, if not all, commons were originally *), but others, for want of due attention in the commoners, are stocked without number or limitation.

* This, I conceive, is very problematical.

tion. When commons are not stinted in proportion
to the stock they are capable of keeping, very little
benefit is derived from them; and though the parties
cannot agree to inclose, they should not omit to stint
and drain the commons: this plan would render
them of some benefit, and introduce a progressive
improvement, until a more beneficial and decisive one
could be adopted. It is not a little extraordinary to
see a starving stock upon a common of five hundred
acres soaked with water, when the expense of a few
shillings for each right, prudently laid out in drains
and bridges, would double its value. Such is the
obstinacy of men, and so difficult is it to induce them
to form the same opinion; though an union of senti-
ment would much more materially promote their interest."

Much credit is due to Mr. Leatham, for those remarks. Until a general law of appropriation be suffered to pass, and in cases in which the appropriation
of commonable lands, by separate bills, is prevented
by lords of manors, tithe owners, or other holders of
abstract rights belonging to them, the regulations
and improvements, suggested by Mr. L. might, in
many cases, be undertaken by owners and occupiers
of common-right lands, with great profit to a township; though they might, in some, be attended with
difficulties.

P. 37.—" Many open fields and commons in this
district have been inclosed; and the taste for inclosing
has been carried on here as rapidly, and to as good
purpose, as in most other countries; and the value of
the land has not only increased proportionably above
the original rent, but has paid five per cent. for the
money laid out; other very salutary consequences
also result from inclosures: but this observation does
not attach to all, either from the proprietor's want of
knowledge, or reflexion on the nature and situation
of the land; or from the sinister views and endeavours
of a solicitor, and from the train of jobs which inclosures

sures when ill conducted needlessly create: much land on the Yorkshire Wolds has been inclosed, which, for the above reasons, might have been with more advantage left open."

PUBLIC WORKS.—*Inland Navigation.*—P. 7.— All the rivers above mentioned" (the Humber, the Ouze and the Derwent) " are navigable, except some part of the Derwent. This Riding is nearly encompassed by a navigation, which, with those from Hull to Beverley and Driffield, and from another part of the Humber to Market Weighton, renders it a situation peculiarly advantageous for agriculture and commerce. The surplus produce of this district finds an easy conveyance by water to every port in the kingdom, and to all the great manufacturing parts of the West Riding of Yorkshire."

Drainage.—Speaking on the subject of draining the low flat lands, on the banks of the Humber, Mr. L. makes the following sensible remarks,——p. 19.—— " When the fall is gentle, width is the great object, and ought to be applied to the drainage of most flat lands. This, peculiarly applicable to the drainage in question, with a little additional depth, would make it navigable, and would very much accommodate a considerable tract of country, and the contribution would be lightened by the double advantage derived from the improvement."

Roads.—Much is said under this head. But I perceive little that is entitled to notice, here;—excepting some judicious observations on what husbandmen might well term the *road tax.* Mr. Leatham is of opinion, with me, that the uncivilized custom of " common-day-works" ought to be abolished. We differ only in the manner of levying the rate to supply their place*.

In the NORTH RIDING REPORT, p. 300, Mr. Tuke says—

---

* See TREATISE on LANDED PROPERTY. Subject *Repairing Roads.*

says—" The roads in the North Riding are almost
wholly repaired by statute days, which is (are) per=
formed under the direction of two surveyors of the
high ways, appointed annually by the respective
townships; but an exception is met with in a township, on the northside of the Howardian hills, where
the practice is to employ a person by the year to do
all the carriage work, and keep the roads in repair;
the expense of which is raised by an assessment laid
upon the inhabitants. This has not been long practised, but it is apprehended that the roads are kept in
better repair at less expense and inconvenience to the
farmers, than by the former method."

Mr. Cleaver, however (who lives in that neighbourhood) says, in a note on the above passage,—" Some
of the townships, between Hovingham and Malton,
are contracted for, by an undertaker; but the work
is miserably done, and the plan does not appear to
answer."

Nevertheless, perceiving the following passage, in
the Report now under Review, and taking for granted
that the experiment above noticed was made in the
parish in which Mr. Leatham resides, I think it right
to let my readers hear his sentiments on the subject.

P. 17 " Although the law furnishes means of supplying the deficiency of supporting the roads, when
the statute work fails, yet when we consider how ill
that work is executed, the additional assessment ceases
to be a matter of surprise; for the farmer's servant
considers this as a holiday:—The stone pit will not
admit all the carriages to load at the same time; in
course, many of them lose time by waiting; frequently
no surveyor attends to direct their work, or keep good
order; and if he does attend, he is either unskilful,
wants authority, or does not sufficiently interest himself in the cause to perform his duty. The above-
mentioned reasons, with many others, have long induced me, and several judicious and respectable
farmers

farmers in this district*, to form this opinion, that a contract made by each township with a proper person, is the cheapest and most effectual method of maintaining the roads; and I find this opinion confirmed by experience. The money should be raised by an assessment proportioned to the value of the statute work; and when more is wanted, by a pound rate, as directed by the act. It may not be unworthy the consideration of Parliament, whether it would not be better to abolish the statute work entirely, and substitute a mode upon the above principles."

Markets.—I have great satisfaction in selecting, from this Report, the subjoined intelligent account of what might be denominated the AGRICULTURAL TRAFFIC of Yorkshire:—furnishing a striking instance of the INTERCOURSE of DISTRICTS†. It is evidently the result of extensive observation, and mature thought: reflecting much credit on the writer.

P. 11.—" The situation of Hull, on a river receiving navigable branches from the most flourishing and trading parts of this and several other counties, is particularly advantageous to trade, and renders this town both populous and opulent, and a market for a large share of the neighbouring produce, not only to support the inhabitants, but also for the victualling of ships. From hence also considerable quantities of corn, butter, and bacon, are daily exported; those articles however are only exported in proportion to that part of the country, which is situated within a convenient distance, as the freight and carriage of such heavy goods, must always induce the vender to avail himself of the nearest market; consequently every navigation will have its share in proportion to the cultivation and surplus produce of the country which

---

* Meaning, doubtlessly, the district in which the Reporter was writing.

† See MIDLAND COUNTIES.

which adjoins it: on this account other places also have their share of trade, and the country derives a convenience from their situation; thus Patterington accommodates the south, and Bridlington the north part of Holdernesse, with the east part of the Wolds; Driffield the west part of Holdernesse, and the south and east part of the Wolds and its vicinity; Malton the north and west part of the Wolds and its neighbourhood; the Derwent various places from Malton to its fall into the Ouse; York takes a considerable share of the produce from the west part of this Riding; Market Weighton navigation accommodates the south part of the Wolds, and each side of its line to the Humber; Howden is very near the Ouse and, with the neighbourhood of Cave, is accommodated by the Humber: thus a communication is established by water not only to the interior part of this large and flourishing county, and to the adjoining counties, but to the sea also, and of course to all the world.

" It is now proper to shew the articles of traffic. In this county the produce of wheat is superior to its consumption, as the manufactures here are not extensive, nor the population more than necessary to carry on the cultivation and trade of this Riding; its exports consist of the following articles: of a very considerable quantity of wool, nearly if not entirely to the amount of its whole produce, of large quantities of grain, of bacon, butter, and potatoes, of a very considerable number of horses, cattle, sheep, and pigs. Most of the horses are bought up at York and Howden fairs, by the London dealers, who attend each fair twice a year for that purpose, and who also buy them frequently out of the stables of the country dealers. The London market takes off a small part of the grain, and a great part of the bacon, butter, and potatoes; the remainder supplies the West Riding. The pigs are bought to keep up the stock of the London distillers; the cattle, both lean and fat, are sent to York and the West Riding; a great number of
sheep,

sheep, chiefly half fat, are bought on the Wolds by the turnip graziers and farmers of the West Riding: The wethers when bought, have turnips given them, and are killed in the winter and spring; the ewes are purchased to produce lambs, and are afterwards fatted.

" This Riding, except on the eastern coast, where Newcastle coal is used, is supplied from the West Riding near Wakefield and Leeds with that article, of which the consumption is very considerable. The lime used in the south and west parts of the Riding, is brought from Knottingley and Brotherton. Thus a reciprocal trade is carried on between the East and West Ridings, particularly advantageous to both, and nature seems to have kindly interposed by so happy a combination, that as each country is adapted to supply the wants of the other, so the most convenient channel of communication is afforded by the adjoining rivers; the navigation of which, with the different branches of trade depending upon it, gives constant employment to a very considerable number of people."

I likewise readily copy the following well grounded proposal, for establishing a Government VICTUALLING OFFICE, at HULL. The thought is happily conceived, and the advantage to arise from it well made out. There cannot be a doubt of its *possitive* eligibility, as a market for the peculiar breed of cattle, with which Government stores are chiefly supplied. But how far it may be *relatively* compatible with—and admissable as a part of—the immense machine of Government, I leave for its executive officers to determine.

P. 33. " Before we leave the subject of provisions, it may be observed that this district, particularly the eastern part, produces and fattens a great number of large cattle. As they are bred and fed in the same district, and as there is no expence or dealer's profit in driving them from the breeder to market, not to

mention

mention the contiguity of Hull, beef can certainly be
afforded as low here as in any other part of the kingdom ; and Government might establish a victualling
office in this Riding with a very considerable advantage, both in respect to supply and price ; to this
office an additional supply would also be furnished
from the other neighbouring parts of Yorkshire, and
from those of Marsh Land and Lincolnshire, all of
which places are situated at very easy distances :
these considerations are certainly sufficient to warrant
Government in making the trial.

" The above plan, if adopted, would certainly save
a very considerable expence, which the nation at present pays; and where such saving can be made,
justice to the public requires it. Competition only
reduces the price of any article to a proper medium.
Government at present is supplied with cattle, generally bought in Smithfield market, many of which are
driven from a considerable distance, within thirty
miles of Hull, and from 80 to 140 from London.
Most of the fat cattle, therefore, purchased by Government, are driven from an average distance of 110
miles, at an expence of nearly 12 s. per head, besides
a loss of weight in driving, moderately stated at four
stone, of 14 pounds to the stone ; and which, at
4 s. 6 d. per stone, amoun;s to 18 s. ; to this again, as
the grazier receives great part of the cattle fed for
the London market lean from the more northern counties, the expence of driving them, with the drover's
profit, must be added, which would not be less than
12 s. did not the country adjoining Hull supply part
of these cattle, on which account I deduct something
saved in driving and waste, or 4 s. ; the total saving,
therefore, amounts to 38 s. per beast, averaged at eight
hundred and a half, or sixty-eight stone. But when
we consider the real variation between the markets in
this district and London, it may be moderately
reckoned at 45 s. per ox : if we farther estimate the
superior quality in the meat of an ox killed after a

journey

journey of a few hours, or of two days at most, and that of an ox driven eight days, the advantage of establishing a victualling office here, must appear still greater. The above calculation, taken only at 45 *s.* on 68 stone, makes a saving of more than 8 *d.* per stone of 14 lb. ; for a great part of the provisions at this office would be sent from Hull to every garrison abroad, at a rate as cheap as from any other office ; but as a supply would be wanted frequently for the navy, and furnished from this port, at a dearer freight than from the victualling-office in London, I deduct for it one penny per stone : the article is therefore cheaper by 7 *d.* per stone, and at the same time better."

Public Shows of *Livestock.*—P. 60. " In September, there is a show at Driffield of rams, bulls, boars, and heifers, and premiums are given to the best ; which excites an emulation, and not only considerably promotes the improvement of the breed of stock, but affords the uninformed an opportunity of seeing such as are deemed good, and of hearing the sentiments of men eminent in the line of breeding."—This was the first show of the kind that fell under my notice. It had been established some years (for bulls at least) before the Petworth Show took place.

SUBJECT THE THIRD.

RURAL ECONOMY.

DIVISION THE FIRST.

LANDED ESTATES; their IMPROVEMENT and MANAGEMENT.

IMPROVING ESTATES.—*Reclaiming rough Grounds.* P. 50. " The system of paring and burning is much practised, and with advantage on strong coarse land,

or

or even upon thinner soils covered with coarse or thick turf, for it certainly brings land more quickly into a vegetative state. The prejudice which some persons have conceived against this mode of cultivation is founded on the abuse of it; for it has often happened in cases where the occupier has had full liberty, that either through interest or ignorance, he has drawn so many crops from the land as to deprive it of every vegetable principle. I need not ask the question,—in what condition land of a thin staple must be left, after one crop of rape, and two or three of corn shall have been taken from it? according to the common practice. If the crops shall be taken proportionably to the goodness of the land, and a suitable supply of manure shall be afterwards given it, the system of paring and burning in this case may be allowed, and is, as I said before, a ready and profitable method of putting strong soils, or even lands of a thinner staple, into good order."

EXECUTIVE MANAGEMENT of Estates.—*Proprietors*, and *Managers*.—Speaking of " Impediments to Improvements," Mr. Leatham makes these strong remarks, p. 60.—" A third impediment results from the ignorance in agriculture of gentlemen of landed property, who do not sufficiently qualify themselves either to superintend their own estates personally, or to enable them to select persons of sufficient skill and experience in husbandry, of general information, candour, discernment, and activity, to whom the care of their estates can be entrusted : such a man will readily discover the condition of each farm, with the disposition of each farmer; he will be able also to advise with and assist the weak, stimulate the indolent, and check the licentious; but, alas, to what unskilful and inefficient characters is this important trust too frequently committed ?"

Tenancy.—Also the following, p. 60. " A second great and real obstacle arises from the want of a proper confidence between the landlord and the
tenant,

tenant, which if not by some means established, agriculture probably will never florish to that degree required."

And, on " Leases," the subjoined observations are well entitled to the consideration of every proprietor of a tenanted estate. P. 58.—" Very few leases are granted in this district; many tenants being even without a written agreement. The granting of leases, it must be confessed, is a circumstance that requires deep and serious consideration and reflection; some landlords, however, are candid enough to grant them. Leases are proper and safe to be granted, when they contain covenants for a mode of husbandry suitable to the demised farm, and affording the tenant a free scope for his skill and abilities in pursuing a stipulated system of husbandry, advantageous to his own interest, and consequently to the improvement of the farm. This system should be composed and drawn out by a person completely skilled in agriculture.

" As little obligation as possible should be between the landlord and his tenant; the improvements of a permanent nature should be made at the landlord's expense; and the tenant should pay interest, and what is reasonable over and above for the money laid out in main and under drains, new fences, roads, and bridges: and if a tenant who shall agree to, and actually enter on a farm out of condition, should quit it before he shall have been repaid the expense of improving it, the landlord himself, or the succeeding tenant, should reimburse him his expenses; and the landlord should agree to such repayment, before the entry of the tenant undertaking to improve his farm.

" If neither leases be granted, nor a condition similar to the above be stipulated, it cannot be expected that agriculture will be carried to the perfection it might be, at least on the farms of many landlords. There are, however, several farms in the district without either lease or agreement, in which the tenants may be secure during the lives of their landlords;

lords; but when a tenant enters upon a farm out of condition, and pursues a true and spirited mode of husbandry, the advantages arising from the term of one life are not" (may not be) " sufficient to reward him. The putting an ill-conditioned farm into complete order, is attended with a greater expense, and requires more skill and attention than many are aware of."

DIVISION THE THIRD.

AGRICULTURE.

FARMS.—*Sizes* of Farms.—P. 40.—" The farms vary in rent from five hundred to one thousand pounds per annum; but generally from five pounds to two hundred."

Fences.—The following hints may be serviceable to those who occupy inclosed lands, near the sea coast;—or in any other bleakly exposed situation. P. 25. " It is necessary to keep the hedges low adjoining the roads, to admit the sun and air, so essentially necessary for their preservation, and for the consequent accommodation of those who travel upon them. It is not only in this case that clipping of hedges has a good effect; I have for some time considered that the injury received by them in exposed situations, particularly near the sea, proceeds from the sharp air which blows through them, when thin and open; but has less effect, and does not injure them so much, when by their thick foliage, they form a barrier against it; some, though exposed to the sea air, have been clipped yearly from their earliest growth, and appear to thrive infinitely better than those which have not received that attention."

Occupiers, in all situations, may profit by another valuable suggestion of Mr. L. P. 27.—" The advantage

tage of proper fences, and good gates, that shut and open readily, is known to every skilful farmer. Flocks are naturally prone to ramble; and where there is a slight fence, or a gate unshut, they are sure to find it : the injury they then do to a field of turnips, corn, or grass, is not the only consideration, for they become unsettled; nor will they be satisfied with their usual pasture for many days, nay, even weeks : this renders them less profitable and thriving; and disappoints the expectation of their owner, who, for want of this attention to his fences and gates, finds himself injured not only in his crops, but in his stock."

Surface Drains.—Equally judicious, as the foregoing, is the subsequent well conveyed admonition. P. 22.—" To demonstrate the necessity of drains being kept clear and free, it is proper to remark, that to whatever height the water may be stopped, or rise, so much of the drain may be considered as if it had never been cut. We daily see many hundred yards in length stopped half way up the drain for days and weeks, when ten minutes work would remove the cause, and effectually clear the, drain. Every farmer" (in a low moist situation) " should frequently perambulate his farm, for the purpose of discovering such annoyances, which he will readily perceive, when his drains shall have previously been put into complete order ; so that even a trace of the crossing mole will not escape his notice."

Mr. Leatham, as well as Mr. Tuke, recommends the *breast draining spade.*—The following are Mr. L's observations respecting it.—P. 30.—" The breast spade used in draining, is found very useful : it is driven forward by a man in the same manner as the paring spade, and is not much unlike a common hay spade turned up on both sides ; it takes out an entire sod, and is very useful in cleaning out furrows, and cutting small grips or top drains in flat lands."—It is the common breast plow, or paring spade, turned up

up on both sides : its width being regulated to the required purpose. It is useful, also, in irrigation.
See MIDLAND COUNTIES, Min. 68.

Homestalls. The Reporter's cast of mind, and
liberal way of thinking, may be caught in the following remarks.—I must however, endeavor to qualify them, in the minds of my readers, by saying,—
in parody of an old proverb,—Great farmsteads are
great evils.—P. 28.—" There are few instances where
money is laid out more commendably, and to better
advantage, than in building farm houses. It would
be sound policy to attach every man to his home, by
rendering it as agreeable to him as possible : neatness
and order promote tranquillity ; and no set of men
are better entitled to this enjoyment than farmers,
fulfilling the duties of their station with propriety ;
munificence no where shines forth with greater lustre
than in the land-owners, when they perform their
part towards promoting the happiness of a respectable
tenantry."

OCCUPIERS.—P. 13. " The cultivation of the mind
is as necessary a preparation for the great and important work of agriculture, as for any other undertaking where information, knowledge, and application
are requisite. Indeed I have the pleasure of saying,
that many in this Riding, by their sentiments and
practice, show that they possess a cultivated understanding, and may be esteemed an ornament to their
profession ; happier still should I be, had I not observed some minds clouded with a degree of suspicion
and prejudice, the constant companions of ignorance.
The farmers in general are opulent, they have the
power, and, I trust, the inclination to carry into execution every desirable system ; as an opposite conduct must not only be detrimental to the community,
but to themselves also."

PLAN of MANAGEMENT.—P. 40.—" Of some"
(farms) " one-third part is arable ; of others the grass
and arable lands are nearly equal ; others again, consist

sist chiefly of grass with a very small proportion of arable. The manner of cultivation varies as much as the nature of the land.

" In the strong and flat lands, most farmers summer fallow for wheat, and afterwards sow beans or oats ; and several not satisfied with two crops, take a third. Others summer fallow for oats, barley, or beans, after one of which they sow wheat and barley, or oats ; some, particularly upon the warp lands, plant potatoes after a winter and spring fallow, which are succeeded by a crop of wheat, and some take two crops after them. Some winter and spring fallow for flax, others sow their fallows with rape for seed, or to be eaten off in autumn ; after which wheat, and sometimes also oats are sown, and one or two crops are taken."

On the *succession*, or course of crops, we find nothing estimable ; though several schemes are set forth. The changes, of which crops, as bells, are susceptible, are endless. And, excepting with respect to some two or three standing rotations, scarcely any two men think alike on the subject :—every one having his own favorite course.

Mr. Leatham allowably prides himself on having been principally instrumental in improving the ancient system of common field farming, in the parish of Hunmanby, upon the Wolds,—by introducing the Norfolk husbandry of six shifts ; thus, intermixing turnips and cultivated herbage, with the corn crops : and, moreover, by establishing a parish flock,— placing them under the care of a parochial shepherd,— and folding them ;—agreeably to the practice long established in the southern counties :—an obvious and great improvement.

Mr. L. mentions an ancient practice, in the Wold husbandry, which had escaped my attention. It is the more entitled to notice, here, as we may not, in going through the English Reports, meet with another instance of the kind. In Scotland, a similar custom was

was common, I believe, to that kingdom; and, at this day, is found in the more recluse parts of it.

P. 42.—" The greater part of the Wold townships which remain open, have a large quantity of *out field* in ley land, that is land from which they take a crop of corn every third, fourth, fifth, or sixth year, according to the custom of the township; after which they leave it without giving it any manure or fallow, in the same situation as when they reaped the crop."

The rule of conduct, in the management of a farm, which is comprised in the subjoined extract, has been, long ago and repeatedly urged. Nevertheless, I bring it forward, here (though not very tersely put); as it cannot be too frequently impressed on the minds of practical men.

P. 61.—" Every farmer should so arrange the plan of his work, that it may proceed gradually and without confusion, that a proper attention and force may be given to every part of it. This conduct will render every farmer master of his time; so that every thing required to be done will be performed in time, not delayed till the season and opportunity shall have been lost. The impediments arising from rainy days, sick servants, from the occasional and necessary absence of the master, &c. will in this case be of little consequence, nor embarrass the operations of the farm, nor prevent the occupier from attending to the smallest concerns of it, that are of very material consequence, in every view of which the keeping the farmer at home is not the least."

WORKPEOPLE.—P. 31. " Farms of considerable magnitude, are generally worked by a foreman (if upon the Wolds, by a shepherd), with from two to four other servant men, and a suitable number of day laborers, according to the size of the farm: the laborers sometimes work by the day; sometimes they take their work, as threshing, ditching, &c. at a fixed price for a certain quantity of work: paring and burning

burning is generally taken, and some corn also reaped
at a certain price per acre; but I think a greater
number perform this work by their own servants, and
by day laborers, men and women, who, during harvest,
come in great numbers to Malton to be hired, from
the North and West Ridings, particularly from the
neighbourhood of Richmond and Knaresborough, and
the western dales of Yorkshire; most of these people
go upon the Wolds, and into the eastern parts of this
district: the redundancy of inhabitants in the North
and West Ridings, thus supplies the deficiency in the
east."

WORKING ANIMALS.---*Oxen.* P. 35. " A considerable number of oxen are used, mostly in yokes and
for carriages, in the farms; very few for the plough,
as they are deemed too slow for that purpose, and in
warm weather cannot stand, with sufficient ease to
themselves, that continued labor for so long a time
which the plough requires. In carriages they often
get short intervals of rest whilst loading and unload-
ing, and as this sort of work best suits them, the
greatest portion of it should be done by them, which
would be a considerable advantage to most farmers."
---In Devonshire, the whole of the ploughing, and
little else, is performed by oxen. Such are the customs and fashions of districts.

Horses.---P. 36. " I have often in this Riding seen a
boy of 15, with a pair of good horses, plough as well,
and more, than a man, with a boy to drive, could do
with four horses in other countries.

" No doubt but in wet seasons and strong clay
land, it is proper that the cattle drawing the ploughs
should walk in the furrow, and consequently must be
harnessed at length, and walk single and move slow.
Oxen may here be used; for there is a coolness in the
air upon the surface of this kind of land which suits
the ox, and the foot of the ox is best adapted to land
which is very wet and stiff, as it *expands when setting
down, and contracts when lifted up;* and therefore does
not

not stick in the soil like that of a horse." For the *breed* of working horses, see the sect. HORSES.

IMPLEMENTS.---The following short extracts will serve as a specimen of the Reporter's want of perspicuity and intelligibleness, when registering the established practices of the country submitted to his inspection.—P. 30. " The *waggons* in the greatest part of the district are drawn by two or four horses. They are generally clumsy, with low fore-wheels that lock under the body, which in course is raised by heavy cumbersome blocks, and runs very heavily."

From these remarks, as well as from what precedes and follows them, we are led to understand that the indiscriminate censure, they contain, is applicable to the whole, or the greatest part, of the East Riding. Whereas, in the East Riding of Yorkshire, as in the county, and the kingdom, at large, the *English waggon* is prevalent; unless on the Wolds and their immediate environs. There, it is true, waggons widely distinct in their constructions, appearance, and method of using them, from the common English waggon, may be said to be almost the only farm carriages in use. But "the Wold waggon" (being emphatically so termed) may, I believe, be considered as peculiar to the Wolds: I have not recognized it in any other part of the island. It is, I am informed, the true Flemish, or *German, waggon*. It is guided by a pole, as the coach; not by shafts, as the English waggon. Four horses are usually put to it, very much in the same way as they are to a stage coach. The driver mounts the near wheel horse, and guides the leaders with reins;—generally trotting, when the carriage is empty; whether in harvest, or upon the road. How a public Surveyor could pass so singular a sight, in England, without intelligibly reporting it, appears extraordinary.

The general principle of the Wold waggon is excellent;—whether for the works of harvest or for going long journies on free open roads. But the prevailing construction

construction of many of its parts, is vile. (See
YORKSHIRE.—*Team Labor* and *Implements* of the
WOLDS.) This, however, appears to be annually improving. And I perceive the implement is slowly
straying from the Wold hills. In regard to roads,
the Wold waggon, with four horses, double, is infinitely preferable to the long *tandem* team of the rest
of the kingdom.

MANURES.—*Lime.*—" P. 54. " Lime is a manure
much used on the Wolds; the average price of it per
chaldron, of 32 bushels, costs as under:

	s.	d.
" Chalk lime of the Wolds, . . .	8	6
Lime near Malton, ...	7	6

Lime of an excellent quality, from Knottingley and
Brotherton, 12s. 6d. per dozen, equal to a chaldron
of 36 bushels—this supplies, by the convenience of
water carriage, the lower parts of the Riding. Seldom
more than three dozen of the Knottingley or Brotherton lime are laid upon an acre, but often only two.
Of the other sorts from three to five, but generally
four."

Sea Sand.—P. 55. " Sea sand is found to answer
well upon strong clay; the quantity laid upon an acre,
is generally from 20 to 40 loads: as the land lying
near the coast is chiefly of this description, this kind
of manure may be used at a moderate expence: it
has the strongest effect when laid upon the fallow, as
it thereby becomes more effectually mixed with the
soil; the best time for using it is while it continues in
a damp state."

Sea Weed.—" P. 55. " A considerable quantity of
sea-weed is often thrown on this coast; it makes an
excellent manure, either when laid fresh upon the
land, or after it has lain some time in a heap to promote fermentation."

Chalk.—P. 55 " Some of the Wold chalk stone has
been used to good effect upon strong fresh land, in the
proportion

proportion of sixty tons to an acre, and is worthy of further trial."

HORSES.—P. 53. "The horses are generally stout, for the light or bay kind, and are equal if not superior, particularly those upon the Wolds and the eastern division, to any others in Yorkshire. Great attention is paid in breeding them, particularly to the stallion; but much to the injury and loss of the breeder, most of the best mares are sent out of the Riding, as more saleable. This economy is delusive; some see the folly of it, and act differently; and the rest no doubt will follow the example. Although a considerable degree of the racing blood is introduced into this breed, yet both the largest coach, and smallest saddle horses are produced in this Riding.

" No horses are better calculated for the plough than this breed, their activity and quick walking give them a superiority over the slow black kind, excellent however for drawing heavy waggons. These two breeds should be kept distinct without any mixture of blood."

CATTLE.—P. 52. "The cattle are of the short horned kind: the oxen at a proper age, and fatted, weigh when killed from sixty to one hundred and ten stone (at the rate of fourteen pounds to the stone); cows weigh from forty to sixty stone (the average of oxen weighs seventy, of cows forty-eight stone). Those of the greater size are bred in the eastern part of the Riding.

" A great improvement might be made in this breed, by the introduction of bulls less coarse, rather thinner boned, and more of a feeding kind."

SHEEP.—P. 51. "A great number of sheep are kept upon the Wolds, and in other parts of this district; most of which are of the long-woolled kind; the breed is a mixture of the old Wold sort and the Lincolnshire, and of late has a cross of the Leicestershire. Some townships upon the Wolds still retain a smaller sort, soft, with a finer and shorter wool, occasioned rather by the scanty pasture, than introduced and kept up by the choice of the farmers, who generally use a long-woolled ram. Three year old wethers of the first kind when fat, weigh from twenty-four to thirty pounds, and the ewes from sixteen to twenty-two pounds per quarter.

" The fleeces of the ewes, wethers, hogs, or hoggits, will, upon an average, weigh from eight to ten pounds. Wethers of the second kind when fat, will weigh at the same age from sixteen to twenty pounds, the ewes from twelve to sixteen pounds per quarter. The fleeces of the wethers, ewes, hogs, or hoggits, upon an average, will weigh from four pounds to six ; a stone of wool in this district weighs sixteen pound."

The Reporter has bestowed some pains on the disease of *rot* in sheep; and I had marked his obser-vations for insertion, here. But they will not bear close examination. Nothing of fact is made out; except that there are lands which will rot in a wet season, but not in a dry one:—nor any thing of opinion offered; except that the " disorder appears to me to be merely a consumption," p. 57. And this without the slightest foundation having been pre-pared on which to ground the theory:—unless by " consumption" be meant that of the liver *.

ON the whole, it seems probable that, in going through the Reports of the Board, we may not find one, in which good sense and futility are so equally and intimately blended, as in that of the East Riding of Yorkshire.

THE

* On RABBITS (a principal species of livestock on the Wolds) not a word; either as to their number, or management !

SOUTHERN MOUNTAINS

NORTHERN DEPARTMENT OF ENGLAND.

THIS extended body of mountain heights has been repeatedly mentioned. Its northern limits are the valley of the Ribble,—Craven,—and the valley of the Ayre;—by which this division of the Alps, or highlands, of England are separated from the more northern divisions;—namely, the northern Morelands of Lancashire, and the western Morelands of Yorkshire. Its western boundary is formed by the lower, or vale lands of Lancashire and Cheshire. Its eastern, by the manufacturing districts of Yorkshire. Its southern, by the upper grounds of Derbyshire and Staffordshire; namely, the uplands, or mountain skirts, that intervene between the mountain, and the vale, lands of those counties. Thus the natural unity, under notice, extends within the political limits of five counties:— namely, Lancashire, Yorkshire, Cheshire, Staffordshire, and Derbyshire.

The extent of those alpine lands,—from their northern extreme, between Colne and Keighley, and the southern extremity of the limestone heights (the wever hills) of Staffordshire,---is above sixty miles. Their width is extremely irregular:---from the feet of the Cheshire hills, to those of the hills near Sheffield, is upward of twenty miles; while at Blackstone Edge, between Rochdale and Huddersfield, they contract to a mere ridge; by which the southern Morelands of Lancashire, and the Yorkshire and Derbyshire hills are indivisibly united.

My OWN KNOWLEDGE, of this tract of mountain, is

by

by no means intimate. The northern parts, however,
I have viewed on every side; and have twice crossed
them,---over Blackstone Edge. Formerly, I traversed
the more central parts, by a devious line, from Stockport, by Buxton ; thence, by Tidswell, to Castleton ;
and from thence, by Bakewell, to Matlock and
Derby. In my excursions, in the midland counties,
I have had opportunities of viewing their southern
skirts. In 1798, I examined with more attention,
the southern declivity of the Derbyshire hills ; and
crossed the limestone heights and morelands of Staffordshire,---from Ashbourn, by Leek, to Congleton.
And, in 1806, I gained a general idea of their southeastern limits, in travelling with that intention, from
Sheffield, by Chesterfield, to Derby.

The whole of the northern, and most of the western,
parts of those high lands, are black moory heathlands ;
resembling the more northerly morelands. But the
southern and southeastern quarters are limestone
heights; rising, northward, to a superior degree of
elevation, as calcareous hills. They resemble the
limestone mountains of North Wales ; showing, at
their most elevated heights, strong, mountain features.
But the surface, in general, is less broken and rugged,
than that of the calcareous regions of Merionethshire.

The produce of the heathlands, from what I have
seen of them in various parts, is of an inferior quality.
But the less elevated of the limestone heights are of a
productive nature. The higher swells are used as
sheep walks ; the lower and better sheltered parts, as
arable lands:---the lower stages being of a valuable
quality.

The stock of the more southerly heathlands are
native mountain sheep, of a light frame;—their faces
mostly grey;—some of them horned, others hornless ; and bear the name of " Peakrils." They
resemble the native breeds of the Cumbrian mountains, &c. &c. See p. 201, aforegoing. What I saw
of the sheep, upon the limestone lands of Derbyshire,

byshire, about Ballidon,—between Ashbourn and Bakewell,—were of the poled, whitefaced, longwooled breed, and of a vile quality: resembling the worst of the old Leicestershire, and Lincolnshire sorts!—The longhorned cattle, however, which I found on those hills, were of a superior quality;—of a better frame and cleaner, than those of the lower lands of Derbyshire.

REPORTS.

ON examining the BOARD'S REPORTS, from the five counties which claim shares of this indivisible mass of mountain, I find, unless in one instance, scarsely any accurate information,—relating either to the nature, or the management, of the lands that cover it!

THE LANCASHIRE Report mentions it, in the following terms:—P. 2.—" The ridge of mountains, which bounds this county on the eastern side, from Yorkshire, and which runs through not only Yorkshire, but Cheshire, Derbyshire and Staffordshire, &c. And called not improperly the back bone of the kingdom, being the most elevated ground on the island (!) skreens Lancashire more particularly from the ungenial eastern blast, frost, blight, and insects, which infest the countries bordering upon the German ocean."

THE WEST RIDING Surveyors penetrated it, as far as Penniston, situated near its eastern confines:—but without noticing it, farther, than by imperfectly describing its breed of heathland sheep (see p. 406,) and making the following observations, on the immediate neighbourhood of Penniston.—App. p. 25.—" Soil very variable, but mostly wet and spongey, and a great deal of moor carrying little but heath. Proprietors small. Mr. Bosville of Gurthwaite the representative of one of the oldest families in the county; being the only large one. Farms likewise small; except

except upon the moors. In the vicinity of the town, about one half is plowed; but in the moors there is little or no tillage at all. The stock is sheep, and long horned cattle of the Derbyshire breed, which are smaller than the Craven breed. Little grain is cultivated; except oats and a small quantity of wheat."

The CHESHIRE Report has the following passage.— P. 8.—" The general appearance of Cheshire is that of an extended plain; but on the eastern side there is a range of hilly or rather mountainous country, connected with the Derbyshire and Yorkshire hills, about twenty five miles in length, and five in width, extending from near Congleton to the north eastern extremity of the county."

The STAFFORDSHIRE Reporter tells us,—p. 7,— " The aspect of this country is various. The north part rises gently in small hills, which beginning, here, run through the heart of England, like the apenines in Italy, in a continued ridge; rising gradually higher and higher into Scotland, under different names: here called Moorlands, then Peak, then Blackstone Edge, then Craven (!) then Stanmore, and then parting into two horns are called Cheviots." (!) How could the Board, and the officers thereof, suffer such egregious nonsense to be re-printed!—He continues—" The Moreland is a rough, dreary, cold tract, the snow lying long on it." And, among the appendices of the reprinted edition, we find a journal of a tour (a botanical tour, it would seem) by the Reporter, in the " Moorlands" of Staffordshire: In which Journal, blended with much desultory and irrevalent matter, are some apt and *strong* remarks, on the southwestern limb of the mountain tract under notice.
P. 188. " The north part of Staffordshire called Moorlands is situate to the north of a line conceived to be drawn from Uttoxeter to Newcastle under Line. The face of this part of the county is various, but in
general

general hilly, with large tracts of the land waste or uncultivated."—P. 189. "These barren wastes are pretty extensive, and not worth, I think, one shilling per acre as pasturage, for sheep or any other animal: they are, I fear, generally too poor and beggarly to be reclaimed, by cultivation, for the purposes of corn or pasturage."—P. 190. "The commons or wastes between Cheadale and Oak Moor, called High-shutt, Ranger, and Alverton Common, consist of an immense number of rude heaps of gravel, upon an under stratum of soft sandy rock, thrown together without order or form, or rather into every form that can be conceived; into sudden swells and deep glens, with scarcely a level perch."—P. 191. "A little north of Oak Moor the limestone country begins, and extends over a great breadth of country to the north, east, and west, in many places rising out of the main surface in huge cliffs. The Wever Hills are of considerble extent. They are composed of immense heaps of limestone, which I was much pleased to find covered with a rich, calcarious, loamy earth, capable of being improved into very good arable or pasture land. They are inclosed in large tracts, by stone walls, but not subdivided, and large breadths have never undergone the least improvement, which I much lament, as the neighbouring lands, which have been improved, are covered with an excellent fine turf, and bear good crops of grain. These hills are a very elevated situation, overlooking, or at least as high as any of the Moorlands, or Derbyshire Peak Hills (?) which may be seen from their summits."—P. 194. "The calcarious part of the Moorlands, or that on a limestone bottom, is pretty extensive, reaching in length from the Weaver Hills to Longnor, and in breadth from the Dove to Morridge, including fifteen or sixteen parishes, and fifty or sixty square miles. The quantity of limestone here is inexhaustible, being in many places in strata of immense thickness. This is the best part of the Moorlands, and the soil seems to have

have a natural aptitude for producing a fine *herbage of grass ;* and, to the credit of the people, here I must observe, that their breed of cows, of the long-horned kind, are generally superior to those in the south of the county, where the land has been longer in an improved state."—P. 198. "At Ecton, is a very considerable mine of copper and lead, the property of his Grace the Duke of Devonshire, and there are other mines of the same metals in this district. The calcareous or limestone bottom ends at Morridge, and the under stratum in the tract of country, west of Leek, and of this waste, is generally sandy or gravelly clay, or gritstone rock. This part of the country, northeast of Mole Cop, is the worst part of the morelands, and of Staffordshire, the surface of a considerable proportion of this land being too uneven for cultivation. Large tracts of waste land here though so elevated in point of situation, are mere high moors, and peat mosses, and of this sort are a part of Morridge, Axedge, the Cloud Heath, High Forest, Leek Frith, and Mole Cop, though ranking amongst the highest land in the county. The summits of some of the hills in this county terminate in huge, tremendous cliffs, particularly those called Leek rocks or roches, and Ipstones' sharp cliffs, which are composed of huge piles of rude and rugged rocks, in very elevated situations, piled rock on rock, in a most tremendous manner, astonishing and almost terrifying the passing traveller, with their majestic frown. Here, single blocks, the size of church steeples are heaped together, some overhanging the precipices and threatening destruction to all approachers, and some of prodigious bulk have evidently rolled from the summit and broke in pieces."

The Reporter of DERBYSHIRE being a stranger in the land, and viewing it, merely, as an enquiring tourist, it were in vain to expect, under such circumstances, much useful information. In speaking of
the

the soils of Derbyshire, the Reporter divides the
county into high peak, low peak, and fertile parts.
On the first (which alone is here to be noticed) we
meet with these *luminous* remarks.—P. 10. " High
peak is chiefly what *the natives* call a corn loam; this
seems to me to consist of virgin earth impregnated
with nitre, on the mountains, and liberally poured
down by them upon the happy vale. (!)   Where this
corn loam is in sufficient quantity, and meets with
a stratum of marl or clay, it forms a most desirable
field for cultivation; but is ever overbalanced by the
vast tracts of barren hills and mountains, from which
this soil is washed.   The sides of these mountains
(forming a considerable part of the whole) present
very little soil to view, being chiefly composed of
rocks.   Where the limestone forms the mountain
(the flats on the tops and where the sides are not too
perpendicular for soil to lodge) the soil, though scanty,
is productive of the finer grasses, which form pasturage for sheep.   Where gritstone abounds, the soil
in general approaches near to the nature of peat moss,
in places forming vast morasses, retentive of water,
and rendered dangerous for either man or beast to
tread upon; except in dry weather; the surface presenting nothing but the barren black moss, thinly
clothed with heath or ling, and every where yawning
out a dreadful rock."

THE END.

Mr. MARSHALL's other WORKS on RURAL ECONOMY.

1.

In two Volumes, Octavo, price 15s. in Boards,

MINUTES and EXPERIMENTS on AGRICULTURE; containing his own Practice in the Southern Counties; and moreover conveying, to practical Men in general, an accurate Method of acquiring Agricultural Knowledge, scientifically, from the Results of their Experience.

2.

In twelve Volumes, Octavo, price 4l. in Boards,

The established Practices of the higher Orders of Professional Men, in the six Agricultural Departments of England:

The Practice of the Northern Department being shown, in the RURAL ECONOMY of YORKSHIRE ; price 12s.

That of the Western Department, in the RURAL ECONOMY of GLOCESTERSHIRE; price 12s.

That of the Central Department, in the RURAL ECONOMY of the MIDLAND COUNTIES; price 14s.

That of the Eastern Department, in the RURAL ECONOMY of NORFOLK; price 12s.

That of the Southern Department, in the RURAL ECONOMY of the SOUTHERN COUNTIES; price 15s.

That of the South-western Department, in the RURAL ECONOMY of the WEST of ENGLAND ; price 15s.

3.

In two Volumes, Octavo, price 16s. in Boards,

A general Work on PLANTING and RURAL ORNAMENT; with the Management of WOODLANDS and HEDGEROW TIMBER.

4.

In one Volume, Quarto, price 2l. 2s. in Boards,

An elementary and practical TREATISE on the LANDED PROPERTY of ENGLAND : comprizing the Purchase, the Improvement, and the executive Management of Landed Estates; and moreover containing what relates to the general Concerns of PROPRIETORS, and to such Subjects of Political Economy, as are intimately connected with the LANDED INTEREST.

5.

In one Volume, Octavo, price 10s. 6d. in Boards,

A general Work on the MANAGEMENT of LANDED ESTATES; being an ABSTRACT of the above Treatise; for the Use of professional Men: including whatever relates to the BUSINESS of ESTATE AGENCY; whether it be employed in the Purchase, the Improvement, or the executive Management of Estates.

INDEX.

Printed at the Office of
THOMAS WILSON & SON,
High-Ousegate, York.